The Practice of Risk Management

Implementing processes for managing firmwide market risk

The Practice of Risk Management

Implementing processes for managing firmwide market risk

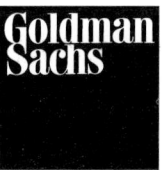

SBC Warburg Dillon Read

Published by Euromoney Books

Note: At the time this book went to press the boards of directors of Union Bank of Switzerland and Swiss Bank Corporation had decided, subject to shareholder approval, to merge both bank groups as equal partners and to form a new business entity. As a consequence, and subject to approval of the merger, the name of Swiss Bank Corporation will have changed by the time of publication.

Published by
Euromoney Publications PLC
Nestor House, Playhouse Yard
London EC4V 5EX

Telephone: +44 (171) 779 8888

Typeset by Julie Foster
Printed by Clifford Press, UK

3 2280 00652 5422

Acknowledgements

In the course of working together on this book, our two firms have discovered far more common ground than we originally expected. The commonality of our views has also led us to believe that our experience may benefit a broader audience of financial and non-financial firms.

Writing a book on a topic as broad and as complex as risk management requires a team effort, particularly a book which draws upon the practical experience of people who actually perform the function, as this one does.

In that light, we would like to recognise the significant contributions of the following members of our team who took time out of their busy days to bring to life the reality of managing market risk:

Robert Gumerlock
Swiss Bank Corporation

Robert Litterman
Goldman Sachs & Co.

who conceived and began writing this book a year ago;

Denise Hayman-Loa
Goldman Sachs & Co.

Tim Shepheard-Walwyn
Swiss Bank Corporation

who contributed vast amounts of personal time and energy to writing and editing these chapters as well as project managing the process; and

Armen Avanessians
Michael Allen
Slim Bentami
Guillermo Bublik
Joseph C. DeLuca
Arnout M. Eikeboom
William J. Fallon
Reinhard Hannak
Karen J. Hladik
Charlene C. Kuo
Chris Matten

Andrew O'Reilly
Peter Reiser
Marcel Rohner
Jay Ryan
Jae H. Sang
Barbara Smigelski Colie
Paul Staneski
Mark Wallace
Susan Waters Lese
Jeffrey Weiss

the writers and advisers from our two firms. We would also like to express our sincere thanks to the many friends and colleagues who have contributed their ideas and feedback during the development of this book.

Preface

E. GERALD CORRIGAN

In one form or another, Risk Management is a phenomenon that can be traced to the very origins of civilisation in that the most basic instincts of mankind, such as the search for shelter, can be seen as the practice of risk management. Centuries later, the early organisation of financial institutions, including banks and insurance companies, marked the beginning of the generalised institutionalisation of risk management in financial affairs, a process that continues to evolve even today. However, while it is probably fair to characterise the pattern of change in banking and finance over the broad sweep of time as evolutionary in nature, it is equally fair to characterise such developments over the past 25 years or so as revolutionary. Indeed, in that latter time frame the intensified application of increasingly sophisticated technology and telecommunications to banking and finance has produced an almost unthinkable surge of innovation in the financial arena that has brought with it vast benefits but also new and extraordinarily complex elements of risk. These developments have ushered in new challenges for risk managers in financial institutions and for those charged with the official supervision of financial institutions.

By the mid 1980s, it became increasingly clear that conventional methods of risk management and official supervision were seriously handicapped in their ability to effectively measure and manage the galaxy of risks facing financial institutions, especially those institutions actively involved in global markets. As a consequence, the art of risk management increasingly turned to sophisticated statistical and mathematical techniques to buttress, if not significantly supplant, more conventional risk management techniques.

Thus, over the past 10 years or so, highly complex management information and risk management systems were forged into mathematical models utilising volatilities, correlations, randomised simulations, non-linear approximations, and other techniques for estimating "capital at risk" in major financial institutions.

While the techniques of risk management have changed, its essence remains much more an art than a science. Indeed, at its core, risk management entails the time honoured task of getting the right information, in the right format, to the right people, at the right time. That in turn is what permits policy makers to ask the right questions and to make informed judgments about risk in relation to returns. However, practitioners as well as policy makers must also understand the limits of contemporary risk management systems, including the inescapable fact that the past is not a remotely perfect guide to the future.

Just as the dictates of practicality have helped reshape approaches to risk management in the private sector, the international community of supervisors have had to adapt their practices and policies. In the broadest of terms, this has entailed a shift in emphasis away from a "black box" approach to regulation toward a more flexible emphasis on supervision which places greater weight on a case-by-case evaluation of individual institutions relative to established prudential standards and norms.

While much has been accomplished by practitioners and policy makers, the task of further adapting risk management systems to the changing dictates of the global marketplace remains formidable. Moreover, developing and maintaining effective risk management systems is also expensive – very expensive. But, while the costs associated with effective risk management systems are large, so too are the costs of cutting corners to "save" money. Indeed, sooner or later the costs associated with inferior risk management systems will reflect themselves in financial or reputational losses that can threaten the very viability of individual financial institutions.

This treatise on risk management, prepared jointly by Goldman Sachs & Co. and Swiss Bank Corporation, has been written by practitioners for practitioners. While it is far from the last word on the subject, it brings together a "real time" overview of the art of risk management as it plays out day by day in two of the largest and most successful globally active financial institutions in the world. As such, it represents a valuable and compelling overview of the practice of risk management which will benefit practitioners and policy makers alike.

Introduction and table of contents

Introduction

Our objective in writing this book is to provide a practical guide to implementing the theory of risk management on a day-to-day basis in financial firms. In this context, we focus particularly on managing market risk, because this is the dimension of risk where the quantitative techniques of modern risk management began and where the discipline is most fully developed at present. At the same time, risk management is an area where ideas and thinking are evolving even as we go to press. Undoubtedly the issues associated with managing other significant risks, such as credit and operational risks, will warrant similar treatment as they reach the same level of development.

In this book, we introduce the main themes at a high level first, and explore them in more detail as the book progresses. At the same time, the book is designed to be accessible to both the technical and the non-technical reader. With this in mind, we have organised it to also allow selective reading without detracting from the overall message. For example, while we have tried to avoid excessive use of technical jargon, some use of specialist terminology is unavoidable in a topic as complex as risk management. Consequently we believe the structure allows the reader to gloss over these more technical sections without losing sight of the book's overall message.

We have attempted to describe the practical application of risk management concepts, as used in our two firms. That being said, we would not presume to suggest that we have thought of everything or documented everything on this vast topic. So what we have tried to do at a minimum is to present a framework for thinking about risk, and to outline some of the key themes our two firms have encountered in our practice of risk management.

The book is laid out in four key sections. Section I places risk management in context, both in the current world, and historically, as well as defining market risk. Section II articulates the various methods and tools currently available to measure risk. Section III describes the risk management process, how to perform the function, and how to report the results. And Section IV concludes by broadening our outlook to consider regulatory and capital allocation applications for risk analysis, as well as taking a stab at looking into the firm of the future.

Table of contents

The concepts of risk management are introduced, giving the reader a sense of the day-to-day operations of a risk management department. The origins of risk management are explored, looking at some of the important events which have influenced its development, and why it is now recognised as a core competence for financial firms. Management and organisational issues involved in establishing a risk management function are defined, and the key themes of the book identified. The section discusses, and begins to focus on, market risk, which is currently the most developed of the risk management disciplines.

This section explores the various issues associated with compiling an effective toolkit for measuring a firm's exposure to market risk. The relative strengths and weaknesses of stress testing, Value at Risk (VaR), and scenario analysis are explained and discussed. The chapter looks at how they can be used as complementary tools whilst recognising that different firms will place different weight on the methods depending on their organisational structures and business mixes. In addition, the main issues associated with the less well developed discipline of measuring specific risk are explored.

Section III   **Risk management in the real world**

This section addresses the practical challenges of implementing and sustaining a risk management function for market risk, and examines the supporting processes, technology and cultural implications. It outlines the interactions within a firm, and with external constituencies. It discusses how to staff and run a risk management function, the type and structure of information that needs to be produced, and the challenges of making sure the data is accurate and the methodology is robust. It particularly highlights the critical importance of instilling a risk management culture throughout a firm. Also considered are some of the issues associated with implementing risk management beyond banks and securities firms.

Section IV **The changing world of risk management**

This final section of the book considers how developments in risk management theory and practice are influencing the wider environment within which firms operate. It looks in particular at adaptations in the regulatory structure, which is placing greater emphasis on the quality of risk management practices. It also considers changes in accounting and disclosure rules to provide investors with more meaningful risk profile information, and the integration risk measures into the performance measurement and capital allocation processes. Finally, in a more speculative vein, it considers what life might be like in the successful firm in the year 2008.

Section I

Risk management in context

The concepts of risk management are introduced, giving the reader a sense of the day-to-day operations of a risk management department. The origins of risk management are explored, looking at some of the important events which have influenced its development, and why it is now recognised as a core competence for financial firms. Management and organisational issues involved in establishing a risk management function are defined, and the key themes of the book identified. The section discusses, and begins to focus on, market risk, which is currently the most developed of the risk management disciplines.

A day in the life of a risk manager

Introduction

This first chapter chronicles the activities of the department which identifies, monitors, analyses and reports risk, in support of senior management, and the front office risk managers who interact directly with the market. This risk monitoring function should be performed in an independent group, as it is depicted here, and should be supported by a flexible system which brings together relevant data from various sources throughout the organisation. The size and composition of the risk monitoring group is certainly dependent on each organisation's structure, but many of the events which we describe in our typical day are broadly applicable.

This chapter has been developed to give the reader a sense of the activities that make up a risk manager's typical day. It should be viewed solely as an introduction to some of the themes and issues that will be explained more fully in later chapters so it is not necessary to understand every term at this stage. Our goal here is simply to familiarise the reader with some of the risk management concepts, and to provide an understanding of what it is really like to manage the risk of a large organisation day in and day out.

Finally, our "risk manager" is really made up of the multiple individuals who are needed to perform the risk monitoring function effectively, as it is a complex and comprehensive role requiring many types of skills. Our imaginary day starts at 7.00am in Tokyo, and ends late in the day in New York, which is certainly the reality in the global world we live in today. So please join us as we start our rather lengthy day, working our way through managing market risk in practice.

The trading day

Tokyo 7.00am

NY

LON

TKY

The day starts by checking the status of the data feeds that come in from the various front and back office systems. Gary and Jay are members of the risk monitoring team based in Tokyo. Gary was a trader's assistant before he moved over to the risk group, Jay was a P&L analyst, so they both have relevant market experience. It is their responsibility to check that the data needed for measuring risk has been received and that any data exceptions are resolved before running the risk model.

Gary's first question is usually, "Are the feeds all in?"

"Actually," replies Jay, "they are. Everything is in from all the Asian offices, both the front office analytics feeds and the back office position feeds."

"There was a delay in the feed from Singapore yesterday, but I guess back office support resolved it. So we can start resolving the exceptions kicked out by the system. Can you take equities?" Gary asks. "I'll take bonds and swaps."

"Sure," responds Jay. "Also, just so you know, I'm planning to check out the equity prices in detail, because I think one of the exchanges had a system problem late yesterday. The system should identify them as exceptions, since they would have been outside of the tolerances."

"I'm also expecting a position discrepancy in the 10-year, based on what the trader told me to watch out for yesterday. It's likely to be just a missing duration, but it won't go through the risk model without one. I'll check it against the break sheet between the desk's view and the back office view."

Gary and Jay spend the next hour reviewing the exceptions produced by the system's filtering process. The system checks for missing data, or data that is outside of certain tolerances, and provides the capability to adjust any data errors. Gary and Jay confirm any discrepancies in positions or prices with either operations or financial controllers before making any changes to make sure they are consistent with the firm's books and records. Once the data is scrubbed, it can be run through the risk model.

Reviewing and scrubbing data is an essential part of the risk monitoring function, as any data problems will cause the results of the risk model to be inaccurate, nullifying the validity of the risk information. In any large trading or investment organisation, there will always be some data discrepancies, which is why reconciliation procedures to tie out to both the front office view and the back office view need to be performed before generating risk reports.

Tokyo 9.00am

NY   LON   TKY

"OK, I've checked out equities," says Jay. "There were some pricing problems, but I called down to controllers and they gave me the correct prices to input, so now everything looks good to review the results in the equities portfolios."

"I'm still working on swaps; but bonds are done, so I'll start running them through the risk model," Gary replies. "There was a missing duration number on the 10-year, but the desk had the information. If you want, go ahead and run your portfolios through the model, just don't forget to monitor the arbitrage desk. They were near their limit yesterday. They might ask for an increase. If they are over, we'll have to prepare a violation memo."

"I'll keep an eye on it. Also, once I'm done with equities, I thought I would take a look at the firm's JGB futures positions across all desks. The Fixed Income division risk manager asked me to monitor it to make sure we don't have a market concentration."

"Just keep me posted".

Tokyo 10.00am

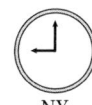  

NY   LON   TKY

"Well, swaps are done now too," Gary mentions. "I'll start running the risk for them. How did equities look?"

"The desk didn't end up reaching their limit," responds Jay. "They put on a position that is negatively correlated with the position which was a large risk contributor yesterday, so everything looks good now. I talked to the trader and to operations just to double check that the results tied with their expectations. The aggregated equities VaR number was well within their limit."

"Bonds look reasonable too," says Gary, "at least for Tokyo. Later on I'll start checking London and New York, once those feeds come in. How did that JGB futures analysis go?"

"Actually, I'm a bit concerned about it. We seem to be heavily overweighted on the short end across several desks; I think we should bring it to management's attention."

"Let's go talk to them right away."

Gary and Jay communicate with the Tokyo Fixed Income division senior risk managers to inform them of the concentration in JGB futures. The team needs to be aware of senior management's comfort level, so they know how carefully to monitor the positions. The risk managers decide they are comfortable with the level of risk, but ask the risk monitoring team to keep an eye on it. If the market looks like it's starting to change direction, they may have some traders adjust their positions.

Tokyo 11.00am

NY   LON   TKY

Once all portfolios are run through the risk model, Gary and Jay can review the aggregated risk across all desks. If the risk looks reasonable, they can then focus on various projects that may be under way, or requests for analyses from traders or senior management. On this particular morning, the aggregated risk does look reasonable for all products and desks in Tokyo, so they respond to a request from a trader who would like to see the impact of a particular trade on the VaR of his portfolio. This type of interaction is helpful for gaining trader buy-in for the VaR numbers.

"What I would suggest we do is load your portfolio into the model," Gary tells the trader, "and adjust the trade quantity to the level you are thinking about. Then we can run the risk analysis process to see how that trade affects the risk. What quantity did you have in mind?"

"How about putting in another five million," the trader responds. "Let's see what that does."

"OK, based on the correlation with the rest of the portfolio, that quantity actually puts you over the VaR limit. We can adjust the quantity to reduce the risk, or we can take a look at something else that is less correlated."

"What about a possible hedge?" asks the trader.

"We can run a hedge analysis to see what the system would have recommended. A recommendation to increase or decrease a position will depend on its covariance with the other positions in the portfolio. In this case, the system suggested a trade of two million to reduce the risk."

"So next time I can do this on my own, right?"

"Sure," responds Gary, "just pull it up from the menu. If you want to enter any of today's trades you can do that also, in order to monitor the changes to the VaR during the day. Then you know what to expect for tomorrow's VaR."

The risk monitoring team is also asked by the head of the bond desk to run an analysis of the views implied by the desk's portfolio. The head of the desk has a bullish view on the 20-year JGB, called the "superlong" bond, but the implied views analysis shows that the portfolio is actually bearish on the superlong, due to its covariance with the other positions in the portfolio. In this case, given the head trader's view, an increase in the superlong position could increase the profitability of the portfolio, while at the same time reducing the risk. Based on the implied views analysis, the head of the desk decides to add to the position.

Tokyo 3.00pm

NY   LON   TKY

Gary and Jay hear back from the head of the bond desk after he adjusted the superlong position. The profitability on the portfolio looks good; he thanks them for their help. This is the kind of positive interaction which demonstrates to the front office that the risk group's role is both to independently monitor risk and to assist in identifying opportunities for increased profits.

At this point in the day, the feeds have started to come in for the London office, so Gary and Jay can begin processing London's data to get a jump start on their day. They contact London via e-mail if they notice any problems that need to be followed up on. They also compose an e-mail which they send to London and New York summarising the day in Tokyo, essentially "passing the book", and letting them know about anything to watch out for, such as the large short in the JGB futures positions.

London 7.00am

NY   LON   TKY

Eric, Maureen and Doug are all members of the risk monitoring team in the London office. Eric and Maureen came from an accounting firm and the internal operations department respectively, and Doug is a technology support person. As London is a larger office than Tokyo, having a dedicated technology resource on site is key for supporting the development of new reports and analyses, for modelling new products or for quickly tracking down production problems.

Just as in Tokyo, the first thing the team does is check the status of data feeds from the various front and back office systems and review the summary e-mail from Tokyo. In London, because the volume and diversity of trading activity is greater than in Tokyo, there are far more moving pieces, thus increasing the likelihood of missing feeds or required data adjustments.

"Doug, the position feed for bonds is missing today. Can you contact the support person and find out when we will get it?" asks Eric.

"Actually, I already called," responds Doug. "That system was running late due to some late trades, but the feed is on its way. But we have another problem with the Eurobond desk; the feed isn't in yet from New York and they were over their limit yesterday. Unfortunately, I'm going to have to wait for New York to get in to handle this one."

"Oh, OK, thanks. Maureen and I will move ahead on the other portfolios then; we'll return to bonds once the feed is in. The only thing I'm worried about is that the Eurobond desk was over it's limit yesterday, and while the trader says he's now under, senior management is putting pressure on us to monitor it. They're not going to be happy with the delay, but I guess until we have round the clock technology coverage, this will happen."

"By the way, Doug," says Maureen, "a couple of new equity positions kicked out this morning. Can you pull in the return data for them so they can be run through the model tomorrow? For today we can map them to the equity index to capture the risk."

"Sure, just give me the security reference data and I can load it in from the historical database."

"Maureen, while you're doing the swaps desk," Eric says, "one of the traders wants to monitor his strategies as two separate accounts. Can you split the positions and set up the new account?"

"OK, I'll follow up with him to see how he wants them split. It's pretty straightforward, as long as the accounts are also changed on the feeding systems. I'll check with operations to make sure they know about it too."

These types of maintenance activities typically occur on a daily basis, and the team needs to stay on top of them to keep the results from the system accurate. And of course the more complex the firm, the more complex this process can become. The team relies heavily on their technology support, and while they are fortunate to have Doug locally in London, there are still constraints imposed by time zone differences which they have to work around. For example, the delay in the feed from the Eurobond desk is a bit uncomfortable, as senior management is watching that one closely.

Just as in Tokyo, the risk monitoring team proceeds to check and scrub the data, and to interact with other areas of the firm, such as verifying the P&L data with financial controllers. Eric does end up calling Gary and Jay in Tokyo before the end of the day in Japan to discuss the JGB futures situation. The London team will need to monitor it, informing senior management in London and New York if action needs to be taken.

London 9.00am

NY   LON   TKY

As feeds and exceptions are processed, the team updates the system. They also review the trader e-mails from throughout Europe to match the traders' information against the results of the risk system. These e-mails are a critical part of the risk monitoring process, providing the team with each trader's view of their positions, some colour on their markets and their estimated profits or losses. The e-mails are used as a check and balance against the results of the risk system; if there is a large discrepancy, this gives the risk monitoring team an indication of where to begin the research process. (See Exhibit 1.1.)

As Eric and Maureen go through the portfolios and the trader e-mails, they begin to develop an English language summary for senior management, which highlights major positions, market exposures and potential risks. Senior management can use this summary to gain a quick understanding of the firm's exposures to major markets across all divisions. The summary supplements the information provided by the risk system, and is one of the value-added services performed by the risk monitoring function.

Once the data scrubbing and trader e-mail reconciliation process is completed, the team reviews the risk of each major business unit to identify potential problems or violations.

"Maureen, did you notice there's a small VaR limit violation on the foreign exchange desk?" says Eric. "It's not an emergency, but we'd better bring it to the attention of the desk head, the division head and the head of risk management as soon as possible, because it seems to be caused by the emerging markets positions."

"Right, they did mention at the last risk committee that they wanted to be informed if that happened," Maureen replies. "Do you want to put together an e-mail?"

"Sure, but I think I'm going to call the desk head directly too, just to give him a heads up."

The e-mail and calls are carried out quickly, and the replies come back recommending an analysis of the desk's positions and historical information. It turns out that the desk has been asking for an increase for some time, and senior management would like more information in order to make a decision.

Eric takes a look at a number of factors to build a picture of their historical patterns. For example, he reviews key indicators such as the P&L history, the risk percentage versus the limit historically, the statistics on how many times they have been over their limit, and their Sharpe ratio (risk/return). He communicates this information to senior management.

Exhibit 1.1 Sample trader e-mail

Text

ARB DESK – RISK REPORT

POSITION SUMMARY:
$125MM 2–5–10yr German Butterfly – long 5yr
$150MM 5–10yr UST Steepener
long $75MM Bunds vs. Gilts
$100MM JGB flattener
long $50MM Philip Morris

FLOWS: Huge two-way flows again with much better buying by global central banks. Speculation surrounding the health of South American and Hong Kong banks, as well as fears of large future broker losses also drew in buyers. Fed Chairman's testimony was neutral to positive and further supported the market.
Russian spreads widened 200bp radically strengthening Vnesh position.

Senior management evaluates this quantitative data, along with additional subjective considerations, such as the desk's reason for the limit increase request and a sense of the desk's good reputation and credibility. Based on all of this information, they collectively decide to increase the desk's VaR limit from four to five. Eric adjusts the VaR limit in the system, putting an expiration date on it for four weeks out, at which point it will be reassessed. He sends an e-mail to the risk group in New York to inform them of the decision.

London 11.00am

NY   LON   TKY

Once the production work is completed for the day, and all the risk for London has been reviewed and updated, the team can turn to other projects. On this particular day, they have received a request from the financial controller's group to review the pricing on a complex derivatives contract. The risk monitoring group is asked to independently model the pricing on the deal. Depending on the complexity of the contract, this activity can be very time-consuming. In addition to his other responsibilities, Eric has some training in modelling derivatives, but complex deals generally need to be forwarded on to the centralised quantitative group in New York for a consistent review.

"Sure, I can take a look at it," Eric responds to a phone call from Jeff in Financial Controls, "but if it's too complex, I'll need to send it on to New York. What's your timeframe like?"

"It's somewhat critical to get it done soon for the audit, but it's more critical to be accurate. So just let me know what you decide on the modelling and I'll communicate it back to the auditors. Thanks for your help," says Jeff.

"No problem. I'll let you know how it looks in a bit."

Eric makes an initial attempt at modelling the deal, but quickly finds that it is too complex for his background and the tools he has available. He sends an e-mail to the quantitative group in New York, attaching a spreadsheet with the terms of the deal. They will call him once their day starts to discuss what he has figured out so far.

While Eric is working on the derivatives contract, Maureen is focusing on a request from senior management to run a historical P&L and VaR risk analysis on a major business unit, with desks in New York, London and Tokyo, for the past month. She starts with an on-line summary graph displaying the two pieces of information together, then she pulls up the daily reports to put together a detailed breakdown of how and why the risk and the P&L of the portfolio changed during the course of the month. Management will use this analysis to help them decide how to allocate capital to this business unit.

London 1.00pm

NY   LON   TKY

By midday in London, New York has already started their day. The London team sends off a summary e-mail to update New York on what has occurred so far. In particular, London needs New York to focus on the missing Eurobond feed, so they can respond to senior management.

Once the feeds start coming in for New York, the London team typically tackles some of the New York portfolios. This is similar to how Tokyo assisted London and is a good way to both maximise efficiency and to keep all members of the global team current on what is happening in the various offices around the world.

In our imaginary organisation, New York is home office, and therefore is responsible for carrying out the final aggregation and reporting of the firm's risk. New York calls London to let them know that they need some help processing one of the major divisions, as they have a risk meeting with that division at 11.00am. The portfolios are divided up for review.

"Eric, can you and Maureen help with the New York Fixed Income desks?" asks Joanne, one of the Risk Monitoring managers based in New York. "We have a Fixed Income risk meeting at 11, and we need to pull the information together and analyse it before then."

"No problem. By the way, we have been watching JGB futures all day at their request. You may want to print out an analysis of those positions for the meeting," replies Eric. "Did Gary post you on that?"

"Gary called me at home last night to fill me in, thanks. Has there been much activity since then?" asked Joanne.

"Not in JGBs, but we did have that small limit violation in FX which you might want to take a look at. They were given a temporary limit increase which we already put in the system. I also passed a derivatives deal on to the quant group for modelling; it was more complex than what I've typically done. Our big outstanding problem is still the Eurobond desk, but hopefully that will get resolved soon."

"OK, I'll follow up with the IT guys on the Eurobond feed, and I'll check with the quant group on that derivatives deal later once production is completed."

London 2.00pm

NY   LON   TKY

London proceeds to assist New York, and to handle periodic requests from traders or risk managers, until their day wraps up. They do finally get the feed from the Eurobond desk and run their risk through the system.

"So how did the Eurobond limit look?" asks Eric. "You know, the trader is certain he's under his limit now, based on some trades he did yesterday."

"Well, actually, things don't look great," answers Maureen. "He's still over his limit, and it looks like he lost some money. I would expect senior management to cut him back a bit after this, and to ask us to watch him closely."

Later in the day, the risk group gives a quick demo of the risk system and the risk monitoring process to an energy client that is starting to set up it's own risk management function. The risk monitoring group has been doing such demos for clients more and more frequently these days, as the industry focus on risk management continues to increase.

New York 7.00am

 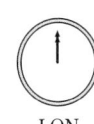 

NY   LON   TKY

As the day cycles on to New York, the New York team needs to check the risk globally. In its role as head office for our imaginary organisation, New York is responsible for monitoring the status across all business units and geographic regions and reporting to senior management.

Using the advantage of the time zones, we saw how Tokyo and London helped with the processing so that some of the results could be ready earlier. The remainder of the portfolios still need to be reviewed and then the aggregated risk can be run for the various levels, such as business units, divisions and the firm overall. The New York team also completes the English language summary of key risk exposures started by the London team.

The group in New York is the largest, as New York is also the largest office. The risk monitoring managers, of which Joanne is one, are based in New York, along with a team of four analysts. The technology staff supporting the system are also based in New York, as this is where most new development happens. It seems that the risk management system is never completely finalised as new products, markets and methods are continuously evolving.

In New York, as in Tokyo and London, the first thing that needs to be done is to check the feeds from the various systems. Today, all the primary feeds are in, but one of the market data feeds used to generate the return database is not in yet. Joanne touches base with Matt, the technology manager who supports the return database.

"Matt, the equities market data feed hasn't come in yet, though we should get it later this morning."

"That's not a problem," Matt replies. "It can be resolved later in the day. The covariance matrix that's generated off the return database is on a day lag, to ensure that the data can be scrubbed properly. I'll have Tim contact the support person in equities and keep an eye out for it."

Because the covariance matrix uses large amounts of historical data, a lag of a day will not have an impact; however it is critical that the data be clean, so that is the team's focus. Just as there are a number of automated filters to identify exceptions in the position and price data, there are also multiple layers of automated checks developed to catch bad datapoints in the return database.

Similar to the other offices, once the feeds are in the exceptions are checked and reconciled with operations and financial controllers. Checking with the trader is done only as a last step, if the exception cannot be resolved otherwise. On this day, there is a price that kicks out on a large municipal bond position based on the tolerance filters. Because munis don't always trade every day, only the trader will know if that price is reasonable. Jacob, one of the risk monitoring analysts, calls down to the trader.

"Bill, the price on the NY City bond, maturing 9/15/2006, was 99, and is now 101. Is that an accurate price for that bond?"

"Yeah, it's fine," Bill replies. "That bond tracks to the 10-year Treasury, with a spread of 100 basis points. The market isn't very liquid, so it's typically only priced weekly, and you will often see that kind of jump."

Next time, Jacob may not need to call the trader, because in his role of being responsible for monitoring the risk of the municipal desk, he will begin to develop knowledge about how these markets behave and how to test for reasonableness.

New York 9.00am

NY   LON   TKY

Once all the portfolios have been scrubbed, the next step is to review where the major risks are coming from across the firm, starting from the top down. As some areas tend to be riskier on a general basis, the team will take a bottom-up approach to reviewing their risk numbers. As we saw in Jacob's dialogue with the muni trader, building product and market experience and knowledge among the risk monitoring team is a key component to effectively monitoring the risk of the firm. Senior management relies on the risk monitoring team to make educated judgments about which risks should be focused on.

The trading desks have grown to rely on the risk monitoring group as well. Joanne takes a call from the Treasury desk – they expect a major announcement today, and they anticipate that they may take a large position. They ask Joanne to help monitor their risk.

"OK, what I can do is to bring your portfolio up, and if you can post me on what trades you want to do, I can easily run them through the system to assess the impact on the risk," Joanne tells them. "If you want, once I get it set up for you, you can monitor it yourselves. That will save you the phone call."

"We can do that," the desk replies. "Also, because we expect this announcement to impact rates, can we pass along some risk factors which go through a few yield curve shift scenarios?"

"You can, but we also take those in from your system every day. Do you expect much variation from those?"

"Yes, we expect something a bit more dramatic, especially on the long end, so we've developed a few additional scenarios. We'll have our systems person send the file up."

While this interaction is under way, the rest of the team is completing the review of the aggregated risk, and preparing the reports for the 11.00 meeting with the Fixed Income risk committee. Overall the risk looks reasonable, but there is a general concern still about the JGB futures positions which the group has been monitoring all day. The team pulls together the summary risk reports that will be handed out at the meeting, and also highlight issues such as the JGB futures, the London Eurobond desk limit violation, the temporary limit for FX and the Treasury desks concern over today's announcement. (See Exhibit 1.2.)

New York 11.00am

NY   LON   TKY

The Fixed Income risk committee meets weekly to review the risk of each desk, globally, and to evaluate requests for limit increases. The reports for the committee to review were prepared that morning, with the assistance of the London office. The FX limit violation in London is discussed, and the temporary increase is agreed

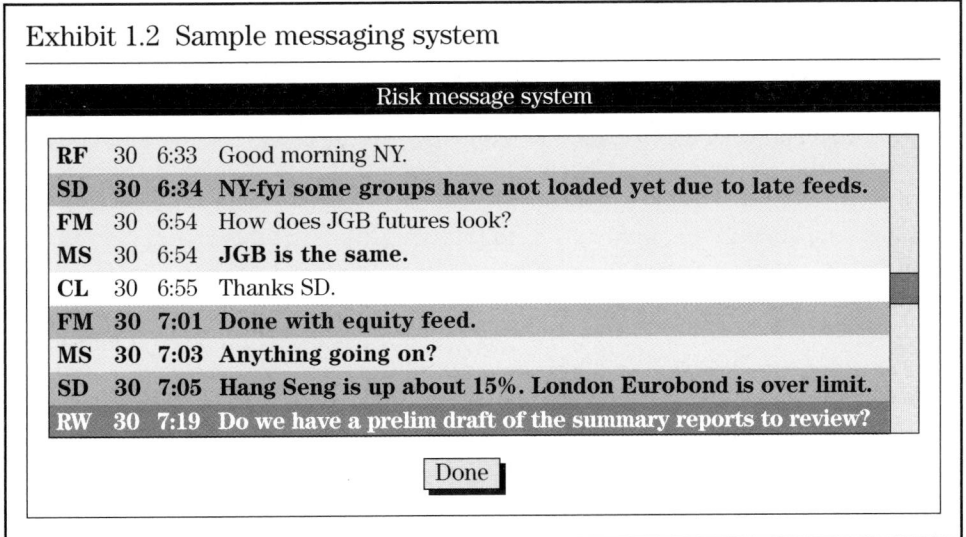

Exhibit 1.2 Sample messaging system

			Risk message system
RF	30	6:33	Good morning NY.
SD	30	6:34	**NY-fyi some groups have not loaded yet due to late feeds.**
FM	30	6:54	How does JGB futures look?
MS	30	6:54	**JGB is the same.**
CL	30	6:55	Thanks SD.
FM	30	7:01	**Done with equity feed.**
MS	30	7:03	**Anything going on?**
SD	30	7:05	**Hang Seng is up about 15%. London Eurobond is over limit.**
RW	30	7:19	**Do we have a prelim draft of the summary reports to review?**

Done

upon. Another desk that is far below its limit is discussed. They have a good Sharpe ratio historically, and that the committee is comfortable with their performance. They will be encouraged to take more risk to increase returns. A major business unit that has consistently been performing well, but is near its limit, is allocated a limit increase to utilise additional capital.

While the Fixed Income risk committee meeting is under way, Jacob and one of the other analysts, Deborah, analyse the preliminary results for a new product type that is being added to the system. There is limited return history for the product, because the firm has not traded it actively, so data will need to be constructed from external feeds. Clean historical return data is often a key challenge when modelling new products.

Jacob notices that the model may be overstating the risk of the product. "Most of the risk in this product is interest rate risk, so they should behave most like the 10-year Treasury. But see here, the risk is significantly different between the two."

"I've reviewed and confirmed the position data and the analytics from the front office," Deborah mentions, "and I think we have the right risk factors based on the trader's feedback. There might be some bad historical data, because we had to build the return database with external price feeds."

"That was it," Jacob says after they research the historical data. "It turns out there were quite a few bad datapoints. I researched those items, and updated the database. Now we can rerun the analysis and continue the test process."

"We'll have to let Joanne know. If this works well for three to four consecutive days, we can probably put it into production, so we can monitor it actively on the system."

New York 1.00pm

NY   LON   TKY

One of the traders on the bond desk calls to argue that his risk is overstated. He has had a spread trade on between a newly issued sovereign bond and the par bond in the same country for four months.

"I think the risk number is too high," says the trader. "These two bonds have been highly correlated for the past four months. I've been watching them ever since I put the position on."

Jacob brings the data up on his screen to review it. "The data we are using is for the sovereign par bond asset class," he explains, "and by using that, we end up going back before the new bond was issued. The par bond had a lot of volatility historically, and what our model is trying to do is to project what could possibly happen based on what has happened in the markets. To do this, we will tend to use more history, and group bonds together under an asset class that's indicative of the volatility of the group. That might explain why the risk number is higher than you'd expect."

The trader is not thrilled, but at least he understands, and feels that the approach is valid. He asks Jacob to show him how to bring up those screens in the system so he can monitor the results for himself.

New York 2.00pm

NY   LON   TKY

The head of the Firmwide Risk committee calls. He needs a summary of all key risk exposures in emerging markets. By pulling up the risk decomposition reports at the highest level of the firm, Joanne is able to quickly assess the key market risk exposure areas. By reviewing the results of the system and the e-mails from the trading desks the summary list that is prepared for emerging markets every week is updated.

After finishing the emerging markets list, Joanne continued a backtesting analysis she had been working on, comparing the historical P&L to the risk results from the model. While reviewing one of the corporate bond portfolios, she noticed a large unexplained P&L move of four million when the VaR for the whole desk was five million. Because matching the risk results to the historical P&L is the best way to test that the risk exposures are being modelled correctly, a difference like that could point to a problem.

Joanne started by taking a look at the market data and the positions in the portfolio for the past two weeks to see if there was an obvious explanation. There didn't appear to be much activity in the market that day, so she decided to probe further by contacting the financial controller's group. She calls Joe, who is the manager of the P&L and pricing process for corporates.

"Joe, I'm trying to track down a large P&L move that differs from what our risk model projected. Can you review that account, and let me know if there was anything that could have caused the move?"

"Sure," Joe responds, "let me take a look." Joe reviews the historical prices for the portfolio. "Well, it does appear that there was a significant price adjustment that day on some of the positions in the portfolio. That market is quite illiquid, so the prices may be static for a week, and then have a large move on one day."

"OK, that's helpful, but I'm not sure it explains everything. Were there any position changes?"

"Actually, there was a large as-of position adjustment on that day that could also have accounted for the jump," Joe noted. "We should put a procedure in place to notify you of those adjustments, so you can tie out to the books and records historically."

"Great, that would be helpful, and thanks for taking the time on this one," Joanne closes, "it really helps us keep our system in line with the firm's books and records."

New York 3.00pm

NY   LON   TKY

Some members of the risk monitoring team are asked to attend a meeting with one of the firm's regulators. Joanne and the other members of the team are quite practised at this type of meeting, as, similar to the client meeting Eric and Maureen conducted in London, they occur frequently. Risk management is receiving enormous focus throughout the industry at the current time and the regulatory agencies are typically very interested in how large global firms manage their risk. The regulators let the team know they are working on developing standards for the industry.

The meeting starts with a discussion of how the firm's risk committee is structured, and what their topics of discussion are, as well as a discussion of how limits are set and monitored. Joanne goes through a description of the risk monitoring group, what their role is and what procedures are followed. She then gives a demo of the system – both the part of the system that helps gather and scrub data, and the modelling and reporting components. The regulators ask a number of questions, mostly focused on the practical and organisational aspects of monitoring risk, as their focus is not only on the quantitative aspects, but also on the qualitative.

The head of regulatory reporting is very pleased with how the meeting went, and calls Joanne afterwards to thank her. A positive response from the regulators regarding how the firm manages risk provides a long-term benefit – risk measures will play an important role in regulating the industry and regulators will increasingly use a firm's risk management capability as an indicator of overall soundness.

Conclusion

So, we have followed our risk monitoring team through their imaginary day. We have seen them process data feeds and scrub the information that comes in from multiple sources, as well as coping with the practical realities of producing meaningful risk numbers. We watched the team interact internally with traders, senior management, operations and financial controllers, and externally with the firm's clients and the regulators.

During our day, it became clear that this team needs to comprise experienced, knowledgeable professionals who understand the markets and the behaviour of different products, so that they can make effective judgments about the firm's risk. Active communication between the members of the team is also key to effectively managing the risk of a large global organisation. And underlying all of these activities, we heard repeated mention of the system playing an important role in supporting the risk monitoring process.

Needless to say, we have only scratched the surface of this very complex topic. Throughout the remainder of this book we will go into far greater detail on these and other concepts. We hope that this initial chapter has provided a glimpse into what managing market risk is all about, and we now go on to lay out the foundations for practising the art, and the science, of managing market risk.

2

The beginnings of risk management

In Chapter 1 we saw a notional day in the life of a risk management department in an investment bank. Risk management departments of the type outlined fulfil a function which is now recognised as critical to the effective management of financial firms. Indeed, the purpose of this book is to explain what that job is; what techniques and skills are needed to do the job effectively and how the tools of risk management can assist in a wider understanding of the activities of financial firms. But we should not forget that this is a very recent development.

Ten years ago, financial firms did not have a function dedicated to the control of market risk. In that sense, the Risk Manager is unequivocally a creature of the 1990s and beyond. So before we move on to consider the practical challenges that are associated with the role, it is worth reflecting on the changes that have given rise to it. What happened in the financial services business to make risk management such an indispensable part of the management of financial organisations today?

The 1970s: Derivatives – the early days

To answer this question, we need to start by going back to 1973. Two events occurred in the spring of 1973 which in retrospect can be seen to mark the beginning of much of modern finance. The first event occurred in April of that year when the Chicago Board Options Exchange (CBOE) began its operations in the smoking lounge of the Chicago Board of Trade (CBOT) – the world's leading market for commodities trading. What the CBOE offered for the first time was the opportunity for traders to deal in standardised contracts for options on individual stocks. The second event of that year was the publication in the May edition of the Journal of Political Economy of the seminal paper by Fischer Black and Myron Scholes[1] on the valuation of options.

With the benefit of hindsight it is not difficult to see the significance of these two events, but at the time this was not at all obvious. Indeed, the early days of the CBOE were extremely modest. The exchange was set up by the CBOT primarily as an attempt to diversify its product range at a time when growth in its traditional commodity business was slowing, but the new market was highly experimental and it was unclear where the interest in the market would come from. Indeed, only 911 contracts changed hands on the first day of trading, representing a value of underlying equity of little more than US$3.5 million and, even by the end of 1975, average turnover was still a relatively modest 57,000 contracts per day.

It was not long, though, before hard commercial experience began to show the potential significance of the quantitative approach to option pricing that had been outlined by Black and Scholes. In its early days the market was run as a traditional commodities market, with a mixture of older traders who had been relatively unsuccessful in trading other contracts and wanted to try their luck with something new, and a number of younger traders for whom this was their first experience in trading. As might have been expected, the older traders tended to have no more success on the CBOE than they had done on the CBOT, but some of the younger traders began to understand the new market. Armed with a pile of sheets that Fischer Black was now producing and selling each week showing the theoretical value of options using his formula, they began to seek out mispriced options and make money as a result.

At about this time, a further impetus to encourage the use of quantitative techniques by traders came from a somewhat unexpected source – a clearing firm called First Options. As a market run on the traditional commodities exchange model, the clearing firms on the CBOE played an important part in establishing the new market because it was they who provided the guarantee to the clearing house on behalf of the individual floor traders. In order to help support the development of the new market, the brothers William F. and Edmund J. O'Connor, who owned one of the biggest clearing firms on the CBOT, set up First Options as a CBOE clearing firm at the outset of the exchange. However, it quickly became clear to the O'Connors that a number of the traders for whom they were providing clearing services were sustaining losses, suggesting that they didn't fully understand the risks they were taking. This worried the brothers because of the credit risk it posed for First Options. So in 1975, in order to limit this risk, they hired Michael Greenbaum, a maths major from Rensselaer Polytechnic Institute in New York to run training programmes for the traders, and they insisted that the traders who were taking losses go through the new training programme before they were allowed to resume their clearing account.

This proved a remarkably far-sighted initiative by the O'Connors. They were not only successful in reducing the credit risk to First Options. More significantly for the development for risk management practice, in 1977 Greenbaum persuaded the O'Connors to support him by establishing a company where he could apply a statistical portfolio approach to options trading. The firm Greenbaum set up with an initial staff of just three young floor traders – O'Connor and Associates – quickly became established as one of the leading firms in Chicago applying quantitative portfolio techniques to financial options. All this coincided with the "golden age" of equity options markets, with new instruments and new markets being established at a remarkable rate. Indeed, by 1985 when Greenbaum retired as an extremely wealthy man, turnover on the CBOE had risen to nearly 600,000 contracts per day, and O'Connor and Associates alone accounted for 7–8 per cent of market turnover. What Greenbaum had shown was that understanding and applying options theory was an essential prerequisite to being able to make money in modern financial markets. It was a lesson that had to be learned in many other firms and in many other ways over the next 10 years.

The 1980s: The changing face of international finance

The successful development of exchange-traded financial derivatives in the late 1970s in Chicago brought a new dimension to financial markets. For the first time products that enabled financial risk to be hedged in a precise manner meant that derivatives began to play an increasingly important part in international finance. The growing volatility in financial markets since the mid-1970s combined with increasing volumes of international financial activity saw demand for derivative products rising at a

Exhibit 2.1 Markets for selected financial derivative instruments (notional amounts outstanding at year-end, US$ bn), 1986–96

	1986	1987	1988	1989	1990	1991	1992	1993	1994	1995	1996
Exchange-traded											
Interest rate products	517	610	1,175	1,589	2,054	3,229	4,298	7,321	8,401	8,605	9,209
Foreign exchange products	49	74	60	66	74	81	98	110	96	82	97
Equity products	52	46	70	112	163	209	238	340	366	502	579
Over the counter[1]											
Interest rate swaps	–	683	1,010	1,503	2,312	3,065	3,851	6,177	8,816	12,811	–
Currency swaps[2]	–	184	320	449	578	807	860	900	915	1,197	–

[1] Data collected by ISDA only; the two sides of contracts between ISDA members are reported once only; excluding instruments such as forward foreign exchange contracts, currency options, forward interest rate agreements, and equity and commodity-related derivatives.
[2] Adjusted for reporting of both currencies; including cross-currency interest rate swaps.

Source: Capital Market Risk Advisors, Inc.

remarkable rate. Derivatives exchanges were established during the 1980s in almost all of the major financial markets, and the outstanding amounts of contracts grew from nothing to a figure in excess of US$4 billion by the early 1990s.

Perhaps more importantly (as Exhibit 2.1 shows), by the early 1990s the market in over-the-counter instruments, particularly the market in interest rate swaps, was growing at a rate exceeding the exchange-traded markets, thus giving rise to additional risks such as credit, legal and settlement risk that were not associated with exchange-traded instruments.

But the emergence of the new market in financial derivatives during the 1980s was itself part of a broader change in the nature of international finance which was moving from a market dominated by banks and bank finance to one where bonds, commercial paper and international equity were assuming a much more important role (see Exhibit 2.2). This process was accelerated in the mid-1980s with the opening up of the UK market in the "Big Bang" of 1987 and the opportunities afforded by the spectacular rise in the Japanese stock market, where foreign expertise in derivatives offered huge profit potential for foreign firms in the Japanese warrant market.

Exhibit 2.2 Bank lending and securities issues (in US$ bn), 1987–96

	1987	1988	1989	1990	1991	1992	1993	1994	1995	1996
Net bank lending[a]	275	250	290	430	185	165	200	190	330	405
	(68%)	(61%)	(61%)	(72%)	(47%)	(52%)	(50%)	(40%)	(51%)	(43%)
Net securities issues[b]	131	159	183	164	205	151	198	285	312	540
	(32%)	(39%)	(39%)	(28%)	(53%)	(48%)	(50%)	(60%)	(49%)	(57%)

[a] Changes in amounts outstanding, excluding exchange rate valuation effects and interbank redepositing.
[b] Net issues (excluding exchange rate valuation effects) of international bonds and Euronotes.

Source: BIS *67th annual report 1997* (based on data from Bank of England, Euroclear, Euromoney, Futures Industry Association, *International Financing Review*, ISDA, ISMA, national data and BIS).

In parallel with these changes, investment banking was taking a much more significant role relative to commercial banking. Banks like JP Morgan, and Bankers Trust in the US, the three big Swiss banks, UBS, Credit Suisse and SBC, and Deutsche Bank in Germany had already set out their intention to establish investment banking as a major international business activity. As a result, trading and investment banking income was representing a much larger proportion of overall bank income, with the provision of risk management services based on the developing derivatives markets an integral part of this trend. At the same time, the US investment banks were changing too: from fundamentally domestic institutions in the early 1980s, they had become progressively more international and were actively establishing extensive networks of overseas offices and businesses.

This process was not without its problems. Indeed there were many warning signs that pointed to the management and cultural problems associated with these changes. These were particularly evident in the events surrounding the Big Bang in the UK in 1986 when minimum commissions on equity trading were abolished and the restrictions on the ownership of member firms of the London Stock Exchange were lifted, offering banks the chance to move into the securities markets for the first time. Many large banks, both from the UK and overseas, purchased brokerage firms for premium prices, only to have to write off their investment within the next three or four years as they discovered, following the 1987 stock market crash, that they were not equipped to manage these businesses effectively. A number of major banks were affected including Lloyds Bank, Midland and Morgan Grenfell in the UK; Citibank, Chase and Security Pacific from the US; as well as Swiss Bank Corporation, all of which shut down their UK brokerage operations. Estimates of the combined cost of the write-offs at that time were as much as £2 billion.

Nor were the problems of handling the risks associated with the changes in financial markets confined to commercial banks. Many securities firms in the US also suffered heavy losses in the 1987 equity market crash, most notably those firms which relied on the theory of "portfolio insurance" or dynamic asset allocation as a means of protecting against falling markets. In 1987, Merrill Lynch announced a loss of over US$200 million arising from trading in mortgage-backed securities. In 1990 Drexel Burnham Lambert, the US investment bank, failed spectacularly as a result of its excessive reliance on the "junk bond" market at a time when the market was seriously illiquid. In 1991 the chairman of Salomon Brothers, John Gutfreund, resigned and the firm was fined US$200 million and came close to collapse when it was found to have submitted fraudulent applications in the US Treasury auctions. In 1994, Michael Carpenter, the chief executive of Kidder Peabody also resigned and Kidder was sold to Paine Webber following the announcement that Joseph Jett, the firm's star trader in US Treasuries, had apparently manufactured false profits in excess of US$350 million by exploiting differences in internal accounting systems. But perhaps more remarkably still, as recently as the first quarter of 1994 a number of investment banking firms were reported to have suffered losses on their interest rate trading activities of over US$500 million each as the US Federal Reserve Board embarked on its policy of raising interest rates.

1992–94: Growing concerns about derivatives

In the light of these problems it is perhaps surprising that the need for a risk management function was not already established and accepted within the financial services industry well before the early 1990s. The reality is that only a small minority of firms had such a function at that time. This can be explained in part by the fact that modern risk management techniques rely heavily on investments in information technology and

Exhibit 2.3 Case note: A lesson in legal risk

The fact that over-the-counter derivatives gave rise to new types of risk was made very clear as a result of a judgment by the House of Lords in London in 1991. The case involved the local authority (the municipality) in the London Borough of Hammersmith and Fulham. At the time, the Conservative central government was imposing tight constraints on the ability of local authorities to raise funds independently to finance their activities. In this political climate, the local authority treasurer in Hammersmith and Fulham had resorted to an innovative method of supplementing the finances by borrowing fixed rate funds as he was entitled to from the central government, and then through the late 1980s entering into swaps with a number of banks to convert the borrowing into floating rate obligations for the authority so that it would benefit from a fall in interest rates. But he then went further, and started taking outright positions in swaps unmatched by any underlying borrowings, building up a portfolio with a notional value of £2966 million.

Unfortunately for Hammersmith and Fulham, in the late 1980s the British economy was overheating. Inflationary pressures were building up and the government was forced into a policy of sharply higher interest rates. Short-term sterling rates rose from 8 per cent in 1987 to 13 per cent in early 1989 and the local authority, which had an annual budget of just £44.6 million was facing a loss on its swap portfolio of around £300 million. This in turn led to a legal action being brought by the official auditor, who had been appointed to review Hammersmith and Fulham's finances. The official auditor asked the courts to decide whether the authority had the legal powers to enter into swap agreements and, if it did not, to nullify the contracts.

The decision of the House of Lords in early 1991 that the local authority had indeed acted outside its powers ("ultra vires") sent shock waves through the swap market in London, not only because the banks which had dealt with Hammersmith and Fulham were facing losses, but because the court's judgment extended to a large number of swap contracts undertaken with other local authorities.[2]

---

advancements in power and capacity. But, more importantly, there was still no general consensus within the industry on the need for a risk management function.

Starting in the early 1990s, the mood began to change. In particular, if there was any doubt about regulators' concerns regarding the impact that the growing use of derivatives was having on the ability of management to control their businesses effectively, the position was made crystal clear in a speech in January 1992 by the then president of the Federal Reserve Bank of New York, Jerry Corrigan.

Corrigan issues a warning

Speaking to the Annual Mid-Winter Meeting of the New York State Bankers Association, Corrigan said "You had all better take a very, very hard look at off-balance sheet activities. The growth and complexity of [these] activities and the nature of the credit, price and president of the Federal Reserve Bank of New York, Jerry Corrigan. settlement risk they entail should give us all cause for concern." He concluded his comments on derivatives with the words which have come to be seen as a wake-up call to the management of financial services firms throughout the industry: "I hope this sounds like a warning, because it is. Off-balance sheet activities have a role, but they must be managed and controlled carefully and they must be understood by top management as well as by traders and rocket scientists."

Jerry Corrigan's speech marked the beginning of a period of significantly heightened official concern about the risks associated with derivative products, and particularly the risks of over-the-counter instruments. Indeed, it was partly in response to Corrigan's concern that the Group of 30 set up a study group under the chairmanship of Dennis Weatherstone, chairman of JP Morgan, to review the implications of the over-the-counter market. The report of the study group, entitled *Derivatives: Practices and Principles*, which was published in July 1993, constituted the first definitive assessment of the state of the market for over-the-counter derivatives. The report recommended a set of 20 best practices for market participants and end-users, including the recommendation that "Dealers should have a market risk management function, with clear independence and authority", which was the first formal recognition of the need for independent risk management.

Nevertheless, despite the significant progress achieved through the G30 report, official concern about the risks associated with over-the-counter derivative products remained at a high level. Investigations were initiated at different times by the General Accounting Office (GAO) and by the House of Representatives in the US, as well as by the Treasury and Civil Service Committee in the United Kingdom and by the European Parliament to consider whether these products were appropriately regulated. The report of the GAO in particular, which was published in 1994, drew attention to the fact that the major US investment banks were conducting a large part of their over-the-counter derivatives activities in firms that were affiliated with their registered US broker-dealer, but were not themselves subject to regulation by the SEC or the CFTC.

This in turn led to a second important industry initiative to respond to official concerns with over-the-counter derivatives – the creation of the Derivatives Policy Group at the initiative of the SEC chairman, Arthur Levitt. Unlike most of his predecessors, Levitt, himself a former investment banker, recognised that the industry needed to participate actively in any solution to an issue where the SEC itself had limited powers of intervention. So he suggested to the six major derivatives dealers with unregulated affiliates – Goldman Sachs, Morgan Stanley, Merrill Lynch, Lehman Brothers, Salomon Brothers and CS First Boston – that they should prepare a voluntary code setting out the standards with which they would agree to comply in order to provide assurance to the SEC that the activities of their unregulated affiliates would not cause any problems.

In response to Levitt's suggestion, the six firms set up a working group called the Derivatives Policy Group (DPG) under the chairmanship of two former banking regulators, Jerry Corrigan, who was working as a consultant at Goldman Sachs, and John Heimann, a former Comptroller of the Currency who had moved to Merrill Lynch. The DPG report, entitled *A Framework for Voluntary Oversight*, was published in February 1995 and set out the standards with which the six firms volunteered to comply under four headings – management controls; enhanced reporting; evaluation of risk in relation to capital; and counterparty relationships.

By the time the DPG report was published, however, a number of significant events had occurred that took the discussion about derivatives and risk control to new levels of urgency. First, official concern about the implications of over-the-counter derivatives was further exacerbated with the announcement in the course of 1994 of significant losses (see Exhibit 2.4), particularly within the US, on leveraged over-the-counter derivatives transactions, notably by two customers of Bankers Trust (Gibson Greetings and Procter and Gamble). Next came the high profile default of Orange County in California as a result of the controversial investment activities of its

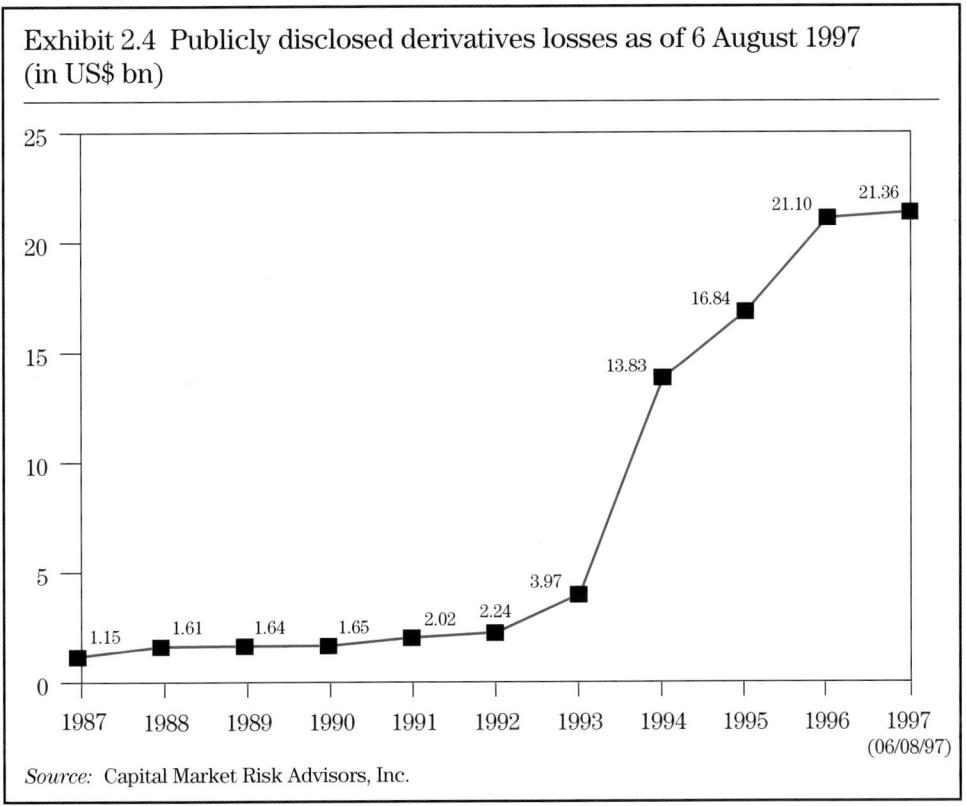

Exhibit 2.4 Publicly disclosed derivatives losses as of 6 August 1997 (in US$ bn)

Source: Capital Market Risk Advisors, Inc.

aptly named treasurer, Robert Citron. The immediate cause of these problems was strikingly similar to the story of Hammersmith and Fulham Council in the late 1980s. The losses arose from positions that were heavily geared against a rise in US interest rates, and the unanticipated decision by the US Federal Reserve to raise interest rates in a pre-emptive strike against inflation at the beginning of 1994 created losses of US$14 million in the case of Gibson Greetings, US$160 million in the case of Proctor and Gamble, and US$1.6 billion in the case of Orange County.

In each case the losing party claimed that the losses were either directly or indirectly the result of misleading advice, and brought actions against their advisers for compensation. This in turn led to a further extensive debate as to the extent to which broker-dealers should be held responsible for any advice given to customers in relation to the sale of over-the-counter derivatives. In addition, a joint official action was initiated against Bankers Trust by the Federal Reserve Bank of New York, the Securities and Exchange Commission and the Commodity Futures Trading Commission. The action criticised the management of Bankers Trust for failing to supervise its staff and to implement its own internal management procedures, and led to the appointment of a new chairman, Frank Newman, previously the Assistant Secretary of the US Treasury, in an effort to restore the company's battered reputation.

FINANCIAL TIMES

MONDAY FEBRUARY 27 1995

3am EDITION   65p

rt | Bank of England set to provide liquidity to system ■ Singapore trader loses group £500m

Barings forced to cease trading

1995: One day in Singapore

Notwithstanding all this, the defining moment in the development of risk management occurred on the morning of Sunday 26 February 1995 when it was announced that Baring Brothers, the oldest and among the most famous names in British finance, had lost over £600 million and was insolvent as a result of its derivatives trading activities in Singapore. In many ways the story of Barings represented a microcosm of the issues that underlie the changes in international finance since the mid-1980s. Established in 1762, by the early 1980s Barings was a typical example of a British merchant bank. Its core specialisation was in corporate finance in the UK, but it also had some success in the sterling Eurobond business, and a moderately sized fund management and private banking business. Like most of the other merchant banks, however, it faced a challenge at the time of the Big Bang if it was to maintain its position as a leading firm in the face of growing competition from the new entrants to the securities markets, both from the bigger UK firms like Barclays, Nat West Bank and Warburgs, but also from the foreign firms moving into the London market.

At the time of Big Bang, Barings avoided spending excessively on developing a securities business, preferring instead to team up with Christopher Heath, a broker who had developed a particularly profitable niche business selling Japanese equities and equity warrants to UK clients at a time when the Japanese equity market was performing extremely strongly. The business, which was renamed Barings Securities, was run by Heath as if it was a traditional independent brokerage firm, with little intervention from the management of Barings. This arm's length arrangement worked well for a number of years while the Japanese market continued to perform strongly, and Heath proceeded to build up Barings Securities as one of the leading securities firms in the Asia Pacific region. But in 1992 the Japanese market turned down, and Barings Securities suffered a loss of £20 million so requiring support from its parent, Barings, for the first time. This led to a conflict between the management of Barings and Heath about the correct strategy for the securities business. Heath wanted Barings to inject additional capital into the business to help it to expand its trading capabilities, while the management of Barings were concerned about the potential costs and wanted the business to be integrated more closely with the rest of the bank. In the event there was a stalemate and a very public disagreement between Heath and the management of Barings. In early 1993, Heath and a number of his key staff left, and Barings began the task of integrating the securities subsidiary into the rest of the bank.

It was against this background of management disruption that Barings was also undertaking its ill-fated derivatives trading business on the Singapore Monetary Exchange (Simex). The business was initially set up purely to undertake deals on the exchange on behalf of clients, but Nick Leeson, the manager of the business, who had never traded on the floor of an exchange before he went to Singapore in 1992, managed to persuade his managers that he could generate "risk-free" profits for

Barings itself by arbitraging between the same contract – the stock index future on the Nikkei 225 Index on the Osaka and Simex exchanges. Indeed, such was Leeson's purported success at this strategy that he was believed to have generated a profit of £10 million in 1993, rising to £28 million in 1994, which constituted some 20 per cent of the total reported profit of Barings Group.

As the subsequent investigations into the collapse of Barings have shown, Leeson never made any money trading on behalf of Barings. He had simply found a way to hide his losses and to generate false profits by the use of an internal suspense account – an account that he had numbered 88888 ("eight" being the Chinese lucky number) – which he managed to maintain for two years without detection. Leeson was able to continue his fictitious trading partly because there was confusion within Barings as to who was responsible for managing him and for understanding how he made his money. Indeed, the simplest of management investigation should have revealed that Leeson's version of how he was making that amount of money with no risk was simply incredible. In particular, no one seems to have asked why, if Leeson was taking no risk, he kept on needing to borrow more and more money from Barings in London to fund his positions.

But at an even more basic level, Leeson was only able to perpetrate his fraud because Barings allowed him to control both the front office and the back office at the same time, so invalidating any independent controls over the business. The bottom line was that Barings lacked the management infrastructure to control the business it was undertaking. It had expanded too fast, and was run by a board of directors who didn't understand and could not control the risks of the businesses that they were running.

Risk management under the spotlight

The collapse of Barings was significant not just from the perspective of the customers of Barings itself, but also for the broader impact which it had on attitudes within the financial services community and among the regulators. Barings was a bank which was supervised by the Bank of England, one of the most highly respected bank supervisors in the world, and which the day before its collapse had apparently been well capitalised and profitable. Indeed, the chairman of Barings, Peter Baring, had recently told Brian Quinn, the director at the Bank of England responsible for banking supervision, that "it is not actually terribly difficult to make money in the securities business". Yet Barings had seen its capital wiped out in a few days by a lack of control over one employee in a relatively small office on the other side of the world.

What Barings showed in the clearest terms was that the real issue was not derivatives in general, or over-the-counter derivatives in particular. The real issue was about the quality of management and control required in modern international financial markets. Over-the-counter derivatives were in fact only the most visible symptom of a more fundamental change which had been taking place in international finance and in the way in which the firms were organised since the mid 1980s.

Barings can thus be seen as a watershed event for both the industry and the regulators. It was significant not so much for its direct effects on financial markets, which were surprisingly small (Barings was acquired for £1 within a period of 10 days by the Dutch bank, ING, and quickly resumed much of its former activities), as for its effect on attitudes more widely. The collapse made clear both to management and to a wider public that the changes which had taken place in the international financial market required an urgent reappraisal of the way in which firms were being managed.

It also led to a substantial rethinking of the regulatory approach both internationally and within the UK, as the events demonstrated all too obviously that the existing national regulatory structures and approaches were no longer appropriate.

In the UK a fundamental review was undertaken to learn why the supervisory system had failed, leading directly to a radical overhaul of the techniques of banking supervision used by the Bank of England. Now the approach concentrates more on assessing the risk profile and control environment of the firms being supervised and less on the financial information received from banks. The subsequent decision by the new Labour government in 1997 to undertake an overhaul of the regulatory structure in the UK and to integrate into the new Financial Services Authority both banking and securities regulation owes much to the reappraisal of the UK regulatory system that Barings initiated.

At the international level, too, Barings had a significant impact, because it highlighted a number of gaps in the existing regulatory arrangements. In the immediate aftermath of the crisis, the supervisory authorities responsible for the world's major derivatives exchanges met to review how international regulation should be strengthened, and ratified the Windsor Declaration which set out a programme for improving regulatory oversight and co-operation in derivative markets. In a parallel initiative, the Futures Industry Association of the US and the Futures and Options Association initiated a project which resulted in a code of best practice for derivatives markets and for firms active in the international markets. It also led to the establishment of a further G30 study involving both industry participants and regulators to determine what steps needed to be taken to reduce systemic risk.

In addition, the collapse of Barings, coming as it did shortly after the Mexican peso crisis of late 1994, led to greatly heightened political interest in the way that international finance and regulation was structured. As a result, the heads of government at the G7 summit meeting in Halifax, Nova Scotia in June 1995 called for the banking and securities regulators to review and strengthen the arrangements that they had in place to oversee the safety of the international financial markets.

The heightened political interest in the regulatory framework for international markets has in turn brought about a significantly accelerated pace of work in regulatory and industrial bodies. In May 1996, in response to the request from the Halifax summit, the Basle Committee and IOSCO set out eight principles for international regulation and announced a new initiative to enhance the arrangements for regulatory co-operation in supervising internationally active firms. In 1997, in preparation for the Denver Summit, the Basle Committee published its *Core Principles for Effective Banking Supervision*, and in preparation for the 1998 Birmingham Summit (at the time of publication) IOSCO was preparing a paper on the core principles for regulating securities markets.

The increasing focus of this discussion has been on the techniques that firms and supervisors can use in order to minimise the risk of problems arising which threaten the stability of the international markets, and all are focusing on the central part that risk management and control plays in financial firms. Thus, for example, in February 1997 the Institute of International Finance published a report entitled *The Supervision of Financial Conglomerates – a Private Sector Perspective*, which argued strongly that regulators and supervisors should adopt a global, risk-based approach to the supervision of internationally active firms. In June 1997, the Joint Forum of banking, securities and insurance regulators produced a report for the G7 heads of government which emphasised the role risk analysis should play in group supervision. Moreover, in

July 1997 the final report of the G30 study group on systemic risk was published, advocating the establishment of an international industry group to set clear standards for risk management against which international financial firms could be objectively judged by both their regulators and their counterparties.

Conclusion

In this chapter we traced the origins of modern risk management from the earliest days of financial derivatives in the early 1970s through the growing trend towards the internationalisation of finance in the 1980s to the present day. We noted that ten years ago financial firms did not have a risk management function. But certain key events, such as Gerald Corrigan's warning that derivatives must be understood by the top management as well as rocket scientists, together with the G30 report on derivatives, and the formation of the Derivatives Policy Group, signalled an increasing official focus on the importance of risk management.

However, it was the collapse of Barings in 1995 which really served to underline in the clearest and most public way the consequences of failing to control an international financial firm effectively. The political and regulatory attention that followed the collapse of Barings has resulted in a heightened recognition of the role and importance of risk management at all levels, both within firms and among financial regulators.

So the journey of financial risk management from the smoking room of the CBOT and the pages of the *Journal of Political Economy* to the agenda of the heads of government and the mainstream of best practice in financial markets is almost complete. The challenge that the industry now faces is how to make risk management work in practice, and that is the subject which is addressed in the rest of this book.

---

[1] Myron Scholes and Robert Merton received the 1997 Nobel Prize in Economic Sciences for their "new method to determine the value of derivatives", which was developed in close collaboration with the late Fischer Black.

[2] The judgment dismissed the banks' argument that swaps were a form of insurance against financial risk in the following terms: "By insurance, an assured sacrifices a premium which when aggregated with premiums from other assured will form a pool from which the insurer will indemnify the unfortunate victim (if any) who suffers from the risk insured against. A swap contract based on a notional principal sum of £1 million under which the local authority agrees to pay the bank £10,000 if Libor rises by 1 per cent and the bank promises to pay the local authority £10,000 if Libor falls by 1 per cent is more akin to gambling than insurance".

3

A framework for firmwide risk management

As discussed in Chapter 2, there has been a significant change in the focus on the risk management process at financial firms over the past three or four years. Starting with the G30 report in 1993, an increasing number of documents and recommendations have appeared from different industry and regulatory bodies about the subject. The purpose of this chapter is to consider the components of an effective risk management process.

The origins of firmwide risk management

Although it has not always been referred to in those terms, risk management is not a new concept for financial firms, and many components of a risk management function have been in place for many years. In the case of banks, for example, where credit risk was the most prevalent, credit policies and procedures have traditionally been accorded a high priority by management; it was common for the senior credit officer to be a member of the Board, and for senior management and the Board to discuss credit issues on a regular basis. Similarly in securities firms where the principal risk was failure to comply with the regulatory and legal requirements of securities markets, the primary risk control function was performed by the compliance and legal departments, which reported to the firm's General Counsel, who again was usually a member of senior management.

Risk management terminology

The term risk management does not have a universally agreed definition.

In this book we use the term risk management to refer to the complete set of policies and procedures which organisations have in place to manage, monitor and control their exposure to risk. We also adopt the market practice of referring to the independent function within companies which is responsible for the monitoring and control of risk as the risk management group or risk management function, although in practice such groups seldom manage risk directly. In our experience, the risk management group rarely has any authority to assume risk positions itself, although in some firms it may have the authority to instruct front office management to alter risk positions.

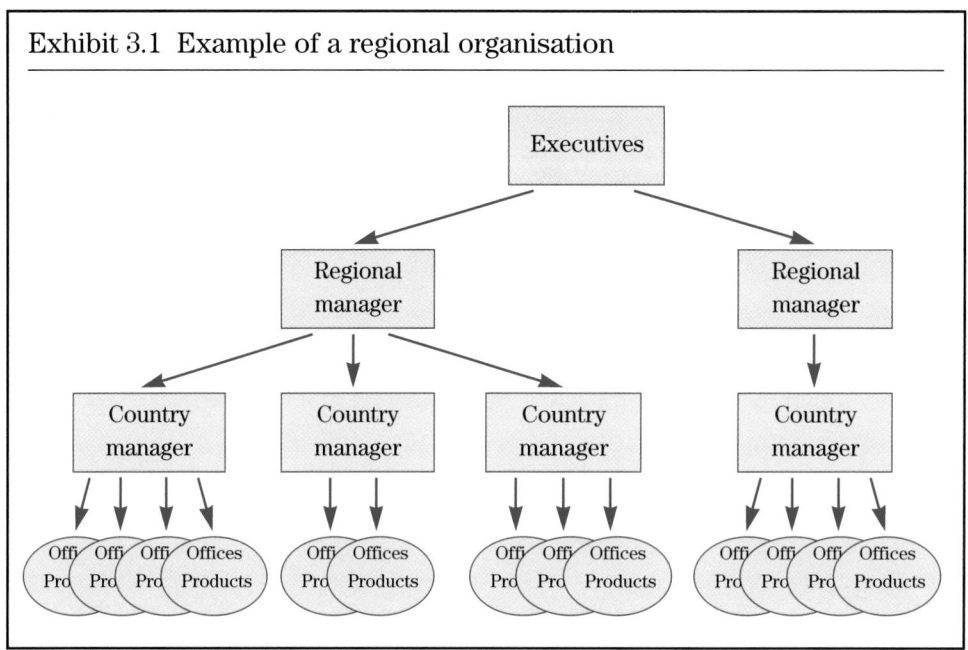

Exhibit 3.1 Example of a regional organisation

Furthermore, when firms operated internationally, they were typically organised on a regional basis (see Exhibit 3.1). In these circumstances firms generally accounted for their business on an office-by-office basis. The primary responsibility for the effectiveness of management controls in the local office lay with the regional or country manager, often assisted by a local internal audit function checking on the local office's operational controls and conformity with internal guidelines and controls.

In this environment, the approach to managing other risks was usually less structured. Control over market risk, for example, to the extent it existed as an identified function, was usually seen as an accounting or P&L issue that was organised as an addition to one of these back office departments. By the beginning of the 1980s some firms had begun to develop what was termed a "middle office" which performed some of the functions now recognised as part of a risk management department's responsibilities.

Arrangements of the type described here were common in the majority of banks and securities firms until comparatively recently, but the change in the nature of international finance in the past 10 years has meant that it is no longer practicable to run the business primarily on a local or legal entity basis. The demands of clients and the need for a consolidated view of business results as well as a portfolio view of risk has led firms increasingly to organise their activities on a functional and global basis. As a result, firms have come to rely on more sophisticated forms of "matrix" management (see Exhibit 3.2). Thus staff employed in the different business activities such as trading, corporate finance, funds management or private banking will typically report to a "functional" manager who assesses their overall contribution to the business line rather than to a particular office. At the same time, a local or regional manager will normally be responsible for ensuring that the different business lines co-ordinate effectively in the relevant region and that the firm is responding effectively to the needs of local clients and regulators.

As a result of this move to matrix structures, the focus within firms has changed from performance measurement and management at the local level to an increased focus on business results at the functional business line and group level, with the

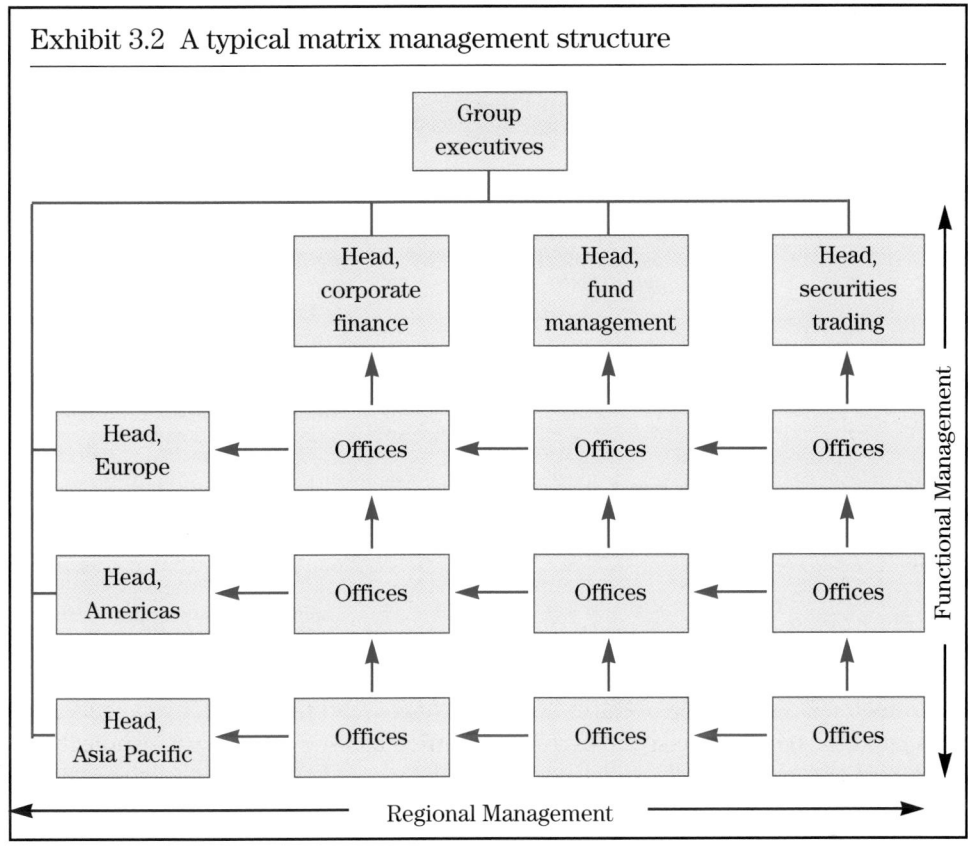

Exhibit 3.2 A typical matrix management structure

activities and performance of regional offices or legal entities more likely to be determined by regulatory and tax issues than by business considerations.

The scope of firmwide risk management

This change in the way that firms are being managed has also led to a recognition that the old structures under which risk was managed primarily at the local level were no longer satisfactory. The risk management function has had to respond to the reorganisation of firms' business on to global lines. Moreover, firms have encountered new types of risk as their business has changed. Banks for example have increasingly become exposed to compliance and regulatory risk as they have expanded their securities dealing and advisory business. At the same time, credit risk has become more of an issue for securities firms as they have become more extensively involved in trading longer dated over-the-counter derivatives. Further, as both banks and securities firms have both become more heavily involved in trading activities, market risk has becoming a substantially more important concern for both.

In consequence, it is now widely recognised both by firms and the official regulatory bodies that an effective risk management function not only needs to be organised on a firmwide basis, but also needs to cover all material aspects of risk in financial markets (see Exhibit 3.3). This inevitably raises the question of what risks should be covered by firmwide risk management, given the great breadth of risks that firms face and the different ways in which risk can be defined.

While there is no single agreed listing of all of the relevant risk factors, the seven risk categories that were defined by the Basle Committee and IOSCO in their 1994 papers on risk management in the over-the-counter derivative markets provide a useful reference. These are:

Exhibit 3.3 The risk management landscape

Risk Dimension	Definition	Managed by
Market risk	The risk to an institution's financial condition arising from adverse movements in the level or volatility of market prices	Providing consistent information of market risk across the organisation at all levels; calculation consistent risk measures (volatilities, VaR); establishing appropriate procedures and monitoring risk limits; and understanding where risk comes from across the organisation.
Credit risk	The risk that a counterparty will fail to perform on an obligation owed to the firm	Monitoring credit exposures relative to limits; resetting limits regularly; and scenario analysis.
Settlement risk	The risk that a firm will not receive funds or instruments from its counterparties at the expected time	Monitoring counterparty activity and settlement limits; and managing presettlement counterparty exposures
Liquidity risk	An institution faces two types of liquidity risk: one related to specific products or markets, the other related to the general funding of the institution's activities. The former is the fisk that an institution may not be able to, or cannot easily unwind or offset a particular position at or near the previous market price because of inadequate market depth or because of disruptions in the market. Funding liquidity risk is the risk that the institution will be unable to meet its payment obligations on settlement dates or in the event of margin call	Actively matching funding horizon of debt to liquidity of positions; and developing liquidity guidelines to limit exposure in asset classes and instruments
Operational risk	The risk that deficiencies in information systems or internal controls will result in unexpected loss. This risk is associated with human error, system failures and inadequate procedures and controls	Establishing proper supervision and segregation of duties; testing all systems in a comprehensive manner; establishing complete reconciliations between internal and external systems; and setting up compete independent backup facilities and systems.
Legal risk	The risk that contracts are not legally enforceable or documented correctly	Carefully contracting and conducting business with external parties and employees; and establishing clear compliance and regulatory structures

- **Market risk:**

  Market risk is in essence, the firm's exposure to the sensitivity of value of a financial instrument or portfolio to changes in market parameters. These parameters include foreign exchange rates, interest rates, equity market indices, implied volatilities, and commodity prices. These are examined in considerably more detail in Chapter 4, and in the balance of this book.

- **Credit risk:**

  The traditional view of credit risk within banks was limited to the risk of the outright default of the counterparty. In an environment where banks were committed to loans for the full term of their life, and could only obtain repayment from the borrower itself, this was an understandable view of credit risk. As a result, banks held loans on their balance sheet at par, and only wrote down the value, in the form of a provision, when the borrower began to default on its obligations. Moreover, the risk of default of a particular borrower was regarded as a random event and few efforts were made to analyse the statistical properties of default risk.

  More recently however this binary interpretation of credit risk has come under considerable criticism as a poor representation of the true nature of credit risk. In particular it has been cited as a major cause of the strong "bunching" effect on banks' reported results over the course of an economic cycle. This effect has shown up particularly strongly in the credit cycle of the late 1980s and through the 1990s when banks in a number of different countries have all reported large profits during the upswing of the cycle, and then have all had to make substantial provisions and frequently report losses as borrowers went into default at the same point in the downturn. This experience has led banks to examine the potential for improving their ability to model the default risk in their portfolios.

  At the same time there has been an increasing interest in the developing the market in traded instruments based on credit. This includes an increasing interest in trading bonds on the basis of credit spreads rather than on interest rates - a development which will be accelerated further by the introduction of the euro in the European Union in 1999. In addition, a secondary market is developing in loans as banks seek ways to economise on their use of regulatory capital, and firms are also now trading credit derivative products such as total return swaps and credit linked notes which allow banks to hedge the credit risk in their portfolio without having to sell the underlying asset. Since all these instruments are traded in a mark to market environment, they are susceptible to daily price movements which are related to improvements or deteriorations in the in the condition of the underlying obligor but which fall short of outright default. In many trading firms this type of issuer-specific risk is one of the larger risks which the firm faces, and is often larger than the firm's outright directional exposure to market variables such as interest rate risk.

  The recognition of the importance of specific risk in securities markets has in turn led to a broader interpretation of the nature of credit risk. Instead of just being the exposure to the outright default of the counterparty, credit risk can be seen in the broader sense as the risk of a loss in the economic value of a firm's assets as a result of a change in the ability of a firm's counterparties to perform on their obligations. Under this interpretation of credit risk the determining factor is not whether any particular counterparty will in fact default in the immediate future, but whether there has been a change in the likelihood of the counterparty defaulting. The agreement by banking supervisors to allow firms to use internal models to calculate the capital required to cover the specific risk in

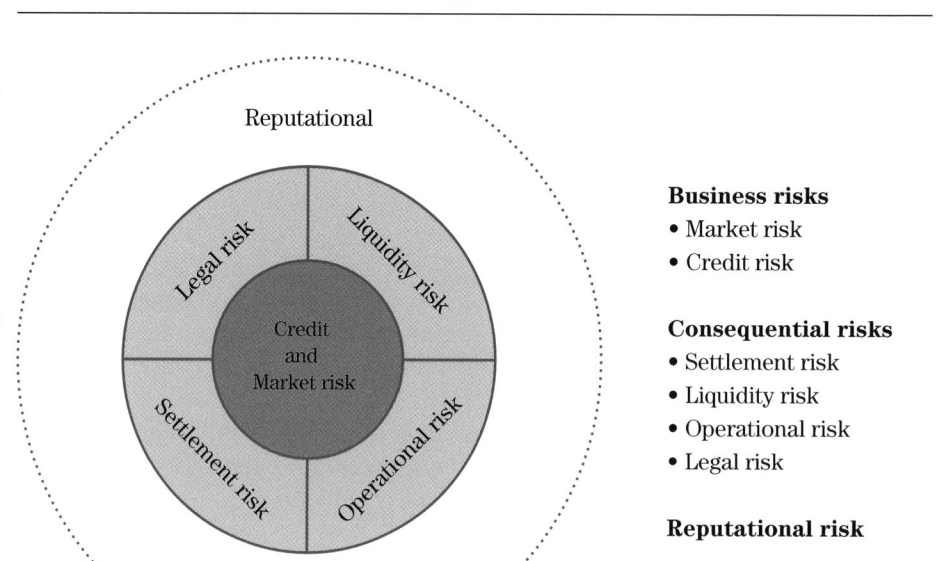

Exhibit 3.4 Business risk vs. consequential risk

Reputational

Business risks
- Market risk
- Credit risk

Consequential risks
- Settlement risk
- Liquidity risk
- Operational risk
- Legal risk

Reputational risk

risk

Market risk and Credit risk can be thought of as "Business Risks", ie, the risks a financial institution chooses to assume with a view of making money. By contrast, the other risks which firms face are not assumed with the view of remuneration but are consequential risks, ie, risks that inevitably arise as a result of being in the financial services business.

their trading books has added a further interest finding ways of quantifying and managing both specific and default risk.

In an attempt to assist the development of techniques for modelling default risk, JP Morgan and a number of co-sponsoring institutions issued Credit Metrics™ in mid-1997, which uses migration matrices to model the probability of default in a portfolio of assets. A short while later Credit Suisse Financial Products issued their own product, Credit Risk+ which offers an alternative methodology based on insurance theory and triggering considerable debate about the relative merits of the differing approaches. From this debate it is clear that credit risk is an area where statistical risk management tools are still being developed, and where firms have to use considerable skill and judgement in managing their overall exposure to the risk.

We examine the issues associated with the measurement of specific risk in more detail in Chapter 9. The broader issue of managing credit risk within a banking business where loans are not traded is clearly also of the highest importance to the management of a bank but is beyond the scope of this book.

- **Settlement risk:**

  Although settlement risk has always been an aspect of financial markets, it has not always received a high level of management attention, despite the fact that one of the most serious crises in international finance, the collapse of Bankhaus Herstatt in 1974, was a result of settlement risk. Although settlement risk is present in all dealing transactions where firms exchange cash for securities or to honour their obligations under trading contracts, it is particularly characteristic of foreign

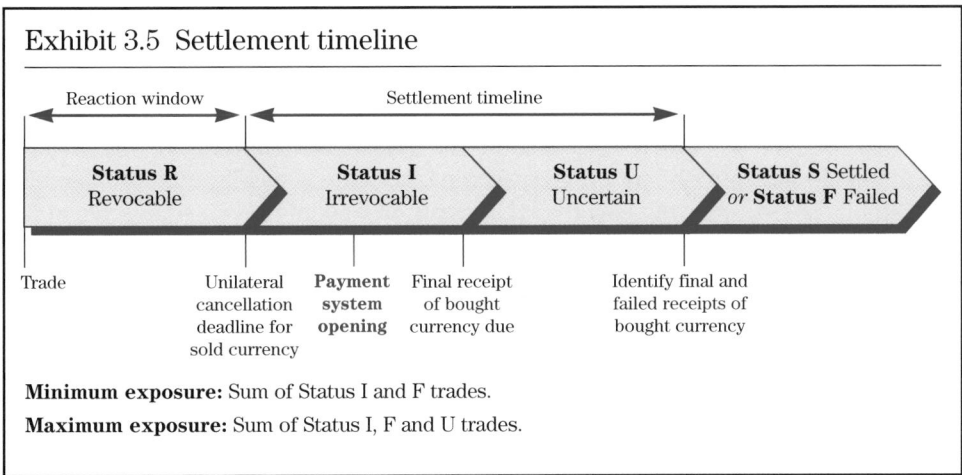

Exhibit 3.5 Settlement timeline

Reaction window

Settlement timeline

| **Status R** Revocable | **Status I** Irrevocable | **Status U** Uncertain | **Status S** Settled *or* **Status F** Failed |

Trade

Unilateral cancellation deadline for sold currency

Payment system opening

Final receipt of bought currency due

Identify final and failed receipts of bought currency

Minimum exposure: Sum of Status I and F trades.

Maximum exposure: Sum of Status I, F and U trades.

exchange trading because of the fact that in a cross border exchange-for-value currency trade (say an exchange of US dollars for Japanese yen) cash payments are made in one currency (Japanese yen) well before funds are received in the other currency (US dollars). Add to this time differential the fact that payment instructions are typically released at least one business day prior to the actual day in which the trade is due to settle and the incoming receipts are only reconciled one business day after the agreed settlement date, and there are multiple days worth of payments lodged in electronic queues awaiting final disposition while outside of the direct control of the issuer of the original payment instructions. This so called Timeline effect on settlement exposure is shown in Exhibit 3.5.

Despite the dramatic growth that has taken place in the volume of foreign exchange business in the intervening 24 years, with daily turnover in 1995 in excess of equivalent US$1.2 trillion, the settlement process has not changed. Moreover, the actual related payments are a multiple of this figure since each

---

Exhibit 3.6 Case note: The collapse of Bankhaus Herstatt, 1974

On 26 June 1974 the Bundesaufsichtsamt fur das Kreditwesen withdrew the banking licence of Bankhaus Herstatt, a small bank in Cologne active in the FX market, and ordered it into liquidation during the banking day but after the close of the interbank payments system in Germany. Prior to the announcement of Herstatt's closure, several of its counterparties had, through their branches or correspondents, irrevocably paid Deutschmarks to Herstatt on that day through the German payments system against anticipated receipts of US dollars later the same day in New York in respect of maturing spot and forward transactions.

Upon the termination of Herstatt's business at 10.30am New York time on 26 June (3.30pm in Frankfurt), Herstatt's New York correspondent bank suspended outgoing US dollar payments from Herstatt's account. This action left Herstatt's counterparty banks exposed for the full value of the Deutschmark deliveries made (credit risk and liquidity risk). Moreover, banks which had entered into forward trades with Herstatt not yet due for settlement lost money in replacing the contracts in the market (replacement risk), and others had deposits with Herstatt (traditional counterparty credit risk).

Source: Bank for International Settlements, Settlement Risk in Foreign Exchange Transactions, March 1996, p.6.

trade will consist of two payments, less the effects of netting which are remain relatively small. This slow progress by the industry in addressing the issue of foreign exchange settlement risk has not gone unnoticed by the banking supervisors and regulators. A report published in March 1996 by the Committee on Payment and Settlement Systems of the Bank for International Settlements footnoted that little or no progress had been made in tackling the problems of settlement risk since the collapse of Herstatt. In view of the potential scale of the risk and lack of progress to date on this issue, the report gave a clear warning to the industry that it should institute steps to reduce the scale of global settlement risk within the subsequent two years if it wished to avoid further regulatory action. Settlement risk is a highly complex issue with many facets, to include: the creation of limits, checking availability prior to committing to a trade, deal capture, trade confirmation reconciliation, excess control reporting, payment release management, receipt reconciliation, failure-to-receive management, activity analysis and stress management. In-depth knowledge of local law and market practice are essential. Settlement risk is an issue which, in an increasingly international market, firms cannot afford to ignore.[1]

Exhibit 3.7 The CLS initiative

Partly in response to the BIS report, various industry groups have intensified their efforts to encircle foreign exchange settlement risk. These efforts include the initiation of the Exchange Clearing House Limited (ECHO) in August 1995, the creation of Multinet International Bank (MIB) which received approvals from both the Federal Reserve Bank of New York and New York State Banking Department in December 1996, the work of the Group of Forty (G 40) during 1996 and 1997, and the work of the Group of Twenty (G 20) culminating in the creation of CLS Services Ltd. (CLSS) in London in July 1997. It was announced in October 1997 that an attempt will be made to consolidate all of these individual efforts under one umbrella beginning with the merger of ECHO, MIB and CLSS. Such a merger will bring under one roof a multiplicity of risk reduction techniques in a single clearing system to include: bilateral obligation netting, multilateral obligation netting, multilateral settlement netting, and continuous linked settlement (CLS) with simultaneous payment versus payment (PVP) in an environment which assures finality.

- **Liquidity risk:**

  The central importance of liquidity risk to financial firms, both in terms of the liquidity of trading positions and the availability of adequate funding, was shown most clearly in the collapse of Drexel Burnham Lambert in February 1990. The reason that Drexel ran into difficulties was because it had built up a sizeable inventory position in illiquid high yielding bonds, which it was unable to sell in the market when it needed to obtain funding for its positions. However, the actual collapse was due to the drying up of Drexel's funding sources. Thus, despite the fact that on the morning of the collapse the US Securities and Exchange Commission and the Federal Reserve Bank of New York confirmed to the market Drexel's solvency, the firm still failed by the close of business that same day because of its inability to meet its funding obligations as they fell due.

  In contrast, when Salomon got into funding difficulties in the market in 1991 as a result of government bond trading problems, it is generally recognised that its well structured liquidity management policy, which ensured that it had adequate recourse to assured long-term sources of funds at all times, played an important part in helping it reduce its balance sheet and thus weather the initial crisis. This in turn provided reassurance to the market that Salomon would survive, which in due course restored its access to other sources of funds.

- **Operational risk:**

    Operational risk covers a broad range of risks that are internal to the firm, and has in the past received rather less attention than other aspects of risk. However, attention is increasingly being focused on this issue because of the scale of the losses that firms have suffered as a result of breakdowns in internal controls. A number of the examples in Chapter 2 can be attributed to a failure of operational controls, but two further examples help to indicate the diversity of operational risk and the scale of the losses that can arise as a result.

    In the first example, Toshihide Iguchi, a US government bond trader at Daiwa bank in New York, created a loss of over US$1 billion for his bank over a period of 10 years because he was able to cover up the losses on his bond trading by switching securities out of clients' custody accounts. In the second, Peter Young, an apparently successful fund manager at Morgan Grenfell Asset Management in London, created a loss of a similar size for Deutsche Bank by failing to follow the investment guidelines for the mutual fund he was managing and investing instead in highly speculative unlisted stocks. When the scale of the problem was finally revealed, Deutsche had to step in and compensate customers for any loss they might have incurred as a result of Young's unconventional actions.

    Partly because of the losses which a number of firms have suffered as a result of their failure to manage operational risk effectively, the subject is now receiving a much higher level of attention than in the past, and firms are beginning to apply the same quality of management attention to what has traditionally been a back office concern as is applied to the more well-developed areas of credit and market risk.

- **Legal risk:**

    The scope of legal risk, and of regulatory risk, to which it is closely related, has increased significantly as firms have moved to enhance their earnings from new instruments and from fee-based and client advisory businesses.

    This risk includes not only the question of whether documentation is enforceable, as in the case of Hammersmith and Fulham (see Chapter 2), but also whether the firm has discharged its own legal and regulatory responsibilities to its customers appropriately. The cost to a firm of such a failure, even in the absence of a formal legal judgment against it, can be significant. Thus Bankers Trust, for example, was reported to have paid some US$150 million in 1996 to settle the cases of mis-selling which it faced from clients such as Proctor and Gamble and Gibson Greetings. But this figure is dwarfed by the judgment under which Prudential Securities had to pay US$1.5 billion to compensate clients for mis-selling of limited partnerships in the 1980s, and the insurance industry in the UK is estimated to face a potential bill of as much as US$5 billion as a result of the mis-selling of private pension schemes in the late 1980s.

In addition to these six risks, a seventh risk category could be added, which is often mentioned in this context but which is not among the categories defined by the Basle Committee and IOSCO in 1994:

- **Reputational risk:**

    This is the risk that any action taken by a firm or its employees creates a negative perception in the external market place.

    Companies increasingly recognise the overriding significance of this risk, which can arise as a result of problems in almost any part of a business, and as a result of any number of risk factors, but can have an impact on a company's standing and its business far in excess of the initial problem.

Conclusions on risk categories

While the above list is useful, it should not be regarded as exhaustive in itemising the risks that firms face. Other risks that firms might wish to include are, for example, interest rate risk and sovereign risk, particularly in the context of banking, as well as tax risk, strategic risk, and business continuity risk that are clearly matters of concern to all businesses. The important point about these risk categorisations is that each firm has to be able to assess the full range of risks that it faces and ensure that they are adequately captured within its risk management process.

The structure of firmwide risk management

In addition to defining the scope of the risk management process, the way in which a firm is structured to undertake risk management is of paramount importance. Perhaps more than anything else, a central theme of all the different recommendations on risk management best practice is the recognition that if risk management is going to be effective it must be a top-down process (see Exhibit 3.8). Unless the risk management process is fully endorsed and actively supported by the Board and by the senior management of a firm as an integral part of the way that the firm is managed, it cannot be effective. This means that the Board needs to set out clearly the firm's attitude towards risk taking, its appetite for risk, and the assignment of responsibility for assuming and controlling risks. In addition, the Board needs to endorse the firm's system of risk policies and risk limits and to review those arrangements on a systematic basis.

Once the firm's risk policies have been endorsed by the Board, senior management also needs to be involved in the implementation of those policies on a day-to-day basis. This means that there needs to be an effective structure for risk management, with appropriate levels of authority for taking risk, and a framework of risk committees and risk reports to ensure that senior management does in practice address risk issues on a regular basis.

In parallel with an effective top-down management process, it is also essential that the risk management function itself must be established independently from the business areas and operate as a controlling or monitoring function. The role of the risk management function is to provide assurance to senior management and the Board that the firm is assessing its risk effectively, and is complying with its own risk management standards. This means that the risk management function has to have an independent reporting line to senior management, and also the skills and resources to enable it to understand and challenge the business lines. (Some of the practical implications of this important consideration are discussed in more detail in Section IV.)

The risk management process

In parallel with the establishment of an effective structure for risk management, a firm also has to ensure that it has in place a comprehensive risk management process. Such a process requires the elements shown in Exhibit 3.9 on page 40.

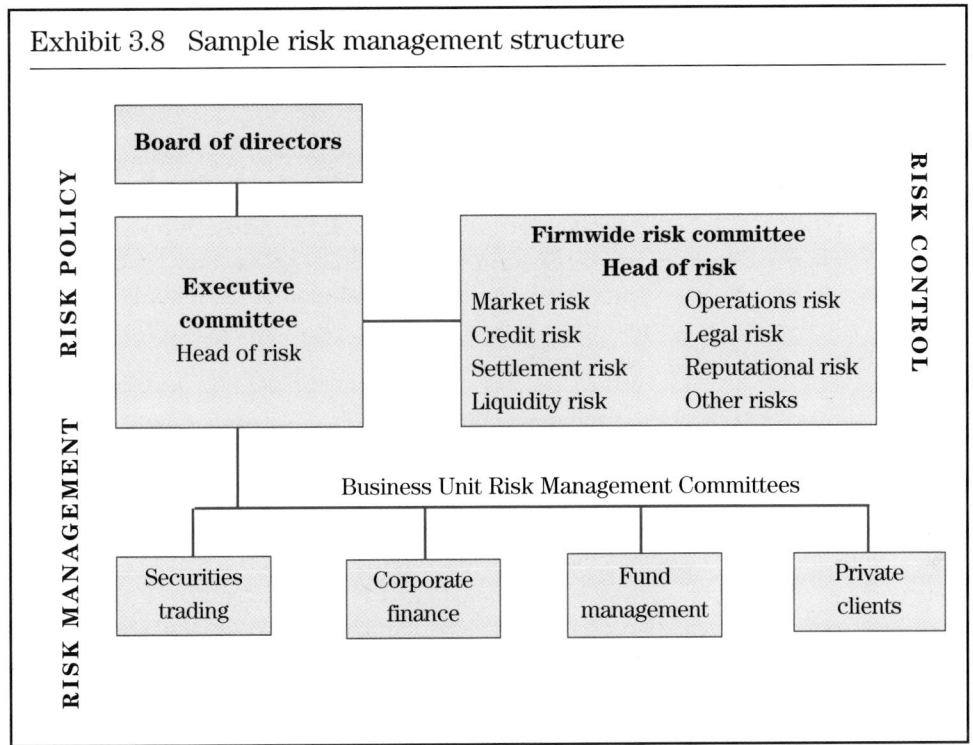

Exhibit 3.8   Sample risk management structure

RISK POLICY

RISK MANAGEMENT

RISK CONTROL

Board of directors

Executive committee
Head of risk

Firmwide risk committee
Head of risk

Market risk	Operations risk
Credit risk	Legal risk
Settlement risk	Reputational risk
Liquidity risk	Other risks

Business Unit Risk Management Committees

Securities trading

Corporate finance

Fund management

Private clients

Risk identification

Although it is often overlooked, risk identification, which refers to the need for a firm to define and understand the nature of the risk which it faces, is an essential part of any risk management process. It is important to recognise that risk management is a dynamic process and much of the progress that has been made in recent years in understanding risk has been the result of effective risk research both at firms and in academic bodies. Advances in the understanding of market risk have been particularly noteworthy, but considerable research effort is also under way on other aspects of risk. There have, for example, been significant advances recently in the development of a common definition and understanding of settlement risk, stimulated in part by the publication of the *BIS Orange Book* referred to earlier.

Risk measurement

A central objective of any risk management system must be that it enables the firm to assess and manage the risk which it faces on a consistent basis. In order to do this the firm has to develop a measurement methodology that allows comparison to be made across the different dimensions of risk, and enables risk considerations to be factored into performance measurement and capital allocation decisions.

This does not imply that risk measurement is in any sense a simple task. Even where there is a good supply of reliable data, as in the case of market risk, there are still considerable challenges (as will be discussed in later chapters), and for a number of risk factors such as operational and legal risk there is still a paucity of information. Nevertheless, effective risk management requires that a consistent methodology be developed for analysing risk, and as firms increasingly look at risk on a firmwide basis it becomes more necessary to be able to compare risk on a consistent "apples for apples" basis even for those risk factors where there is limited data available.

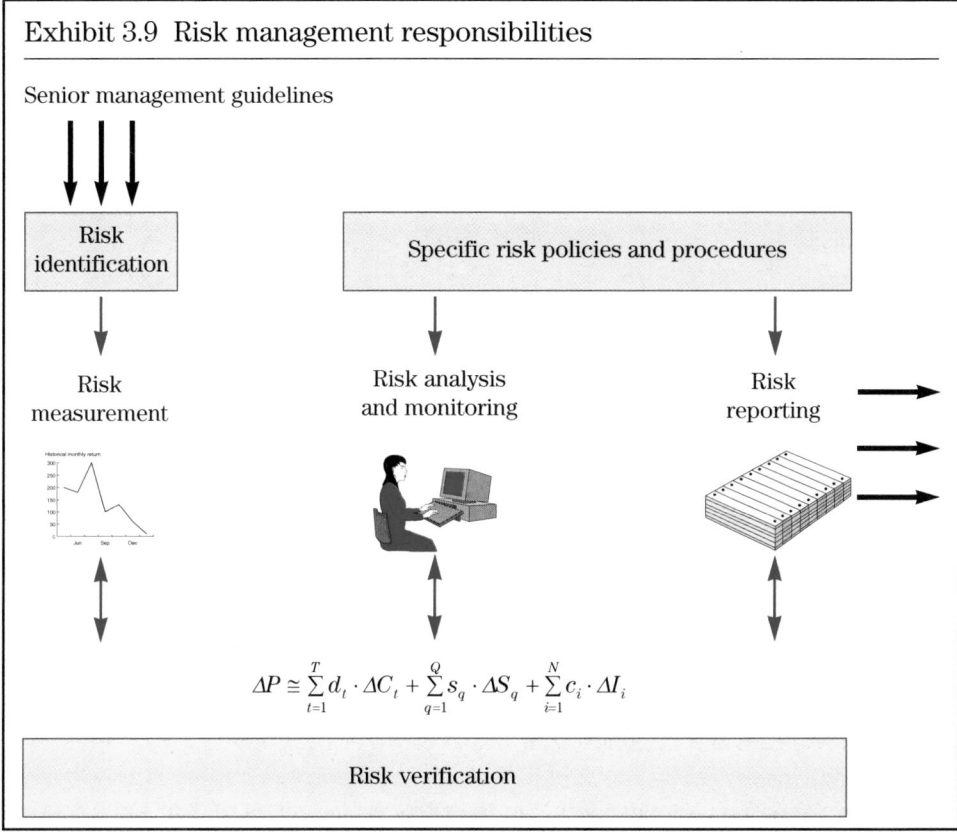

Exhibit 3.9 Risk management responsibilities

Senior management guidelines

Risk identification

Specific risk policies and procedures

Risk measurement

Risk analysis and monitoring

Risk reporting

$$\Delta P \cong \sum_{t=1}^{T} d_t \cdot \Delta C_t + \sum_{q=1}^{Q} s_q \cdot \Delta S_q + \sum_{i=1}^{N} c_i \cdot \Delta I_i$$

Risk verification

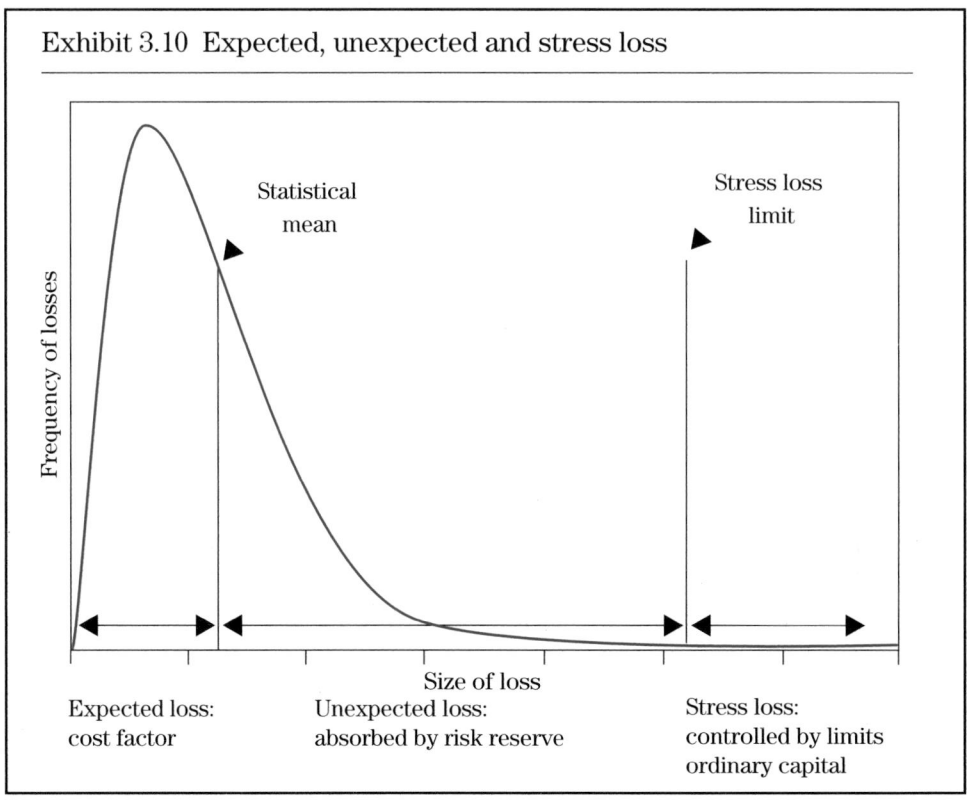

Exhibit 3.10 Expected, unexpected and stress loss

Statistical mean

Stress loss limit

Frequency of losses

Size of loss

Expected loss: cost factor

Unexpected loss: absorbed by risk reserve

Stress loss: controlled by limits ordinary capital

Expected, unexpected and stress loss

One framework for comparing risk factors, which has been developed at Swiss Bank Corporation, seeks to look at all dimensions of risk under three different measurement categories (see Exhibit 3.10). The first measure is the **expected loss,** which is associated with the predicted cost to the firm of its exposure to the risk factor on an ongoing basis. Thus, for example, the expected level of loan losses is the expected cost to the bank of its exposure to credit risk. In the same way, the cost of purchasing building insurance can be seen as the expected loss or cost of exposure to physical risk, and a similar analysis can be made with respect to most other risk factors. The expected loss is treated as a direct charge to the business like any other business cost.

The second risk measure is the **unexpected loss** associated with a risk factor. This is a measure of the potential variability of the expected risk cost over time. Provided the risk measurement methodology is accurate, unexpected losses will average out to zero over time. Nevertheless, the unexpected loss can be significant in any particular time period, so the bank has to be able to fund such a loss if it were to arise, and therefore has to have capital allocated against the unexpected losses in order to protect against this happening.

The third risk measure is the **stress loss** associated with a risk factor. This is the worst case loss that the bank might face as a result of its exposure to a risk factor, but must nevertheless be able to plan for and to survive if it were to occur. Stress losses such as the market crash of 1987, or the collapse of a significant trading partner, or the loss of a major operating centre, are by their nature extremely unusual events. As a result, the quantification of a stress loss for each risk factor is not easily measured by reference to past experience, and has to rely as much on professional judgement as on statistics. However, the important point about stress loss is that, because it identifies and quantifies the worst case scenario for the bank, it also provides a basis for establishing a framework of policies and limits that help to minimise the likelihood of the stress event occurring. Nevertheless, the bank has to have sufficient capital to enable it to survive if such an event were to take place.

Risk policies and procedures

As emphasised in all the best practice guidelines (see Chapter 2), in order to be effective a risk management system has to be based on a set of written risk policies and procedures that are endorsed by the Board and implemented by the senior management of the firm. The firm therefore not only has to set standards for its risk policies, but also has to ensure that they are disseminated to and understood by the staff who are affected by them. In addition, regulatory authorities are increasingly using the availability and completeness of adequately documented risk policies as a strong indicator of the overall quality of a firm's internal control environment. Indeed, one of the strongest criticisms of management in the regulatory investigation into Bankers Trust's OTC derivatives activities related to its failure to disseminate and enforce its internal policies effectively.

In financial firms that are subject to frequent staff turnover, management has to pay particular attention to the arrangements in place for ensuring that new staff are made aware of and comply with its risk policies.

Risk analysis and monitoring

Risk monitoring is the operational process whereby the firm ensures that it is operating within its defined risk policies and procedures. This includes, for example, advising on the interpretation of the firm's policies as well as the monitoring of limit excesses and the investigation of breaches of policy, plus ensuring that those policies are appropriate and up to date. Risk monitoring is the day-to-day responsibility of the risk management group, and is discussed in detail in the context of market risk in Section III.

Risk reporting

Risk reporting, which is closely linked to risk measurement, is the process under which the firm reports on risk internally through its MIS systems as well as to its regulators and to its shareholders. It is an increasingly important part of the risk management process, as firms seek ways to improve their ability to measure their performance and return on equity on a risk-adjusted basis. It is also an area where there has been significantly heightened official attention, given the lack of transparency about a firm's risk profile provided by traditional accounting conventions.

There have been a number of initiatives by banking and securities regulators in recent years to encourage improved regulatory reporting and risk disclosure in annual reports. There have also been a number of efforts by the accounting profession to update the process of accounting for financial assets, with the most radical being a proposal from the International Accounting Standards Committee for a complete overhaul of the accounting methodology for financial instruments to move to a comprehensive mark-to-market basis.

Risk verification and audit

The final component of a risk process is the need to ensure that the risk management system and techniques that the firm is using are effective. This has led to greater focus on the importance of a formal review or backtesting procedure as an integral part of a risk management process.

Risk verification and audit also includes the requirement for an audit of the risk management process, by internal and external auditors. The development of risk management as a discrete discipline within firms has had a significant impact on the role and responsibilities of both external and internal auditors. In the case of the external auditors it means that the focus of work has to extend from verifying the integrity of the financial records to an approach that also assesses the integrity of the risk information. In the case of the internal audit, the change is perhaps even more significant, because that portion of the traditional role of internal audit which consisted of checking compliance with internal guidelines and procedures has now been assumed by the risk management function. Consequently, the role of internal audit has to be focused more on the review of the integrity and completeness of the risk management process. This means that a much higher level of technical skill is now required in the internal audit function, given the type of technical skills that are now required to understand and review the effectiveness of the risk management functions.

Conclusion

As discussed in Chapter 2, there has been a significant change in the focus on the risk management process at financial firms over the past three or four years. Starting with the G30 report in 1993, an increasing number of documents and recommendations have appeared from different industry and regulatory bodies about the subject.

In this chapter we used the six risk categories defined by the Basle Committee and IOSCO in 1994 as the basis of outlining the scope of a firmwide risk management. We then discussed the elements of an effective risk management process which draws on the experience of SBC and Goldman Sachs and shows how, despite very different starting points, our two firms have adopted a remarkably similar approach to firmwide risk management. One of the most important points arising from this analysis is that risk management must occur and be supported from the top of an organisation. Policies and methodologies for risk identification, measurement, procedures, monitoring, reporting, review and audit must be endorsed and actively supported by the Board and senior management.

This chapter looked at the considerations which are involved in establishing a firm wide risk management process, viewing risk management in the broadest sense. In the next sections of the book we move on to look at the practical challenge of putting these principles into effect, specifically in relation to the management of market risk. We will, however, return to some of the broader issues raised here when we discuss the additional benefits of risk management in Section IV.

---

[1] A more detailed assessment of the issues associated with settlement risk can be found in: *Risk Reduction in Payments, Clearance and Settlement Systems*, Goldman Sachs & Co 1996.

4

A taxonomy of market risk

Introduction

In the preceding chapters we presented a series of vignettes that illustrate the various tasks of a risk manager, considered the environment that prompted risk management to be developed as a professional endeavour and introduced the concept of effective firmwide risk management. We now begin to examine in greater detail the practice of risk management as it has developed within financial firms, with particular reference to market risk where the discipline is currently most fully developed.

Before launching into a more detailed analysis, however, it is important to establish a working meaning for the term "market risk". For the remainder of the book then, we shall define market risk to mean "the sensitivity of the value of a financial instrument or portfolio to changes in market parameters". In this chapter we attempt to categorise the elements that underpin this definition.

Classifying financial instruments

In order to understand market risk we need to start with a clear definition of a "financial instrument". In a recent discussion document on accounting for financial assets and financial liabilities, the London-based International Accounting Standards Committee described a financial instrument in the following terms:

A "financial instrument" is any contract that gives rise to both a financial asset of one enterprise and a financial liability or equity instrument of another enterprise.

A "financial asset" is any asset that is:

(a) cash;
(b) a contractual right to receive cash or another financial asset from another enterprise;
(c) a contractual right to exchange financial instruments with another enterprise under conditions that are potentially favourable; or
(d) an equity instrument of another enterprise.

A "financial liability" is any liability that is a contractual obligation:

(a) to deliver cash or another financial asset to another enterprise; or
(b) to exchange financial instruments with another enterprise under conditions that are potentially unfavourable.

An "equity" instrument is any contract that evidences a residual interest in the assets of an enterprise after deducting all of its liabilities.

This definition, which now commands a wide consensus among accountants and financial controllers, is appropriate for viewing market risk as well. However, embedded in this brief description is a set of categories essential to understanding market risk, which would benefit from further elaboration. We will start with that most basic of financial elements – cash.

The lifeblood of all financial instruments is **cash**. However complex the chain of rights and obligations, and however far in the future an asset exchange is scheduled, all financial instruments eventually lead to cash flows of some sort. Even equity instruments ultimately result in dividends or return of cash upon wind-up. But cash can come in currencies of various denominations, and here arises the first element of market risk: every firm has its equity capital specified in a particular currency. (We can overlook the handful of exceptions which have issued equity in more than one currency.)

The currency of the equity capital is most often the reporting currency of the entity as well, which can also be referred to as its "base" currency. Any firm holding assets or liabilities only in the cash of its base currency does not incur any market risk; it goes without saying that such a firm would not require very much analysis. For example, a firm that raised cash with an equity offering and placed it in a vault would have no market risk; although, on the other hand it would also have no revenues. However once the firm accumulates assets or liabilities in foreign currencies, it must value those in relation to its base currency for inclusion in its financial reports.

Virtually every allowable accounting technique relies on the exchange rate between the foreign currency and the base currency either at the close of the reporting period or averaged throughout it. As those exchange rates fluctuate, a firm with cash assets or liabilities in currencies other than its base currency is exposed to valuation changes, whether favourable or unfavourable.

Future cash flows

As revealed by the balance sheet of any active corporation, cash comprises a very small fraction of the assets of almost all firms. A much larger segment of assets or liabilities consists of contractual rights or obligations to receive or deliver cash from or to another enterprise. These include accounts receivable or payable, certificates of deposit, notes and bonds held or issued, loans and other standard financial products. The cash flows that discharge the rights and obligations under these contracts will each occur at some point in the future, giving rise to uncertainty about the value of that future cash flow in relation to a similar amount of cash received today.[1] This restates the obvious, that a dollar, pound, mark or yen received today is worth more than one received one day, week, month or year hence. The challenge, of course, is to quantify the discount for increasingly distant receipts and payments in all relevant currencies.

As with foreign exchange, the accounting literature on net present value (NPV) techniques is voluminous, but the increasingly common theme is that future cash flows must be discounted by an appropriate yield for the given term. Because the "appropriate yield" is itself subject to market exigencies, any firm with rights and obligations in the future ("forward" rights or obligations) is exposed to changes in valuations due to changing yield curves in the currencies of its financial activities.

For government bonds in top-quality countries, the market value of a bond is the NPV of its future cash flows using the risk-free yield curve.[2] Once this was recognised, enthusiastic auditors began using risk-free term structures to NPV future cash flows from all obligors, not only sovereigns, but that blunt prescription stumbled on the following anomaly. The market price of a corporate bond will generally be less than the NPV of its cash flows discounted by the risk-free yield curve, simply because the corporate is not as creditworthy as the sovereign. Hence there developed the concept of a yield curve appropriate to high-quality non-sovereign obligors – the Libor curve.

As high-yield debt became fashionable, it was then recognised that each rating category deserved its own yield curve, with Libor reserved for AAA and AA obligors and higher yields for weaker counterparties. Traders began to routinely speak of "spreads" between the yield curves of various rating categories. It is now recognised that every obligor theoretically has its own yield curve, which is deducible from the market prices of its publicly traded obligations (ie debt), and consequently that the NPV of the cash flows it owes should be discounted using this particular yield curve. However, the practical limitations in determining yield curves individually and the broad acceptance of rating categories (such as investment grade and non-investment grade) has led to a convention whereby future cash flows are discounted by a rate that the market has determined is appropriate for obligors of similar credit quality.

This definition blurs the line between market and credit risk, and it indicates the direction of convergence between the two disciplines. Nevertheless, until sufficient instruments for each obligor are publicly traded so that the yield curve for each can be calculated, implementation of the theoretically correct approach is probably beyond reach; it seems that the instruments needed to allow observable yield curves will include secondary trading of loans and individual credit derivatives, in addition to publicly traded debt. Until these are widespread for a majority of firms, market risk and credit risk will remain largely distinct.

Futures

The IASC definition of financial instruments, in addition to covering cash and rights or obligations to receive or deliver cash, includes a somewhat technical phrase that encompasses virtually every type of derivative financial product, namely "... a contractual right to exchange financial instruments with another enterprise under conditions that are potentially favourable." This part of the definition at first appears circular, but upon reflection is creatively recursive. Once a financial instrument has been constructed, it can become the underlying instrument for a further financial product. It is these "derived" financial products that make modern finance so endlessly prolific. An infinity of products is imaginable; of course, each ultimately resolves itself at some point in the future with one or more cash flows.

The "exchange of financial instruments" covers two types of derivatives that are important to distinguish for risk management reasons – forwards and options.[3] Forwards are instruments where both parties are obliged to make an exchange at some point in the future; at the time the contract is agreed, it is unknown which party will be favoured when the exchange does take place. (This is one weak spot in the IASC definition, for it treats the final exchange as a right of the favoured party, when in fact it is legally an obligation, albeit a pleasant one.)

Forwards are valued directly from the relation between the future values of the financial instruments being exchanged. Where the exchange involves only cash in two different currencies (such as foreign exchange forwards), the value of the forward is a simple calculation, combining the future value of each currency cash flow viewed individually. Thus, a forward is a logical extension of the concept of a single future cash flow, linking two such individual cash flows inextricably. Where the exchange involves more complex financial instruments, the value of the forward is always computable, as long as the future values of each leg of the exchange are known.

In any event, a forward contract is exposed to all of the factors that impact the valuation of either leg, and either future cash flow. It is not possible to say whether forwards are more or less risky than single future cash flows, because sometimes the effects of market forces on either leg may offset each other, and sometimes they may reinforce each other. However, because a forward is subject to two sets of market factors, one for each leg of the contracted future exchange, it is definitely more complex than a single future cash flow.

Options

These are instruments where only one party (the option seller) is obliged to abide by the exchange, whereas the other party (the option buyer) can choose what to do at exchange. As a result, if the exchange favours the option buyer, they will likely insist on completing it (ie the option will be exercised), but if the exchange does not favour the option buyer they will not call for it to take place and the option will expire worthless. In other words, while all forward contracts are destined from the outset to result in a future exchange, only about half of all option contracts – those favouring the option buyer – are destined to be exercised, although of course, it cannot be known at the outset which ones those will be.

As a result, the valuation of options is one of the most difficult questions in finance, for it involves specifying in advance a probability for each possible future value between the two legs of the options. Not only are options exposed to all of the factors that influence forwards, they are also exposed to any change in the probabilities of future events. In general, as the future becomes more uncertain (more possible outcomes, each with less individual probability), options increase in value. Conversely, as the future becomes more certain (fewer possible outcomes, each with more individual probability), options decrease in value. Option values are therefore a function of time as well as factors like interest and exchange rates.

This direct relation to uncertainty about the future often causes options to be considered as identical to insurance. It is also important to note the fundamental asymmetry between the buyer and the seller of an option, particularly from a risk standpoint. If the option expires without having been exercised, the buyer only loses the amount of premium paid for the option. However, should the buyer exercise, the seller may undergo significant financial hardship to effect the required exchange, and in an ordinary option there is contractually no upper limit at which such losses are capped.

Equity

Equity or shares are among the most volatile financial instruments, representing "a residual interest in the assets of an enterprise after deducting all of its liabilities". Indeed, market risk management can properly be said to have been born in the attempt to quantify exposure to equity instruments. Equities are interesting not only in their own right, but also as underlying instruments for creating derivatives. Virtually every major industrial country has a liquid market in forwards and futures on its domestic equity index (eg the S&P 500 in the US, the FT-SE 100 in the UK, and the Nikkei 225 in Japan), and many countries allow public trading in options on individual shares.

Equities are also challenging because, unlike debt instruments, they do not yield cash flows continuously, but rather in uncertain, "chunky" dividends. This problem is further compounded by the constant changes in capital structures, resulting in rights offerings, share splits and buy-backs, which may require an adjustment to a preexisting equity derivative contract. In short, equities are themselves among the riskiest financial instruments, and derivatives based on equities have additional dimensions of risk.

Commodities

The IASC definition of financial instruments makes no mention of commodities, in spite of the fact that certain commodities (eg precious metals and energy products) are frequently held by intermediaries who are neither producers nor end-users in the traditional sense. Perhaps physical commodities themselves are not financial instruments, but derivative products built on top of commodities as underlying instruments certainly are, particularly those which are "cash settled".

In broad terms, commodities can be divided into precious metals, base metals, oil and energy, and agricultural products. Precious metals are the closest to being considered financial products. Base metals markets and derivative products are used mainly by producers and end-users. Energy markets undergo periodic volatility due to geopolitical events and then become of interest to investors. Agricultural products face complexities of seasonality, quality, storage and spoilage for any participants other than insiders.

Real estate

Few would suggest that real estate itself is a financial instrument. Generally, real estate is viewed as integral to a business (eg a factory) and extremely individualistic. Nevertheless, real estate has spawned several successful financial instruments, from mortgage-backed bonds to real estate investment trusts, and these are subject to risks uncommon elsewhere in the financial universe (eg prepayment risk). However, we will not establish a separate category for real estate, given that mortgage-backed bonds are essentially interest rate instruments and publicly traded real estate funds can be considered in the class of equities already established.

Classification by ownership and asset flow

The list in the previous section becomes clearer still if decomposed along two independent axes. The first axis indicates whether a financial instrument:

- is owned outright (a "spot" instrument);
- will be owned at some point in the future (a "forward" instrument); or
- may be owned at some point in the future (an "option" instrument).

For example, cash in currencies and equities are "spot" positions. Forward instruments include future cash flows in a single currency or any pair of currencies (foreign exchange forwards), or where an equity or commodity will be exchanged for a currency. Option instruments include any forward instrument where the receipt or delivery is subject to a contingency.

The second axis describes the type of asset flow that underlies the instrument. Where cash in the base currency comprises a spot position, or where cash in any single currency underlies either a forward or option product, the instrument can be said to be an interest rate (rate) instrument. Thus, bonds (sequence of future cash flows in one currency), forward rate agreements, and interest rate swaps are all examples of interest rate instruments. A foreign exchange (forex) instrument would include cash other than the base currency comprising a spot position, or pairs of

Exhibit 4.1 Classification of financial instruments

Instrument type	Rates category	Forex category	Equity category	Commodity category
Spot instruments	Base cash	Foreign cash	Shares	Not considered financial instruments
Forward instruments	Bonds, forward-rate agreements, interest-rate swaps	Forex forwards, cross-currency swaps	Forwards on baskets	Commodity forwards and swaps
Option instruments	Swaptions, bond options	Forex options	Index options, convertible bonds	Commodity options

currencies underlying a forward or an option product. A rate–forex hybrid occurs with cross-currency swaps, but since the forex risk is greater than the rate risk, it is more prudent to consider them to be forex instruments.

Where equities underlie a spot, forward or option position, the product is said to be an equity instrument. In this manner, shares, forwards on baskets of shares, and equity index options are all examples of equity instruments; convertible bonds are rate–equity hybrids and should be included in the equity category unless the value of the embedded equity warrant is minimal. Where a commodity underlies a forward or option position, the product is said to be a commodity instrument. So forward contracts in crude oil and gold options are commodity instruments.

This classification is best illustrated with a table, where the first axis is called "instrument type" and the second axis is called "risk category" (see Exhibit 4.1).

It should be noted that no categorisation covering an area as dynamic as market risk will remain fixed. As new instruments are created and new types of risk are traded so new issues in risk management will arise. For example, the nascent market in insurance-based products such as bonds with a pay-out linked to the occurrence of catastrophes such as hurricanes and earthquakes, or futures and options on new underlyings such as electricity or industrial emissions give rise to new concerns for the risk manager. Indeed as mentioned in Chapter 3, the identification of such new classes of instruments and their attendant risks forms a key part of the risk management process.

Classification of major market risks

The preceding taxonomy of financial products leads to a complementary classification of various market risks. Exhibit 4.1 suggests that market risks emanate from both the instrument type and the risk category, with many commonalties among instruments of the same type or the same risk category. With respect to risk category, however, few instruments are influenced by the behaviour of more than one risk category. The exceptions are instruments like cross-currency swaps or convertible bonds, and they usually have one dominant risk category and one subordinate one. With respect to instrument type, the risks increase going from spot to forward to option; in other words, forwards are exposed to spot risks as well as some risks unique to forwards, and similarly, options are subject to spot and forward risks as well as certain risks peculiar to options.

Spot instruments

For spot instruments, the major risk is that the spot market in a given risk category moves significantly. In the case of the spot rate instrument, namely cash in the base currency, there is no market risk at all because every other value is stated in terms of this instrument. In the case of spot forex instruments, which consist of cash in currencies other than the base currency, the major risk is that the forex rate between a given currency and the base currency moves adversely. Currencies generally move quite independently, so it is difficult to come up with any systematic treatment for them.

In the case of spot equity instruments, the relevant risk is to movements in share prices, but the number of such equities is enormous. Fortunately, equity prices display considerable systematic behaviour, with the risk of each individual equity able to be decomposed into a segment that relates to the market as a whole and a segment which is specific to that equity. The former segment is called general market risk and the latter is specific risk. General market risk may be further decomposed into a segment relating to the performance of the national market and a segment relating to the firm's industry sector. In the case of spot commodity instruments, which are not considered to be financial instruments in themselves, the major risk is to a sharp move in the commodity price itself; commodities, with the exceptions of the precious metals group and the crude oil distillate group, do not generally move in a systematic way.

Forward instruments

These are influenced by all of the spot risks attendant on the underlying assets. In addition, forward instruments are exposed to changes in yield curves and other financing variables. These risks, which govern the relationship between the spot price and a forward price on the same asset, are broadly termed "basis risks". Basis risk has subtleties in each risk category. The values of cash forward instruments like bonds, swaps and forward rate agreements are all very sensitive to changes in yields, which can vary in relation to four basic factors:

1. The levels of all interest rates may change in concert. This overall shift in yields is known as absolute rate risk.
2. The yields in certain maturities may change in one direction while yields in other maturities remain unchanged or change in a different direction. This change in the shape of the yield curve is called curve risk.
3. The yields of corporate issuers may change in a different way to the yields of sovereign issuers. This differentiation among issuers by quality is called spread risk.
4. The yields of a single issuer may change in a non-systematic way, influenced either by a change in the perceived quality of that issuer or some other individual reason. This non-systematic risk is called specific risk.

The values of forex forward instruments are influenced by the combination of Libor yield changes in the two underlying currencies with maturity equal to the term for the forward contract. An equity forward instrument faces risk arising from any changes to the dividend stream from the equity that is scheduled to be paid over the term of the forward contract. In addition, the value of an equity forward is influenced by the repo rate for the underlying shares. The repo rate, which is a standard proportion of Libor yields for much of the time, and therefore subject to Libor yield risks, can also react to particular supply/demand concerns for the particular shares in question. Because commodities do not yield anything themselves, unlike stocks with dividends or bonds with coupons, a commodity forward has risk primarily do to financing concerns (eg Libor yields) and to supply/demand considerations in the commodity itself.

Option instruments

These instruments are exposed to all the risks of forward and spot instruments in the same risk category, plus two risks peculiar to options. These risks are similar for options in each risk category and are therefore better discussed without reference to a particular risk category. These risks grow out of an option's unique sensitivity to the probabilities of various outcomes. As explained earlier, increasing uncertainty raises the value of an option, while decreasing uncertainty lowers its value.

The most common tool to describe uncertainty is a frequency distribution of outcomes. The well-known normal distribution is an example of a standard frequency distribution, though by no means the only one. It is true that return distributions of many financial parameters can be approximated using a normal distribution, and therefore a normal distribution is found at the heart of many option valuations. Once an appropriate distribution has been selected, a useful measurement of the dispersion of outcomes is the standard deviation of that distribution;[4] in an intuitive sense, the standard deviation measures the "girth" of the distribution – the width of the portion of the distribution containing most of the probable events. For financial parameters, the standard deviation of the distribution of changes in a given parameter is also called the "volatility" of that parameter.

It is natural, then, to inquire into the relationship between the volatility (ie uncertainty) of a market parameter and the value of an option based on that market parameter. That sensitivity is the volatility risk of the option. (The standard nomenclature for volatility risk, "vega", creates a mysterious aura without shedding additional light. Vega – which is not even Greek – grew out of option floor traders' insistence that every option risk have an appropriate handle. We think "volatility risk" is sufficiently intuitive.)

The second esoteric option risk is curvature risk, which should not be confused with curve risk already discussed in the context of various interest rate risks. Curvature in options also arises from their sensitivity to uncertainty. If an option purchaser exercises the option it becomes identical to a forward contract containing the same terms. On the other hand, if the option is allowed to lapse it will be identical to no position at all. As a consequence, the sensitivity of an option with respect to spot market risk fluctuates between the sensitivity of an identical forward contract (anticipating the option exercise) and zero (anticipating the option expiration). Curvature risk is the name given to this fluctuation of an option's sensitivity to spot market risk. As would be expected, this fluctuation is high when uncertainty is high and low when uncertainty is low. (Curvature risk also has a Greek name, "gamma", which is as unhelpful to intuitive clarity as vega.) Both volatility risk and curvature risk are inherent in all options, regardless of risk category.

The market risks described above can be arranged in a table similar to the one built for financial instruments (see Exhibit 4.2).

Exhibit 4.2 Classification of market risks

Instrument type	Rates category	Forex category	Equity category	Commodity category
Spot instruments	No risk	Forex spot risk	General market risk (country and industry), specific risk	Specific risk
Forward instruments (basis risks)	Absolute risk, curve risk, spread risk, specific risk	Yield risk (currency 1), yield risk (currency 2)	Dividend risk, repo-rate risk	Repo-rate risk, supply/demand risk
Option instruments (uncertainty of exercise)	Volatility risk, curvature risk	Volatility risk, curvature risk	Volatility risk, curvature risk	Volatility risk, curvature risk

Additional market risks

The classification in Exhibit 4.2 covers the major market risks of financial instruments; these are the risks that manifest themselves throughout the portfolio. However, the proliferation of new and exotic instruments continues to create additional sources of market risk, some of which can be significant for given instruments, if not for the portfolio as a whole. Here is a description of some of the better known minor risks.

Pin risk

This is a special option risk that creates heightened uncertainty near expiration. Because the basic uncertainty in an option is whether or not it will be exercised and because the strike price of an option indicates the ratio between the two assets that will be exchanged if the option is exercised, it follows that the closer the spot price is to the exercise price, the more difficult it is to anticipate whether the option will be exercised or not. (When the spot price is equal to the strike price, parties to the transaction should be indifferent whether the exchange takes place or not, because the two assets to be exchanged have identical value.) If the spot price hovers around the exercise price as expiration approaches, it becomes very difficult to manage because with a small move in one direction it behaves exactly like a forward and with a small move in the opposite direction it behaves exactly like a nil position. This is made even more difficult if the market in the underlying instrument is itself illiquid or suffers from discontinuities as may happen for example in the case of emerging markets. The danger of managing an option position whose exercise continues to be uncertain down to the final moments in the life of the option is termed pin risk, because it is most problematic when the spot price seems to "pin" itself to the strike price of the option.

Rollover risk

This grows out of a mismatch in maturities between a derivative position (forward or option) and its related hedge. If the derivative position expires before the hedging instrument does (and for this purpose spot positions are considered to have infinite maturity) and if the derivative does not have physical settlement (which would preserve its risk profile through exercise), the trader must either unwind the hedge or find a new derivative instrument that has a similar risk profile to the expiring one. If the liquidity in the hedging instrument is sufficient, the trader can simply unwind the hedge. However, if that liquidity is insufficient, the trader must then acquire a position in a derivative of longer duration with a similar risk profile to the one he or she currently has. This is generally done by acquiring an amount of longer-term derivatives and the unwinding a similar amount of shorter-term derivatives, thereby "rolling" the risk position out to a later maturity. The success of this tactic depends on the liquidity in the derivative market, which cannot be counted upon, particularly if other participants in the market are aware of the need to "roll", which is the situation that caused Metallgesellschaft such agony in the crude oil markets.

Prepayment risk

This is a special risk commonly associated with the mortgage practice in certain countries, including the US. If the standard mortgage contract allows prepayment without penalty, the debtor possessing such a mortgage actually owns a free option to refinance. That option goes in the debtor's favour if mortgage interest rates fall, but it is notoriously difficult to determine when the average homeowner will choose to refinance. For those securities that pay based on a mortgage pool, the very time that the yield of the instrument is in favour of the security owner is the very time that the homeowners of the underlying mortgages are considering refinancing. Prepayment risk is the risk that a security with a favourable coupon is prepaid earlier than anticipated due to the behaviour of the debtors of the underlying mortgage pool.

Quality risk

This arises when more than one asset is eligible for delivery in satisfaction of a derivative contract. If an obligor to a derivative contract has several alternative assets to deliver in satisfaction of the derivative contract, it is rational to assume that they will choose the one with the least value relative to what they will receive in exchange. For those derivatives where the value for alternative assets is based on complex formulas, it may well happen in the days leading up to settlement that the "cheapest to deliver" asset may in fact change from one alternative to the other. If a derivative trader is not careful to always base the derivative valuation on the "cheapest to deliver", it may well happen that at delivery they find themselves out a substantial amount of money on the settlement over what they were expecting to pay.

Location risk

This concerns mainly physical commodities and agricultural products. Because these products, unlike financial instruments, cannot be transferred by wire instruction, but must be physically removed from one location to another, the discharge of derivative contracts where they are required for delivery in a certain location necessitates considerable attention. A trader who has hedged a contract with delivery in one location with a contract specifying delivery in a second location can generally count on the prices being equivalent in the two delivery locations, but occasionally supply and demand considerations in a particular location may result in wide divergence in commodity prices between alternate delivery locations. (This is one of the features that keeps commodities and physically settled commodity derivatives from being classified as financial instruments.)

It is possible to continue a litany of such additional risks indefinitely. But with each new risk, the concern becomes more specific to particular details of the contract and less relevant to the entire portfolio. And since the goal of risk management at the firm level is to measure the risk of the entire portfolio – a subject taken up in subsequent chapters – it seems appropriate to draw the curtain on the elements of market risk right here.

Conclusion

We have now begun to examine in greater detail the practice of risk management as it has developed within financial firms. We have focused particular attention on market risk, as the discipline is the most fully developed today.

We have defined market risk as *the sensitivity of the value of a financial instrument or portfolio to changes in market parameters*. We have classified financial instruments loosely as spot, forward, or option instruments. We also very broadly categorised market risk categories as being rate, FX, equity, or commodity related.

We now move to the crux of the risk management problem. Assuming we have an understanding of many of the market parameters that comprise a firm's risk profile, how do we approach assessing risk to those parameters in a useful manner. We will begin to examine this issue in Section II where we consider how to measure market risk.

---

[1] This "forward valuation" problem exists whether the future cash flow is in the base currency or not. If it is not in the base currency, then the problem is to relate a future foreign cash flow to the same amount of foreign cash received (paid) today, with the relation between foreign cash today and base currency cash today having been addressed by the methods outlined in the previous subsection.

[2] More philosophically, it is actually the converse which is true: the risk-free yield curve is defined to be the term structure of interest rates that results in the current market price of each issue of outstanding government debt to be equivalent to the NPV of its future cash flows.

[3] For the purposes of this discussion, futures traded on public exchanges may be thought of as a subgroup of forwards, because they differ mainly along the dimensions of financing and credit.

[4] The standard deviation is less useful as a risk measurement on some non-normal distributions.

Section II

The toolkit for measuring market risk

This section explores the various issues associated with compiling an effective toolkit for measuring a firm's exposure to market risk. The relative strengths and weaknesses of stress testing, Value at Risk (VaR), and scenario analysis are explained and discussed. The chapter looks at how they can be used as complementary tools whilst recognising that different firms will place different weight on the methods depending on their organisational structures and business mixes. In addition, the main issues associated with the less well developed discipline of measuring specific risk are explored.

5

The challenges of risk measurement

Introduction

The preceding chapter defined market risk as the sensitivity of the value of a financial instrument or portfolio to changes in market parameters. In addition, we described qualitatively the risks of individual financial products. This chapter moves from the qualitative to the quantitative, investigating the challenges of trying to assign a number to the risk of a portfolio. We also examine why it is so difficult to use any one number to characterise meaningfully the risk of a portfolio.

At the outset, it is important to understand that every measurement algorithm has its intended purpose. Leaving aside risk for a moment, consider the measurement of human size. Everyone knows qualitatively what "large" and "small" mean, but life gets more difficult when we want to express size in a single number. Either height or weight can be useful, depending on the problem being addressed. A basketball coach, for example, will be most concerned about height, while a rugby coach is more interested in his players' weights. The point is that each metric is appropriate for a given problem, and neither serves all purposes. Indeed, if one asks for a definitive answer to the question of which metric is the "best" measure of size, the answer is that neither height, nor weight, nor a linear combination of them is the "best" measure of size. The best measure of size is the one most appropriate to the purpose for which it is intended.

As with human size, so with market risk. *Risk is not one dimensional, and no one algorithm for measuring risk will serve all purposes.* In this context it is worthwhile to consider the two dimensions of risk that firms care about most. Financial institutions have established independent risk management units because the boards of those firms want to understand and control the risks taken. During most market conditions and most of the time, risk management can provide measurement and analysis that aids the understanding of financial risks taken and thereby leads to higher profitability.

This better understanding of risk is an important dimension of risk measurement. But the other dimension, control, cannot be ignored. The complexity of modern global capital markets, the rapidity with which risks can change, and examples set by firms like Barings and Sumitomo have combined to motivate senior managers to take risk management seriously from a control perspective, and they have done so. By funding risk control, these firms are trying to insure against the possibility of unwarranted loss due to market risk. Indeed, the truth is that what shareholders would probably desire most from risk management is insurance against losses greater than some size.

In a basic sense this desire for understanding as well as control of risks taken is sensible; senior managers now realise that in financial markets there are no excess returns without risk, and that to insist on zero risk tolerance is to condemn their firms to zero excess returns. If the returns that shareholders demand are to be made, risk must be taken; hence, some losses cannot be prevented. The task of risk management is to monitor those risks and to contain those losses to pre-specified tolerances. *In other words, although risk management cannot prevent losses, it can ensure the firm's awareness of and comfort with the level of risk.*

However, in a deeper sense the paradigm is simplistic. No risk group can guarantee absolutely that losses above a certain amount will never happen; market risk cannot be absolutely contained within such boundaries, particularly in financial institutions. Open market risk positions can potentially produce a wide array of outcomes, depending on the size of moves in various market parameters. The history of market movements confirms that, despite extended periods where market volatility conforms with historical averages, there will always be circumstances where inordinately large market moves do occur. The best that can be hoped for is a quantification of the probability of losses of a given size. Unfortunately, we are least able to quantify the probabilities for the large losses of greatest concern. Thus, complete control of financial risks is an unattainable goal. What we will see, however, in this chapter is that there are a variety of risk measurement tools that complement each other and help to illuminate different aspects of the risk management challenge.

Risk normalisation and cumulation

The financial firms that have embraced risk management most enthusiastically are those with a multiplicity of business units, operating in many locations across the globe. These firms realise that in the global financial market-place, when market shocks occur they affect the related risk exposures wherever they may be housed in the firm. Unless a firm is alert to where the various risks reside, it is impossible to identify concentrations of risk and to achieve meaningful ex ante control of its exposures. Closely related to the question of where risk is being taken is the question of how much risk is being assumed. How much equity general market risk is being assumed by the London trading room? How much foreign exchange risk is being taken in the Singapore office? How much duration risk is being taken by the US government bond trading desk?

The answers to these questions require a common language for comparing each category of risk across the firm. So the first challenge of risk measurement is to identify the risk factors to which the firm is exposed. This is the importance of a classification scheme such as that discussed in the previous chapter. Given such a classification, it is a responsibility of the risk monitoring function to discover where in the firm these risks are being taken. Where is spot forex risk being taken? Where is equity general market risk being assumed? Where are there exposures to commodity prices or Japanese interest rates? It is then the responsibility of the risk monitoring function to quantify the risks and distribute this information. Finally, it is up to the senior management of the firm to clearly identify those responsible for each type of risk and for making decisions about how much of each risk is acceptable.

These issues are of much more than purely academic interest. Understanding the organisational structure of the firm is at the core of understanding how a firm needs

Exhibit 5.1 Case note: Contrasting organisational approaches to risk taking

Swiss Bank Corporation and Goldman Sachs have adopted somewhat different management approaches in deciding on the organisation of risk taking. At Swiss Bank Corporation, the majority of the firm's market risk is assumed within the SBC Warburg Dillon Read business, where there is a clear division of responsibility between the different product areas. Consequently, foreign exchange risk is only assumed within the foreign exchange trading area, interest rate risk within the rates area and equity risk in the equity area. Other business areas are required to hedge out the non core risks they are taking (ie interest rate risk in the equity books) with the respective product areas. There are an extremely limited number of individuals within the firm who are allowed to trade outside their product specialisation. As a result, the line management interest in risk is for information at the product level first, and at the cross-product level as a secondary interest.

Goldman Sachs, by contrast, has traditionally had a more open approach to cross-product trading. Different departments and traders, although focused on their particular area of specialisation, are allowed a greater latitude to trade other products. So, for example, a government bond trader may be allowed to take foreign exchange risk – something that would never occur at Swiss Bank Corporation. Similarly, a larger number of traders at Goldman Sachs than at Swiss Bank Corporation have the authority to trade widely across a broad range of products. And given the various product lines and proprietary desks that may trade in emerging markets, there could be as many as half a dozen different trading desks with exposure to a given emerging market on a particular day.

This organisational difference between the two firms is one reason why there has been a different emphasis on different measurement techniques. Swiss Bank Corporation has emphasised risk measurement and analysis within product types as its first priority to meet the needs of the desk heads, and has only recently moved to cross-product analysis using full VaR as a management reporting tool. Goldman Sachs, by contrast, has chosen from an early stage to use VaR as its primary measure of exposure at all levels within the firm in order to meet the requirements of the trader, the desk, the business unit and senior management.

to approach the challenge of risk control. Whether the firm is organised fairly strictly along product lines so that the foreign exchange department only ever deals in foreign exchange products and the equity department only in equity products, or whether different parts of the firm are allowed to trade across different products – for example, if an arbitrage desk can choose to take forex, interest rate, equity or emerging market risk – will affect the way that the risk manager approaches the challenge of monitoring risk across the firm. In any case, of critical importance at the outset to effective risk management is that the risk-taking parameters of different parts of the firm must be clearly set out and enforced by senior management, so that each business unit as well as the risk management department know exactly which risks it is allowed to assume.

Risk measurement must service various levels within the organisation in a coherent fashion. A trader may want to see his or her positions and risk broken out into various different accounts – a market-making account, a proprietary account, a quantitative trading account and so on. A desk head will want to see measures of risk for each of the traders. In order for each of them to discuss risk meaningfully, the trader and the desk head should see the same risk measure for the trader's positions. Similarly, a business unit head will want to see the risk he or she is responsible for broken out by desks, and that measure needs to match that shown to the desk heads.

The business unit head will also, of course, want to be able to "drill down" to the trader or account level to better understand where particular risks are coming from and why they are being taken. Business unit heads will need to be able to communicate with division heads, division heads with senior management and the risk committee, and so on. Thus, there has to be a tree structure for aggregating risk throughout the organisation and there has to be common units of risk from the lowest to the highest level. We discuss this further in Chapters 10 and 11.

Having identified where risks are being taken within the firm, the next challenge of risk measurement is to cumulate the risk exposures for a given risk dimension. (To keep terms clear, we will always speak of "cumulating" risk within a given risk dimension – "adding apples to apples", so to speak. We will refer to "aggregating" risk across risk dimensions – in other words, "adding apples to oranges". Aggregation is much more difficult than cumulation because it requires consideration of correlations – one of the more difficult notions in risk management.)

Correct cumulation depends on the risk management unit being aware of each location where a particular market risk is being assumed. The "ticket in the drawer" conundrum has caused endless speculation, but it is relatively rare these days. With counterparties taking great care to confirm trades and with most firms now employing strict segregation of duties between front office and back office, the chance that a significant position can be assembled outside of proper settlement channels is small. Much more likely is the chance that a position is traded and correctly settled in a business unit that does not have authority and/or appropriate systems to trade that particular market risk. The position may be settled and show up in back office records, but if it is not a standard product for a particular desk the systems may not recognise it and it may not show up in the risk system. Firms must instill a culture in which front office traders and management, as well as back office personnel, are responsible for identifying and highlighting significant risks. It is imperative that the risk management unit be aware of any trading desk or business unit that is taking material risk, and this necessitates excellent information systems (see Chapter 15) and teamwork between the front office (see Chapter 10), the risk unit, and the operations and controllers departments.

In addition, correct risk cumulation requires data integrity. It is one thing to know which desks are taking which risks; it is quite another to obtain from each of these desks on a regular basis accurate and complete risk data, normalised to the firm's standard. Since much of the exposure information is calculated in front office systems, which may not be accessing the same database of trades where settlements are logged, care must be taken to ensure that the front office database is frequently reconciled with the settlement database. Technological progress continues to hold the promise that someday all information – risk, settlement, accounting, financial control – will be obtained from a single "data warehouse", and that the days of arduous reconciliation will come to an end. In the meantime, firms must ensure that the various databases are synchronised and reconciled. (These challenges are discussed in more detail in Chapter 15.)

Any firm that has established a common unit of market risk measurement (risk normalisation) and that combines the worldwide information for each risk dimension (risk cumulation), has surmounted one of the most difficult practical challenges of risk measurement. It is very easy at that point to identify the level of risk along each core risk dimension, and if desired to set a limit on it. Such a multi-dimensional risk limit structure will protect the firm against all but the most systemic events – ie those cutting across many risk dimensions.

Risk aggregation

Risk management has always been an important component of trading, while management of traders has always required some understanding of risk. Traditionally, however, the most detailed understanding of risk took place at the trading desk, and the higher up the level of management in the organisation, the less likely management was to understand the risks being taken. In recent years, however, four circumstances have served to change this state of affairs:

1. **Senior managers** of financial institutions have become more concerned about market risk, especially risks created through derivative instruments. These senior managers want a perspective of risk that encompasses the entire portfolio and is broadly intuitive.
2. **Risk capital performance** – The attempt to maximise shareholder value has led firms to try to find risk measurements that might be consolidated to produce a measure of risk capital. Such an internal measure of capital utilisation by various business areas is an essential step toward the optimal allocation of capital across businesses.
3. **Supervisors** of financial institutions, having promised their constituents that a companion document addressing market risk would follow their historic 1988 Capital Accord which dealt only with credit risk, have begun to accept internal models to compute regulatory capital for market risk.
4. **Advances in information technology** have given firms the ability for the first time to consolidate positions and compute risk at an enterprise level.

The common hallmark of these influences is that each contributes to the desire and the ability to create a consolidated picture of a firm's risk profile. In the 1980s the focus of risk management was increasingly detailed measurements of a number of risk types in individual portfolios. Indeed, traders prided themselves on the number of "Greeks" (ie risk types) they had mastered, and the ultimate achievement was to invent a new, previously unappreciated "Greek". But the focus clearly changed in the 1990s. The challenge of aggregation and consolidation became dominant. Firms realised that all of the "Greeks" together could not answer simple-sounding questions like, "What would happen to our portfolio if US interest rates rose by 50 basis points?" or "What is the chance that the trading portfolio loses US$100 million tomorrow?"

Of what use was all the financial apparatus to senior management if it could not provide answers to such reasonable portfolio-wide questions? And, more frighteningly, might the firm as a whole be vulnerable to a set of risks that none of the traders or trading managers could see individually, but which together could imperil the institution? In short, senior management demanded meaningful aggregation.

Stress testing

A relatively intuitive way in which to approach the challenge of senior management for meaningful aggregated exposure information was to use the techniques of "stress testing" the aggregate portfolio. In stress testing, the risk manager selects a set of moves for certain major market parameters and then subjects the current portfolio to those moves, measuring the simulated change in portfolio value. Such as stress test has many attractions compared to other methods:

1. It can be performed with market parameter moves of any size.
2. Because the risk manager specifies which parameters are moving and by how much, there is no need to worry about correlations.
3. Anyone examining the results of a stress test can see exactly what caused the value of the portfolio to change.
4. Stress testing does not waste analytical energy creating the entire distribution if the true area of interest is what happens in the case of an extreme event.
5. It does not require the assignment of probabilities to events; all that stress testing does is assign "possibilities", however remote, to events.
6. Stress testing does not take an advanced mathematics degree to understand and is therefore easily communicated.

As a tool for communicating risk to senior management, stress testing has considerable attractions, and in addition offers management themselves the opportunity to participate in the discussion about which risk factors they are most concerned about. In the case of Swiss Bank Corporation, for example, the board has endorsed the table of market moves for use in computing valuation changes and risk sensitivities set out in Exhibit 5.2. These rather large market shock factors were requested by the Swiss Bank Corporation board, who insisted out of prudence to simulate for each risk category the largest market moves that have been observed in recent years – eg the Crash of '87 for equities, the ERM breakup for foreign exchange, the bond crash of '94 for interest rates and the Mexican "Tequila" crisis of 1993–94 for emerging markets.

The basic shortcoming of stress testing, however, is that it does not readily facilitate decision making. Stress tests can only be conducted on a finite set of parameters. This leads immediately to the question of how a risk manager decides for which handful of events to stress test the portfolio. Moreover, even if it were possible to achieve a full set of stress tests for all material risk factors, the results would be so extensive that they would be of little use as management information. Moreover, because stress tests do not take into account probabilities or correlations between different risks it is very difficult to know what to focus on. What senior management needs from the risk manager is filtered information, not piles of printouts. The challenge of risk aggregation is to be able to show in as summary a form as possible the most relevant indication of the risk profile of the firm. On this standard, stress testing, while useful, does not satisfactorily resolve the problem of meaningful risk aggregation. Stress testing is discussed in greater detail in Chapter 6.

Exhibit 5.2 Market moves in valuation and risk sensitivity calculations at Swiss Bank Corporation

Country ratings	Interest rate shocks	Equity shocks	Foreign exchange shocks	Commodity shocks
(all countries)				
AAA	60–100 bp	8–6%	4–10%	Gold 8%
AA and A	160 bp	20%	10.0%	Platinum 12%
BBB	240 bp	25%	12.5%	Palladium 12%
BB	320 bp	30%	20.0%	Silver 16%
B	420 bp	40%	30.0%	

Value at risk

The limitations of stress testing, as well as the increasing pressures, both externally from the regulatory community and from shareholders (discussed in detail in Chapters 17 and 18) and internally, for higher quality risk reporting at the aggregate level, led firms to explore the possibility of measuring risk another way. An approach was developed to calculate the statistical distribution of trading returns over a given time horizon – for example, one day. Creation of return distributions for a portfolio of financial instruments is referred to under the general heading of "value at risk" (VaR), which has now become synonymous with the subject of risk management and therefore warrants further consideration of its strengths and weaknesses.

Building a model of the return distribution of a portfolio is quite straightforward. We must first understand what risk factors affect the value of the portfolio. We must then make an assumption about the distribution of the outcomes of those risk factors. We might use historical returns or some parameterised distribution based on the historical returns. However, once this distribution is determined we simply create repeated draws of the risk factors and revalue the portfolio. The resulting values are draws from the distribution of the portfolio returns. Although simple in concept, it is unfortunately the case that practical issues make this computation more difficult than it sounds.

Risk taking is a dynamic activity. Volatilities and correlations of risk factors are constantly changing. New securities often appear, and sometimes, as was the case with the inflation-indexed Treasury notes issued recently for the first time in the United States, the new securities will incorporate new risk factors. Thus, even if a very accurate risk measuring scheme could be devised at a point in time, it would slowly degrade in terms of accuracy. It is best to realise that risk measurement is always an approximation and requires constant attention to keep it as accurate as possible.

Exhibit 5.3 Three types of VaR

There are three basic types of VaR:

- **The "covariance matrix" method** uses the volatilities and correlations of risk factors. Exposures are generally assumed to be linear, though higher order approximations are available. Although very efficient in terms of computer time, this method is often inadequate to capture the effects of non-linearities associated with options and other derivatives. If a normal distribution is assumed, this approach will not capture the fat tails of financial return distributions.
- **The "Monte-Carlo" method** also employs a covariance matrix, and using techniques developed to compute gambling odds, the simulation engine then runs a large number of possible outcomes and aggregates the results. This method is very flexible but uses enormous computer power.
- **The "historical simulation" method** takes the normalised risk profile in all of its multiple dimensions and runs it through the actual market prices over some recent interval of time (usually the past two to five years); the simulated value changes of the portfolio are then assembled in a return distribution. This method is a moderate user of computer power, but requires very accurate historical price data to be constantly available.

It is premature to say which is the "best" method. Swiss Bank Corporation uses historical simulation for its VaR and Goldman Sachs uses all three approaches. (The issues involved in calculating a VaR are discussed at length in Chapter 7.)

In this context, the process of backtesting plays a particularly important role in verifying the validity of the underlying models that firms are using. Backtesting is a general term for any technique that seeks to systematically link *ex ante* risk profiles with actual ex post P&L. Because both senior management and the supervisors are concerned with developing a useful measure of how much a firm could lose in a given circumstance, any algorithm that purports to do this needs to be compared on a daily basis with the actual trading profit (or loss) of the portfolio. Many firms have come to realise that a good daily mark-to-market P&L is the most effective tool in risk management, eclipsing even the best *ex ante* risk profiles. Any *ex ante* risk measure that can not be validated by backtesting is a candidate for the rubbish heap.

Unfortunately, the backtesting challenge is complicated by a number of factors. In particular, on an ordinary day the P&L of any decent size portfolio may easily be dominated by random factors not captured by the risk system. These factors may be as simple as intra-day trading, fees, or valuation adjustments.

There are various forms of backtesting. One simple approach is to see whether the actual P&L is adequately approximated by applying the risk factor changes to the risk system exposure measures. Success in such a backtest is best determined on a day which involves large market moves. Another approach is to assemble a large number of days, to adjust the P&L for factors such as those mentioned above which should not be captured in the daily risk, and to scale the adjusted P&Ls according to the *ex ante* risk measure so that in theory they should be drawn from a common distribution. Then, the empirical distribution of the adjusted, scaled P&Ls can be compared with the hypothesised distribution. Nonetheless, this can be quite complex to carry out in practice. (Backtesting is described in more detail in Chapter 12.)

Scenario analysis

We have discussed two of the standard tools of risk analysis – stress tests and VaR. Stress tests provide information about how much money could be lost along many different risk factor dimensions, while VaR provides a probability of losing a given amount of money. But because these two approaches may often miss the biggest risks facing an organisation, we need another tool as well. Scenario analysis goes beyond these two approaches by looking at not only the direct impact of a particular set of market moves, but also at the direct and indirect impacts on revenues over a period of time of a constellation of events associated with a given scenario.

At Goldman Sachs, for example, as part of the annual budgeting exercise each of the business units is asked to forecast its revenues for the coming year unconditionally, and then again conditional on a significant decline in equity and other asset values. The firm is looking in particular for the impact on revenues associated with lower commissions, fewer equity underwritings, fewer investment banking fees and so on. This "down market" scenario is typically estimated to have an order of magnitude larger impact on revenues than any conceivable short-run impact of market factors on the value of positions in inventory. Understanding the implications of such a scenario thus may have a much more profound impact on risk management than any stress test or VaR analysis, which focuses only on the valuations of current positions. Indeed, events in Asia around the end of 1997 forcibly underline the importance of undertaking such analyses.

Scenario analysis is difficult to do because it is about the effect on the firm as a whole of a constellation of significant events. In order to be effective, it needs to involve business managers from across the firm. If the firm really wants to know how it would be affected by a collapse of confidence in, say, eastern European equity markets, the exercise needs to take into account not only the immediate effects on the value of the trading portfolio, but also how the change would affect its revenue stream from fixed income, from lending business and from corporate finance in the same circumstances. In order to achieve this, the risk manager needs to draw on the skills not only of the risk management department, but of the rest of the firm. Each business manager will be tempted to interpret the scenario differently, so a key aspect of creating a meaningful analysis is for the risk manager to standardise the parameters of the analysis. Nonetheless, the business managers will also have useful insight into the impacts on their business of the scenario, which the risk manager will need to incorporate.

Thus, in this context the risk manager needs to move outside the realm of pure statistical measurement into the world of judgement and market experience. A well-designed and developed scenario analysis can bring interesting insights to guide a firm's consideration of its future direction. We discuss scenario analysis in greater detail in Chapter 8.

Conclusion

In this chapter we have passed from the qualitative to the quantitative, investigating the challenges of trying to assign any one meaningful number to the risk of a portfolio. These difficulties arise because risk is not one dimensional, and no one algorithm for measuring it will serve all purposes. In this context we have considered the dimensions of risk with which firms are most concerned. Financial institutions have established independent risk management units because the boards want to understand and control risk taking. Similarly shareholders look to the risk management function for assurance against losses.

Management now realises that there are no excess returns in financial markets without risk. If zero risk tolerance condemns firms to zero excess returns, then shareholders naturally demand that risk be taken; hence, some losses cannot be prevented. The task of risk management is to contain those losses to pre-specified tolerances. In other words, although risk management cannot prevent losses, it can ensure the firm's awareness of and comfort with the level of risk taken. We have shown that while complete control of financial risks is an unattainable goal, there are a variety of complementary risk measurement tools that help illuminate the market risk management challenge.

We return to the question we posed at the outset of this chapter – "Measurement for what?". There are many reasons for firms to measure their risk, whether to establish a common language within a firm, to ensure the optimal deployment of risk capital in pursuit of ordinary business opportunities, to determine defensible regulatory capital and report on risk to shareholders, or to establish a set of processes strong enough to prevent an aggressive trader or an extreme market event from putting the firm's viability at risk. However, as we have seen, the risk manager is not limited to the use of just one measure. Indeed modern technology provides an almost limitless array of such measures. A well-designed risk measurement methodology should capture all significant exposures through normalising, cumulating and aggregating risk information. It should also employ the complementary combination of stress testing, VaR measures, and scenario analyses. This comprehensive set of techniques enables the risk manager the ability to address the manifold measurement challenges which are central to the function. In the rest of this section we shall consider the issues that arise in implementing each of these techniques as well as some of the particular issues associated with measuring issuer specific risk.

6

Stress testing

Introduction

If one could encapsulate the most fundamental concern of any part of a firm involved in taking market risk, from the individual trader right up to the board of directors, it could probably be summarised in the one question, "How much could I lose?" The challenge for risk management is to be able to find a way of answering that question.

As explained in Chapter 5, effective risk management recognises that there is no one "right" way to answer the question. It requires a combination of the different techniques of stress testing, VaR and scenario analysis, each of which has its place in the risk management tool kit. We start in this chapter by considering the role of stress testing, by which we mean looking at the effect on our portfolio of large predefined moves in a single market variable. It addresses in a relatively direct and intuitively accessible way the question "How much could I lose?" based on a major change in a particular dimension.

In the following discussion, we take a highly pragmatic approach to this topic, examining how to design, implement and analyse stress tests. The chapter continues with a review of some of the limitations and cautionary notes that accompany the process of stress testing and interpreting results. As is often the case with other powerful analytical techniques, stress testing provides an important tool in the overall arsenal for managing risk, but its real power comes from knowing how best to integrate stress tests into a balanced and effective overall risk management system for the organisation. The chapter therefore concludes with some thoughts on how stress testing can be combined with other types of risk analysis discussed throughout the rest of this book.

Definition

What if the Fed announced a 50 basis point increase in US interest rates? What would be the effect if the price of oil doubled? How would a 35 per cent devaluation of the Mexican peso relative to the US$ affect P&L?

While none of these events is very likely to happen on a given day or even year, they are all certainly possible. In October 1987, for example, the US stock market fell over 20 per cent. In contrast to the rule of thumb in most financial markets where 4-standard-deviation events happen approximately once per year, the October 1987 crash was a 25-standard-deviation event.

Stress testing deals with these "outlier" events. It addresses the large moves in key market variables that lie beyond day-to-day risk monitoring but that could potentially occur. The process of stress testing, therefore, involves first identifying these potential movements, including which market variables to stress, how much to stress them by, and what timeframe to run the stress analysis over. A number of assumptions need to be clarified as they can affect the structure of the testing and the interpretation of the results. For example, strong existing correlations between key variables (eg 2-year, 5-year, and 10-year bonds) may indicate stressing a whole family of related variables together (eg the whole yield curve). On the other hand, one might believe that under "catastrophic" conditions even these strong correlations may break down, which may indicate stressing individual variables alone.

The key starting point in establishing stress testing is to define the key changes in market variables that make up the set of stress tests to be performed. Changes in interest rates and their volatilities are very common. In fact, changes in the underlying price of an instrument (eg interest rate, equity index, exchange rate, commodity price, etc) and changes in its volatility can be everyday analyses in financial markets. A broader definition of what can be stress tested could cover any variables that impact market prices and thus a firm's portfolio valuation. One could well imagine, for example, particular markets where key variables driving market prices included changes in the weather or labour productivity, and if the sensitivities were available, these could also be included in a series of stress tests.

Once these market movements and underlying assumptions are decided upon, "shocks" are applied to the portfolio. Revaluing the portfolio allows one to see what the effect of a particular market movement has on the value of the portfolio and the overall P&L. Stress test reports can be constructed that summarise the effects of different shocks of different magnitudes. Normally, there is then some kind of reporting procedure and follow-up with traders and management to determine whether any actions need to be taken in response.

Regulatory requirements

Stress testing also plays a key role in certain regulatory requirements affecting the financial community. The Derivatives Policy Group (DPG), for example, was formed in 1994 to address derivatives activities by US brokerage firms. In its 1995 *A Framework for Voluntary Oversight*, DPG proposes certain standards for models used in analysing risk. Part of the periodic assessment of these models includes specifying large moves in core risk factors and computing their effect on P&L. Exhibit 6.1 details the stress tests involved.

The DPG analysis highlights some of the more typical tests carried out on financial portfolios. Even at this basic level, however, the number of analyses can be quite large. Here, each of the stress tests is done not only for the US but for a range of other countries as well. Also, in most cases, these stress tests isolate movements in individual risk factors. Once combinations of factors such as a change in the yield curve combined with exchange rate movements are considered, the volume of output can grow at a very rapid pace.

Some stress testing issues

While stress testing can be a very straightforward process – and is, in fact, often used as a quick and dirty form of "risk management" – certain issues concerning the validity of the results are not always clear. In particular, stress test reports are often run showing progressively larger movements in the variables being stressed (eg

Exhibit 6.1 DPG stress testing standards

(a) Parallel yield curve shifts of 100 basis points up or down.

(b) Steepening and flattening of the yield curves (2s to 10s) by 25 basis points.

(c) Each of the 4 permutations of a parallel yield curve shift of 100 basis points concurrent with a tilting of the yield curve (2s and 10s) by 25 basis points.

(d) Increase and decrease in all 3-month yield volatilities by 20% of prevailing levels.

(e) Increase and decrease in equity index values by 10%.

(f) Increase and decrease in equity index volatilities by 20% of prevailing levels.

(g) Increase and decrease in the exchange value (relative to the US dollar) of foreign currencies by 6% in the case of major currencies and 20% in the case of other currencies.

(h) Increase and decrease in foreign exchange rate volatilities by 20% of prevailing levels.

(i) Increase and decrease in swap spreads by 20 basis points.

Source: DPG, *A Framework for Voluntary Oversight*, February 1995, p.30.

increases/decreases in interest rates by 5 bp, 10 bp, ..., 50 bp). Using stress test results to make decisions in the more "normal" range, however, can be a naive substitution for more rigorous VaR analysis. On the other end of the range, stressing a variable by a large amount beyond the status quo raises questions about whether an independent jump by this variable is realistic or whether correlations with other market variables in the model need to be taken into account.

A second concern is that although stress tests are an excellent example of something that sounds easy to do in theory ("Sure, we can run some quick stress tests on interest rate changes") this can quickly multiply in practice into reams of output and analysis (parallel interest rate shifts up and down by increments of 10 basis points, concurrent with various degrees of steepening or flattening across the yield curve, etc). Finding a useful and practical way of integrating stress testing into risk management requires considerable skill and judgement. The risk manager needs to be aware of the types of questions that stress testing is best suited for and where other techniques may be more appropriate.

Thirdly, there is always an issue as to whether the predefined stress tests have in fact identified the risk factors that are most appropriate to the firm. A good example of this is the predefined table of stress tests agreed as part of the DPG reporting framework to the SEC (outlined in Exhibit 6.2). Although this report contains information on the effect of stressing over 100 factors, when Goldman Sachs filed its first report for positions held in May 1995, the largest risk in its swaps business was not one of those listed. It happened to be a large position in the spread between municipals and swaps. A year earlier the firm lost over US$10 million from changes in the spread between the prices of natural gas in two different locations in North America. There are thousands of such spreads that could be significant risk factors in the energy market alone.

Fourthly, it is important to remember that stress testing, while providing one answer to the question "How much could I lose?", cannot provide an answer to the equally important question "How much am I likely to lose?" In other words, while providing a good measure of a portfolio's sensitivity to a significant move in any one

Exhibit 6.2 Sample DPG stress test table

Core risk factor scenarios
As of 1 November 1997

Country	Risk factor	Move size	Impact in US$ million	
			Up	Down
Australia	Parallel yield shift	100bp	-0.209	1.129
Australia	Curve steepening	25bp 2s to 10s	-0.009	0.057
Australia	Yield shift + steepening		-0.090	0.647
Australia	Yield shift + flattening		-0.231	1.387
Australia	Interest rate volatility	20%	0.703	-0.809
Australia	Equity index shift	10%	0.000	0.000
Australia	Equity index volatility	20%	0.000	0.000
Australia	Currency	20%	0.824	-0.727
Australia	Currency volatility	20%	0.000	0.000
Australia	Swap spread	20bp	0.009	-0.008

risk factor, it does not provide any information about the probability of such a one-factor move happening in practice. In this sense stress testing helps to define the boundaries of a firm's risk profile, but treats each event as if it has an equal likelihood of happening, which is clearly not the case. VaR techniques (discussed in detail in Chapter 7) are much better able to address the question of the probability of a particular loss arising, but are less well able to respond to the question of how bad things could be in an unlikely extreme scenario.

Consequently, despite its shortcomings, stress testing is still one of the best lines of defence in calculating a firm's potential exposure to catastrophic loss.

Stress testing vs. scenario analysis

Before moving on to consider the practical issues associated with stress testing, we should also comment briefly on the relationship between stress testing and scenario analysis. These two techniques are often referred to interchangeably, and they do have a number of similarities. Both hypothesise a future state of the world and test the effects on the current portfolio, and neither technique assigns probabilities to the events involved.

In practice, however, there are important differences between the two techniques. Stress testing takes a good hard look at the market variables driving the value of a portfolio and asks what would happen if one or more of these variables moved in a specified way. Scenario analysis, on the other hand, typically starts with an hypothesis about an alternative state of the world and deduces what this implies about the underlying market variables. New market values are then run through the model with subsequent effects on the value of the portfolio. In this sense, stress testing can be thought of as a bottom-up analysis technique, while scenario analysis is by its nature a more top-down approach.

More complex states of the world, however, often blur the distinction between stress tests and scenario analysis. When the situation troubling risk managers is relatively contained to large movements in one or a few key variables, stress tests are normally run. When the catastrophic situation is more complex with related assumptions or implications, one is usually better off tackling it top-down through scenario techniques. Major regulatory changes, wars, earthquakes and strikes are all examples of events that lend themselves to scenario analysis. In reality, though, many states of the world, such as a stock market crash, fall somewhere in between, so the appropriate technique to use is not so clear-cut. Nevertheless, the two techniques, when used properly, should be complementary.

Step-by-step approach to stress testing

Having defined what a stress test is and how to choose the variables to be tested, we can now turn to the actual step-by-step considerations in setting up, running and evaluating stress test analyses. Exhibit 6.3 summarises some of the issues involved.

1. Picking what to stress
- *Choice of market variables:* Sometimes it is not clear which market variables to stress and whether this should be done individually or in groups. It may be helpful to consider which collections of market variables move together and which move independently. Are there natural "families" of variables such as groups of currencies or the yield curve that could be stressed at the same time? Some examples of types of variables to consider include: individual market variables (eg interest rates, volatility); relative values of variables (eg 10-year/30-year rates); "families" of variables (eg the entire yield curve); and two-dimensional combinations of variables (eg interest rates and volatility).

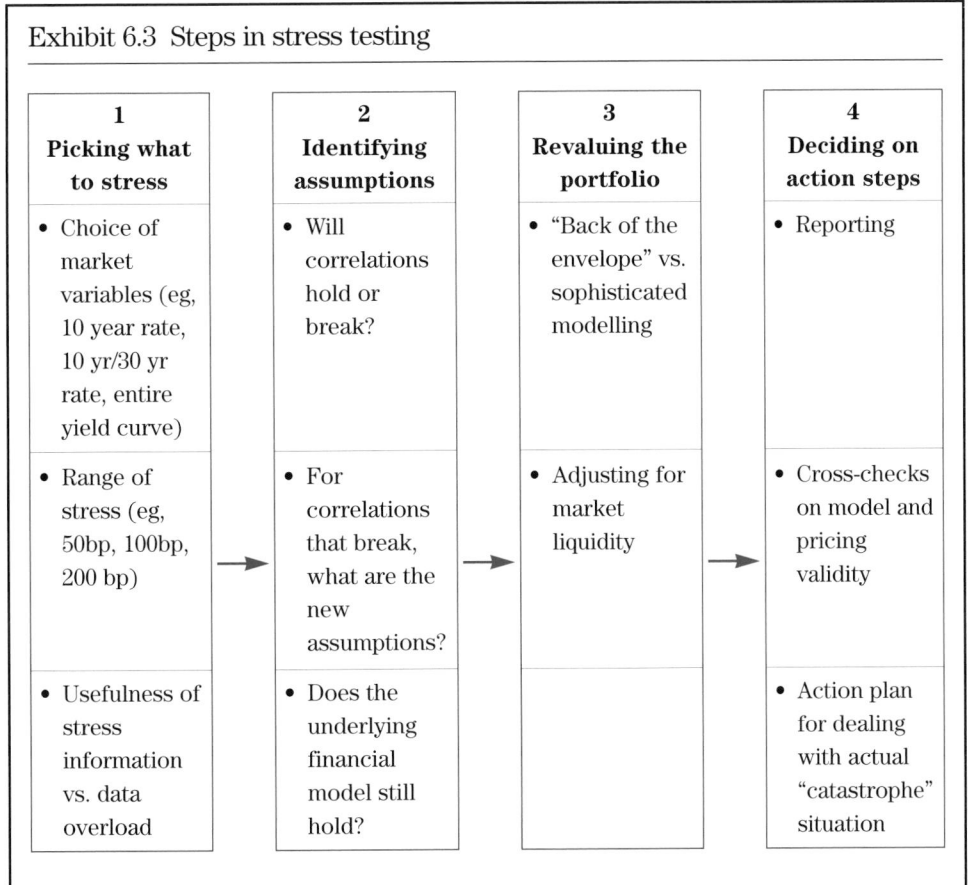

Exhibit 6.3 Steps in stress testing

1 **Picking what to stress**	2 **Identifying assumptions**	3 **Revaluing the portfolio**	4 **Deciding on action steps**
• Choice of market variables (eg, 10 year rate, 10 yr/30 yr rate, entire yield curve)	• Will correlations hold or break?	• "Back of the envelope" vs. sophisticated modelling	• Reporting
• Range of stress (eg, 50bp, 100bp, 200 bp)	• For correlations that break, what are the new assumptions?	• Adjusting for market liquidity	• Cross-checks on model and pricing validity
• Usefulness of stress information vs. data overload	• Does the underlying financial model still hold?		• Action plan for dealing with actual "catastrophe" situation

- *Range of stress:* As discussed earlier, care should be taken at both ends of this spectrum. Small stress tests around the current position should not be a substitute for VaR. Very large ranges in stress tests, however, may be discounted as improbable or beyond the realistic assumptions of the underlying model.
- *Usefulness of stress information vs. data overload:* For the above inputs, it may be tempting to conclude that when in doubt, do more. In practice, however, it soon becomes clear how quickly "possibly useful" stress tests can multiply. An effective risk manager needs to keep in mind that stress tests are a supplemental risk technique. If the time spent running, analysing, and distributing the results begins to approach anywhere near the majority of time spent on risk monitoring, data overload may be a problem and the number of stress tests being run may need to be cut back.

2. Identifying assumptions

- *Will correlations hold or break?* Should we assume, for example, that correlations that hold under normal circumstances also hold when markets crash? Deciding on how much faith to put in correlations is largely a matter of judgement concerning the nature of the particular market in question. For example, crises may break the usual correlations among the European currencies – the Italian lira may drop dramatically while the Deutschmark remains relatively strong and stable. On the other hand, it is difficult to imagine a circumstance in which the three-month price of oil collapses while the two and four-month contracts still hold firm. Assumptions about correlations between different market variables should be a cross-check against the choice of which variables to stress. In the case of the three-month oil contract, for example, it may be advisable to stress all short-term oil contracts together, much in the same way that the entire yield curve rather than individual bond rates often appears in stress reports.
- *For correlations that break, what are the new assumptions?* For example, can we look to other countries, markets, or industries for proxies and histories of similar events? Stress tests typically assume zero correlation among the variables being stressed and other market variables affecting the portfolio. Correlations that are still assumed to hold are treated, as mentioned in the point above, by stressing the two correlated variables together – effectively assuming a correlation of 1. For correlations that break, however, more sophisticated techniques may be employed when we can replace the zero correlation assumption with better estimates. Scenario analysis, for example, works top-down to explicitly consider which variables will be affected by the scenario and then considers their combined effect on P&L.
- *Does the underlying financial model still hold?* Stress testing is most reliable if it is based on an objective assessment of historical market movements and actual market data are used. Nevertheless as we have seen, stress testing is often used to "push beyond the envelope" into hypothetical situations, in part because these can be the most worrisome. The extent to which a market variable is stressed far beyond its historical range is based on certain assumptions that the underlying financial model remains robust and still holds in this range. In extreme hypothetical situations, scenario analysis may again be the better technique as it deals head on with the analytical problems of new states of the world and a top-down assessment of the model and the assumptions that drive its results.

3. Revaluing the portfolio

- *"Back of the envelope" vs. sophisticated modelling:* For most stress tests, sophisticated theoretical modelling is probably unfounded. There are more complex techniques such as scenario analysis or Monte-Carlo simulations for when the assumptions get complicated, as described earlier. Time may also be critical in arriving at an answer. If it takes too long to write the code and analyse the results, people will lose interest.

4. Deciding on action steps

- *Reporting:* In many large brokerage firms, stress reports may be circulated every day to the traders. As mentioned above, it is important to avoid data overload such that people feel like they are buried in paper. As regards what is reported, risk managers and management are often most concerned about the impact of various stresses on the P&L. Traders on the other hand, tend to focus on the "Greeks" – ie mostly delta along with gamma and vega. Traders want to know, for example, if delta shifts how difficult will it be to buy or sell the underlying security and whether they could be caught on the wrong side of an illiquid market. They are often more concerned with smaller stresses while risk managers tend to look at larger moves and typically want practical, boiled-down version of stress reports. The risk manager's temptation, on the other hand, may be to analyse and report a large variety of possible stresses – just in case the bad event happens, the risk manager did his job and reported the potential loss. There is no simple answer to resolving these different objectives. It does, however, point out the need for careful up-front planning involving both traders and the risk management department to agree on mutually useful reporting content and procedures.

- *Cross-checks on model and pricing validity:* Stress tests often reveal sizeable vulnerabilities in P&L, especially for extreme movements in key market variables. In many cases, this can indicate a flaw in the model or pricing algorithm rather than an actual market sensitivity. Stress tests, in fact, are one of the most important cross-checks on model accuracy. Where stress testing reveals unusual results of this sort, it is often a good policy to check the underlying model. Risk management departments in large brokerage firms, in fact, often employ quantitative experts whose job includes an independent check on model validity.

- *Follow-up with traders:* When models and pricing have been confirmed to be accurate, there is often an issue of how much follow-up with traders is needed or even appropriate. In many instances, delivering the stress report to the trader, no matter how startling the results are, is the final step in the process. The trader is assumed to take any necessary actions concerning his or her trading strategy. A closer working relationship between risk manager and trading desk, however, will often lead to a dialogue and follow-up. This can include such issues as possible diversification or hedging strategies to reduce the areas of greatest downside risk as revealed in the stress analysis.

- *Action plan for dealing with actual "catastrophe" situations:* Clearly, it is a matter of experience and judgement as to whether normal VaR monitoring has any usefulness during these periods. Stress tests, however, can help determine an action plan before catastrophe strikes. For example, stress testing may be used to identify "discontinuities" or "breakpoints" in likely P&L impact. In a stock market crash, for instance, losses may tend to accumulate at a greater rate after the stock market drops 100 points and at an even more alarming rate after 200 points. By identifying possible inflection points in returns, stress tests can help establish credible benchmarks for dealing with potentially difficult situations.

Some cautionary notes

While stress tests have a useful and important role in risk management, they also come with their own particular type of warning label. We have seen some of these issues in earlier parts of this chapter. Here we summarise the main limitations.

On the surface, stress testing can appear to be a deceptively easy technique. In practice, however, stress tests are based on a relatively large number of subjective choices. It is not always clear what to stress, including what market factors to pick (either individually or in combination with other factors), what range of values to consider, or what timeframe to analyse. This is the most serious barrier to the effective use of stress testing as a day-to-day risk management tool. The large number of possible stress tests that one could run (and, by definition, the unlikely possibility that any of them could actually materialise) can be overwhelming.

Another serious limitation of stress testing is that there are no probabilities attached to the outcomes. Where VaR is a measure of how much we could gain or lose with a specified degree of confidence, stress testing is strictly a focus on how much we could gain or lose. History is, in fact, so thin for these extreme movements in risk factors that assigning any probability estimates would be an inexact process at best. Lack of probability measures, however, only exacerbates the issue of data overload and the subjectivity mentioned previously.

A related issue is that market variables typically do not move independently but rather are correlated in various degrees with other market variables. In the "normal" range of market movement, a history of observations allows precise calculation of the correlation matrix. On the outer edges of the range, where stress testing is most often applied, there may only be a few if any observations. This "thinness" of data makes it impossible to calculate historic correlations. Likewise, lack of any correlation may be an equally extreme assumption, though the one that is most typically made in stress testing.

A further pragmatic concern in running stress tests is the extent to which the data and models involved in the testing all reside on the same system and/or in the same part of the firm. A risk manager needs to assess not only the feasibility of running and analysing a potentially large number of stresses but the mechanics of this process as well. This includes feeding stress factors into multiple systems to reprice portfolios and then aggregating the results from these systems into total P&L effects. Even in the most compatible environments, this process can add significantly to the turnaround time that is necessary and needs to be addressed in the up-front planning process.

Reliance on stress testing

To the reader the complementary nature of stress testing to other risk measurement methods (introduced in Chapter 5) may seem clear. In practice, however, the right balance is often difficult to achieve. The following brief description of the extremes may serve as a reminder against any possible bias towards either over-reliance or under-reliance on stress tests.

In this chapter we have described how stress testing can provide useful insights into P&L impact in the event of large moves in key market variables. Stress tests are an effective complement to other risk management techniques such as VaR and scenario analysis. To the reader this complimentary nature may seem clear. In practice, however, the right balance is often difficult to achieve. The following brief description of the extremes may serve as a reminder against any possible bias towards either over-reliance or under-reliance on stress tests.

"What if" mentality (over-reliance on stress testing)

It is easy to fall into the trap of trying to cover an ever-expanding set of risks and catastrophes. Particularly as the risk management function gains visibility in an organisation, the commentary from traders and other parts of the firm may take the form of "Yes, but what if ...". An active imagination combined with the relative ease of running "just a few more" stress tests can steer a risk manager towards growing and perhaps excessive use of stress testing techniques.

To counter this tendency, it is worthwhile to reiterate one of the main shortcomings of this method – namely the absence of any probability measure associated with the particular stress test. A focus on the catastrophe (eg we could lose US$1 billion, but with an extremely low probability) will eventually yield a mountain of stress tests that never materialised into reality. The backlash is then that these results get heavily discounted and the credibility of the risk monitoring role may be tarnished.

"Let's just deal with it when it happens" (under-reliance on stress testing)

The other extreme, and possibly result of the backlash described above, is simply taking a reactive approach to market concerns. This approach has its drawbacks as well. The more obvious include a lack of understanding or preparation for any adverse moves in the market. Every organisation has its breaking point, and it is simply good business practice to know to what extent one is "betting the bank". Stress tests may reveal an organisation that is too exposed to certain market events or even possibly an organisation that is too risk averse.

The less obvious drawbacks to avoiding or downplaying stress tests may be that this also shuts down potentially important lines of dialogue with traders. Isolating specific market risk factors through individual stress tests can help both identify and address specific concerns.

The happy median, as we have discussed throughout this chapter, is to use stress tests as one of several risk management tools.

Conclusion

This chapter described how stress testing can provide useful insights into the P&L impact of changes in portfolio values in the event of large moves in key market variables. Stress tests are an effective complement to other risk management techniques such as VaR and scenario analysis.

Beyond its value for management purposes, we have shown that stress testing has become a regulatory requirement. The major steps in stress testing include: picking what to stress; identifying your assumptions; revaluing your portfolio; and choosing action steps required based on your analysis.

The following chapters give more detail on VaR and scenario analysis. None of these techniques is good or bad in itself but rather different in the assumptions it is based on and the types of questions it is best suited to answer. It is the role of the risk manager in an organisation to be able to pick and choose among these techniques knowledgeably.

Appendix – Stress test examples

Here we take a look at several different stress tests. These are all typical analyses that might be run for a currency trader or to monitor risk for a foreign exchange desk.

Linear payoffs

In the simplest case, let us start with a single dimensional stress test on one currency, the German Deutschmark. Suppose that its spot exchange rate is 1.50 Deutschmarks (DM) per US dollar (US$). Let us take the case where we hold a forward contract on a spot transaction of DM150 million, which is equivalent to US$100 million. Exhibit 6.4 shows the profit or loss associated with a change in the exchange rate of up to +/- 6 per cent. For example, a 6 per cent depreciation of the DM relative to the US$ would result in a loss of US$6 million. In this case, the P&L impact is strictly linear. For linear payoff structures, stress tests are easy to calculate and can be extrapolated across different stress ranges in a very straightforward manner.

Non-linear payoffs

Payoffs, however, are not always linear. In Exhibit 6.5, a single one-month call option on the Deutschmark is stressed, again by running stress tests of up to a +/- 6 per cent change in the exchange rate. Assuming volatility of 10 per cent, no discounting, and a strike price of 1.5 DM/US$, we can calculate the P&L impact. As is shown, the payoffs are no longer linear. In fact, the payoffs are convex around the current spot rate, increasing at a progressively faster rate for each percentage point of currency appreciation. For negative stresses, the convexity results in a flattening slope as the currency depreciates (for more on stress tests see Chapter 11).

Non-Linear payoffs with convexity reversals

Exhibit 6.6 shows a stress test on a portfolio of options. The same one-month call option as above is combined with a short one-month call position of DM250 million. The volatility remains at 10 per cent, the strike price is 1.47 DM/US$, and again there is no discounting. The stress test now reveals a much more complex pattern of

---

Exhibit 6.4 One currency stress test with linear payoffs (DM150 million)

| | % change in DM/US$ exchange rate | | | | | | | | |
	-6%	-3%	-2%	-1%	0%	1%	2%	3%	6%
DM/US$	1.5957	1.5464	1.5306	1.5152	1.5000	1.4851	1.4706	1.4563	1.4151
Profit & (loss)	(6.00)	(3.00)	(2.00)	(1.00)	–	1.00	2.00	3.00	6.00

Exhibit 6.5 One currency stress test with non-linear payoffs

DM150 million, 1-month call = 0.0077; volatility = 10%; strike = 1.5 DM/US$; no discounting.

| | % change in DM/US$ exchange rate | | | | | | | | |
	-6%	-3%	-2%	-1%	0%	1%	2%	3%	6%
DM/US$	1.5957	1.5464	1.5306	1.5152	1.5000	1.4851	1.4706	1.4563	1.4151
Profit & (loss)	(1.14)	(0.94)	(0.74)	(0.44)	–	0.57	1.27	2.08	4.87

Exhibit 6.6 One currency stress test with non-linear payoffs and convexity reversals

1 DM150 million; 1-month call = 0.0077; volatility = 10%; strike = 1.5 DM/US$; no discounting.

2 DM250 million; 1-month call = 0.0028; volatility = 10%; strike = 1.47 DM/US$; no discounting.

	-6%	-3%	-2%	-1%	0%	1%	2%	3%	6%
				% change in DM/US$ exchange rate					
DM/US$	1.5957	1.5464	1.5306	1.5152	1.5000	1.4851	1.4706	1.4563	1.4151
1 Profit & (loss)	(1.14)	(0.94)	(0.74)	(0.44)	–	0.57	1.27	2.08	4.87
2 Profit & (loss)	0.69	0.62	0.52	0.33	–	(0.51)	(1.23)	(2.17)	(6.12)
∑ Profit & (loss)	(0.45)	(0.32)	(0.22)	(0.11)	–	0.06	0.04	(0.09)	(1.25)

payoffs. Negative changes in the exchange rate continue to have a non-linear convex shape. Positive stresses, however, result in profit, but only up to a point. Between a 2 per cent and 3 per cent appreciation of the DM, there is an inflection point beyond which losses begin to accumulate.

7

VaR

Introduction

In the previous chapter we attempted to answer the question – "How much could we lose?" – with stress testing techniques. VaR attempts to provide a meaningful answer to the important question for senior management – "How much am I likely to lose?"

In the past 10 years VaR (value at risk) has emerged as the most important concept in risk management. How did this happen? What does it mean? How does one compute and use VaR? And where do we go from here? These are the questions we will address in this chapter.

Value at Risk – simple definition

Although "VaR" has a narrow meaning, as a unit of risk, we will follow the general convention and use VaR more generally to refer to any model that combines an ability to mark-to-market with an ability to assign probabilities to the future states of underlying risk factors.

The motivations for VaR

As we saw in the previous chapter, one way of looking at risk is to use stress testing techniques to assess potential exposure to predefined moves in individual risk factors. Indeed, although it may not have been formalised in this way, in practice most major financial institutions managed their market risk for many years by using variants on single factor stress testing techniques. These techniques hinge on setting individual position and risk factor limits, combined with a number of capital constraints such as limits on the size of the balance sheet, the degree of leverage and regulatory capital usage. These approaches worked very well in the simpler environments that existed in the past. Although there was some modernisation of the limits approach to reflect new risk measures – introducing duration limits for fixed income or limits on the "Greeks" in option trading – it has only been comparatively recently that there has been pressure to change the fundamental approach to measuring risk and setting risk limits.

The pressure for change in this area came from a number of different sources. First, the senior management became increasingly aware that, because of the growing complexity of their business, their system of risk limits and exposure reports was not providing a reliable measure of aggregate market risk. This requirement was famously encapsulated in the demand from Dennis Weatherstone, the chairman of JP Morgan, for a report to be on his desk at 4.15pm which showed in a single number the market risk that the firm was assuming over the next 24 hours.

Furthermore, measuring the risk-adjusted returns on a business brings with it the need for a common unit of measurement enabling different risks to be assessed and compared in a consistent way across the firm. Secondly, pressure from the banking regulatory authorities meant that banks were forced to consider how the market risk they were assuming could be encapsulated in a single number. Thirdly, external pressure on financial firms to describe the nature of their risk profiles more clearly to their shareholders and counterparties forced firms to some consensus on the best way to present this information.

All these pressures have led to an increasing focus on VaR as the answer to the problem of measuring market risk, and in response to this the criticism that it results in an oversimplification of risk analysis. Risk certainly cannot be summarised in a single number. Risk management is a complex task, and a complete understanding would at the very least require knowing the VaR for many different horizons and many different levels of probability, not to mention knowing the exposures to underlying risk factors and their volatilities and correlations. But, of course, such an observation should not be seen as a criticism of VaR.

It is obvious that no single number can convey the richness of the potential for future losses. Indeed, if someone were required to use one single number, some VaR statistic might be the best solution. Luckily, though, we live in a world today where there is virtually no constraint on the number of statistics that can be computed and examined. The usefulness of VaR has everything to do with the fact that it recognises and quantifies the uncertainty of future outcomes. VaR was never intended to summarise everything in one single number, and its usefulness has little to do with being one number.

Understanding VaR

As we saw in Chapter 6, although measures of exposure such as stress tests can answer the question "How much could I lose?", they are not able to provide any meaningful answer to the more important question for the manager of a trading business – "How much am I likely to lose?" The difference between these two questions is the essence of VaR. Answering this question forces a firm to quantify the probability of a multitude of possible outcomes rather than just listing a set of worst case scenarios.

To make this point clear, consider the following thought experiment. Suppose there existed a very sophisticated computer program that could model the value of any financial instrument in any state of nature. Let us call this the "ultimate mark-to-market machine", or UMM for short. Inputs to UMM would include any combination of relevant data about all those uncertain factors that affect security valuations. Of course a computer program like UMM would not be easy to create. But if UMM did exist, then among other things it would be able to produce all the above-mentioned exposures and any others that might be wanted. Given any change in one risk factor, UMM could measure the change in value of any instrument; given any scenario, UMM could reprice a portfolio.

Unfortunately, despite all the sophistication and power of UMM, a risk manager needs something more in order to quantify risk. Given any state of nature, UMM can do its thing, but what risk management is all about is quantifying the uncertainty of future outcomes. UMM can only quantify the valuations for a given outcome. The key additional input that is needed is a specification of the possible future states of nature and their probabilities. This quantification of the uncertainty of the future states of nature is the statistical basis of risk management. The recent recognition of this fact by the financial industry is the real substance of the VaR revolution in risk management.

Indeed, recognition of the impracticality of managing to worst cases has led to the widespread adoption (not only in finance, but in many disciplines) of an emphasis on managing risk relative to infrequent, but regularly recurring outcomes. In many fields a statistically measured quantity forms the basis for risk management. Most people are familiar with the concept of a "100-year flood" to describe a standard for readiness. The idea implicit in this standard is that a community should be able to withstand most, but not all conceivable outcomes. This is a reasonable approach to risk management, and has recently been extended to the financial community, where the measure of preparedness is "value at risk."

There are only two basic tasks to achieve this. First, one must be able to value one's positions in all states of nature; this is the mark-to-market requirement. Second, one must be able to specify the likelihood of all future states of nature; this is the probability model requirement. A probability model for the future distribution of underlying risk factors together with an algorithm for marking-to-market then creates a distribution of future values of a portfolio. This distribution is the object of interest in risk management. A complete understanding of risk requires a complete specification of this distribution.

Nonetheless, for most purposes we try to summarise the salient features of this distribution in a single number. As we mentioned in Chapter 4, the most common summary statistic for measuring the width of a distribution is the standard deviation, which quantifies the size of a typical random outcome. Risk management, however, is often not so concerned with typical outcomes, but rather with rare or "worst case" events. Unfortunately, in most contexts there is no "worst case". Most often there are simply larger and larger potential losses with decreasing likelihoods of occurrence.

Statisticians have long studied the properties of quantiles – points in the distributions of outcomes that are greater than a certain fraction of the outcomes. For example, outcomes are said to be in the upper quartile if they lie above a certain point. That point (the point below which three-quarters of the outcomes lie) is the top of the third quartile of the distribution and is an example of a quantile.

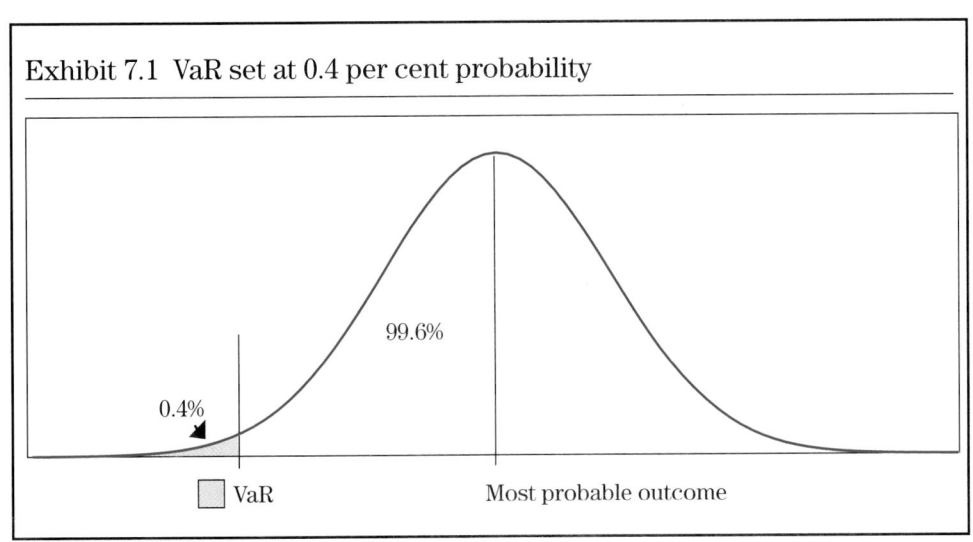

Exhibit 7.1 VaR set at 0.4 per cent probability

99.6%

0.4%

☐ VaR   Most probable outcome

VaR is also a quantile. The probability used to define the VaR statistic is generally quite small, because it is designed to refer to "rare" events, but the actual value chosen varies from one application to another. For example, often it is chosen to be the point in the distribution that is greater than all but one per cent of the outcomes. But in other contexts it might be the point in the distribution which will be exceeded only one business day per year, that is 1/252, which is a probability of 0.4 per cent (see Exhibit 7.1). In general, the VaR is an amount of loss which should be exceeded only a small, prespecified percentage of the time.

At this point we need to recognise an additional degree of complexity. When we speak of the distribution of future outcomes we need to specify exactly what horizon we are referring to. One could imagine looking at the range of outcomes one day ahead, two days ahead, a week ahead, a year ahead and so on. Just as there is no single point in a distribution that accurately represents the entire distribution, there is no single horizon that accurately represents the entire future. Like the probability associated with a VaR statistic, the horizon used to define the distribution from which the statistic will be computed also varies depending on the context of the application.

Thus, perhaps unfortunately, a VaR per se does not have a generally accepted meaning. To specify that a financial institution has a VaR of US$100 million is meaningless. At the very least, one needs to specify a horizon and a probability in order to interpret a VaR. Once these quantities are specified, the VaR indicates the size of loss that is likely to be exceeded over the given horizon with the given probability.

Despite the above mentioned hazard of trying to summarise risk in one single number, there has been a natural tendency toward standardisation of a definition of VaR, especially as it has been applied to regulatory reporting and capital standards. The financial regulators have in most contexts focused on the computation and reporting of a VaR associated with a two-week horizon and a one per cent probability. Interestingly, in most contexts this computation will not accurately measure the one per cent point in the true distribution of outcomes for the institution. The computation is almost always made holding positions fixed, which will rarely be the case in practice, and is usually made without ageing the positions. The latter qualification is generally not important unless there are short dated options.

In any case the regulatory definition of VaR can better be viewed as a standard rather than a reflection of the true distribution of outcomes. Perhaps the best interpretation of the regulatory VaR is that it is intended to measure a quantile in an artificial distribution of losses that would occur if we sample only over large events. These events are assumed to happen in such a short period of time, or with such illiquidity, that a firm's positions could not be materially changed. In that context the "large" event is defined to be an event drawn from the distribution of typical two-week events.

Five steps to VaR

Stated in the dry fashion of Exhibit 7.2, the task sounds quite manageable. If only it were so easy. In fact, in risk management perhaps more than most endeavours, the devil is in the details. We now briefly discuss in turn each of these five steps.

1. Identify the positions held by the institution

The challenge associated with this topic is discussed at length in Chapter 15. It is, for many firms, one of the hardest tasks. The number of practical problems is large, but high on the list are the following:

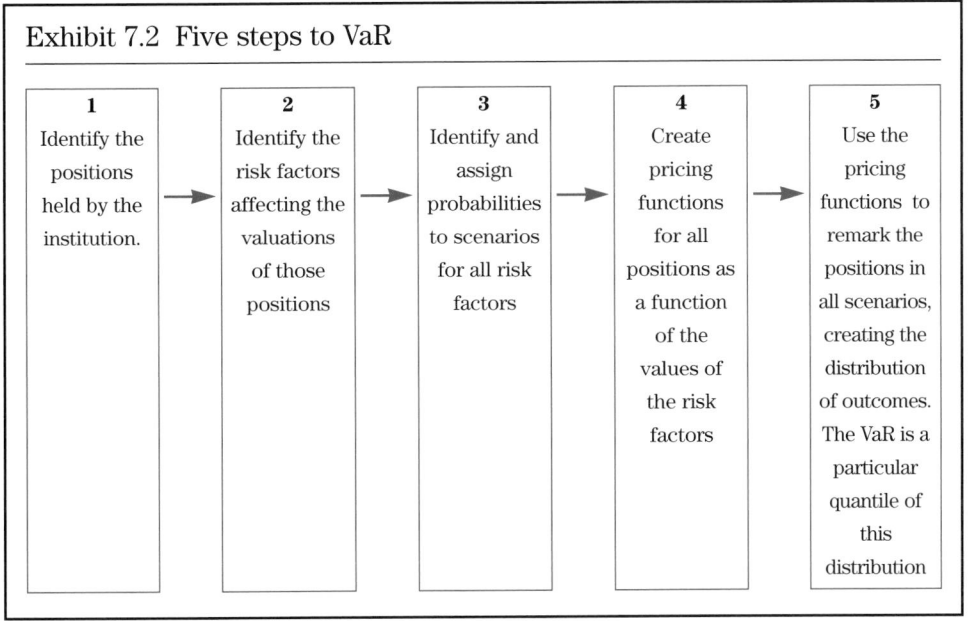

Exhibit 7.2 Five steps to VaR

1	2	3	4	5
Identify the positions held by the institution.	Identify the risk factors affecting the valuations of those positions	Identify and assign probabilities to scenarios for all risk factors	Create pricing functions for all positions as a function of the values of the risk factors	Use the pricing functions to remark the positions in all scenarios, creating the distribution of outcomes. The VaR is a particular quantile of this distribution

- many different trader and back office systems;
- no consistent definition of securities in the different systems;
- no ability to capture the full description of derivatives in back office systems; and
- no control over the accuracy or completeness of positions in traders' systems and spreadsheets.

Although it is not ideal, a first approximation to the positions is often created by obtaining a feed of exposures to risk factors from traders' systems. Because they need this information for hedging purposes, traders typically have access to such exposure information. There are problems with this type of solution, however. Often such exposures are created on a portfolio basis, not for individual securities. There would typically be only very limited ability to audit the completeness of such a feed because traders' systems are often not tied to the books and records maintained by the back office operations and control staff.

The best solution would be to obtain a complete feed from the firm's back office systems. The problem with this approach is that back office systems typically do not keep enough information, especially about derivatives, to allow either complete repricing in different scenarios, or at least calculation of exposures to the relevant risk factors. When such complete information is not available the risk function must obtain the pricing information from a front office system and match it to the back office position information.

In practice a risk system will generally have to take multiple feeds from a variety of front and back office systems and somehow manage to create an accurate and complete database of positions, valuations, and the information that allows repricing in different scenarios or "position analytics". It includes exposure information such as duration for bonds, deltas, vegas, and gammas for options, but also, in the case of difficult to price derivatives, may need to be a fairly complex and complete description of all the contingencies that might affect the value of the derivative in different future market conditions.

2. Identify the risk factors affecting the valuations of those positions

In much the same way as we saw in Chapter 6 in the discussion of how to identify the factors that should be stress tested, one of the more difficult judgement issues in creating a VaR model is deciding how many risk factors to include. The more factors included, the more accurate the valuations can be for any given security. However, more risk factors requires more data and more complicated systems. For example, if the portfolio includes individual equities one might hope to capture the main risk by using an equity index as a risk factor. In many contexts, however, such an approach will not capture the primary risk in the portfolio. Perhaps the portfolio is dominated by a few concentrated positions, which may not behave at all like a market or sector index.

Equity markets are often modelled as being a function of a small number of risk factors together with the idiosyncratic or "specific" risk of the individual equities. Such "factor" models can be estimated using prespecified "observable" factors, or can be estimated through statistical identification of "unobservable" factors that account for the correlations of returns of different equities. In either case any particular position is not completely determined by the movements of the factors. Rather, it is hoped that the factors explain most of the returns of the positions, and that the remaining change in value is small and uncorrelated across positions. Depending on the nature of the portfolio, any given set of factors may be more or less adequate in explaining the changes in value, and thus in modelling the risk. It is very difficult to determine in advance whether a particular set of factors will be adequate, and whether it will continue to function well over time.

Similar issues come up in other markets. For bonds, how many points are needed to model the yield curve? How many industries, ratings categories and maturities are needed to model corporate spreads? How many dimensions of mortgage products are required? How many currencies? How many different types of emerging markets securities? How many different types of commodities, forward prices, locations, etc? These are the issues that must be answered, but there is never a complete or even an adequate answer. For any given set of risk factors, a trader can almost certainly find a position that has significant risk along a dimension that is not captured.

A VaR model must try to capture as many of the risk factors affecting the valuations of positions as possible. Typically this will be a process requiring constant monitoring and updating. However, no set of risk factors will ever be complete. There will always be approximation error. Whether any given set of risk factors is adequate depends on the context of its use.

3. Identify and assign probabilities to scenarios for all risk factors

There are many issues that arise in creating a distribution for risk factors. We need to estimate volatilities and correlations, and specify the shape of the distribution – for example, whether it has fat tails. Does it change over time? To simplify the discussion and be concrete, let's start with only one risk factor, say the 10-year US Treasury bond, and one horizon, say one day. We then need only to specify a distribution for daily returns on the US Treasury bond. Even in this context there are many alternative approaches.

Do we look at historical data? For example, we might look at returns on actual Treasury bonds in the past; but which bonds, and how do we treat the data. Most trading of bonds does not take place on exchanges. Whose prices do we use? Do we look at historical returns or yield changes? Do we convert returns to excess returns? If so, do we use a risk-free rate (and if so, which one?), or do we subtract a mean return (and if so, how is it estimated; does it vary over time?). Do we take into account the lower than normal financing costs that often arise in the Treasury market? Do we take into account the change in duration that occurs when we roll from an older bond to a newer bond? Perhaps we try to estimate the price of a constant maturity bond; but if so, how?

We might also want to recognise that the distribution of Treasury returns has changed over time. During the three years from October 1979 through October 1982 there was a much higher than normal volatility in the Treasury market. While not so dramatic (volatilities rise and fall all the time), should we take that into account? Do we focus on recent historical volatility, or do we look at the implied future volatilities embedded in options on Treasury bonds? If we are really focused only on a one-day return, do we also take into account the impact of any economic data releases or other events that are scheduled to occur on that day?

Even if we assume that we know the volatility, we still need to know what the shape of the distribution of Treasury returns is. Historical data for most financial securities shows a pattern of "fat tails" – evidence that every so often a very large shock hits the market; shocks that are larger than those anticipated by the "normal" bell-shaped distribution. We should probably take those into account; after all, risk management is all about preparing for large shocks. But there is relatively little information on the size and frequency of large shocks. If the issue at hand is how often does a five standard deviation return occur, reasonable people may differ by a factor of two or more. We don't have enough observations to estimate such quantities precisely, and the data itself is subject to differences in interpretation. Should we, for example, include the data from 1979 through 1982 in the calculation today? Is it relevant, or not?

When we add more than one risk factor, then of course the number of issues increases. We now need to add estimates of correlations – the degree to which any two risk factors move together. All of the issues that affect estimates of volatilities affect estimates of correlations, and more. For example, what do you do when the historical returns on two different risk factors are measured at different times; for example the returns on Japanese government bonds and US Treasury bonds? What do you do when the historical returns on different series differ in length? What do you do with holidays and other missing data?

We have raised many issues, and provided no answers. Unfortunately, for most of the questions we have raised there are multiple possible answers and a thorough treatment would require a book in itself. More positively, though, we might add that the reason there are many answers is because in most contexts one approach is just about as good as another. Most of the time it doesn't matter much, for example, whether one uses historical returns or yields, or how the mean is removed, or exactly what sample is chosen.

On the other hand, the fact that "most of the time it doesn't matter much" is not a very satisfactory answer. Sometimes different approaches give very different answers and it is important to understand those differences and the uncertainty inherent in any statistical estimate. Such uncertainties are especially apparent in new and emerging markets where data is scarce and the structure is changing rapidly over time. There is really no simple set of rules to follow. At the end of the day, creating a realistic probability distribution for the future values of risk factors is a hard problem that needs to be worked through.

4. Create pricing functions for all positions as a function of the values of the risk factors

Earlier we imagined an "ultimate mark-to-market machine" (UMM) that can mark-to-market any given security in any given state of the world (read "values of risk factors"). This step is where the UMM is needed, but unfortunately, it doesn't exist.

In practice a variety of different approaches is used. For many securities the mark-to-market is a relatively simple function of the change in the risk factor (sensitivity approach). For example, if we use relative durations to represent a particular bond as a slightly larger or smaller position in a benchmark Treasury which is a risk factor, then the mark-to-market impact on the given bond is just the return on the Treasury bond applied to that adjusted position size. In other more complex securities, such as a derivative, the approach might be to run a derivative pricing model and use the risk factor values as inputs to the model (mark-to-market approach). For example, a bond option might be marked-to-market using a model that adjusts the value of the underlier based on a benchmark bond return and adjusts the volatility by some volatility risk factor change. In this type of situation one is confronted with a requirement to map model inputs into risk factors, which may be difficult in complex derivatives books. Another difficulty is often the time it takes to reprice derivatives in complex computer models.

For these reasons, one approach is to approximate the impact on security or derivative valuations by using exposures and Greek letter sensitivities. The delta, or delta-vega approximations are based on linear sensitivities to risk factors. The delta-gamma or delta-vega-gamma approximations are quadratic functions defined by the delta, vega and gamma sensitivities of a derivative to the risk factors. These approximations may be useful in many contexts, but can give misleading results when the reasonableness of the approximation breaks down. Such problems typically arise in exotic options that may have discontinuities in the price function (such as a knock-out or barrier option) or other significant non-linearities such as options close to expiration.

5. Use the pricing functions to re-mark the positions in all scenarios, creating the distribution of outcomes: the VaR is a particular quantile of this distribution

Given that steps 1 through 4 have been accomplished, step 5 is really quite easy. The probability distribution of risk factors is given in step 3; thus, we use one of the many well-known numerical algorithms to draw scenarios from that distribution. Then we apply the mark-to-market approach given in step 4. This combination produces one change in value for the portfolio. We then repeat these two steps many times and create a distribution for changes in portfolio value. The VaR is a quantile of the distribution. Thus, if we define the VaR to be the 0.1 per cent point in the distribution, then we simply order the outcomes and find that point. For example, if we have created one million samples of changes in portfolio value we would choose the 1000th largest loss to represent the 0.1 per cent quantile of the distribution.

The trade-offs with VaR

The reader will have realised by now that there is no simple formula for computing a VaR. Rather there are some simple to understand, but rather complex to implement steps that have to be undertaken. In this context we will spend the final part of this chapter discussing some of the important trade-offs that can affect the desirability of different approaches to the VaR model.

One important trade-off is between the likelihood of the outcome and the accuracy of the VaR measure. It is easier to measure and validate the accuracy of an estimate of the once-per-year loss than an estimate of the once-per-century loss. The problem is that management really cares about rare events – and rare events are, by their nature, more difficult to predict accurately. We can accurately measure reasonably frequent outcomes, but those are of less interest; so where do you focus attention – on what you can measure accurately or what you care about?

Another similar trade-off is between measuring risk in "normal" environments versus risk in "extreme" environments. We have ample data on normal environments; almost every day we get another datapoint to use. We can estimate the volatilities and correlations of risk factors in that environment relatively well. In many contexts we are comfortable that we are prepared for the normal environment. The problem that we worry about is the "market crash" or "currency devaluation" or other extreme outcome. These scenarios are difficult to characterise completely, we have very little data to go on, and we generally have an uncomfortable suspicion that the data from normal days tells us very little about what will happen in the extreme case. For example, normally bond and equity returns have a small positive correlation. In the market crash of 1987 the bond and equity markets both had extremely large moves, but they went in opposite directions. It's hard to say whether the next time there is a market crash bonds will go up or down, but they probably will have a big move. The small positive correlation of normal days is of relatively little help in thinking about our risk or the impact of bond exposures in an equity market crash scenario.

There is also a trade-off involved in trying to track the time-varying volatilities and correlations in the market. In general, the accuracy of a statistical measure is an increasing function of the amount of data used. Thus, if we use only recent data in order to capture the current state of the market we may have greater estimation uncertainty. Conversely, as markets change over time, it is also important to recognise that recent data may in certain portfolios be of greater significance. The changes in daily volatility that occurred in October of 1997 highlight the necessity for appropriate risk modelling time horizons.

Traders care about volatility and correlations over a holding period of a position. When holding periods are short, they care about the volatility today, which may be different from the volatility in the past. When we focus on the recent period, however, we have, by definition, less data – thus our estimates are less precise. To put it another way, we have a forecasting problem. To the extent that volatilities and correlations are unstable (and we have ample evidence that they do change over time), more data does not necessarily provide more accurate measures. On the other hand, when holding periods are long, then we are not so interested in the current state of the market but rather on returns over the holding period horizon. In that context we may well want to use a long data sample to more accurately measure the average return distribution likely to be in effect over the longer horizon, rather than today in the market.

Another trade-off exists between the amount of data required and the type of analysis being made. Sometimes all you care about is the volatility of a portfolio. In that context you can get away with using much less data. For example, the past 10 days P&L may give a pretty good idea of the current volatility of a portfolio; if, on the other hand, you want to understand the portfolio better, understand sources of risk, or perhaps find potential hedges, then estimates of the full covariance matrix are necessary, which generally will require significantly more data. Portfolio optimisation requires the most data – enough to understand the potential impacts of changes in positions in all different dimensions. Note that estimation error in the covariance matrix not only adds "noise" to the measurement of the risk of a portfolio, but also adds bias to the risk of a portfolio optimised relative to the affected covariance matrix. The reader may ponder whether risk management is more often concerned simply with risk measurement or rather with activities that either directly, or indirectly, are concerned with portfolio optimisation.

Finally, there are trade-offs that exist in alternative choices of the probability distribution for the risk factors and the approach to marking positions to market. With respect to the former, the two basic approaches are historical simulation, which uses the actual historical changes in the risk factors, versus estimation of a parametric distribution such as a normal distribution with an estimated covariance matrix.

There are many positive features about historical simulation. The actual data includes the extreme events to the extent that they have occurred. It does not require any distributional assumptions (other than that the future will be similar to the past). Also, it can be used effectively to focus attention on the types of events, in terms of particular historical scenarios, that may cause large losses.

On the other hand historical simulations have some important limitations; most significantly, there is always a relatively limited sample from which to choose. If the environment has changed, either because of market or political events, then historical data may be less relevant – and it takes a long time to build up a new sample. Because the historical data is limited, it tests only certain scenarios. Relative to particular historical data it may be possible to create a risky portfolio that would not have blown up over the historical sample, but which might in the future.

Parametric approaches have their positive features as well. A covariance matrix may allow a fast, simple analytic measure of VaR. This can be particularly attractive when there is a need for rapid processing of many large portfolios. Even in environments that require Monte-Carlo sampling, such as might be the case with non-linear pricing functions, a covariance matrix can provide a distribution from which thousands, or millions, of scenarios may be drawn. In other words, a parametric approach can provide a richer source of scenarios and therefore more thoroughly search the outcome space.

It is also important to realise that one need not assume normality in using a parametric approach. It is quite easy to create fat-tailed distributions with a given covariance structure. For example, one simple approach is to draw from a mixture of normal distributions. However, there is deeper criticism that parametric approaches do summarise distributions through some set of parameters. In doing so they generally "smooth" the data in some form. While it is possible to devise a parametric solution that will avoid any particular problem, there are many strange features of financial market data, and the extreme scenario that will lead to the most significant future losses is unlikely to be a probable event from the parametric distribution that is used in practice. Given the various positives and negatives associated with these two approaches, one may want to apply both and look deeper, using a bit of judgement when the results differ.

Conclusion

As we have seen, there are multiple approaches to assessing a firm's risk profile, which we view as complementary. We have used VaR generally to refer to any model that combines an ability to mark-to-market with an ability to assign probabilities or confidence levels to the future states of underlying risk factors. This chapter has shown a five step process for VaR, in which we: identify the positions held by the institution; identify the risk factors affecting the valuations of those positions; choose and assign probabilities to scenarios for all risk factors; create pricing functions for all positions as a function of the values of the risk factors; and use the pricing functions to remark the positions in all scenarios, creating the distribution of outcomes where VaR is a particular quantile of the distribution.

As we have suggested, VaR techniques, while essential in the modern art of risk management, have drawbacks as well. The extreme scenarios that result in the most significant future losses, tend not to be represented in your data (eg, the 25 standard deviation 1987 US stock market crash). In Chapter 8 we will discuss scenario analysis – an important risk management technique used in conjunction with stress tests and VaR to understand the effects of the unlikely, yet possible scenarios.

8

Scenario analysis

Introduction

Stress testing and VaR techniques, as discussed in the two preceding chapters, are designed to look at the risk to a firm's trading portfolio from changes in market prices over a short period of time. As we have seen, these are valuable tools for the risk manager and provide important information to traders and management about the risk in the trading portfolio. They cannot, however, account for those events that are potentially most catastrophic to a firm – namely major changes in the external macroeconomic environment that have an effect well beyond their immediate impact on the value of the trading portfolio. This is the stuff of scenario analysis. When used in combination with stress tests and VaR calculations, this methodology serves to round out a firm's risk management practice.

This chapter will alert the "proactive risk manager" to the role of scenario analysis, its subjective nature and its limitations. The first section of this chapter provides a definition of scenario analysis, partly by a comparison and contrast with its look-alike technique, stress testing. This will lead into an explanation of how to prepare a scenario analysis, interpret it and, finally, recognise its shortcomings.

Defining scenario analysis

Scenario analysis is a strategic technique which enables a firm to evaluate the potential impact on its earnings stream of various different eventualities. It uses multi-dimensional projections, and helps the firm to assess its longer term strategic vulnerabilities.

In this context, it is important to distinguish between the respective roles of scenario analysis and stress testing. Both are forward looking techniques which seek to quantify the potential loss which might arise as a consequence of unlikely events. Stress testing is designed to evaluate the short-term impact on a given portfolio of a series of predefined moves, in particular market variables. Scenario analysis on the other hand seeks to assess the broader impact on the firm of more complex and inter-related developments. Huge losses often occur due to a sequence of several adverse events. Scenario analysis can help to identify such potential problems well in advance.

The purpose of scenario analysis is to help the firm's decision makers think about and understand the impact of unlikely, but catastrophic, events before they happen. The Mexican peso devaluation in 1994/1995 and the Thai baht devaluation with the subsequent contagion effects to other emerging markets in 1997 are typical examples of such extreme situations where the assumptions valid in the past break down. A

Exhibit 8.1 Scenario examples

Risk	Example
Political risk	A significant political upheaval occurs in a country where a business has a large investment. The firm needs to act very quickly to evaluate what kind of impact this would have on the investment.
Operational risk	A new settlement system has been implemented at a bank and it cannot be reconciled back to the original system to ensure data integrity. Thus, payments cannot be made and trades cannot be booked.
Legal risk	A large corporation sues an investment firm because they did not disclose all necessary risks associated with a particular transaction in the prospectus.
Credit risk	A business looks at its top 5 credit exposures, all with varied liquidity problems and the market moves 10 per cent against them.
Reputational risk	An employee of a bank embezzles funds for an extended period of time before being caught.

Exhibit 8.2 Scenario analysis vs stress testing

Stress testing	Scenario analysis
Bottom-up approach	Top-down approach
One dimensional	Multi dimensional
P&L impact on a portfolio if one or more of the market variables moved in a specific way	Hypothesis an alternative state of the world and implies the underlying market variables
Tactical	Strategic
Short-horizon	Long-horizon
eg: S&P500 index move by 10 per cent	eg: What would be the impact if there is a "Middle-East Crisis"?

management team that learns its lessons from these situations is more likely to avoid losses in the future. Scenario analysis is an effective tool to assist management in that process. Exhibit 8.1 gives some scenario examples.

Due to its holistic view, scenario analysis is usually initiated by the senior management and is recognised as a very subjective way of assessing risk. Stress testing in contrast is usually done from the bottom-up. (See Exhibit 8.2.)

Scenario preparation and issues

The scenario analysis process

The process of generating a scenario analysis can be decomposed into five steps as shown in Exhibit 8.3.

Exhibit 8.3 The scenario analysis process	
Scenario definition	• Description of the starting scenario • Basic assumptions • Definition of the time horizon
Scenario-field analysis	• Identification of the scenario fields: the risk dimensions and risk factors which are affected and relevant for this scenario analysis
Scenario projections	• Estimate the likely movements of the identified scenario factors and determine the potential loss in that case
Scenario consolidation	• Consolidate the results • Check for consistency errors, double counting, • Independent validation checks
Scenario presentation and follow-up	• Summarise results • Analyse and evaluate • next steps: eg, put on a hedge

Step 1: Scenario definition

The first step in the process is defining a plausible scenario. Although recognising relevant scenarios is more an art than a science, there are two principles of scenario selection: knowing your portfolio and understanding the relevant events in the marketplace. Numerous factors could affect a portfolio -- major events in the markets, political elections, world banking crises, major tax reforms, severe flooding, the US stock market at all time highs, or high unemployment to name a few. For example, if a business was invested heavily in municipal bonds in late 1995, management might have been concerned about the possible impact of the flat tax reforms proposed during the 1996 presidential election campaign. This tax reduction would have reduced the advantage of holding municipal bonds over other taxable investments. Thus, running different tax reform outcomes would have been useful information for large holders of taxable or tax-exempt securities.

Scenarios are typically requested and broadly defined by senior management because they are most familiar with the firm's business and the external factors that affect the firm's earnings. These scenarios ask the question: "What is the impact of ..." and are often accompanied by specific scenario conditions and basic assumptions. Exhibit 8.4 outlines a scenario requested by a CFO concerned about a downturn in both the debt and equity markets and the impact that it might have on current and future earnings.

Sometimes the risk group itself initiates and develops scenarios in order to identify potential weaknesses in their risk management concept and to make sure that the firm is capable to survive even unlikely but catastrophic complex events. For this purpose one might:

• Take historic scenarios like the 1987 crash, the 1993 Tequila crisis, the Kobe earthquake;
• Or develop new scenarios, eg,
  – single events triggering unfavourable changes eg, a war, a natural disaster, an unexpected economic event;

> ### Exhibit 8.4 An example scenario requested by a CFO
>
> *The CFO would like to know what the impact would be on the firm's earnings over the year if:*
>
> - US interest rates were to rise 125 basis points in the long end;
> - US interest rates were to rise 100 basis points in the short end; and
> - the US equity market declined 25 per cent.
>
> **Key assumptions:**
>
> - international bond markets decline on average a similar amount;
> - international equities decline a similar amount;
> - no precipitous event causes this scenario – the market moves occur more or less smoothly over the year; and
> - credit spreads, business conditions, inflation, exchange rates or other economic variables develop in a manner consistent with the above.

- long-term market scenarios eg, recession in a group of determined countries, failure of EMU; and
- ask managers for the worst thing they could imagine regarding their business and extend this scenario to the whole firm.

It is advisable to specify enough detail and key assumptions in order to ensure that the all of your experts interpret the scenario in the same way. For example, it is very important to specify the time horizon of the scenario. If the objective is to find out how much the firm would lose if it had to liquidate its inventory in an emergency, then the time frame might be five days. A time horizon for a scenario of a portfolio's worst mark-to-market would be one day. A longer time horizon of three months might be appropriate for the scenario of holding a large inventory position during a steady market decline.

Step 2: Scenario-field analysis
Having defined the scenario that we wish to analyse, the next step in the preparation phase is an extensive interview process. This process incorporates the appropriate business areas and other experts within the organisation in order to further refine the scenario compiling the relevant data needed. This step is very closely linked to the next steps, which are usually integrated in this interview process as well.

The interview process should be standardised to ensure consistent feedback. To give a clearer picture of the interview process consider the sample scenario in Exhibit 8.4. One approach, would be to give all of the interviewees a written description of this scenario, along with a list of questions, and ask them to respond by a specific date.

The purpose of the scenario-field analysis is to identify all relevant risk dimensions and risk factors, also called "scenario fields" which are affected by the scenario. For example strong movements in the stock market might trigger defaults of some firms causing substantial credit losses and vice versa, interest rate or stock market movements which themselves might not be severe might trigger movements in other markets with severe consequences. Also second order and third order effects have to be taken into account, eg, effects on future earnings, upon staffing, etc.

It can be seen that establishing meaningful scenario analysis is a complex process which requires the expertise of many people with diverse backgrounds in various departments. In a financial services firm, these may include: market research analysts, traders/salespeople, technologists, accountants, lawyers and senior management.

Although it is always possible that business people may participate in developing scenarios in order to design an analysis that gives an attractive appearance to their own business, this risk can be largely diffused by ensuring that a broad enough range of people are involved in the process. Moreover, by entrusting the risk management department to conduct scenario analysis at the firmwide level, an appropriate degree of independence from the business areas can be built into the process.

Often scenarios have major themes in common with historical events. For example, one could argue that the 1997 Thai baht crisis looked like the 1994 Mexican peso devaluation. Many similarities exist such as over-borrowing abroad, limited guidance from banks, and both countries' reluctance to acknowledge that they needed aid from the IMF. But there were also important differences. The Mexican problems were isolated in one country, while the Thai problem spilled over into a whole region. Nonetheless such historic events might give important insights into identifying scenario factors.

Step 3: Scenario projections
This is the heart of the scenario analysis. For each scenario field identified a prognostic of the potential development within the given time horizon and of the associated potential losses have to be determined. Again this step should be carried out by or in close contact with the appropriate business areas and experts. In this context it should be mentioned that it is not the goal to find the most likely development but to identify adverse or extreme scenarios. Therefore this process will sometimes result in more than one estimate of the potential returns. Furthermore it should be emphasised that the process is not an exact science, but rather requires best estimates.

During the information gathering process the scenario will itself become more clearly defined as feedback is received. For example, you may find out from a fixed income specialist that interest rates in a specific country would be affected as well, which would then be incorporated into the analysis. The scenario analysis process, therefore, has to be flexible enough to incorporate refinements and updates to the initial scenario as the analyses and interviews proceed. It must be an iterative process.

Step 4: Scenario consolidation
Here the projections developed for each scenario field are consolidated into one consistent scenario. However, the scenario has not only to be checked for consistency errors but also for double counting or contradictory assumptions. Results must also be checked for reasonableness: start by looking for any outliers and make sure the feedback is consistent. If there are one or two outliers, go back to the person questioned to make sure they understood what you were asking them. Inconsistent information is frequently caused by misunderstood questions. In order to prevent receiving such information, it is a good idea to conduct some background research prior to the review (see Exhibit 8.5). When checking market move projections over a certain time period, it may be useful to ask them what a typical move in their market would be in order to find out if the scenario results makes sense.

If you have received inconsistent information, it may be time to redefine the scenario. Whenever possible, leverage off historical data to compare the results from the interview process.

Analyse the profit and loss history for the various business units for clues that your results make sense. Examine the market value of the portfolio for any significant

---

Exhibit 8.5 Key information for interview process

- Know the current and prior years actual earnings, this is a good barometer for the estimates you will be given
- Understand the current market conditions in order to compare to the projected conditions
- Obtain future revenue projections from the budgeting department, this is a good independent check against the results
- Ask for a baseline revenue projection, this will give you an indication as to whether or not the impact to earnings due to the "scenario" market conditions is a fraction or all of earnings

---

changes. Take a look at the volatility of the P&L to see whether it is in line with what you would have expected, given the results. It may be helpful to consider questions such as:

- were the right people interviewed?
- did they have the appropriate level of experience?
- and how long have they been in the current position?

Independent checks on the results may give an indication that the questions were not clear or that the wrong questions may have been asked. Here you may need to redefine the scenario in order to obtain more meaningful results. Sometimes it may also be appropriate to ask more than one person to review the results in order to check them for reasonableness.

Step 5: Scenario presentation and follow-up
The final analysis and presentation of the results is a critical step in the process. Evaluating the results and drawing conclusions can be quite challenging, as it is a highly subjective process and therefore requires an interpreter with both experience and judgement.

Scenario results are frequently surprising and sometimes doubted. Often people are shocked at the magnitude of potential loss. While the probability of a scenario event is typically very low, the results should not be discounted. Since the analysis is subjective, it is easy to poke holes at any to the assumptions being made. Given the circumstances surrounding most scenario discussions, the dialogue is iterative. Therefore, when presenting the results it is very important to state clearly what the assumptions and objectives of the exercise were before the results of the analysis in order for the reader to correctly interpret the results and understand their value.

The primary goal of a scenario analysis is to get the audience to recognise that damaging losses can happen. But more importantly, to allow management to take appropriate action to prepare for the unlikely outlier events. The presentation should be a learning experience for everyone involved. As a result of the successful presentation some plan of action must be developed. Follow-up can be as simple as:

- put on a hedge;
- put on a specific trade;
- unwind a position modify the analysis;
- develop a repeatable process;
- do nothing.

Traps to avoid

There are several traps to avoid when developing scenarios:

- *Overkill:* In developing robust scenarios it is important to avoid including too many variables, which unnecessarily complicate the scenarios. Only take into account the really relevant risk factors.
- *Over-evaluating the results:* Interpreting and evaluating the results is definitely an important step. However, the results of scenarios should not be evaluated too extensively as each scenario is only one of many possible outcomes. The additional benefit after a certain point may not be worth the effort.
- *Inconsistent assumptions:* A very common cause of inconsistent information is confusion about the time horizon. The time horizon in regards to volatility can be misinterpreted. While volatility is usually quoted on an annualised basis, some think of it in terms of one week. For example, in the scenario in Exhibit 8.4, business unit heads were interviewed about the impact the scenario might have, the analysis time horizon was 12 months. It is difficult to know if they made the correct translation as they scaled the number. It is easy to pick out the large outliers but it is not so obvious when the differences are closer in range.

Repeating scenarios

Frequently senior management will request the same scenario be repeated on a regular basis, either weekly, monthly or quarterly. These scenarios represent the greatest challenge to the preparer because it is easier for a interviewee with very tight time constraints to give the same or similar answer as the prior analysis. Regular scenarios run the risk of becoming meaningless very quickly because the interview candidate is not challenged with a new scenario, they just need to give an update. Therefore, scenarios that need to be updated on a regular basis should be structured in a way that provides some type of independence. Exhibit 8.6 is an example of a simple scenario that can be updated on a regular basis and remain meaningful. The reason is because the updates on the inventory values can be obtained from the accounting department (an independent source) and the market value impact can be re-computed. The volatilities of the specific bonds must be updated over time, but this is a specific question that is readily answered.

Other uses for scenarios

Budgeting tool

Scenarios are useful during the budget planning process because they can give insight

---

Exhibit 8.6 Example of a simple scenario

Corporation Z

Scenario analysis: What is the impact of a general deterioration of credit quality on the inventory values, assuming a widening of credit spreads by one standard deviation over a one-month time horizon?

Product	1 StDev.	Inventory value
Utility bonds	5bp	US$375 million
Yankee bonds	8bp	US$550 million
Finance bonds	4bp	US$985 million

into what could happen in an economic downturn. It is quite useful to compare a baseline budget to a budget that takes into account an extreme change in the market environment. If the scenario is defined clearly, decision makers can get a better handle on the budgeting process and will be prepared for unexpected events in the year ahead. For example if a company's revenues are generated primarily from equities it would be very useful to know how a 15 per cent decline in the equities market would affect business.

Regulatory reviews

As regulators increasingly come to rely on the output of firms' internal models and risk management processes in place of traditional, prescriptive regulatory capital requirements, it is likely that they will also be interested in reviewing the output of firms' scenario analyses to supplement VaR and stress test information. Regulators are particularly concerned about the risks arising in extreme systemic crises, which may not be highlighted by a risk model, and it is precisely these events which scenario analysis is designed to examine.

Conclusion

Stress testing and VaR techniques may not account for those events that are potentially the most catastrophic to a firm (see Chapters 6 and 7). Scenario analysis is an essential complement to the risk management tool-kit, which helps management understand the effects of major changes in the external environment that often have repercussions well beyond their immediate impact on the value of the trading portfolio.

As we have seen, the process involves defining a scenario, including all assumptions and our time horizon. The second step is the identification of scenario fields, eg, risk factors. Scenarios are then projected based on the likely movements of identified variables under the given scenario. The results are consolidated, validated, presented, and analysed. Most important is the follow-up, the action taken or not taken by the firm.

Scenario analysis hinges on effective pre-analysis, interviews, and necessarily the ability to envision a wide range of possibilities. Because firms must leverage off inputs from various departments throughout the organisation, the scenario analysis has a final feature that is of critical importance: It focuses management from different areas on the idea that, while unlikely, events such as the 1997 Asia crisis can happen at any time. The effects of such catastrophes, however, can be largely mitigated through anticipation and effective planning.

9

Specific risk

Why specific risk matters

Until comparatively recently, the term "specific risk" had not assumed any particular significance in the development of market risk modelling. A review of the financial literature shows little written on the topic of specific risk measurement. To the extent that firms' market risk models sought to capture the effects of exposure to factors that were specific to an individual issuer, this was seen as a logical extension of the techniques which were used to model the firm's exposure to changes in general market parameters such as equity indices and interest rates. Moreover, because price risks which are specific to an individual issuer are by definition independent between different issuers, issuer specific risk of this type posed no particular theoretical or technical problem. Consequently there was little attention paid to this dimension of risk modelling in the academic literature either.

More recently, though, a number of developments have led to an increased focus on the topic of issuer specific risk, which justifies considering it as a separate risk measurement challenge. In the first instance, the stimulus for firms to develop specific risk models has come from the banking regulators, who have made a distinction in the use of VaR models for regulatory purposes between models that measure a firm's exposure to what are termed "broad market risk factors" and models that measure a firm's exposure to the "specific risk associated with individual securities positions".

The benefit to firms of being able to develop and have such models approved is considerable. Prior to the approval of specific risk models, for a bank, or for a securities firm operating in the European Union, issuer specific risk was captured under the regulatory guidelines for credit risk capital adequacy. These rules dictate an 8 per cent capital charge against the risk weighted value of a security (referred to as the standardised approach). Given that corporate securities have a risk weight of 100 per cent, these positions therefore attract a minimum 8 per cent capital charge. As is evident from these percentages, the current capital requirement is excessively large for high grade issuers whose annual probabilities of default are well under 1 per cent. This highlights one of the great weaknesses of this approach – it does not differentiate between issuer qualities in a portfolio. The same sized positions in a "AAA" issuer and in a "B" issuer attract the same capital charge, which is clearly at odds with the true exposure.

This methodology also fails to reward a portfolio for diversification which is one of the few ways an institution can protect itself from large credit losses. Currently, a US$100 million securities portfolio will have the same capital charge whether it is at risk to one issuer or one hundred. The introduction of a VaR-based approach to calculating the capital adequacy requirements for market risk will go a long way toward rectifying these problems by allowing the issuer specific risk of these portfolios to be captured by models rather than the crude standardised approach. The end result will be lower capital charges for high grade, diversified portfolios and higher charges for low quality, concentrated portfolios This is an extremely encouraging development, but it only has benefits if robust models are in place to quantify the risk.

While regulatory developments have, without question, been the primary driving force behind the recent evolution of specific risk models, a secondary, but still important, influence relates to the growing industry emphasis on developing credit as a tradeable product. This move toward commoditising credit, via the credit derivatives market, is rapidly moving us into a world where issuer specific risk cannot be assumed to be diversified away. In fact, it is likely that we will increasingly see the reverse situation developing, where exposures to general market risk parameters such as interest rates and equity market indices is a secondary risk factor and some combination of credit spread and specific risk assumes the dominant risk position in a firm's trading risk.

Adding further momentum to this paradigm shift is the upcoming move to a single currency in Europe. This development will crystallise credit differentials across countries and lead the industry to focus on relative value trading in credits, not currencies, as it searches out new ways to generate profits. Trying to isolate and capture this "credit edge", whether through spread trading or laying off the EMU interest rate risk through swaps, will serve to concentrate portfolio risks in the issuer specific dimension.

Issuer specific risk is thus very much the bridge between the two traditionally distinct disciplines of credit and market risk management. In its most complete sense, we can define specific risk as incorporating all the variance in a portfolio that is attributable to issuer related events. This includes gradual changes in the market's perception of a firm's economic prospects or credit worthiness, along with the catastrophic event of default. The measurement of the former for equities, and to a slightly lesser extent corporate bonds, is well understood – even if it has often been ignored in practice because diversification effects are assumed to diminish its importance. This is contrasted with the most extreme source of specific risk – default – which is rarely included in portfolio-wide risk measures. One reason for leaving default risk out of these measures is the belief that, in a trading environment, default risk is not a material issue. If a security trades in a continuous market, then it can be assumed that its value will decline in line with any deterioration in the perceived quality of the issuer, so that as default becomes more likely, the value of the security will tend to approximate the expected recovery rate. In addition, until recently the methodologies for measuring and aggregating default risk have not been particularly well developed or well understood. Default risk has also been considered as falling within the domain of credit risk, not market risk, so its treatment has gone neglected during the development of advanced market risk measurement techniques.

So why not retain this historical separation between market risk and credit risk measurement? It would certainly make life easier for the market risk manager, but it ignores the fact that losses due to default are also part of a trading portfolio's overall risk profile. This is particularly the case for a firm holding less liquid types of instruments, such as emerging market securities or OTC derivatives where the assumptions of continuous liquid markets no longer apply. In these circumstances, if risk is defined as the uncertainty in value of an asset or collection of assets, then all risk dimensions that influence this value should be included and accounted for in a consistent fashion. Risk, unavoidably, comes in many shapes and sizes. This should not deter us from trying to fit these diverse pieces into a seamless mosaic, it simply makes it harder.

The remainder of this chapter therefore seeks to establish a framework for the measurement of issuer specific risk in securities portfolios and identifies the key implementation issues. A technical appendix is included at the end of the chapter for those interested in the quantitative details of these models.

A simple model of specific risk

In considering how we might approach the task of modelling specific risk, we can start by describing the total risk of a security in terms of two components: general risk and specific risk. General risk is the variability in a security resulting from exposure to "common" risk factors such as equity index levels, exchange rates, interest rates, etc. These generic risk dimensions are not dependent on the issuer of a security. Specific risk, on the other hand, is the variability in a security driven exclusively by events tied to the issuer. This leads to the simple equation:

TOTAL RISK = GENERAL RISK + SPECIFIC RISK

The identification, measurement, cumulation, and aggregation of general risk has been discussed in Chapters 5 and 7, so we can focus here exclusively on the specific risk element. In general, specific risk is derived from two sources: normal, day-to-day events which affect daily market prices and can be modelled using traditional statistical methods, and the more rare changes in values related to default which require non-standard techniques. These sources of variation are referred to as residual risk and default risk, respectively. With these distinctions in mind the definition of specific risk expands to:

SPECIFIC RISK = RESIDUAL RISK + DEFAULT RISK

Residual risk – Residual risk captures the "well-behaved" issuer specific variability in the prices or yields of securities. This component of risk reflects the day-to-day changes in the market's perception of credit worthiness of an issuer, changes in earnings expectations, etc, but is not intended to capture the most extreme of these events – default. Filtering out the rare, but extremely large jump events, allows residual risk to be modelled using standard statistical techniques based on the normal distribution.

Default risk – Default risk captures portfolio variability due to sudden and extreme price jumps because of significant credit events. These discrete events cannot be modelled directly using "normal distribution" theory, but it is possible to develop reasonable approximations using other statistical distributions.

The residual risk term in this equation is frequently viewed as synonymous with specific risk, and its quantification is driven by the model of general market risk for the relevant product category (equity or fixed income) since changes in value not attributed to general risk are by definition the residuals. (The technical appendix goes into more detail on the calculation of this term). More generally, the term "residual risk" could also be thought of as a bucket that catches everything left over once

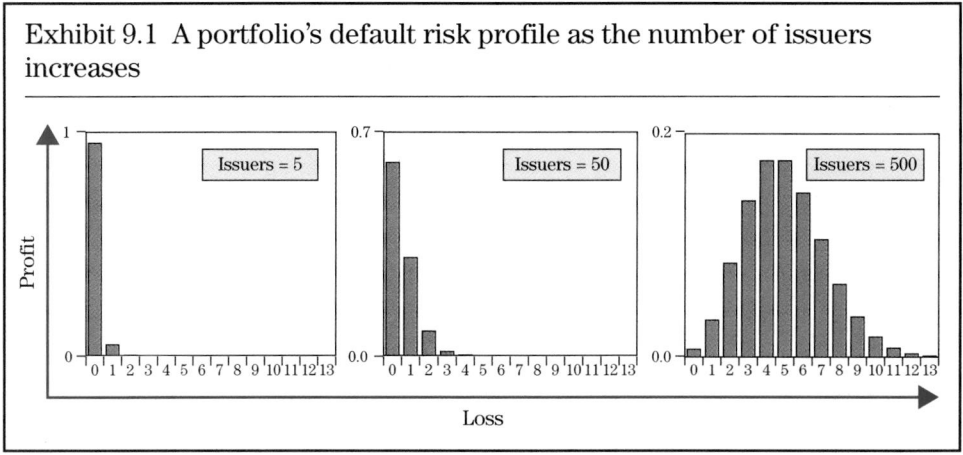

Exhibit 9.1 A portfolio's default risk profile as the number of issuers increases

general market risk is accounted for, so in theory, this term could also catch default risk. In practice though, the default risk component of issuer specific risk has in the past generally gone neglected for the reasons discussed earlier, so we have chosen to identify it as a separate term here, and we now turn our attention to the particular issues associated with its measurement.

Modelling default risk

The application of portfolio-based measurement techniques to default risk in a portfolio context, is a comparatively new area of research. The most notable indication of this is J.P. Morgan's CreditMetrics™ initiative launched in mid-1997. Given the infancy of this field there is not yet a market standard model, so various approaches are being tried. CreditMetric's™ approach uses a simulation approach that captures both residual and default risk in one distribution. Alternatively, we could opt to clearly distinguish between these two terms by modelling each separately using analytical methods. We avoid a debate here on the merits of these two approaches, but it is fair to say that either can deliver the intended results if utilised properly. The detailed formulation of our model is included in the technical annex. Here, we will only highlight the unique distributional characteristics of default losses which lead to the modelling difficulties.

Exhibit 9.1 displays the evolution of a portfolio's default risk profile as the number of issuers increases from 5 to 500. These histograms are based on a probability of default for an issuer of 1 per cent and a loss given default for an issuer of "one unit of value". These plots highlight two important characteristics of default losses. First, the loss distribution is extremely peaked and one-sided when the portfolio is concentrated in a small number of issuers (N=5 and N=50). Second, as portfolio diversification increases (N=500) the distribution becomes more symmetrical while still retaining skew to the downside.

The dynamic and asymmetrical characteristics of the loss distribution force the use of a non-normal statistical distribution to capture these features (refer to annex). It should also be noted this distribution is dependent on the probability of default and the expected loss in default of the issuers and issues in the portfolio, respectively. The determination of these parameters presents an additional challenge. Rather than attempting to estimate these parameters ourselves, we can choose to use historical default and recovery rates published by agencies such as Moodys or S&P.

Time horizon and confidence level

In order to quantify risk, there needs to be a scenario defined which specifies the time horizon and confidence level over which it is measured. From a regulatory perspective these standards have been set for market risk at two weeks and 99 per cent confidence, though many firms use shorter time periods for internal purposes. This regulatory benchmark is used for residual risk. Including default risk under this standard, however, presents a problem. Risk should be measured over a horizon which reasonably maps to its frequency of occurrence. Short time periods for market risk are reasonable because this risk is being realised and observed in near continuous time as prices evolve. The default event, however, occurs far too infrequently to measure over a short time horizon. Another scenario is required. What is the correct time horizon and confidence level? There is no single right answer to this question, so we need to opt for one that balances prudence with reason. Given the fact that annualised defaults for non-investment grade issuers occur with enough frequency to have default rates in the range of 1 per cent to 10 per cent, most models seem to adopt one year as a baseline time horizon (prudence). However since this time period is long we can also lower the confidence level to 95 per cent or 97.5 per cent whilst still retaining a suitably conservative risk measure (reason). This still results in a suitably conservative risk assessment, since we would expect annual losses to exceed this value only once every 20 years. This is compared with once every 3.8 years for market risk (once out of every hundred, two-week periods). The potentially large magnitude of the event risk and the inability to incrementally hedge this exposure on the way down, as well as the relative newness of default modelling techniques is however an appropriate justification for the additional conservatism in this scenario. This is just one example of the many reasonable possibilities for a risk scenario. Ultimately, this decision must be guided by a thorough understanding of how the end result is used. This same reasoning applies to the aggregation of residual risk and default risk.

The final step: putting it all together

Once both components of specific risk are estimated there remains the important question of what we want to use these different measures for, and in what circumstances it might be appropriate to try to add these different risk measures together. This issue needs to be handled with care. The underlying scenarios for residual and default risk are different, as are their associated loss distributions. This makes any form of direct aggregation problematic and an area for future research. Nevertheless, practical interim solutions can be adopted, provided they are well understood, and are appropriate for the purpose for which they are being used.

For example, for internal performance measurement purposes we might wish to use the default risk value as the floor to the specific risk component of a VaR calculation for a trading business. This would help to ensure that the internal risk capital consumed by the business is large enough to sustain its "default loss" potential. This same approach could also be adopted for determining regulatory capital requirements for specific risk.

On the other hand, if the usage of a specific risk model is related to backtesting daily VaR measures against daily P&L outturns, then clearly only the residual risk component should be incorporated in the daily VaR calculation. This is because default losses do not normally appear in daily P&L figures so the inclusion of a default risk amount would unnaturally inflate the VaR measure relative to the P&L outcome, so distorting the assessment, the accuracy and the VaR estimate. Obviously, good judgement and a clear understanding of the different purposes for which risk measures are being used as well as the appropriate aggregation methods, is needed to guide these decisions.

Conclusion

As we have seen in this chapter, the techniques for analysing and measuring specific risk, particularly default risk, are young in comparison with the techniques used for general market risk. Nevertheless, as firms increasingly seek opportunities to trade and hedge credit risk, and as the market for credit derivatives develops, specific risk will become a more dominant dimension in the risk profile of a firm's trading portfolio.

However, while we have provided some indications of the use that can be made of developments in the application of portfolio techniques in default risk to modelling specific risk in a trading business, it is important to recognise that these techniques are themselves developing at pace that is beyond the scope of this book to discuss in any detail. Indeed, they almost certainly justify a book of their own. Consequently, it is safe to predict that, as further advances occur, specific risk models will increasingly come to enjoy the same broad level of acceptance as their general market risk counterparts, and the barrier between what is market risk and what is credit risk will become ever more blurred.

This discussion of specific risk concludes our review of the techniques which are available to risk managers to measure the risks in a trading portfolio. In the next section we move from theory to practice and consider some of the organisational and management issues which arise when using these measures as an integral part of a day-to-day risk management process.

Technical appendix

Measuring residual risk

In order to quantify the residual risk term in the specific risk equation we start with the model of "market structure" used for the particular product category. This model describes changes in value (or equivalently yield) of an individual security in terms of its general and specific risk components. This model is then generalised to a portfolio of securities to arrive at a portfolio level measure of residual risk.

Equities

In equities, the most commonly used model of "market structure" is based on a single risk factor, appropriately named the "market", and an issuer-specific term.

$$R_i = \beta_i \cdot R_M + \varepsilon_i \tag{1}$$

where Ri = return on stock i, RM = return on the market index, βi = beta of stock i on the market index and εi= issuer-specific return on stock i.

This model describes the percentage return on an individual stock as the beta-weighted return on the "market" index, $\beta_i \cdot R_M$, plus an issuer specific return, εi. A broad-based equity index is typically chosen as the proxy for the "market" risk factor.

Generalising this model to a portfolio of securities, and considering the actual change in prices rather than returns, results in the following description of P&L for an equity portfolio:

$$\Delta P \cong \sum_{i=1}^{N} d_i \cdot S_i \cdot \beta_i \cdot R_M + \sum_{i=1}^{N} d_i \cdot S_i \cdot \varepsilon_i \tag{2}$$

where $\Delta P \cong$ total change in portfolio value, di= expected change in portfolio value given a one-unit change in value of stock i (ie, delta), Si = price of stock i and N = number of issuers in the portfolio.

The first term captures the change in value due to the "market" risk factor and the second term due to the specific risk of the N issuers in the portfolio. Because we are only considering residual risk at this time, it is treated as synonymous with the specific risk term. The risk of this portfolio is calculated by taking the variance of Equation (2) which results in:

$$\sigma_{\Delta P}^2 = \text{general risk} + \sum_{i=1}^{N} (d_i^2 \cdot S_i^2 \cdot \sigma_{\varepsilon_i}^2) \tag{3}$$

where $\sigma_{\Delta P}^2$ = total variance of the portfolio and $\sigma_{\varepsilon_i}^2$ = residual variance of issuer i.

The key parameter in this calculation is residual volatility, σ_{ε_i}, because delta, di, and stock price, Si, are available from any trading system. The best source for residual volatilities is the regressions used to estimate the betas needed for the general risk portion of the calculation. This assures consistency between all estimated parameters used for determining portfolio risk.[1]

This approach does have one shortcoming – it is inability to account for curvature (gamma and higher order derivatives) in an options portfolio. This is evidenced in the risk calculation by the presence of only delta terms in the equation. The methods available for addressing this deficiency are the same as those utilised for general market risk measurement, but an explanation of these techniques goes beyond the scope of this book.

Exhibit 9.2 Yield curve decomposition

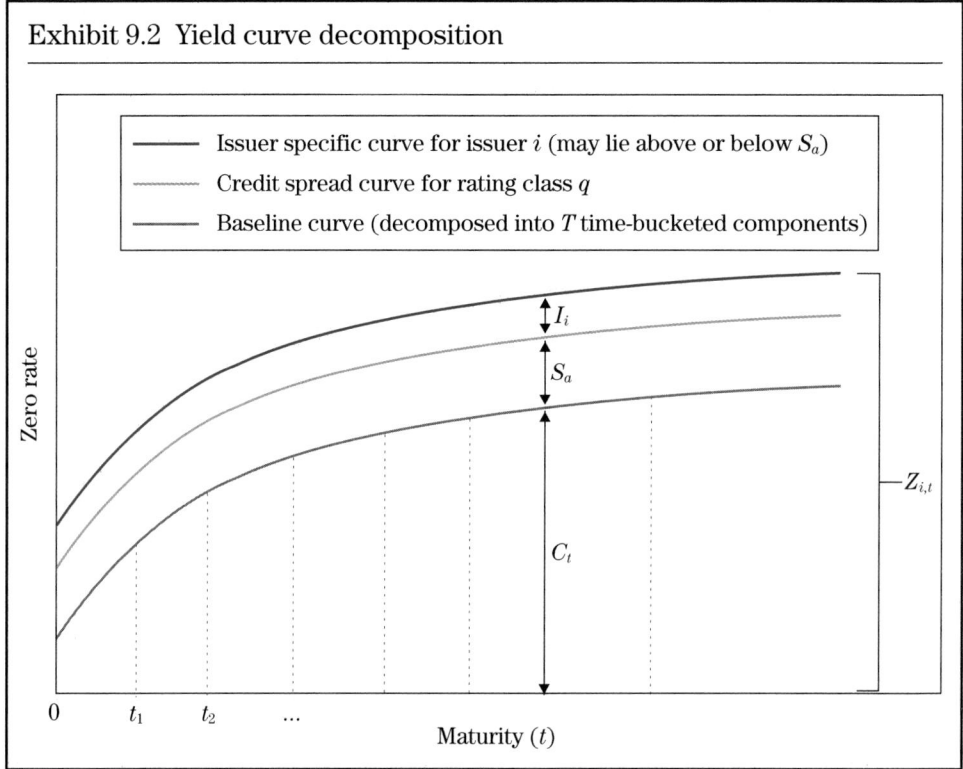

Fixed income

For fixed income securities, the overall risk decomposition is slightly more complicated. We start with a model of yields on a bond issue that expresses the change in its zero rate at any maturity point as the sum of the changes in three distinct yield components: the baseline curve (C), the credit spread (S) and the issuer (I) specific spread (see Exhibit 9.2).

$$\Delta Z_{i,t} = \Delta C_t + \Delta S_q + \Delta I_i \qquad (4)$$

where $Z_{i,t}$ = zero rate for issuer i at maturity t, C_t = government zero curve rate for maturity t, S_q = credit spread required for an issuer of quality q, and I_i = issuer specific spread required for issuer i.

The baseline curve captures the general level and shape of the yield curve for a currency. In this example it has been defined as the government yield curve, but a Libor curve works as well. Credit spreads are defined by rating class and measured relative to the chosen baseline curve (eg, spread to Treasuries or spread to Libor). And lastly, the issuer-specific spreads are relative to the generic credit curve applicable to the issuer's rating class (q). In addition, we make two simple assumptions to complete the model:

1. The credit spread and issuer-specific yields do not have a time structure. In other words, their changes are included in the model as a parallel shift to the baseline curve. In reality there is some structure here, but building in the additional complexity would not materially influence the results of this analysis.
2. The changes in curve, credit spread and issuer-specific yields are independent.

Again, this is only an approximation. In practice, you would expect to see some correlation between these yield components but including these interaction terms would add needless complexity to what is intended to be a simple model.

Applying this yield generating process to a portfolio of securities results in the following description of P&L for a bond portfolio:

$$\Delta P \cong \sum_{t=1}^{T} d_t \cdot \Delta C_t + \sum_{q=1}^{Q} s_q \cdot \Delta S_q + \sum_{i=1}^{N} c_i \cdot \Delta I_i \qquad (5)$$

where, $\Delta P \cong$ total change in portfolio value, dt = expected change in portfolio value given a one basis point (1 bp) change in the zero rate at maturity t, T = number of time buckets used to describe the baseline curve, sq = expected change in portfolio value given a 1 bp change in the credit spread for rating class q, Q = number of rating classes, ci = expected change in portfolio value given a 1 bp change in the issuer-specific spread for issuer i and N = number of issuers.

The first two terms capture general market risk and the last term specific risk. The key characteristic of this equation is that it identifies three different measures of interest rate sensitivity that we will refer to as yield delta (expressed through dt), spread delta (sq), and credit delta (ci). It is important to differentiate between these measures to ensure the correct sensitivity is used in the residual risk calculation. For fixed rate bonds these measures are equivalent, but for floating rate instruments they can diverge depending on the floating rate index of the security.

For example, take a floating rate bond that yields a fixed spread to Libor. Also assume our baseline curve is defined as Libor. This bond's yield delta is based only on the cash flow occurring on the next reset date, while the spread and credit deltas are based on the cash flows all the way out to maturity. The rationale is as follows: for the yield delta, a shift in the baseline Libor curve alters the size of all floating rate cash flows, as well as the associated discount factors for those flows. These two effects cancel each other out precisely. The only risk that remains is to the one fixed cash flow set to occur at the next reset. Now let us assume Libor does not change but that the credit or issuer-specific spread does. The size of all future cash flows remains the same (they are indexed to Libor), but the required discount rate for those cash flows does change because they are based on the full-in yield (Libor + credit spread + issuer-specific spread). This results in an interest rate sensitivity to cash flows all the way out to maturity and demonstrates why multiple sensitivity measures are sometimes needed.

Now moving back to Equation (5), taking the variance of ΔP leads to the following description of risk in a bond portfolio:

$$\sigma_{\Delta P}^2 = \text{general risk} + \sum_{i=1}^{N} (c_i^2 \cdot \sigma_{I_i}^2) \qquad (6)$$

Though the residual risk term in this equation is computational simple, there are potentially two practical obstacles to its calculation. The first is that trading systems do not commonly provide a credit delta measure for floating rate instruments, which can mean systems development work for an organisation. The second is that residual yield volatilities, by issuer, are not readily available or easy to calculate.

Conceptually, the method for calculating residual yield volatility is straightforward. A complete history of an issuer's bond yields along with an historical time series of generic yields for each rating category are needed. The generic yield

109

Exhibit 9.3 Example exposure sizes and default possibilities

Issuer	Exposure size	Default probability
A	200	0.02
B	100	0.05
C	50	0.10

Exhibit 9.4 Example results

Default event	Probability	Loss
None	0.838	0
A	0.017	200
B	0.044	100
C	0.093	50
A and B	0.001	300
A and C	0.002	250
B and C	0.005	150
A, B, and C	0.000	350

associated with the credit quality of the issuer is subtracted from a bond's actual yield to produce a time series of issuer-specific spreads. The volatility is then calculated from this series. The lack of good, clean, high-quality data, however, makes an issuer-by-issuer calculation impractical to implement.

The next best option is to select a representative group of issuers within each rating class, perform the calculations and define a residual volatility for each credit quality based on these values. This reduces the estimation burden significantly by assuming all issuers of similar quality share the same level of residual risk. Data is still an issue, but the magnitude of the problem is significantly reduced.

Measuring default risk

We begin this section with a very simple model of default risk and show how the distribution of losses is generated using this function. We then incrementally add complexity to the model until a version is derived that is both practical to implement and descriptive of the true loss distribution.

The loss function

In the simplest of terms, a portfolio's loss due to default is describable by the following equation:

$$L = \sum_{i=1}^{N} x_i \cdot \tilde{B}_i(p_i) \tag{7}$$

where, L = portfolio loss due to default, xi = the loss, given default, on issuer i's obligations, Bi = Bernoulli random variable with parameter pi, pi = probability of default for issuer i and N = number of issuers.

B is defined as a Bernoulli random variable with parameter p, where p is the probability of default for an issuer. This variable can take on only two values: 1 with a probability of p and 0 with a probability of $(1–p)$. Therefore, when a default occurs the Bernoulli variable takes on the value of 1 and the portfolio loses x. When no default occurs the variable takes on the value of zero and no contribution is made to the loss total.

There are two key assumptions underlying this equation:

1. The loss resulting from an issuer default is a known amount. In practice, the recovery rate on a security is not known, making losses a random variable. This is an initial simplification that is relaxed later in this section.
2. The probability of an issuer default is known. This is also a random variable, but it is treated as a deterministic parameter throughout this section. More complicated models can be built to accommodate this uncertainty, but they are outside the scope of this book.

A simple example

Using this function, we begin by creating the distribution of losses for a simple portfolio comprising exposures to only three issuers – A, B, and C. The exposure sizes and probabilities of default are shown in Exhibit 9.3. Assume the exposures result from positions in their tradable debt and reflect the market value of those securities.

Because default is a binary event for each issuer (it either happens or it does not), there are a finite combination of events that can occur among these issuers. Assuming a zero recovery rate on each issuer's securities, and a zero correlation between their defaults, the loss resulting from each of these events and the associated probability is easily calculated. The results are shown in Exhibit 9.4.

This technique is effective in building the complete loss distribution of a portfolio, but it becomes computationally unwieldy as the number of issuers increases. The number of distinct combinations of events that are possible from N issuers is 2 raised to the N power. This means that for a portfolio of only 20 issuers there are 1,048,576 portfolio events to consider if this approach is utilised. Rather than focus on ways to efficiently extend this methodology to work on large portfolios we will use the results of portfolio simulations like this to establish an understanding of the distributional characteristics of default risk. This insight will guide the subsequent development of an analytical solution to the problem.

The distributional characteristics of default risk

Case I

Let us first examine the evolution of the default distribution as the number of issuers in the portfolio increases from 5, to 50, to 500 (see Exhibit 9.5). The loss in default and probability of default constants are kept constant and set to 1 unit (units are defined as a normalised measure of value) and 1 per cent, respectively.

This clearly shows the distribution begins as very peaked and one-sided. As the number of issuers increases, however, the shape evolves into a more symmetric distribution, while still retaining some skew to the downside.

Case II

We now examine what effect the probability of default has on the loss distributions, and what characteristics a portfolio takes when its issuers have different default rates (see Exhibit 9.6). This example uses two portfolios of 50 issuers each. The loss given default is still held as constant (1 unit), but the default probabilities are set at 0.5 per cent and 10 per cent.

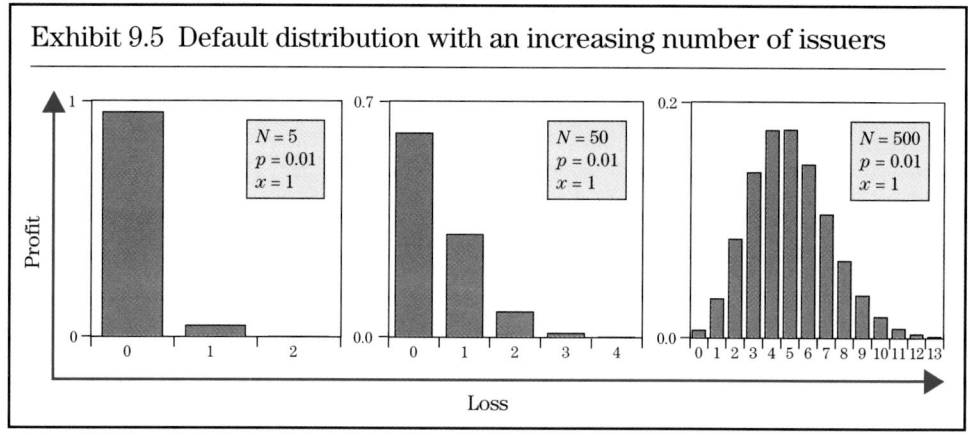

Exhibit 9.5 Default distribution with an increasing number of issuers

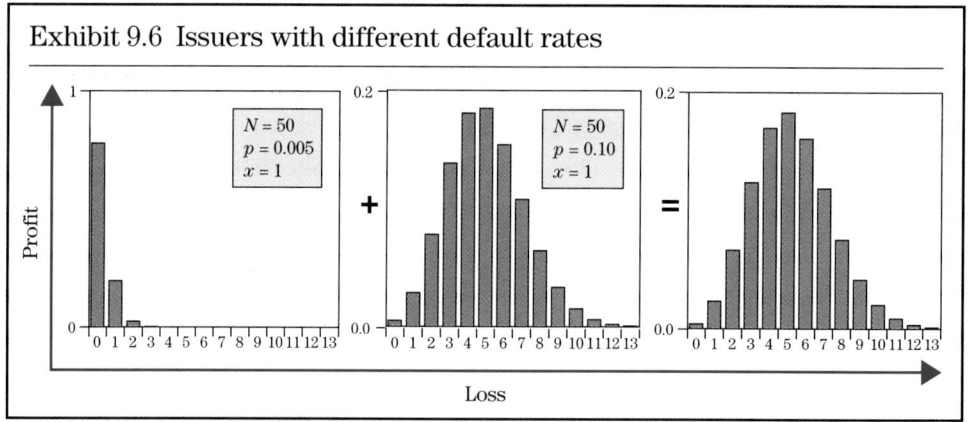

Exhibit 9.6 Issuers with different default rates

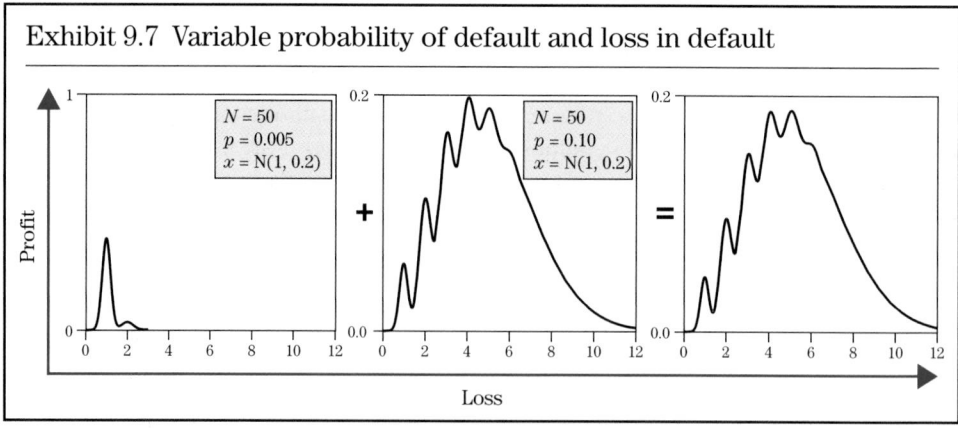

Exhibit 9.7 Variable probability of default and loss in default

This simulation shows a low default rate portfolio is slower to lose its asymmetric shape than a high default rate portfolio. Also, when combined together into one portfolio, the hybrid distribution inherits the characteristics of the lower credit quality issuers.

Case III

Lastly, we allow both the probability of default and loss in default to vary. The two portfolios examined in Case II are used, but this time the issuer loss is assumed to be normally distributed with a mean of 1 (see Exhibit 9.7).

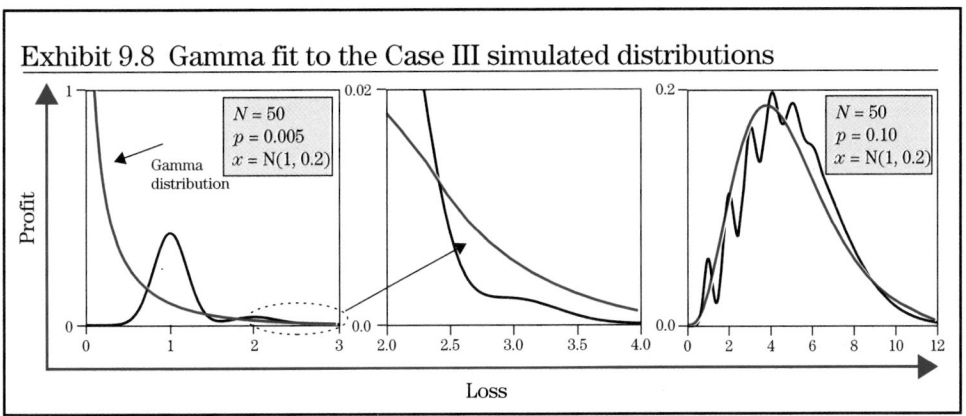

Exhibit 9.8 Gamma fit to the Case III simulated distributions

These results show that allowing losses to vary randomly generates a distribution very similar to the deterministic case presented in Case II – albeit a continuous one.

An approximation to the distribution of default risk

The characteristics of default losses captured by these simulations – a peaked, one-sided distribution evolving into a somewhat symmetric but still skewed one – suggests fitting it with the gamma distribution. This distribution may be unfamiliar to the reader, but all that needs to be known is it is a very flexible continuous distribution that is determined by only two parameters. The ability of gamma to fit the simulated distributions of Case III is used to demonstrate its reasonableness as an approximation. These fits are shown in Exhibit 9.8. In particular, note how well gamma does in capturing the tail of the one-sided loss distribution, as well as the overall shape of both the one-sided and two-sided distributions.

The parameters needed to fit this distribution are called the shape and scale parameters (alpha and beta, respectively) and can be calculated in a two-step process. First, calculate the mean and variance of the portfolio's "loss distribution". These formulas are derived from the "loss function" given in Equation (7). However, keep in mind that variable x, the loss in default, is now a normally distributed variable. You'll remember it was originally defined as a deterministic quantity in the initial model. For this function, the expected loss and loss variance are given by:

$$\mu_L = \sum_{i=1}^{N} \mu_i \cdot p_i \tag{8}$$

$$\sigma_L^2 = \sum_{i=1}^{N} (\mu_i^2 + \sigma_i^2) \cdot p_i - \sum \mu_i^2 \cdot p_i^2 \tag{9}$$

where, μL = expected loss of the portfolio, σL = volatility of loss of the portfolio, μi = expected loss in default of issuer i, σi^2 = volatility of loss for issuer i, pi = probability of default for issuer i and N = number of issuers.

Second, use these values to derive the shape and scale parameters of the gamma distribution according to the following conversion formulas:

$$\alpha = \left(\frac{\mu_L}{\sigma_L}\right)^2 \tag{10}$$

$$\beta = \frac{\sigma_L^2}{\mu_L} \tag{11}$$

$$\Gamma(x, \alpha, \beta) = \frac{1}{\beta \cdot \Gamma(\alpha)} \left(\frac{x}{\beta}\right)^{\alpha - 1} e^{-x/\beta} \tag{12}$$

The gamma distribution function itself is available in most spreadsheet programs (including Excel) and statistical packages. This function is robust enough to handle most portfolio distributions that will be encountered, with the exception of extremely high-grade portfolios with few issuers. The peaked, one-tail distribution in these cases is so extreme it is difficult to fit with any type of continuous distribution. Intuition also suggests that care must be taken anytime a few issuers comprise the majority of the risk. A portfolio-based approach to measuring default risk does not negate the need for a stand-alone analysis of large risk concentrations to individual issuers.

A portfolio example
To demonstrate this approach let's apply it to a hypothetical bond portfolio composed of 18 issuers. The composition is as follows:

1. Total face value of US$90 million split evenly across rating classes BB, B and CCC.
2. Within each rating class there are six positions of size US$5 million. Each position represents exposure to a different issuer.
3. The probabilities of default are 1 per cent, 5 per cent, and 20 per cent for rating classes BB, B and CCC.
4. A mean recovery rate applied of 40 per cent for all securities with a standard deviation of 10 per cent.

Based on the formulas provided in the previous section, the default distribution for this portfolio is shown in Exhibit 9.9. The statistical parameters used to derive this distribution are also shown so readers can test their understanding of the calculation. Based on a one-year time horizon and a 95 per cent level of confidence, this analysis calculates the default risk of the portfolio to be US$11.5 million.

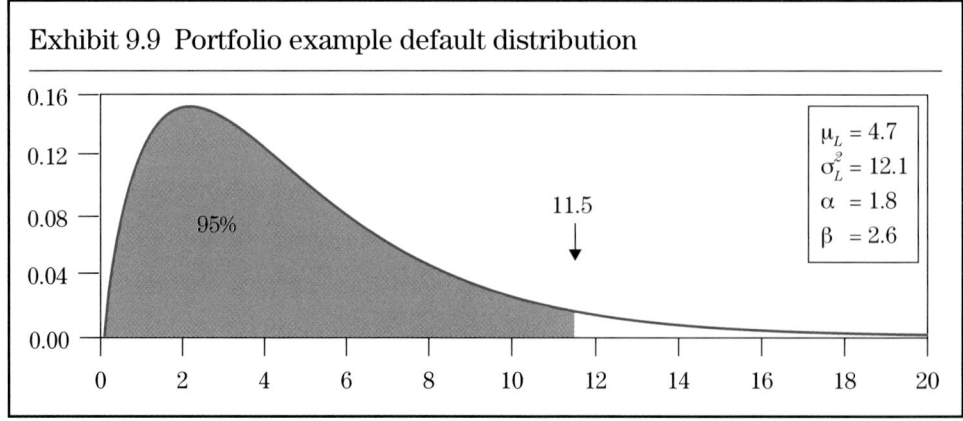

Exhibit 9.9 Portfolio example default distribution

---

[1] For more information about regression technique, see the literature on portfolio theory – eg, Diana R. Harrington, *Modern Portfolio Theory: The Capital Asset Model and Arbitrage Pricing Theory*, Prentice Hall Inc., 1987.

Section III

Risk management in the real world

This section addresses the practical challenges of implementing and sustaining a risk management function for market risk, and examines the supporting processes, technology and cultural implications. It outlines the interactions within a firm, and with external constituencies. It discusses how to staff and run a risk management function, the type and structure of information that needs to be produced, and the challenges of making sure the data is accurate and the methodology is robust. It particularly highlights the critical importance of instilling a risk management culture throughout a firm. Also considered are some of the issues associated with implementing risk management beyond banks and securities firms.

10

The risk management function

Introduction

In earlier chapters we discussed the various categories of risk, defined market risk in greater detail, and identified the key methods and tools for measuring market risk. These techniques are fundamental to supporting the analysis of market risk, yet they alone do not assure a firm's ability to effectively manage market risk. Measurements are not an end in themselves; they need to be accompanied by a mindset oriented on identifying potential risks, the knowledge of how to interpret the numbers, and the supporting processes and technology to produce meaningful, consistent results.

First and foremost, the ideas we outline here are based on a strong belief that the risk management function needs to be independent. This belief in independence then drives many of the subsequent organisational and process decisions. However, once that assumption is made, implementing and sustaining effective risk management still requires an array of supporting elements. We discuss such elements as:

- commitment from senior management;
- carefully designed policies and procedures;
- properly staffed risk analysis and monitoring functions;
- access to reliable technology;
- high integrity data;
- validated models; and especially
- experience and judgement.

We also describe how a risk management group needs to interact with diverse areas of the organisation and external entities, to gather, verify and report information.

Perhaps most important of all is that these supporting elements need to be accompanied by a *risk culture* that is consistent throughout the organisation. This risk culture needs to permeate to every level and every area because, in their own way, each individual can help foster an environment that is aware of both risk and return in all business activities. In this chapter, we discuss these elements of effective risk management, examining in more detail the concepts first introduced in Chapter 3.

Senior management commitment

Risk management is more than a regulatory reporting exercise; if carried out effectively, it can increase business profitability by focusing capital and attention on those areas with a higher risk/return ratio. We have all heard about the disasters caused by inadequate management attention to risk (indeed we described some in Chapter 2), but risk management should not be seen as a strictly defensive activity. The information produced by the risk management process can actually be used as a tool to enhance profitability. Managing risk can be most beneficial to a firm when senior management recognises and acts on its profit enhancing potential.

In this context then, an effective risk management function requires commitment from the highest levels of the organisation. Senior Management should view as one of its primary responsibilities the clear determination of the firm's attitude towards risk taking, and its appetite for risk. To obtain buy-in and compliance with risk management principles by all members of the firm, senior management must clearly believe in it. They need to communicate and act on the risk management principles consistently throughout the organisation, otherwise those who would rather not be under scrutiny will continue to avoid it. Senior management should demonstrate concern for risk management by sending a consistent message on the subject, and the mandate of the risk management group should be clear and widely known.

Consider the following scenario: a swaps desk is constantly over its VaR limit day after day. Although duly reported by the risk management function and highlighted to senior management, no steps are taken to either grant a temporary increase to the limit (if appropriate) or to require the desk to reduce its risk. Other desks, observing this casual attitude toward limit violations, soon adopt the same stance. This type of action clearly breaks down any advances that were made as a result of acceptance of the risk management process.

To incorporate senior management's role in profitability, capital allocation decisions should be based not only on the performance of a business unit but also on the risk taken to achieve that performance. (See Chapter 19 for further discussion of capital allocation.) When risk measures are used to evaluate a business unit, senior management sends the message that each business unit is truly held accountable for its risk. Likewise, when a new product or business venture is proposed, the business risks must be assessed by the risk committee as part of the overall approval process. If the risk committee agrees that the risks outweigh the benefits, other members of senior management need to support that decision.

Senior management should be informed regarding risk exposures in a timely and accurate fashion, but with information that is appropriately summarised and is in common risk measurement terms, such as VaR. (See Chapter 11 for more details on specific types of reports for senior management.) This information should be available both on-line and in hard copy, depending on preferences, and should also be summarised, both in numbers and in text, to present key highlights or exposures. It should also be analysed and scrubbed by the risk monitoring group before distributing it to senior management (see Chapters 11 and 15 for more details on data quality) so that there are no concerns about the accuracy of the data which would negatively impact both acceptance and credibility.

Developing a proactive risk culture

When considering the importance of risk culture, it should be asked why some firms are better than others at risk management. It remains true that Nick Leeson's actions at Barings would have been less likely if a meaningful "risk culture" had been in place which upheld a segregation of duties, and a closer monitoring of risk/return trade-offs in a book that appeared suspiciously profitable. Risk culture is important today because the complexity of modern financial instruments makes it possible for even a single, unsupervised trader to wager, and lose, the entire capital of a firm.

That being said, a key indicator of an effective risk culture can be defined as an awareness of risk which permeates the actions and words of all the members of the firm. In their actions and words, senior management demonstrates to all business areas that they pay attention to the risk reports, and hold the business areas accountable. Every time the head of a desk has a dialogue with a trader asking for an explanation of why a limit increase is needed; every time a trader calls the risk management group for analysis on a programme trade; or every time the financial controls group contacts the derivatives price verification group to analyse a complex derivative; these are the types of actions which demonstrate the presence of a risk culture.

Although senior management support and appropriate policies and guidelines are of fundamental importance to effective risk management, the real test for any firm is how the risk management function works with other areas of the firm on a day to day basis. A risk management group that interacts in partnership with the business areas plays a critical role in developing and reinforcing a positive risk culture. Conversely, a risk management group which takes a confrontational or bureaucratic view of its role can truly detract from the acceptance and propagation of a risk culture.

A strong risk culture does not imply a rigid one; on the contrary, a strong risk culture should be flexible, and should balance risks and rewards, as outlined in Swiss Bank Corporation's mission statement (see Exhibit 10.1). The primary responsibility of a risk management department is to protect the capital of the firm. However, too great a fixation on the "protection" axis may easily lead to a stifling imbalance. Because efficient markets ensure that returns can only follow in the wake of risk-taking, a culture that insists on "zero-loss-tolerance" for risk will only produce a string of missed business opportunities.

For example, if market risk is not assumed at all, the firm will obtain no revenue; if market risk is taken improperly, the firm stands a good chance that losses will outweigh gains. Therefore the risk management group needs to assist the trading desks in employing risk properly. If the group does this well, they are seen as adding value, rather than just being perceived as police, thereby facilitating the buy-in process, and enabling risk management to be more smoothly integrated into the firm's culture.

As we discussed earlier in this chapter, the risk department typically will have developed the risk management policies and guidelines. Once the policies have been written and approved, the risk unit needs to ensure that the policies have been understood at the desk level. The process of developing policies involves obtaining buy-in from the business side; in firms with good risk culture, policy proposals need to have support from both the business people and the risk group. Support can be achieved because the business side understands that the risk culture is enriched by carefully drafted policy proposals and the risk group appreciates that it is far easier

---

Exhibit 10.1 Swiss Bank Corporation's Risk Control Mission Statement

Swiss Bank Corporation's risk control mission statement focuses on both protecting capital, and allowing room for appropriate risk taking:

"... the interests of Swiss Bank Corporation's shareholders are paramount; the value of the capital they have invested in the business must be preserved and enhanced. Swiss Bank Corporation should be compensated for the risk it underwrites, whether at the individual transaction, the portfolio or the relationship level."

to gain acceptance for a policy once the business input has been incorporated into it. A valuable by-product of all this is reinforcing the common language of risk throughout the firm.

Risk culture is one of those elusive notions that seem to evade every attempt to give it an explicit definition. The themes of a good risk culture can be inferred from the manner in which the risk group functions: mutual respect between traders and risk management, pragmatic judgment exercised by risk managers, seamless teamwork between risk control and financial control, availability to the client base, and continuous interaction with senior management. The firms which have these traits in abundance find that they are constantly improving their already strong risk cultures. These firms appreciate the lessons of a Barings, a Daiwa, or a Sumitomo, and they understand that a single risk management mishap can tarnish a firm's reputation for years.

The responsibilities of risk management

As introduced in Chapter 3, it is the responsibility of the risk management function to identify, monitor and measure the risk of the firm. This function is performed by collecting, processing, verifying, monitoring and distributing risk information (see Exhibit 10.2). In that role, the group is accountable for the integrity of the inputs and outputs of the risk system, and for reviewing risk model results in the context of the portfolio as well as recent market events (see Exhibit 10.3). To perform this role effectively, they therefore need to be knowledgeable about trading products and strategies, and the external market-place – and to have solid judgement and experience in these areas.

The risk management group reports risk to senior management, and communicates risk exposures to the appropriate levels within the business units. The group is responsible for monitoring compliance with risk limits and risk policies, as well as interacting with the regulators during risk reviews. In support of this role, the group is also responsible for gathering, scrubbing and reconciling the data received from the front office and the back office, and for acquiring, developing and maintaining the systems required to measure risk. (These activities are detailed in subsequent chapters in this section.)

A key function performed by risk management is the monitoring of risk limits. Every organisation must have some ceiling on its risk appetite. Sooner or later, either risk limits, risk capital or regulatory capital will become a constrained resource requiring allocation. When a limit exception is requested, the risk group may be asked to gather information that can facilitate a decision, record the exception if it is granted and alert management when the time limit has been reached.

Once a limit structure is in place, the risk management group is then tasked with monitoring limit utilisation compliance. This requires the production of a daily risk profile

---

Exhibit 10.2 Excerpt from Goldman Sachs' Firmwide Risk Mission Statement

"The mission of the Firmwide Risk Department is to gather, analyse, monitor and distribute information pertaining to the market risk of the firm's positions in order to allow traders, their managers, other personnel throughout the organisation, and especially the Risk Committee, to understand and make informed decisions concerning the management and control of the risks taken."

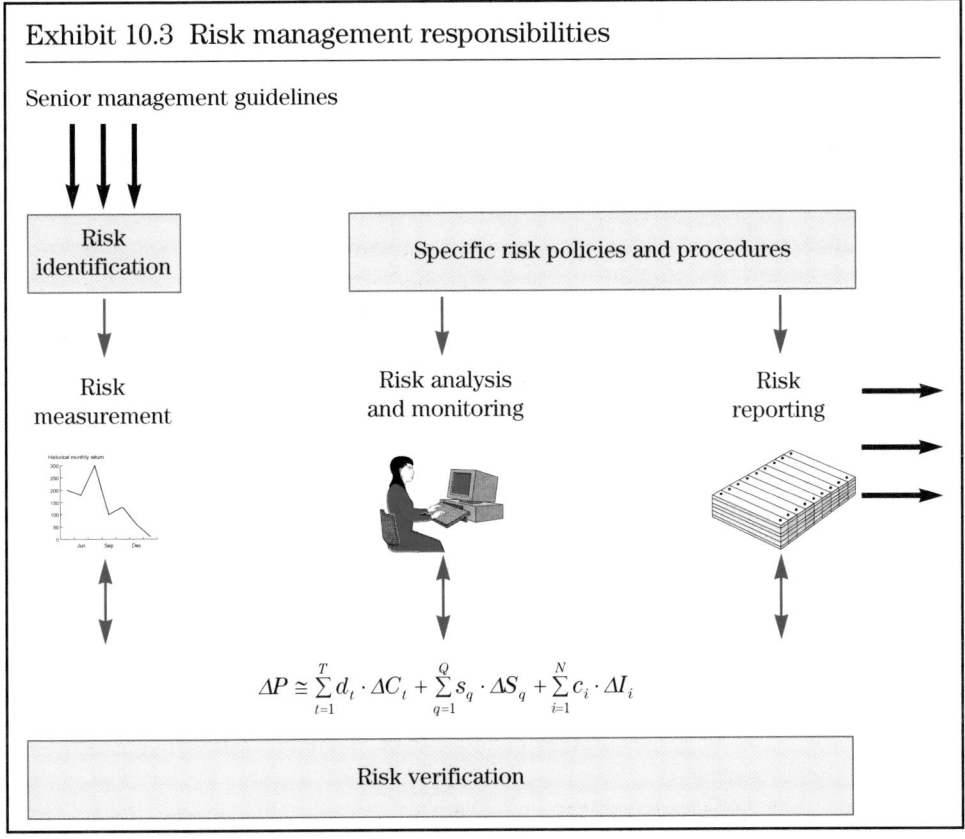

Exhibit 10.3 Risk management responsibilities

Senior management guidelines

Risk identification

Specific risk policies and procedures

Risk measurement

Risk analysis and monitoring

Risk reporting

$$\Delta P \cong \sum_{t=1}^{T} d_t \cdot \Delta C_t + \sum_{q=1}^{Q} s_q \cdot \Delta S_q + \sum_{i=1}^{N} c_i \cdot \Delta I_i$$

Risk verification

for the firm, which automatically compares the risk utilisation against various limits and identifies key risk exposure areas. (See Chapter 11 for more details on risk reporting.) The daily risk profile ranks alongside daily P&L as one of the two most important reports in a firm. Once the risk profile is available, monitoring compliance with policies is a relatively straightforward matter of reviewing limit excesses and following up on those that are judged significant, based on the guidelines (as we saw in Chapter 1).

The group should also have responsibility for verifying the models that are used to price complex instruments, supporting the controller's price review activities. This effort helps to identify potential model risk, by performing an independent verification of the accuracy and appropriateness of the pricing models. The group may also be given responsibility for documenting and monitoring changes to pricing and analytic models. (This topic is discussed further in Chapter 14.)

The risk management function can be a monitoring and reporting function, or it can actively take positions to manage the risk of the organisation. In some firms, the risk management function may actually put on hedges that offset certain overall risks, such as to the equities market, or specific risks, such as to a particular large transaction. This role should be defined based on the needs and structure of the organisation. Our discussion here focuses on the monitoring and reporting approach, because that is how the function is performed in both of our firms, in particular due to the strong belief in the need for independence.

In some cases, the risk management group can be uniquely positioned to have a full picture of the firm's exposures, increasing the group's responsibility for maintaining accurate information. An example of this may be when multiple desks or business units take positions in a particular instrument; the overall firm could either have a significant market concentration (if everyone is long), or the positions could net each other out (if some are long and some are short). The risk management group is likely to be the only function looking broadly across business units for this type of trend, and thereby providing a valuable overview for senior management. In the capital allocation process, for example, information from risk management can be used broadly to compare the risk/return ratios of the business units.

Another event that frequently occurs is for "new" risks to be identified. These new risks might come to light through a major problem at another firm, as a result of a question from the risk committee or because a particular P&L difference highlights a risk exposure that is not fully modelled in the risk system. Once a new risk has been identified, it should be incorporated into the standard procedures and models that the risk management group utilises.

Structure and skills required

Risk management does need to be performed as an independent function, sponsored and supported by senior management, and staffed by dedicated professionals with risk management expertise. The group needs to be separate from the front office, because otherwise there could be conflicts of interest and the firm's risk would not be

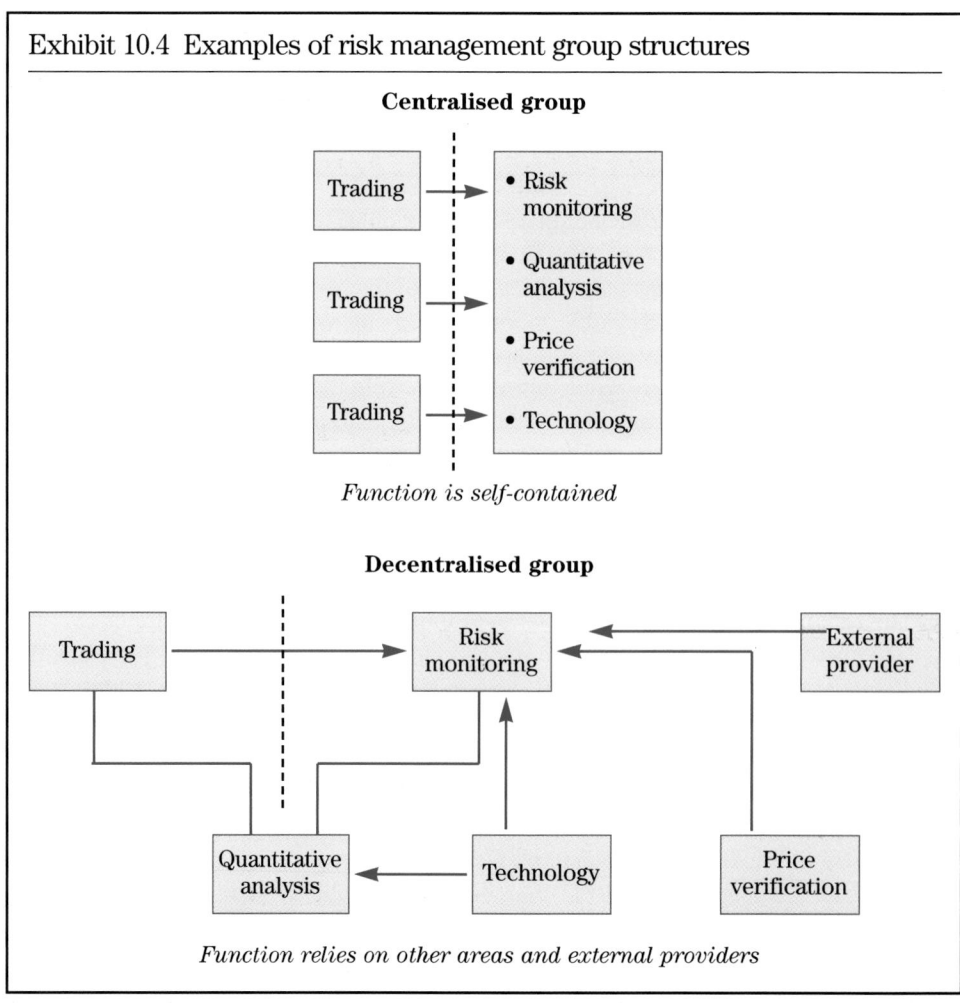

Exhibit 10.4 Examples of risk management group structures

independently measured. However, this independence is a delicate balancing act because the risk group should also service the needs of the front office in order to be effective at interpreting the firm's risk.

At the highest level, corporate risk management includes reviewing all aspects of risk – market, credit, legal, operational, settlement/payment, reputational, etc. In practice, monitoring these risks may require different expertise and skills, and so may be delegated out to different areas of the firm (such as legal), but summarised for senior management in consistent terms by a central group. For the purposes of maintaining independence, the risk management function typically reports to the CFO or the CEO of the firm.

The market risk management function can be organised in two main ways – as a large centralised group, or as a smaller group responsible strictly for summarising the results of decentralised risk groups (see Exhibit 10.4). This decision is highly dependent on how a firm is organised, as well as the technology that is in place. For example, in a firm where proprietary trading activities occur in multiple divisions, a centralised group and system may be needed to bring the information together. In a firm where proprietary trading is all in a single division, a smaller risk group may be able to take consistent information from a single system.

Staffing the market risk management group requires covering a diverse set of skills, such as quantitative modelling of investment product risk, practical knowledge of the trading and valuation processes, and the ability to develop systems to model risk and take feeds of data from multiple sources. In our experience, all of these skills are necessary to perform the function comprehensively. Risk management staff can come from different areas of a firm, such as trading, research or financial control. In

Exhibit 10.5 Structure and skills of a centralised risk management group

Role	Responsibility
Risk monitoring and analysis	• Monitor position and price data • Evaluate risk exposures • Identify and monitor limit violations • Analyse potential scenarios • Summarise and report on risk exposures • Reconcile with other areas • Perform backtesting
Quantitative analysis	• Determine modelling for new products • Design new quantitative models • Test new models
Price verification	• Verify prices on complex derivatives • Track changes in pricing models
Model development	• Develop new models for system • Develop risk analysis tools • Maintain historical return data
Systems development and integration	• Develop infrastructure to support processing • Accept feeds from other systems • Automate data scrubbing and translation • Develop database to support risk data

fact, integrating staff from other areas can enhance the group's understanding of the business implications of risks, and its ability to interact with other areas that either feed the risk analysis process or are impacted by its results.

The size of the group will be dependent on how the risk management function is structured, on the size of the firm, the complexity of the products traded, and the efficiency of the supporting technology. The skills required will also depend on how the function is structured and the group's responsibilities. Exhibit 10.5 summarises the structure and skills of a centralised group.

In some cases, a firm may not require a large risk management function internally, and therefore may decide to outsource some aspects of the function to an external provider. It is still recommended, however, that the firm has a core independent group that is responsible for analysing the results of the process, and for maintaining a centralised view of the risks of the organisation.

The relationship between risk management and other groups

The risk management group does need to be independent, but it also needs to interact and communicate with other parts of the firm. Typical interactions might be with the front office, the back office, controllers, legal/compliance and senior management. The risk management group is also often called upon to meet with external entities such as regulators, auditors, ratings agencies and investors. (The primary interactions are depicted in Exhibit 10.6.)

Internal interactions
Front office
The interactions with the front office entail receiving their views of their positions, markets and P&L, as well as on how to model the products they trade or invest in to properly capture the risk. As stated earlier, there is generally a delicate balance to be maintained with the front office because they can be both the users of risk information and the group whose activities can most be affected by it. They know their products and their markets, and in this capacity it is important for the risk group to interact with them. However, since the risk group must also take an independent view of risk, the relationship with the front office needs to remain at arm's length.

The risk monitoring group will often be asked to prepare analyses for the traders (see Exhibit 10.7) or need to ask the traders for assistance in modelling a complex new product. In order to accurately assess risk, the risk monitoring group does need to have a clear understanding of the traders' views on their markets, positions and strategies. This type of dialogue can only take place if the traders' needs are considered and supported, always provided that the independence principle is maintained.

To support this kind of positive dialogue with the front office, the risk group should furnish the front office with a copy of its own risk data in exactly the form it will be circulated to management; this basic courtesy keeps the desk prepared in the event management raises questions on specific positions. It is beneficial to encourage the design of joint risk reports, where a single report services both the trading desk and the risk unit. In fact, some of the best ideas for reports often come directly from the traders. The risk group can also be of service to traders in helping them see how their desk or portfolio contributes to the firm's overall risk profile.

The risk group can also assist in the trader evaluation process by providing data on their risk-adjusted returns. Before accurate risk profile data was routinely collected, it was very difficult for the managers of traders to quantify the average

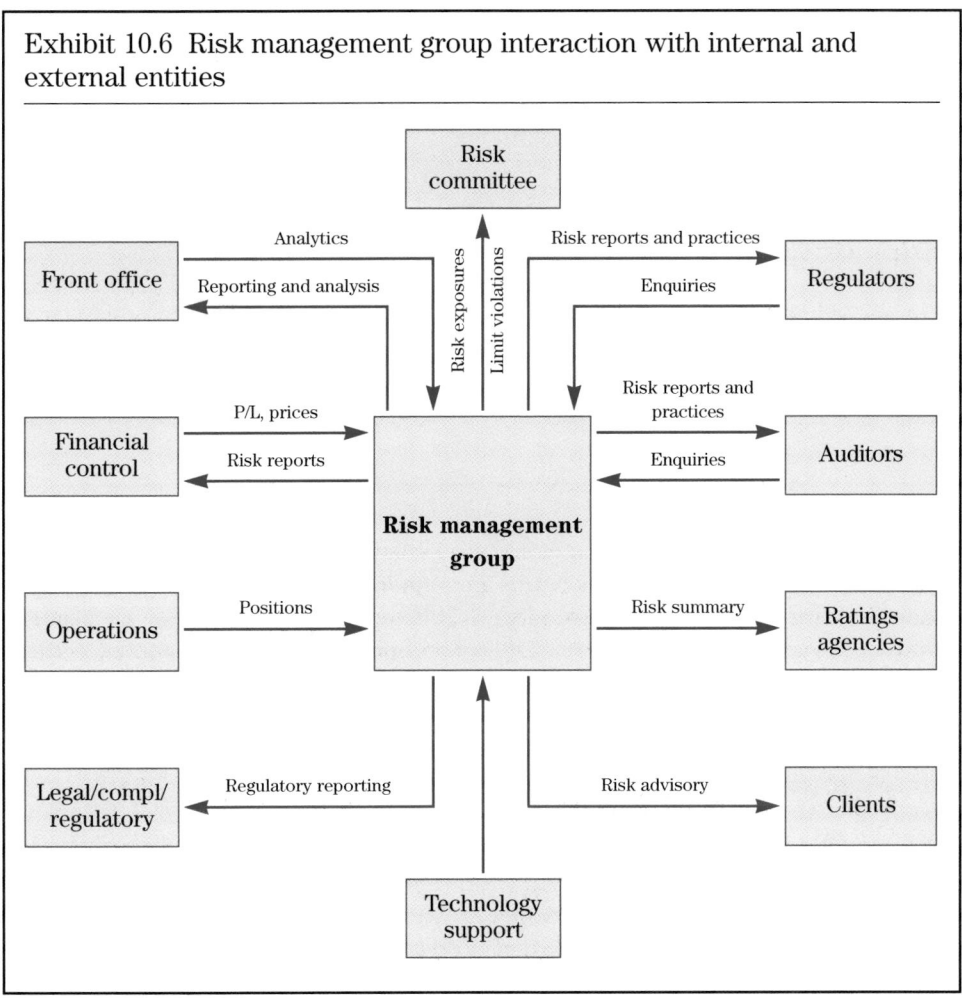

Exhibit 10.6 Risk management group interaction with internal and external entities

amount of risk taken by each trader, but with an historical database containing daily risk profiles and daily P&L all the way down to the trading desk level, it is a straightforward matter to assemble Sharpe ratios and other risk-adjusted performance metrics. Hence, management no longer needs to rely only on total revenue when evaluating a trading desk. This development is as revolutionary in terms of influencing trader behaviour as the advent of management accounts to supplement financial accounts was over a decade ago.

As stressed before, it is critical that the front office and the risk management function maintain a positive working relationship. This may not always be easy to achieve because, typically, the risk management group acts as a control over the trading units. An adversarial relationship can develop if the risk management process is not designed correctly or if senior management does not adequately back the risk management group's endeavours. The risk management group's efforts can also be aided by effective communication from the front office. For example, traders' views on strategies, positions, markets and P&L generation are crucial in making an accurate risk assessment. Further, traders' input on modelling techniques for the products they trade should be sought for two important reasons – they have an expertise in that particular product or market and active two-way communication facilitates front office acceptance of the VaR methodology.

> ## Exhibit 10.7 A request to the risk group
>
> A trader might send an e-mail to the risk group along the following lines:
>
> > "The trade we discussed yesterday did not trade because of market volatility and wide prices from the dealers. But, they plan to do the trade tomorrow. Is it possible to do the analysis we discussed? This is an equity trade where the customer buys US$110 million and sells US$115 million. Because the trade will be bid while the US market is open and the rest of the world is closed, we would like to have a rough idea of whether the buy portfolio or the sell portfolio is more correlated with the US. Thanks."
>
> The risk group would run the portfolio through the system to provide a response to the trader on the correlations. This project clearly has a time constraint, so the risk group must turn it around quickly in order for the analysis to be beneficial.

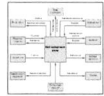

Financial control

The interaction with financial control encompasses taking feeds of P&L and reconciling that the earnings reported in the risk system, and used for backtesting purposes, are accurate. The daily mark-to-market performed by the financial control group is clearly the front line of effective risk management. Also, if the risk group identifies a potential error in either position or pricing data, this must be communicated back to financial control so that it can be addressed. Financial control may also require the assistance of the quantitative analysts in the risk group to provide an independent valuation of complex derivative instruments. The relationship between risk numbers and profit and loss numbers is both strategic and essential, and is likely to grow in the future.

Risk management and financial control must have a close relationship. In the first place, performance evaluation can no longer rely simply on returns or total profit, but should increasingly incorporate risk-based adjustments. Because financial control maintains the books and records with respect to P&L and risk control has responsibility for risk data, the two departments must work closely together. Secondly, as regulatory capital moves from being exclusively based on the balance sheet, as under the original 1988 Basle Accord, to being far more related to actual risk measures, as in the 1996 amendment allowing model-based capital for market risk, it becomes impossible for the finance department to produce regulatory capital using traditional general ledger systems. Indeed, the finance department is now absolutely dependent for regulatory capital computations on parameters that are routinely calculated during creation of the firm's risk profile. This is another way of saying that the databases overseen by risk management are actually now part of the books and records of the institution. The risk department supports finance by keeping them up to date on developments in model-based capital approaches and by ensuring that the normalised risk data for the firm is built in such a way that finance can conveniently extract whatever it needs to complete supervisory reports.

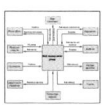

Operations

The relationship with operations is not dissimilar to that with financial controls. The risk group relies on accurate back office data to generate risk results. If the risk group discovers errors in the data, this must be reported back to the operations function in order for them to be fixed for the next day.

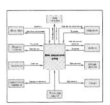

Legal/Compliance/Regulatory reporting

With the growing focus on risk management in the financial industry, the role of the risk management group in producing regulatory reports will increase for all types of businesses (not only banks and investment firms). The risk group produces certain regulatory reports (such as the DPG reports and ultimately, risk capital).

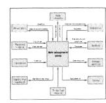

Technology

Due to the high degree of technology capability required to perform the risk management function, as well as the large amounts of data required from diverse systems, the risk management group must interact extensively with the technology areas that support both the front office and the back office.

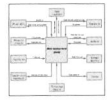

Across the firm

In some cases, the risk management system may be the only source for fully consolidated data across an entire firm, which means it may be relied upon by other areas for the purpose of looking across business units. For example, there may be foreign exchange positions in international fixed income and in international equities, but it could be that only in the risk system are the positions reported together.

External interactions

The risk management group is often called upon to interact with external entities, and as the capability of the risk management function can be indicative of a firm's overall attitude towards risk and sound business management. The following are examples of external interactions.

Regulators

Proper risk management is increasingly viewed by regulators worldwide as critical to a firm's soundness and as an essential tool for mitigating overall systemic risk, especially in view of the globalisation of markets. With the increased regulatory focus on risk management and risk management standards (as discussed in Chapter 2 and later in Chapter 17), the regulators are consistently looking to assess a firm's qualitative and quantitative risk management capabilities. We anticipate this role increasing in the future, as regulatory scrutiny of risk management grows.

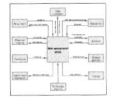

Auditors

External auditors now frequently include an assessment of risk management in the annual audit, in part because of the trend to include risk management information in the annual report and to comply with the regulatory approach of ensuring the soundness of the financial institution. The risk management group must work closely with the auditors to demonstrate clearly the measurement methodologies used, as well as the completeness of the supporting procedures. The quantitative analysis group may also be called upon to work with the external auditors on the more complex pricing models.

Ratings agencies

As with the regulators, the risk management in place in a firm is a key criteria for the ratings agencies in evaluating its soundness and long-term viability. In addition, we are starting to see a trend towards evaluating risk management capabilities in companies that are going public and insurance companies that are going through a demutualisation process.

Investors

Investors will also begin to review a firm's risk management capability as one of the key criteria for assessing soundness. This has historically not been common practice, but we are starting to see a trend in this direction.

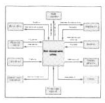

Clients

With the heightened awareness of risk management in the public arena, in particular among institutional investors, risk reporting on client portfolios is already becoming a key requirement. Effective use of quantitative models to assess risk/return can also be perceived as a competitive advantage. Depending on the structure of the firm, this function may be performed by the risk management group or by a specialised client reporting group. The models that support this type of reporting can be provided by the risk management group.

As risk management becomes more widely understood, sophisticated corporate clients often express an interest in financial risk management. The client's relationship manager will frequently ask the risk managers to describe their processes within the firm. As more public pressure is placed on corporations to make transparent market risk disclosures (eg, the SEC directive for increased derivative disclosure in corporate filings), there will be increasing demand from clients for risk advisory services. For firms that choose not to place this new risk advisory function in a separate business unit or subsidiary, the risk unit is the most logical candidate to provide such services. Some firms sense a marketing advantage in making available to clients the very same people who actually conduct risk management as part of their daily jobs. Clients have enquired about every risk aspect, from the basic structure of a risk department to complex Monte-Carlo VaR algorithms. Few professionals anywhere else in the firm have the breadth of knowledge to deal with such a wide array of questions.

General policies and guidelines

In the changing regulatory environment, many organisations are rushing to produce a VaR number purely to comply with the regulatory requirement. However, firms which merely focus on satisfying regulatory requirements are unlikely to gain the benefits which can be derived from understanding and managing risks. In conversations with various central banks and regulatory bodies, we have heard this concern expressed, as well as the concern that firms will focus strictly on quantitative risk measurements, and will not develop the qualitative aspects of risk management which facilitate using the results as a business decision-making tool (see Chapter 17 for more discussion on this point).

In a similar vein, firms often take the approach of implementing a system to measure market risk without putting the accompanying policies and guidelines in place, and without obtaining buy-in from the business areas. The result of this approach is that the system may be ineffective, basically being run in a back room somewhere, without relevance to the business, or it may produce numbers which are not accepted by the very people whose activities are being monitored.

Based on this premise then, another critical step towards effective risk management is to agree upon a set of policies and guidelines describing how risk management will be performed within the organisation. Discussing policies and guidelines, and gaining consensus on them, can also improve the effectiveness and the applicability of the risk management process. And it encourages the development of a risk culture (discussed earlier) by expanding the number of people thinking deeply about risk and its implications.

Policies and guidelines for risk management should define the responsibilities of the risk committee and the risk management group. They should document how the function will be structured and performed, what the frequency of reporting will be and how the resulting information will be used (for example for monitoring limits or for capital allocation). These policies should then be communicated at various levels of detail to all individuals who either feed the process, or are impacted by it, so they can understand their role and how they will be measured.

The process of developing policies and guidelines can be challenging, and the effort should not be underestimated, either in terms of how much work it can be, or in terms of the impact of the decisions that are made. For example, a decision as apparently simple as deciding whether the risk management group is called a "controlling" function or a "monitoring" function can actually have significant implications on acceptance of risk management within a firm, depending on the firm's culture. So, while we discuss a general framework for policies and guidelines as derived from the combined experience of our two firms, significant customisation is always necessary to apply them to each organisation's unique requirements.

When establishing a risk management function, the first activities might be to identify the structure that suits the organisation (eg, centralised or decentralised), to establish a risk committee with the appropriate representatives, to articulate the firm's risk appetite, and to develop a table of contents for a policies and guidelines document (see Exhibit 10.8 – Sample Guidelines). The risk committee can assign the task of designing the policies and guidelines to a sub-group for further development, but the committee then needs to review and condone the results. For example, as limits are determined, it becomes important to integrate them in a coherent view of risk-bearing-capacity, or risk appetite. The risk committee must then make an independent decision on how much risk-bearing-capacity they will delegate to the business managers.

Many of the risk policies will contain some form of quantitative limits. Senior management relies on the risk group for an explanation of the algorithms themselves and how they meet their intended purpose, which necessitates strong mathematical skills in the risk department. The responsibility for setting the size of the original limits lies with the risk committee, but they will often rely on recommendations of the risk group, particularly when defining these initial limits.

Another policy issue is the development of escalation procedures to be followed when there is a risk condition that senior management needs to respond to (see Exhibit 10.9). If a specific trader is over their limit, perhaps notification only needs to go to the desk head, who can then decide to increase the limit, or to direct the trader to unwind the position. However if a desk is over its limit, the head of the business

---

Exhibit 10.8 Sample guidelines

- How the risk management function will be organised
- Which risks will be covered by the group
- How risk will be measured
- What are the group's responsibilities
- What is the structure and meeting frequency of the risk committee
- How will limits be set, and what happens if limits are exceeded
- What escalation procedures will be in place (see example below)
- What approvals are necessary for various situations

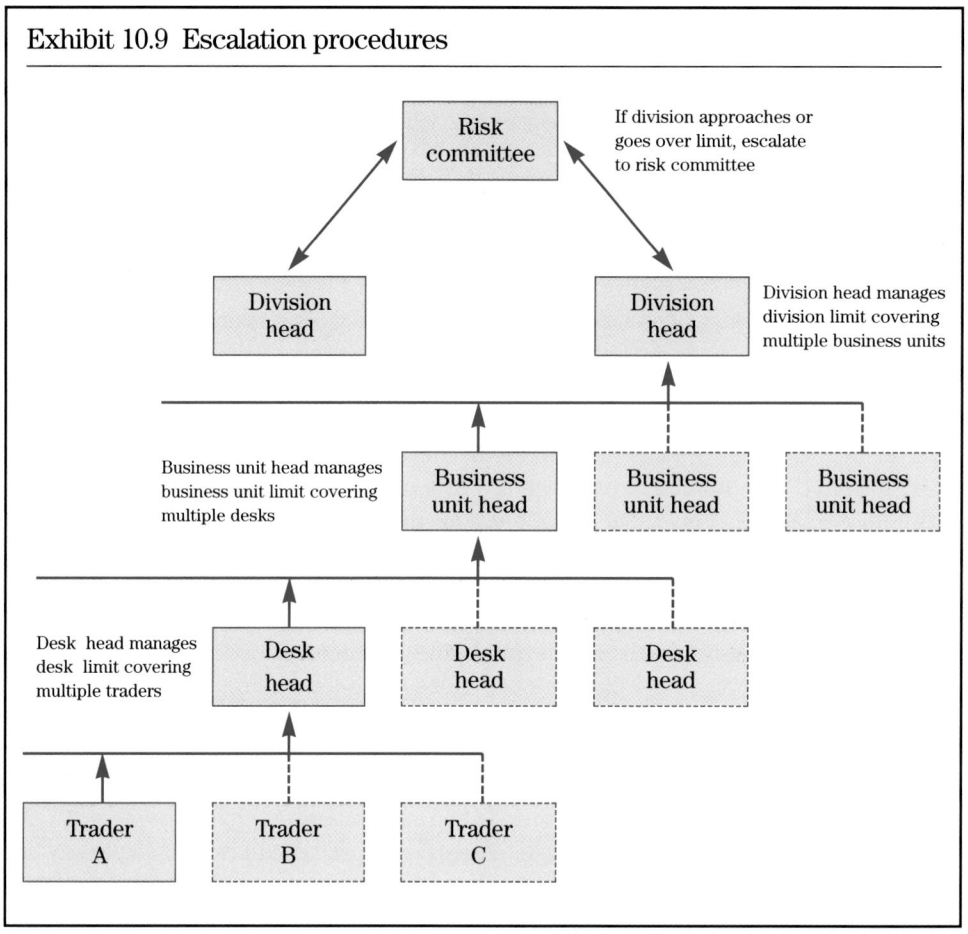

Exhibit 10.9 Escalation procedures

unit would need to be alerted, and would need to decide whether to give the desk a temporary increase based on the business unit's overall limit. Depending on the organisation, at some point the level and magnitude of the risk will need to be brought to the attention of the risk committee for a decision.

Specific policies might also need to be developed for different functions or business areas. Questions that could be asked to stimulate the thought process might include:

- *Risk limits* – how will they be set, will they be set close to the existing risk level or will a larger buffer be put in place? Will the limits also be used to encourage certain low-risk, profitable businesses to take more risk (see next section) ?
- *Valuations* – how will the accuracy and timeliness of valuations be ensured?
- *High risk products limits and control* – will an extra layer of focus be placed on businesses which have a higher risk profile?
- *New business or new products review* – will they be required to go through a review ? If they go without that review, will there be a penalty? What constitutes the review – legal, operational, profitability, other risks?
- *Model review and release control* – will all models be reviewed before being used for valuations or hedging strategies? How will model versions be managed, for consistency, to eliminate error introductions via ad-hoc changes?
- *Regulatory reporting* – will the risk management group participate actively in

regulatory reporting activities? Will specific reports be developed for the regulatory process? How will regulatory issues be handled?

Again, it is advisable to use these questions as a starting point only, and to customise policies based on what will work within a particular organisation's culture and structure. It is also advisable to maintain a flexible approach and mindset, so that as businesses change and grow, policies and guidelines will remain responsive to those changes.

Setting risk limits

As already discussed, an institution must establish a solid risk culture and define its risk appetite and procedures. A major step in implementing effective procedures is the establishment of risk limits.

Why VaR?

Assigning risk limits in terms of VaR has many advantages: it is comparable across products, desks, and units within the organisation; it is currency denominated; it can be validated through backtesting (see Chapter 12); and it facilitates the formation of a common risk language across the organisation.

Determining the limit structure

As discussed earlier, senior management should begin the process of determining the appropriate limit structure for the firm. In particular, they must first determine the risk appetite of the firm and the overall framework with which the risk limit operates. Limit setting is a dynamic, ongoing process which relies upon input from many areas.

Typically firms want to know and be in a position to control their aggregate risk. Therefore, a firmwide limit may be a valid starting point. Limits can then be set for any level of business across the firm.

A typical aggregation and limit structure is depicted in Exhibit 10.10: there is a firmwide limit at the top, giving senior management a clear idea about the amount of exposure to the organisation as a whole. Disaggregating that risk into divisional separations gives the division head an idea of the risks under management. A further breakout may be developed along geographical lines, if appropriate. Business unit limits are designed to help the manager of the area control the business unit's risks as well as to offer a sense of which areas are taking significant or conversely insufficient risks. Finally, limits could be assigned to individual traders. Some consider individual trader limits micromanagement. Many firms leave risk limit allocation to the discretion of the business level management.

One thing to bear in mind, however is that limits should be set where responsibility is clearly defined. A case in point: if a limit is set for a trading area with several different managers with some accountability (such as in organisations with matrix management structures), it may become difficult to manage limit enforcement. Consider this example:

Exhibit 10.10 Typical aggregation and limit structure

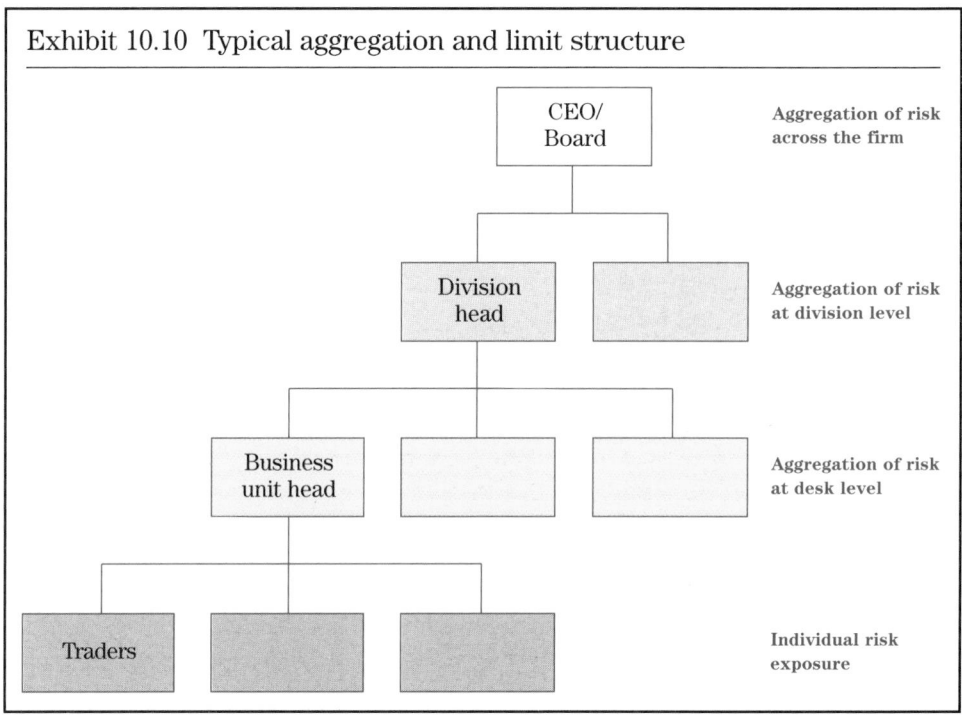

An Asian swaps desk has a NY-based global swaps manager as its head. However, the desk's risk flows up to and counts against an Asian geographical trading risk limit. The head of the Asian office is responsible for controlling the geographical limit. When the Asian geographical limit is breached, the natural person to hold accountable is the head of the Asian geographic trading business. However, he or she would typically point to the swaps trading desk as the culprit and say "talk to them about the limit violation. I don't manage them, I can't do anything about the violation."

In a situation such as the one described above, there should be a separate risk limit for the global swaps trading areas, if this is indeed how swaps trading is managed and the risk of the swaps desk should not count against another area's limit when that area has no control over the trading. This seems simple enough, but with today's trend towards matrix management, these situations are increasingly common.

Things to consider when setting limits

As stated previously, setting risk limits is an ongoing, dynamic process. Changing markets, trading responsibilities and risk appetites will lead a firm to adjust limits accordingly. In general, the things senior management tends to consider when setting limits for trading areas are as follows:

- *At what level of risk is senior management comfortable?*
  VaR represents real dollars at risk. If a US$4 million daily VaR limit is set and VaR is defined as a once a year event, then senior management must be prepared for a US$4 million loss occurring in a single day once a year. If this is not an acceptable daily loss, then the limit should be adjusted accordingly.

- *Depth of trader experience*

  Large risk limits are generally not given to new, inexperienced traders without a proven track record. However risk limits can and should be adjusted as conditions change or as traders prove their abilities.
- *Past performance of a trader or business unit*

  If the business unit or trader has been profitable and senior management would like to encourage more risk taking there, the limit should reflect that level of comfort and confidence.
- *Projected revenue of desk or business unit*

  Senior management should consider the profit potential of a desk when establishing its risk limit. Setting a limit for a desk that is significantly larger than their projected revenue would probably not be very effective.

Finally, there are some further subjective considerations. Although a firm might wish to keep desks from knowing others' limits, word does tend to spread. Senior management does send a message when setting varying limits for different business units and should assume that these limits are common knowledge and may influence behaviour.

Risk limits – establishing policies and procedures

Before limit monitoring and enforcement can take place, appropriate policies and procedures must be clearly defined and communicated throughout the organisation. Some of the typical issues regarding policies are:

- *How often are limits monitored?*

  Limits are typically monitored on a daily basis, if they are to be at all effective. However, this depends on the nature of the trading and how comfortable senior management is with the trading areas' risk taking activities. Some institutions monitor limits on an intraday basis. However, this is often time-consuming and costly and the results are sometimes misleading (see Chapter 15). In the heat of a trading day, there might be delays in booking trades and their associated hedges. If a risk system were to calculate risk by using an intraday portfolio, there is the potential for grabbing an "incomplete" portfolio, one that is missing part of a trade. Penalising traders for breaching limits when limits were not actually violated leads to loss of credibility for the risk management process.
- *How should limit violations be handled?*

  First and foremost, the policies and procedures regarding limit violations should be clearly defined and then scrupulously followed. Careless practices lead to a breakdown in the process. In other words, whatever the method of handling limit violations, the procedures must be adopted uniformly throughout the firm and followed at all times. If not, once people realise that these limit violations are not taken seriously by everyone, the entire risk culture will be ineffective.

  However, this is not to say that limit policies and procedures should be inflexible. Quite to the contrary, bureaucracy and inflexibility should be avoided at the outset. The firm must establish procedures that the firm's members can live with, but which incorporate the risk management principles and ideals of the firm. The severe market moves in late October 1997 are a case in point. A plunge in the Hong Kong market had global reverberations. On Monday, 27 October, the DJIA dropped 554 points, a 7.2 per cent move. The sell-off triggered the first and second shutdown of US stock markets under rules put in place to prevent a repeat of the 1987 stock market crash.

Many professionals felt that constraining and inflexible risk limits actually contributed to the day's steep market drop as traders, particularly those managing volatility books, struggled to get back under risk limits. When the market reopened after the first shutdown, the ensuing panic selling in part was attributed to traders attempting to flatten market exposures. Many lost more money in this endeavour than they would have if they had managed the risks of their books in a manner appropriate for the prevailing market conditions. The moral of the story is that risk management policies should never take the place of sound judgment.

In order to facilitate orderly yet flexible risk management, firms can set limits fairly tightly, perhaps some percentage above typical trading activity, but grant temporary increases to limits on a case by case basis as needed. By establishing tight limits, risk taking is kept in line with normal trading conditions. However, when a business unit wants to put on specific large trades or accommodate customer activity causing a limit violation, the desk head might approach the division head or risk manager to seek a temporary limit increase with a set end date. It may be desirable to have one or several point people for each business unit, ideally individuals well-known to traders, so that the process remains flexible.

There may be occasions when a trading unit needs a permanent increase to a risk limit. This situation may arise when there has been a fundamental shift in a particular market, a change in focus or purview, or a desire on the part of senior management to assume more risk. Whether temporary or permanent, once a limit increase has been granted, this information needs to be communicated back to the trading unit, the risk management department and if mandated in a firm's policies, senior management and the risk committee. Exhibit 10.11 below depicts a typical violation and response process. The risk management system should be able to track the limits on line and be able to receive updates to limits, both temporary and permanent, and monitor expiration dates for temporary limits, reverting back upon expiration. This lends credibility both to the system and to the process.

- *Who should be notified of limit violations, and when?*
There should be clear lines of communication for effective risk limit monitoring. As we stated above, someone should be responsible or accountable for each limit. When a limit violation takes place, it must also be clear who should be notified. As

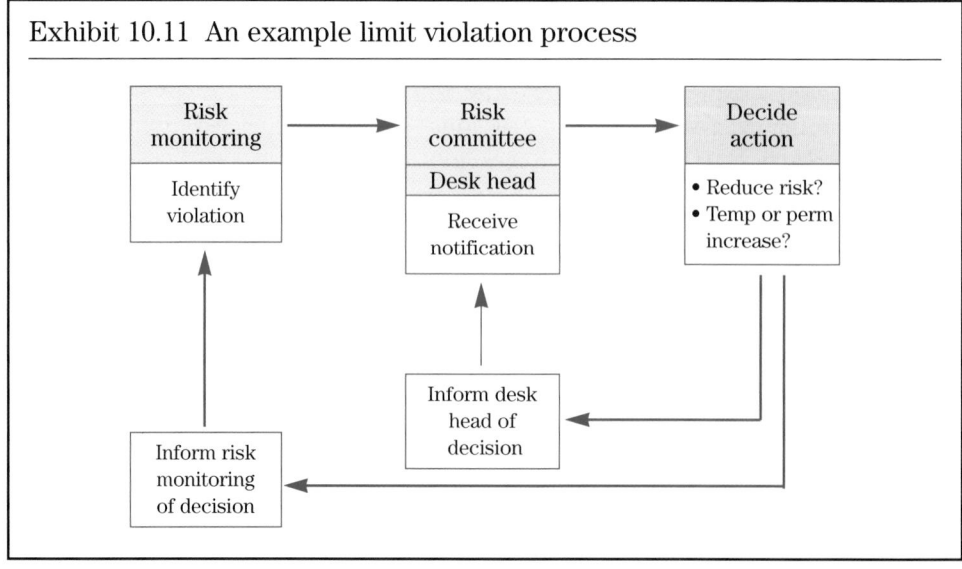

Exhibit 10.11 An example limit violation process

we depicted in the the discussion of escalation procedures in 10.9, for a violation on an individual desk, the desk head and the head should be notified. It would be up to the firm whether or not senior management be notified for each and every violation, or just those occurring at higher levels, say at the divisional level. Whoever the appropriate parties, notification should take place as soon as the violation has been discovered and confirmed. Reporting delays tend to lessen the effectiveness of the risk monitoring process. Further, those individuals with limit approval authority must be made known to all those involved in the process, including the risk management function, who must know who has authority to change limits and who does not.

- *How should "habitual offenders" be treated?*

  A firm should have procedures in place to handle persistent limit abuse. If a trader or business unit has been told not to exceed a limit, or has been told to reduce risk to below the limit and fails to do so, there should be a standard way of handling such incidents. Some firms take a hard line stance – persistent limit violators are dismissed. This is up to the firm; however, whatever policy is adopted must convey the seriousness and spirit of the risk management culture to which the firm aspires.

Conclusion

In summary, market risk management is more than a quantitative measurement function; it is also a qualitative function requiring policies and guidelines be set in place. It requires sponsorship from senior management and a risk culture that permeates the organisation.

The risk management function must by definition be independent. Another critical step towards an effective risk organisation is the agreement by senior management upon a complete set of policies that determine the character of a firm's risk management function. These guidelines should include well-defined risk limits, valuation methodologies, new product and model review and validation practices, and reporting policies, to name a few.

The skills required for the risk monitoring function are diverse but include quantitative analytical skills, strong communication and consensus building skills, product knowledge, and expertise in multiple technology environments. And the key underlying premise is the risk culture – which both enables and sustains a firm's ability to perform effective risk management.

In the next chapter, we describe the information and analyses required to perform risk management, and a number of report examples which can be used to present risk results.

11

Risk analysis and reporting

Introduction

In this chapter we address the critical process of analysing and reporting risk that is performed within the risk management function. Reporting is a key component of any risk process, because it is basically the window into the risk management results and the means of communicating the risks the firm is exposed to. Presenting complex risk information to a broad diverse audience is a significant task.

This being said, developing effective reports is an evolving process that always benefits from individual insights and the test of time. At Goldman Sachs and Swiss Bank Corporation over the years we have developed reports that are effective in our environments, although we are constantly adding reports and presentation mechanisms as markets, businesses and methodologies change.

In this chapter we outline the types of reports that we have found effective to present risk management results both to traders and to senior management. These are meant to be indicative only, our goal being to demonstrate what is possible and what has been useful to us. Different organisations certainly will require different information views; the focus should be on developing presentations that work for your firm in order to facilitate the acceptance of, and the comfort with, risk management. In this chapter we also describe risk analysis in greater detail then covered in Chapters 1 and 10, as well as the complex task of maintaining data integrity. Finally, we detail the information flows required to and from the front office.

The fundamentals of risk analysis and reporting

Effective risk analysis answers two key and often asked questions that arise from the review of risk results: "What does this number mean?" and "What should be done about it?" The goal of practical risk analysis is to take the mystery out of the numbers.

Risk models are often labelled as black boxes, implying that the results come out based on some magic that is performed within an opaque box. Indeed, senior management may justifiably be concerned that excessive emphasis and trust have been placed on a number that comes out of a model. In some cases this is true – for example when too much reliance is placed on a single VaR number. For this and other reasons, it is advisable to have the ability to "decompose" the results of the risk model, producing reports and analyses that help the user interpret the results, thereby reducing the "mystery" quotient.

Multiple measures of risk

As discussed at length in Section II of this book ("Measuring market risk") there are a number of risk measurement methods and tools that can be used in a complementary fashion. Taking advantage of multiple tools contributes additional dimensions to the analysis of risk.

For example, consider the risks in an option portfolio. An option trader might want to calculate the delta (sensitivity to changes in the underlying price or rate), gamma (the change in delta with respect to changes in the underlying price or rate – ie, the degree of non-linearity), vega (net volatility sensitivity) and theta (time decay). The trader might also use stress tests that provide information about profit and loss profiles by stressing a single dimension over a short time horizon. At the firm level scenario analyses, which measure the effect of stressing multiple dimensions over a longer time horizon, might be more appropriate. Stress testing and scenario analysis are discussed in greater detail in Chapters 6 and 8.

Typical risk analysis questions

In the previous chapter we discussed how providing a value-added service to traders and senior management facilitates acceptance of the risk management process. The key is that the analysis provided must be useful to all levels of users so that informed trading and risk management decisions can be taken.

In a diverse global firm, typical queries can run the gamut from simple to complex. We saw some examples in Chapter 1, and others might be along the following lines:

- *Why did my portfolio risk change when I did not change my positions significantly?* Often, changes in the underlying asset returns can cause a change in the risk if a covariance matrix is recalculated each day. An analyst would first check whether the positions are being captured correctly and would then look at asset returns for a possible explanation.
- *What would happen to my risk if I made the following trade?* A risk system should allow the ability to manipulate positions in order to run sample portfolios to answer this question. Ideally, the trader should be able to easily run current positions through the risk model for ad hoc risk calculation.
- *My risk is too high – there must be something wrong with your model.* This question most often arises when a trader is at or over a limit. Rarely does a trader complain that the calculated risk is too low! In this case, the risk analyst would check to make sure that positions, analytics and model return data are correct. There might be different assumptions used in the model, such as the horizon of the historical data. For example, a trader might observe that recent volatility is low. However, if the risk system is incorporating a significant history of data, recent lower levels of volatility will not have an immediate strong impact to the calculation, unless the data is decayed sharply.
- *Where is my risk coming from?* This query arises so often that perhaps the most effective way to address it is to create a report that decomposes the risk of a portfolio. The resulting report helps a trader or risk manager understand where the drivers of risk are. Decomposition of risk is discussed in more detail later in this chapter.
- *Given this large, complex portfolio, what should I be concerned about?* Again, this is an often asked question. A risk manager of several trading desks with complex portfolios may not be able to discern easily what the main strategy or bias of the

overall portfolio is. In this case, a replicating portfolio, which reduces a complex portfolio down to a simple portfolio can aid in this analysis. The best-replicating portfolio concept is also discussed in more detail later in this chapter.

For the number of typical queries, there are as many atypical questions as well. Indeed, this is what makes risk analysis challenging and interesting. Successful and valuable risk analysis is highly dependent upon experience, the availability of good analysis and diagnostic tools, and access to the required data.

Data integrity
As we discussed in Chapter 15, the reports that are produced to measure and decompose risk are only as good as the data fed into the risk model. An effective risk monitoring function is responsible for the integrity of the inputs and outputs of the risk system. Data "scrubbing" is the essential, albeit unglamorous, key to a credible risk management process. Bad data issues can arise in a number of ways – incorrect or incomplete historical data used to measure risk, incorrect or missing position data, or incorrect analytic information (such as option deltas).

For example, if a portfolio's risk has jumped from the previous day due to a significant outright short position for a trader that rarely takes one-sided bets, there is a good chance that the risk calculation is incorrect, probably due to missing positions or position breaks. This is a shortcoming of many risk systems that run risk calculations overnight in a batch process without a review. Manual intervention is critical to ensuring the integrity of the information.

Reporting of risk numbers, therefore, needs to be preceded by a careful process of reviewing and reconciling the data coming from potentially multiple feeding systems. For example, consider the following scenario: if a particular desk is net long the market, this is probably something that senior management should be informed of, unless it is commonly accepted practice on that desk. The desk might dispute the number, particularly if the position held goes against senior management's thinking. This can lead to disagreements about the risk system positions, potentially damaging the credibility that has been built up. This demonstrates why it is critical to treat the risk data with the same degree of care used in reconciling the firm's books and records.

Reporting
Risk information is really only useful if the right information is available to the appropriate people at the right time. Data collection and processing needs to be highly efficient so that accurate risk results are available as early in the day as possible. Distribution should occur without delays, eg, via on-line risk management systems, but within the necessary level of confidentiality.

Furthermore, reporting requirements vary widely: as we outlined in the previous chapter, the risk management group interacts with a variety of areas across the firm – eg, the back office, middle office, front office and senior management. Assessing the information needs of such a variety of groups is challenging. What might be important information for a trader may not be relevant for the chairman of the firm. One person may need very high-level information, while another may require finer granularity. Frequent dialogue between the risk management group and the users of risk information is key to accurately assessing information requirements. Just as in any other function, risk reporting must be targeted and selective in order to be appropriate for its audience.

Backtesting

Backtesting (see Chapter 12) is an important step in ensuring the integrity of risk reporting because it serves to validate the model. It compares the daily risk calculated by the model to the actual daily profit or loss recorded on the books, and should be performed on a regular basis. Action should be taken based on the results of backtesting, either to fine tune the risk model(s) or to evaluate the pricing and P&L process.

Tools for effective risk management

In order to provide useful value-added information to senior management and the front office, a risk management group should have access to a set of effective tools. The key is to develop tools that appeal to all the users of risk information – traders, senior management and risk management professionals. To accomplish this, an effective risk system should provide the ability to disaggregate or "drill down" to the level pertinent to the user. For example, a trader might use risk tools to analyse a specific portfolio, while a firmwide risk manager might use the same tools for the firm's trading book as a whole.

It is also beneficial for a risk management system to provide additional analyses such as risk decomposition, identifying potential hedges and demonstrating simple representations of complex portfolios. The following describes tools that assist in the analysis and interpretation of the risk of a portfolio.

Portfolio reports

The portfolio report shows, both in a summary and detailed way, a portfolio's holdings. A trader might use this report to confirm that the risk system is capturing all of the portfolio's exposures. At a higher level, a firmwide risk manager may wish to see how much the firm is holding in a particular asset, such as with large or suspected market moves. For example, in February 1994, US–Japan trade talks broke down over the weekend and the Japanese yen moved 3.4 per cent. A firmwide risk manager would have wanted to know the firm's $/yen position before leaving on the Friday before so that the firm could make an educated decision about whether to hedge the yen holdings during this period of uncertainty.

A portfolio report can provide position information at the asset class level as well as measures of risk. It may be helpful to include a summary page along with the detailed breakdown of a portfolio's holdings, particularly when the portfolio is large and diversified. A sample summary report is shown in Exhibit 11.1, and the various currencies are listed along the top with asset categories listed down the left-hand side. In the summary report, fixed income instruments are bracketed into maturity bands, and the positions are expressed in terms of US 10-year equivalents. Currency, commodity and equity positions are expressed as US dollar market value and all amounts are presented in millions. The fixed income portfolio presented is long eg, Italy (US$21.4 million 10-year equivalents) and ECU (US$46.5 million) and short eg, France (US$145.2 million) and the UK (US$47.1 million). In total it is short US$123.7 million 10-year equivalents.

A trader might also want to see a more detailed position report, as displayed in Exhibit 11.2, which shows all information broken down to the individual asset class level. The way in which information is displayed should also be customised to user specifications – eg, currency denomination and bracketing of information – for different desks and business units.

Exhibit 11.1 Sample portfolio summary report

Global risk system
Positions as of: 10/6/97
All positions in US$ millions

XYZ portfolio
US-10 year equivalent
Summary

Portfolio risk*: 0.444
Value at risk**: 1.774

Mkt exposure:*** (ger10)-83.3
% or risk explained = 19.6%

Assets held	Totals	us	uk	ger	fra	bgm	ita	spn	swe	fin	nor	ecu
Currency exposure	0.18		0.00	11.62	45.23	0.00	0.00	0.00	0.00	0.40	-0.08	-56.98
1–12 months totals	-91.47	-5.19	-93.52	1.86	-2.13	-0.13	0.00	0.78	6.73	0.12	0.00	0.00
1–12 months (3m equiv.)	2654.81	-150.62	-2714.09	54.09	-61.96	-3.63	0.00	22.56	195.41	3.42	0.00	0.00
2–5yr totals	209.54	0.00	138.31	80.19	-20.54	-0.15	0.00	7.78	2.08	1.86	0.00	0.00
7–12yr totals	-195.45	0.00	-25.31	-135.40	-117.52	2.15	21.38	2.23	-1.12	11.67	0.00	46.47
15–30yr totals	-25.43	0.00	-66.56	46.12	-4.99	0.00	0.00	0.00	0.00	0.00	0.00	0.00
SWAP	-20.91	0.00	0.00	0.00	0.00	0.00	0.00	-20.91	0.00	0.00	0.00	0.00
FI US 10yr equiv	-123.72	-5.19	-47.08	-7.22	-145.18	1.88	21.38	-10.11	7.69	13.66	0.00	46.47

* Standard deviation of daily P&L in US$ millions.

** Value at risk is defined to be the expected daily loss in a given year in US$ millions.

*** Current position in specified asset minus the risk minimising position.

Exhibit 11.2   Sample detailed portfolio position report

Global risk system **XYZ portfolio** Portfolio risk*: 0.444
Positions as of: 10/6/97 Portfolio position report Value at risk**: 1.774
All positions in US$ millions

Mkt exposure: (ger10)***:-83.3
% or risk explained = 19.6%

Assets held	Totals	ger	fra	uk	spn	ECU	ita
Currency	0.18	11.62	45.23	0.00	0.00	-56.98	0.00
Futures (3M # 1)	-9.21		2.21	-11.42			
Futures (3M # 2)	-42.11	-5.19	1.51	-50.51			
Futures (3M # 3)	-25.79	-15.58		-15.58			
Bond (2yr)	-22.12	-1.79	-10.84	-10.35			
Bond (3yr)	23.80	-28.75		-8.26	1.76		
Bond (4yr)	2.05	5.87		-3.82			
Bond (5yr)	158.45		-9.70	160.74	6.02		
Futures (5yr)	47.36	47.36					
Bond (7yr)	73.88		101.32	-70.33		23.31	
Bond (10yr)	-123.81	2.10	-135.95	-48.45	42.21	23.16	
Future (10yr)	-145.51	-137.39	-82.89	93.47	39.98		21.38
Bond (20yr)	-40.25		11.46	-51.71			
Bond (30yr)	14.82	46.12	-16.44	-14.85			
Swap (8yr)	-18.17						

* Standard deviation of daily P&L in US$ millions.
** Value at risk is defined to be the expected daily loss in a given year in US$ millions.
*** Current position in specified asset minus the risk minimising position.

In the upper right-hand corner of the report, the portfolio risk measures are displayed. Risk in this report is stated in terms of:

- *Portfolio risk:* A one standard deviation measure of risk – that is, the amount of profit or loss that could be expected to be exceeded, in a given day, approximately one-third of the time given the current positions.
- *Value at risk (VaR):* The amount of loss that could be expected to be exceeded, in a given day, no more than once per year given the current positions (see Chapter 7 for more about VaR).

The portfolio risk, or volatility of the portfolio, is obtained by combining measures of exposures in a set of asset classes with a covariance matrix that provides numerical estimates of the volatilities and correlations of the returns of those asset classes. It is a measure of the standard deviation in the return distribution, providing an estimate of the size of a "typical" return over a particular period. The fact that it is typical makes it easy to validate through observation. However, also because it is typical, the number may not be of great concern to a risk manager.

The VaR is a measure of a point in the distribution of possible outcomes (gains and losses). In this model, the VaR horizon is a one-day, once-a-year event, and a non-normal distribution is assumed.

The last line in the upper right corner is the market exposure, representing the portfolio's exposure to the overall market expressed in terms of one asset[1]. Market exposure is computed by explicitly accounting for the volatilities and correlations of different assets. It could be presented in terms of one or several assets (eg, US 10-year bonds, JGB futures, German 10-year bonds, etc). The market exposure explains how much of that asset could be purchased or sold in order to make the portfolio have zero market exposure; in other words, to be market-neutral.

The market exposure in Exhibit 11.2 is short US$83.3 million German 10-year bond equivalents, indicating that this primarily European fixed income portfolio is short the overall market. The reader might notice that the 10-year equivalent for the German sector is not nearly that short (US$7.2 million). The market exposure in this portfolio is merely expressed in terms of exposure to the German 10-year; however, it could as easily been defined as French or ECU bonds. In order to take the short market directionality out of this portfolio, the holder should buy US$83.3 million of the German 10-year bond. The "% of risk explained" indicates that the market exposure explains 19.6 per cent of the calculated risk of US$0.444 million.

The usefulness of this report notwithstanding, it does not give an indication as to which assets are contributing the most to the risk of the portfolio. The following report does so by displaying a decomposition of risk.

Decomposition of risk – hot spots reports

Risk is not additive, which makes it difficult to create a simple decomposition of risk. The total risk of a portfolio is the sum of the marginal impacts on the portfolio's risk from small percentage increases in each of the positions. The computation of the decomposition of risk is a function of percentage changes in position size.

A sample "hot spots"[2] report is shown in Exhibit 11.3. It displays the decomposition of the risk of a portfolio. The decomposition is sorted according to the countries and asset classes that create the largest contributions to risk. Positive numbers indicate the position adds to the risk of the portfolio, while negative numbers indicate that the position acts to reduce the risk of the portfolio. The report is shaded to indicate "hot spots", or large contributors, and "cool spots" which represent risk reducers. The contribution is displayed in percentage terms. The subscript numbers represent the size of the position in millions of US dollars.

In this report, France is contributing 80.70 per cent to the volatility of the portfolio, with the 10-year future contributing 40.51 per cent with a position size of short US$101.4 million of 10-year futures, the 10-year bond contributing 63.73 per cent with a short position of US$126 million and the 7-year bond as a risk reducer (–48.82 per cent) with a position of US$147.1 million. The ECU is also a risk reducer (–34.76 per cent).

This decomposition report enables a portfolio or risk manager to clearly see where the risk lies in a particular portfolio. The next obvious question – what to do about it?

Best hedge reports

A best hedge report can be created by measuring the purchase or sale of each individual asset required to reach the risk-minimising position and then calculating and sorting on the percentage risk reduction achieved through that purchase or sale. A sample best hedge report is shown in Exhibit 11.4. The subscript number represents the best hedge or the actual purchase or sale of that particular asset required and the other number represents the percentage reduction in risk obtained by putting on the best hedge.

Exhibit 11.3 Hot and cool spots

Hot spots: Largest contributions to volatility sorted by asset class and country

XYZ Portfolio 10/6/97 Daily risk = US $0.444 million

% of risk, *Position*	Total	France	ECU	Germany	United Kingdom	Spain
Total	100.00	80.70	-34.76	28.75	26.77	8.65
Futures (10yr #1)	65.63	40.52		63.76	-46.60	15.31
		-101.37		-137.47	96.92	-51.01
Bond (10yr)	67.48	63.73	-10.07	-0.87	24.35	-11.84
		-126.02	25.51	2.04	-47.96	44.25
Bond (7yr)	-27.46	-48.82	-9.68		36.97	
		147.12	30.64		-101.10	
Bond (5yr)	-77.32	3.95			-79.26	-1.67
		-17.12			283.26	11.45
Currency exposure	3.87	14.83	-15.00	3.94		0.00
		45.23	-58.98	11.62		0.00
Bond (30yr)	-2.81	8.38		-17.91	6.72	
		-9.24		26.64	-9.44	
Bond (20yr)	19.03	-5.83			24.96	
		7.58			-43.95	
Futures (3M #2)	23.53	-0.46		-0.60	22.31	
		43.03		343.72	-1437.26	
Futures (3M #6)	18.99				18.99	
					-840.77	
Futures (5yr #1)	-14.15			-14.15		
				86.09		
Bond (3yr)	-1.29			-5.21	4.47	-0.34
				80.64	-26.23	5.20
Futures (3M #4)	-6.18	1.82			-8.00	
		-172.06			382.65	
Futures (3M #3)	9.42			1.12	8.30	
				-290.68	-443.19	
Other	21.36	2.57		-1.34	12.64	7.19

For the European portfolio we have been following, this report indicates that the best hedge is the French 30-year bond. If the portfolio holder purchased US$54.34 million of the 30-year, the portfolio risk would be reduced by 28.78 per cent. If, however, the portfolio holder did not wish to trade the French 30-year, other assets in the portfolio are listed, with the risk-minimising position for each and the percentage reduction achieved by putting it on as a hedge. Note that the risk-minimising position or best hedge for the German 10-year is US$83.3 million, matching the market exposure described in (Exhibit 11.2). Recall that the definition of market exposure is the risk-minimising position in a particular asset. At the risk-minimising position, the portfolio is uncorrelated with the asset, representing a market-neutral position

Exhibit 11.4 Sample best hedge report (US$ millions)

Best hedge: **XYZ Portfolio** Best hedge sorted by asset class and country
10/6/97 Daily risk = US$0.444 million

% change risk, *best hedge*

	Max	France	Germany	United Kingdom	ECU	Spain
Max	-28.78	-28.78	-25.56	-18.41	-15.76	-6.62
Bond (30 yr)	-28.78-	28.78	-17.41	-16.94		
		54.34	47.30	43.57		
Bond (20 yr)	-28.51	-28.51		-13.50		
		63.43		44.50		
Bond (10 yr)	-27.53	-27.53	-19.61	-14.89	-15.76	-4.09
		93.89	83.31	54.24	73.53	29.95
Futures (10Y #1)	-25.56	-25.43	-25.56	-12.68		-5.25
		111.05	96.12	49.41		34.04
Bond (7 yr)	-22.30	-22.30		-15.96	-14.67	
		119.42		85.90	86.04	
Futures (3M #6)	-18.41			-18.41		
				1480.12		
Bond (5 yr)	-18.04	-18.04		-14.85		
		142.28		98.24		

relative to that asset. The percentage reduction is 19.6 per cent, which matches the percentage of risk explained by market exposure.

Best replicating portfolio reports

The best replicating report is a generalisation of the best hedge report. For most portfolios, it is unlikely that one asset can hedge it fully. A small combination of assets, replicating the primary risks of the portfolio, may help identify a series of trades that would provide an effective hedge. Further, in order to better understand the dynamics in a complex portfolio, it may be helpful to describe it in terms of a simple, replicating portfolio.

This simplified portfolio view can be derived by using an algorithm to identify and compute a sub-set of assets that best replicate the risk of the portfolio. An example of a best replicating report is illustrated in Exhibit 11.5.

The report shows the weights of the selected assets, the percentage contribution to risk for each asset and the percentage of the portfolio's risk explained by that asset. The replicating portfolio, by taking into account the entire portfolio and summarising the risk in just a few assets, can demonstrate what market views are represented in the portfolio.

Both the best replicating portfolio and the hot spots reports provide similar information – where the risks are coming from. The hot spots report provides more detail or disaggregation while the best replicating portfolio report is most useful in summarising large complex portfolios. However, the hot spots report can reveal the role a particular asset is playing within the portfolio, which the replicating portfolio may not.

Exhibit 11.5 shows the best replicating portfolio report for the portfolio outlined earlier. There are three best replicating portfolios calculated, with three, five or ten assets. Note that as the number of assets in the replicating portfolio is increased, more of the risk is explained. The "% of risk explained" is an indication of the degree of diversification. For example, if one could explain greater than 95 per cent of the risk of a large portfolio with just three assets, that portfolio would not be very diversified.

In this example, the three-asset portfolio comprises the French 10-year bond, the

---

Exhibit 11.5 Sample best replicating portfolio report

10/06/97   Best replicating portfolio report   1
17:18:03   **XYZ portfolio**
Portfolio risk = 0.444

Replicating portfolio consisting of 3 assets:

Country	Sector	Equiv. weight	% Contribution
France	Bond (10yr)	-180.29	132.87
ECU	Bond (7yr)	131.61	-60.61
United Kingdom	Future (3M #2)	-1226.49	27.74

Replicating portfolio risk = 0.367, Residual risk = 0.248, % of risk explained = 43.99%

Replicating portfolio consisting of 5 assets:

Country	Sector	Equiv. weight	% Contribution
France	Bond (10yr)	-138.03	91.11
Germany	Futures (10yr)	-78.72	47.66
ECU	Bond (7yr)	108.43	-44.73
United Kingdom	Future (3M #2)	-1182.56	23.96
Germany	Bond (3yr)	213.46	-18.01

Replicating portfolio risk = 0.388, Residual risk = 0.215, % of risk explained = 51.64%

Replicating portfolio consisting of 10 assets:

Country	Sector	Equiv. weight	% Contribution
UK	Bond (5yr)	353.98	-112.82
UK	Bond (7yr)	-169.76	66.13
Germany	Futures (10yr)	-109.97	58.1
ECU	Bond (7yr)	118.67	-42.72
France	Future (10yr)	-89.54	40.77
France	Bond (10yr)	-66.11	38.08
UK	Future (3M #6)	-1407.32	36.21
UK	Future (3M #2)	-1991.55	35.21
Germany	Bond (3yr)	201.72	-14.85
Italy	Futures (10yr)	13.28	-4.11

Replicating portfolio risk = 0.416, Residual risk = 0.155, % of risk explained = 65.06%

ECU 7-year bond and the UK 3-month future. This is not surprising, because all three assets appear in hot spots as large contributors to risk. The best replicating portfolio summarises the portfolio concisely by showing that it is basically short France and UK and long the ECU. If more detail is needed, the 5 and 10 asset portfolios provide more colour.

Implied views reports

Often positions are the aggregate of many individual decisions by traders operating in many different markets, rather than the result of a large portfolio optimisation. As such, an individual trader's stated views on a particular position may be different from those expressed in the overall portfolio. Or a portfolio manager may have specific views on the market, but the portfolio is not behaving in a manner consistent with those views. It can be beneficial to be able to interpret the views implied by the portfolio itself.

An implied views report reverse engineers the portfolio. Instead of taking a portfolio holder's view on the markets as the input, the portfolio itself is used as the input and, from that, a set of implied views of expected asset returns is created. In general, the neutral position for any given asset is a function of all the other positions in the portfolio. A long position (or overweight the benchmark) can represent a bearish view; similarly, a short position can represent a bullish view. It all depends on the relationship of that position to the other positions in the portfolio. A long position can represent a bearish view if the position is negatively correlated with the returns of the rest of the portfolio. In order to understand what view a particular asset represents, the risk manager must understand the volatilities and correlations of the returns of all of the assets in the portfolio. This can be a difficult and counter-intuitive analysis without an implied views report.

To understand how an implied views analysis might be used, consider the following scenario. A European trader had a large short position in Deutschmarks. In the same portfolio the trader was long the US long bond in a lesser, but still significant amount. On looking at the implied views report, the trader saw that the implied view on the bond position was a bearish outlook. Of course this was not the trader's view at all – the trader was bullish on the US bond market, hence the long position, so naturally the risk model was believed to be wrong. What actually happened was that the trader was looking at these two trades separately, as two distinct trading strategies, although he or she was holding a portfolio of positions. In this case, the negative correlation of the two assets and the weightings in each implied a bearish view on the US bond market. In order to express its bullish view, the desk had to increase the bond position three-fold.

In Exhibit 11.6 the sample implied views report shows the annualised expected excess returns of each asset class for the portfolio we have been following. The annualised expected excess returns for the French, UK, German and Spanish bonds are all negative. This is fairly intuitive because the portfolio is overall short in these countries. What are not so intuitive, however, are the negative returns for the ECU and Italian sectors, since the portfolio is long these bonds. As stated earlier, it is the relationship of the returns of each of the Italian and ECU bonds with the rest of the portfolio that determines the views expressed in the implied views report.

147

Exhibit 11.6 Sample implied views report

| Global risk system | | **XYZ portfolio** | | Portfolio risk*: 0.444 | |
| Positions as of: 10/6/97 | | Implied views | | Value at risk**: 1.774 | |

Assets held	ger	fra	uk	spn	ECU	ita
Currency	0.07	0.07	0.02	0.07	0.05	0.06
Bond (2yr)	-0.01	-0.01	-0.02			
Bond (3yr)	-0.01		-0.03	-0.01		
Bond (4yr)	-0.03					
Bond (5yr)		-0.05	-0.06	-0.03		
Futures (5yr)	-0.03					
Bond (7yr)		-0.07	-0.07		-0.06	
Bond (10yr)	-0.08	-0.1	-0.1	-0.05	-0.08	
Futures (10yr)	-0.09	-0.08	-0.1	-0.06		-0.05
Bond (20yr)		-0.15	-0.11			
Bond (30yr)	-0.13	-0.18	-0.14			
Swap (8yr)				-0.06		

* Standard deviation of daily P&L in US$ millions.

** Value at risk is defined to be the expected daily loss in a given year in US$ millions. Annualised expected excess returns.

Stress test reports

So far we have described a few of the VaR reports that might be helpful in analysing risk. Undoubtedly there are many more possibilities, such as for treatments of specific products or markets that require different views of information, or for customised views based on a firm's organisational structure. We now turn to examples of stress tests, which, as discussed in Chapter 6, typically apply a significant stress to a single risk dimension.

Exhibit 11.7 is an example of a stress text report for the Interest Rates book. It shows gains and losses per risk factor (currency) in the case of an instantaneous market move by -100, -50, -5, +5, +50, +100 basis points respectively. The gains and losses do not increase in a linear fashion: for French francs (Ffr) a move of 100 basis points would result in a gain regardless of the direction of the movement (US$47.6 million and US$51.5 million respectively). Such non-linear behaviour is typical for a portfolio with a high proportion of derivatives. The traditional derivatives risk measures Δ (change of the portfolio value for a given change in the underlying price or rate, here 1 bp) and Γ (the change of Δ for a given change in the underlying price or rate) and τ (sensitivity of the portfolio value to changes in the volatility) are given additionally in the last three columns.

For the purpose of limit control an individual risk factor loss shock (RFL Shock) is defined for each currency. The loss resulting from an upward or downward movement by this amount may not exceed the limit defined for each currency. In the given example the risk factor loss shock for DM is +/- 60 bp. An upward movement would result in a loss of US$17.0 million, a downward movement in a gain of US$43.4 million. The risk factor loss utilisation, ie, the utilisation of the RFL limit, is therefore US$17.0 million, well below the limit of US$50 million.

For aggregation across the currencies perfect correlation is assumed within all

Exhibit 11.7 Stress test report

In US$ million — Risk factor info - interest rates

Risk Factor	Limit info		RFL shocks	Exposures		Shock slides						Derivatives		
	Limit	Util	Shocks	Down	Up	-100 bp	-50 bp	-5 bp	5 bp	50 bp	100 bp	Δ	Γ	τ
Total	**250**	**-121.8**												
Industrialised	**200**	**-113.3**												
Core Europe	**100**	**-45.7**		**127.0**	**-45.7**									
Sfr	50	-13.7	+/-60 bp	27.3	-13.7	57.3	20.7	1.5	-1.2	-10.9	-24.4	-0.25	0.04	9.81
DM	50	-17.0	+/-60 bp	43.4	-17.0	79.5	34.6	2.6	-2.3	-15.3	-24.9	-0.48	0.01	31.80
Ffr	50	0.0	+/-60 bp	21.4	18.4	47.6	16.2	0.6	-0.2	11.4	51.5	-0.07	0.01	11.97
XEU	50	-33.4	+/-100 bp	34.8	-33.4	34.8	17.2	1.7	-1.7	-16.8	-33.4	-0.34	0	-0.01
North America	**100**	**-33.6**		**77.5**	**-33.6**									
C$	50	-7.4	+/-100 bp	4.4	-7.4	4.4	2.7	0.3	-0.3	-3.5	-7.4	-0.06	0	0.67
US$ million	50	-26.3	+/-80 bp	73.1	-26.3	96.5	38.7	2.7	-2.6	-20.1	-28.8	-0.54	-0.02	23.10
Other	100	-34.0		--	--									
Pta	30	-2.1	+/-100 bp	-2.1	0.9	-2.1	-2.0	-0.1	0.2	-1.1	0.9	0.04	0.01	-2.15
S	50	-18.6	+/-100 bp	-18.6	70.7	-18.6	-12.9	-1.7	1.7	23.4	70.7	0.32	-0.02	2.28
L	30	-13.3	+/-100 bp	-13.3	16.2	-13.3	-6.5	-0.7	0.7	7.9	16.2	0.14	0.00	-0.92
¥	50	0.0	+/-60 bp	27.5	34.6	51.8	22.2	0.9	0.0	22.4	97.9	-0.03	0.12	-2.30
Em Markets	**75**	**-8.5**		**1.8**	**-1.5**									
Asia Pacific	**30**	**-1.5**		**1.8**	**-1.5**									
HK$	20	-2.5	+/-160 bp	-2.5	2.3	-1.5	-0.8	-0.1	0.1	0.8	1.5	0.02	0	1.00
Rp	20	-6.6	+/-160 bp	6.9	-6.6	4.3	2.1	0.2	-0.2	-2.1	-4.1	-0.04	0	0
M$	20	-3.3	+/-160 bp	-3.3	3.3	-2.0	-1.0	-0.1	0.1	1.0	2.0	0.02	0	0
Ps	20	-2.1	+/-320 bp	2.1	-2.1	0.7	0.3	0.0	0.0	-0.3	-0.7	-0.01	0	0
Bt	20	-1.5	+/-160 bp	-1.5	1.6	-1.0	-0.5	0.0	0.0	0.5	1.0	0	0	0.36
Emerging Europe	**30**	**-4.9**		**5.2**	**-4.9**									
$	10	-0.9	+/-160 bp	1.3	-0.9	0.8	0.4	0.0	0.0	-0.3	-0.6	-0.01	0	0.05
Kr	20	-0.9	+/-160 bp	0.8	-0.9	0.5	0.3	0.0	0.0	-0.3	-0.5	-0.00	0	0
Ft	10	-1.8	+/-240 bp	1.8	-1.8	0.8	0.4	0.0	0.0	-0.4	-0.8	-0.01	0	0
PLN	20	-1.3	+/-240 bp	1.3	-1.3	0.5	0.3	0.0	0.0	-0.3	-0.5	-0.01	0	0
Latin America	**30**	**-2.1**		**1.2**	**-2.1**									
ARS	20	-1.7	+/-320 bp	-1.7	1.3	-0.5	-0.3	0.0	0.0	0.2	0.4	0.00	0	0
MXN	20	-2.1	+/-320 bp	2.1	-2.1	0.7	0.3	0.0	0.0	-0.3	-0.6	-0.01	0	0
VEB	20	-1.3	+/-320 bp	0.7	-1.3	0.3	0.1	0.0	0.0	-0.2	-0.4	-0.00	0	0

currency groups except for the group "Other", which is calculated as worst case in each individual currency. The utilisation of each of these groups is then added to give the Industrialised and Emerging Markets utilisations. These totals are then combined to give the overall total utilisation.

The total utilisation derived from such a stress loss analysis should not be compared with the total VaR number. As discussed in more detail in Chapter 6, stress testing is to prepare for extreme situations with strong risk factor movements and a breakdown of historical correlations. The total utilisation generated above should therefore be seen more like a highly conservative assessment of potential stress losses which might arise from our portfolio.

Information display

At both Goldman Sachs and Swiss Bank Corporation it has been our experience that risk management, and therefore the reporting of risk results, is a continuously evolving process that benefits from the contributions of numerous thinkers. To facilitate that kind of cross-fertilisation of ideas, in addition to performing a comprehensive risk management function, it is essential to distribute the risk information effectively. We now turn to describing how the information might be displayed and aggregated for various users throughout the firm.

As stated earlier, the key to effective risk management is getting accurate information to the right people on a timely basis. Ideally, this risk information is communicated via an aggregation vehicle that displays information at various views and levels.

Exhibit 11.8 An overview of information requirements

Management Level	Level of aggregation	Design characteristics
CEO, Board	Aggregation of risk across the firm	– focus on overview – highly aggregated assessments – only the largest or riskiest strategies/positions listed – trend reports – bar and pie charts, overview tables – use of 'traffic lights' – weekly, monthly, quarterly, rarely daily reports
Division Head	Aggregation of risk at business unit level	– highly aggregated assessments, but additionally ability to delve into details – daily, weekly, monthly reports
Business Unit Head	Aggregation of risk at desk level	– detailed summary tables – often focus on only one risk category – real time and daily reports
Traders	Individual positions and risk exposures	– individual positions – detailed – mainly tables – real time and daily reports

Design of information

The information requirements for risk management vary depending upon the audience. Good risk reporting should appeal to users at all levels within an organisation, from the CEO downwards. All levels of an organisation should be able to see a consistent view of information, tailored for their functional needs (See Exhibit 11.8). Perhaps the most important consideration here is that there must be absolute consistency between the different levels of reporting. The high level reports should always be built up from the reports used at the lowest level and it should be a simple matter to drill down from the most aggregated report to any level of detail. Nothing undermines the integrity of reporting more quickly than reports at different levels which can not be reconciled.

The information displayed should not be restricted to showing a VaR calculation alone. While relaying VaR versus established limits is important, limit monitoring is not the complete picture. Other pieces of information might be market concentration, the P&L, standard deviation, the Sharpe ratio of a particular portfolio, or a particularly large market move. Reports for senior managers are strongly focused on providing overviews. Details are mentioned where it is necessary to draw senior managers' attention to particular areas of interest or concern. Exhibit 11.9 shows an example of a typical high level risk report.

The information requirements of the front office, or of anywhere within an organisation, are typically dynamic. The personnel providing risk information should be sensitive to, among other things, a changing organisational structure or changing market conditions when assessing what should be communicated. For example, a small currency position in the Philippine peso may not normally warrant a highlight to senior management on any given day. However, that peso position, even if insignificant in comparison with the rest of the portfolio, should be on top of the highlight list on the day the currency is devalued by roughly 8 per cent, as it was in July 1997.

As we stressed earlier, establishing a common language is also critical for effective risk management. Portfolio risk and risk limits should be expressed in common units so that they are comparable. Consider, for example, if one trading desk reported risk in terms of a weekly VaR with a confidence interval of 99 per cent, while another used a daily VaR with a confidence interval of 67 per cent. It would be difficult to compare the two risks without taking out a calculator to adjust the numbers to a comparable standard. Ideally, a limit structure and the subsequent limit reporting should be on a consistent basis across an organisation.

Information flows to the front office

Laying a foundation

As we introduced in Chapters 1 and 10, the integration of effective risk management in an organisation requires a proper dialogue on all aspects of risk. When a risk management framework is put in place, the policies and procedures that will be followed must be communicated to the front office (traders, risk managers and portfolio managers). The same thing is true for VaR limits. Traders and risk managers must know what limits have been placed on their businesses. Ideally, there should be a two-way conversation between senior management and the trading heads at the time the limits are set. This is not to say that the traders themselves set the limits, but rather they have some input in the decision-making process. This exchange might be in the form of a discussion of the business strategy, expected revenue and past performance.

Exhibit 11.9 High level risk report

| **Executive Summary** | **Market Risk** |

General Assessment      Green: no measures necessary at the moment
Yellow: there are issues which require closer attention
Red: Urgent action necessary

Material Developments

There was substantially increased volatility in all equity markets in the last reporting period. As a consequence the standard deviation of total daily revenue increased to US$41.5 million. However, mean daily total revenue remained stable. Market risk in FX increased slightly, mainly due to new long positions in DM against US$ and Ffr against US$. Widening of the spreads in Russian and Mexican bonds increased risk in the rates book, however, utilisation is still within the risk limits. Long position in US Treasury bond futures remains unchanged. See Appendix for more details.

in US$ million	1st quarter	2nd quarter	3rd quarter	YTD
Mean daily total revenue	38.4	48.9	47.1	44.8
Standard deviation of total daily revenue	35.7	38.7	41.5	38.7

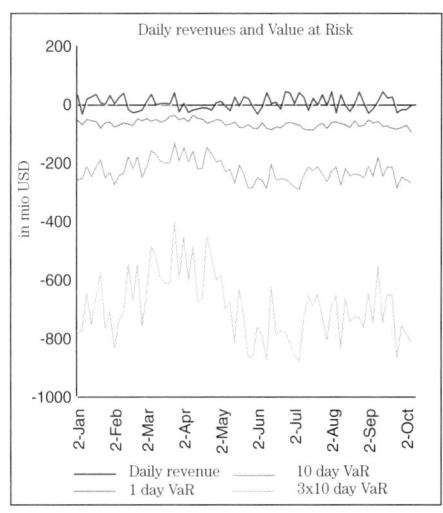

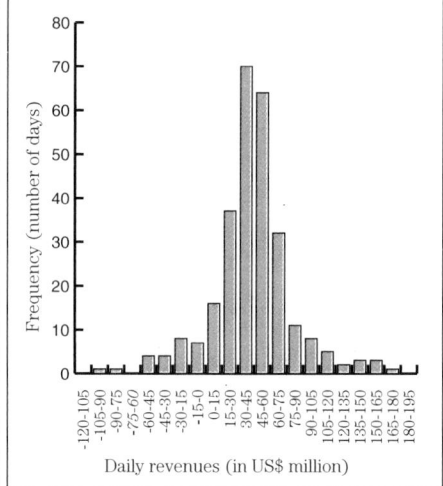

This chart shows the trend of daily revenues and Value-at-Risk measures since the beginning of the year

This chart shows a histogram of daily revenues over the past 12 months

Value at Risk and limits

Backtesting confirms that excesses against the 1-day VaR observed so far this year are in accordance with the statistical properties of the model.

Holding period	Confidence interval 99%	95%	90%
1 day	-88.5	-61.3	-45.3
10 day	-290.5	-198.8	-150.8

VaR limit utilisation in US$ million

	Total	Rates	EQ	FX
General market risk	-290.5	-196.8	-120.8	-199.7
Residual risk	-75.7	-39.3	-56.0	0.0
Total risk	-366.2	-236.1	-176.8	-199.7
Limit	950.0	350.0	550.0	550.0

Stress Loss Limit Utilisation

RFL utilisation and limits in US$ million

	Total	Rates	EQ	FX
Utilisation	1149.1	461.2	288.6	399.2
Limit	1500.0	500.0	450.0	550.0

The methodology used to calculate VaR and the theory behind any accompanying analysis should also be conveyed. Without an adequate understanding of the underpinnings of the VaR calculation, the traders and other front office personnel will not be able to manage to a VaR limit effectively, which can weaken the credibility of the risk model.

If VaR and accompanying risk analyses are displayed on a front-end user interface, all users should receive adequate training in the use of the system. Additional reports, such as those discussed earlier in this chapter, should be explained to the users so that they can use the information correctly and effectively.

Essential elements

There are some essential elements of risk information that the front office needs on a daily basis. First and most obvious, the daily (if appropriate) VaR limit report should be made available as soon as possible after the day's trading is over. If there are significant changes to a portfolio's risk profile from the previous day, some explanation may be required.

Some organisations set their limit policy so that a trader or portfolio manager must be within a VaR limit at all times, rather than just at the end of the day. In this case, the ability to calculate intra-day VaR is critical. Real-time VaR may not be easy to implement, however, depending upon how many systems feeds are required and the quality of the data coming from those systems as discussed later in Chapter 15. In addition, if the data is not accurate and reconciled, it can just introduce "noise" in the risk exposures, setting off unwarranted alarms.

A compromise might be to allow positions and analytics to be fed from a trading system to a segregated area in the risk model for an individual trader. The trader could then run risk anytime during the day. Ideally, the trader or portfolio manager should be able to put in potential trades to see how VaR is impacted. In this way, accidental violations of VaR limits can be reduced by the traders' awareness of their VaR profile throughout the day.

An essential function performed in the risk management area is backtesting (discussed in Chapter 12). The results of the model backtesting should be conveyed to the front office as an important step in obtaining their acceptance of the risk models used. One of the first questions asked when a new product is modelled for risk purposes is "How does this compare to the actual P&L?"

Information requirements of senior management

As we saw in Chapter 1, an accurate risk analysis is facilitated when the front office and senior management communicate their concerns. While some of these concerns may be obvious to the risk group, such as the effect of a Mexican peso devaluation, others may be subtle. For example, senior management might wish to monitor the risk for a particular trading unit because of concerns over that area's trading strategies. They might desire relative-value trading as the general strategy as opposed to outright speculation, and would therefore ask risk management to track where the risk is coming from in that trading unit.

The information requirements of senior management are easily summarised – "Give me everything I need to know accurately and immediately". Of course, this is not as easily achieved. So, the risk management group must strike the right balance in terms of depth and breadth of information. Generally, if risk-taking authority at lower levels has been delegated to risk managers, senior management is concerned with higher level VaR information and limit violations. Relaying a summary of global trading strategies to senior management can also be important. It is difficult to "add up" the hundreds of separate strategies across a firm. For example, the best replicating report, detailed earlier in this chapter, is a good tool for senior management to assess the firm's overall positions. Still, senior management might wish to view more detailed information at the business unit level. Ideally, a combination of aggregated and disaggregated information should be made available.

Additionally, they may want detailed P&L analysis to answer the commonly asked question, "How did we make our money?" This sounds like a simple exercise but may not be so. For example, not knowing that a large part of the firm's earnings are generated from outright speculative positions leaves senior management ignorant of the firm's exposure to a large market move.

Performance measurements such as Sharpe ratios or returns on capital are also important, especially in making compensation and resource allocation decisions. For example, would one allocate more of the firm's capital to a business unit taking less risk but making a small but steady income, or to the desk with high risk and volatile earnings? The proper performance measures can be helpful when making such difficult decisions.

Senior management is typically also interested in stress testing and scenario analysis, addressed in some detail in Chapters 6 and 8. Other helpful information, depending on the policies in place, might cover such topics as trading outside one's purview (eg, a US government bond trader trading municipals), aged inventory (see Chapter 13 for details), opposite views across desks (eg, a flattening vs. steepening trade on the same segment of the yield curve) or unusual trades or structures.

Finally, senior management must be adequately trained in both the methodology used to assess risk and the language used to express it.

Other risk categories

In the discussion above we have focused mainly on reports analysing market risk. However, as described in Chapter 3, there are many more categories of risk which should be regularly measured and reported. As firms recognise more and more the importance of those other risks, substantial effort is now put into developing similar analysis methods to cover credit risk, operational risk and other risk categories. However, the statistical management tools for these risks are still in an early development stage.

Conclusion

We have addressed several aspects of the critical function of reporting and analysing the information that results from the risk management process. Designing meaningful reports to present complex risk information to a broad audience is a significant task. Reports intended to present risk results should assist in interpreting and decomposing risk. The data that feeds these reports must be accurate and timely in order to be credible and useful. Two-way communication between the risk group and the front office is crucial to this process. In fact, good risk reporting must enhance this communication.

We have also outlined the types of reports that can be used to present risk management results, both to traders and senior management. While these reports are indicative only, we sought to demonstrate several important analysis options and we have discussed the complex task of managing data integrity and detailed some of the critical information flows between risk management and the front office.

While we have shown some of the reports that our two firms have found useful over the years, clearly different organisations will require different information views – those that facilitate the acceptance of, and the comfort with, their risk management process. We have found that risk reporting is an evolving process, and one which always benefits from the insights of multiple people across the organisation. At Goldman Sachs and Swiss Bank Corporation we have fine-tuned reports over time that we have found most effective in our environments. And we have regularly added reports and presentation mechanisms as markets, businesses, and methodologies change. In the next chapter we turn to the issue of ensuring that our risk results are accurate and appropriate.

---

[1] See Goldman Sachs' Risk Management Series, *Managing Market Exposure*, Robert Litterman and Kurt Winkelmann, January 1996.

[2] For more on hot spots, see Goldman Sachs' Risk Management Series, *Hot Spots and Hedges*, Robert Litterman, October 1996.

Backtesting

Introduction

As discussed in previous chapters, it is crucial for every financial institution to know whether it has an accurate, complete and consistent description of the risks in its portfolio. This is important not only as an internal risk management tool, but will also be a central consideration when complying with VaR-based market risk regulatory capital requirements. What is therefore essential is systematic backtesting to compare the expected changes in portfolio value as calculated by internal risk management models with the actual revenues that are generated by a firm's portfolios.

The backtesting process has two separate elements:

- Checking whether the VaR methodology the firm is using for aggregating and measuring the risks present in the global portfolio is appropriate when compared with the actual experienced P&L.
- Checking whether the individual models used to value and control the risk of the firm's positions provide a consistent and complete description of all the risk factors through comparing theoretical versus actual P&L.

In both cases the P&L calculations that every institution performs can provide the basis for testing. The first check compares the firm's VaR calculation against the actual P&L generated by its portfolio. The second compares the theoretically expected P&L generated by the pricing and risk control models with the actual change in the market value of the portfolio.

Additionally, the latter goes deeper into the individual components that add up to the theoretical P&L. It breaks down the calculations into many different terms, each one reflecting the change in one set of parameters at a time (eg, yield curves, volatility curves, etc). It then analyses each of these terms separately in order to determine whether the models are including all the relevant risk factors consistently. As well as testing the risk models, this process also provides a better understanding of the different sources of revenue and their relative importance.[1]

VaR vs. actual P&L

In statistics, backtesting generally refers to the process of examining the performance of a model by feeding it actual past data and examining how its predictions compare with the true, known outcomes. Preferably, the data used for this exercise should be different from that which were used to estimate the parameters of the model. In this

Exhibit 12.1 Assessing distribution

In the example below, a statistical test is performed to assess the accuracy of fit of observed P&L data to the distribution of returns of a given portfolio. This helps evaluate how well the entire probability density function of the portfolio is modelled. This test shows the agreement between the distribution of the observed P&L and the distribution used in forecasting VaR.

This particular test relies on the fact that percentiles are uniformly distributed for any probability density function to verify the 'goodness of fit' of the selected distribution. The assumed distribution is a critical feature to the predictive accuracy of the VaR model.

From the observed P&L and the corresponding assumed mean and standard deviation of the portfolio, we calculate the percentile in which the observed P&L falls. If the model for forecasting the portfolio distribution is good, the percentiles of the observed P&L should be uniformly distributed as observed in Portfolio A. The test of portfolio B shows that the assumed distribution is a poor fit causing the model to underestimate the VaR for the portfolio.

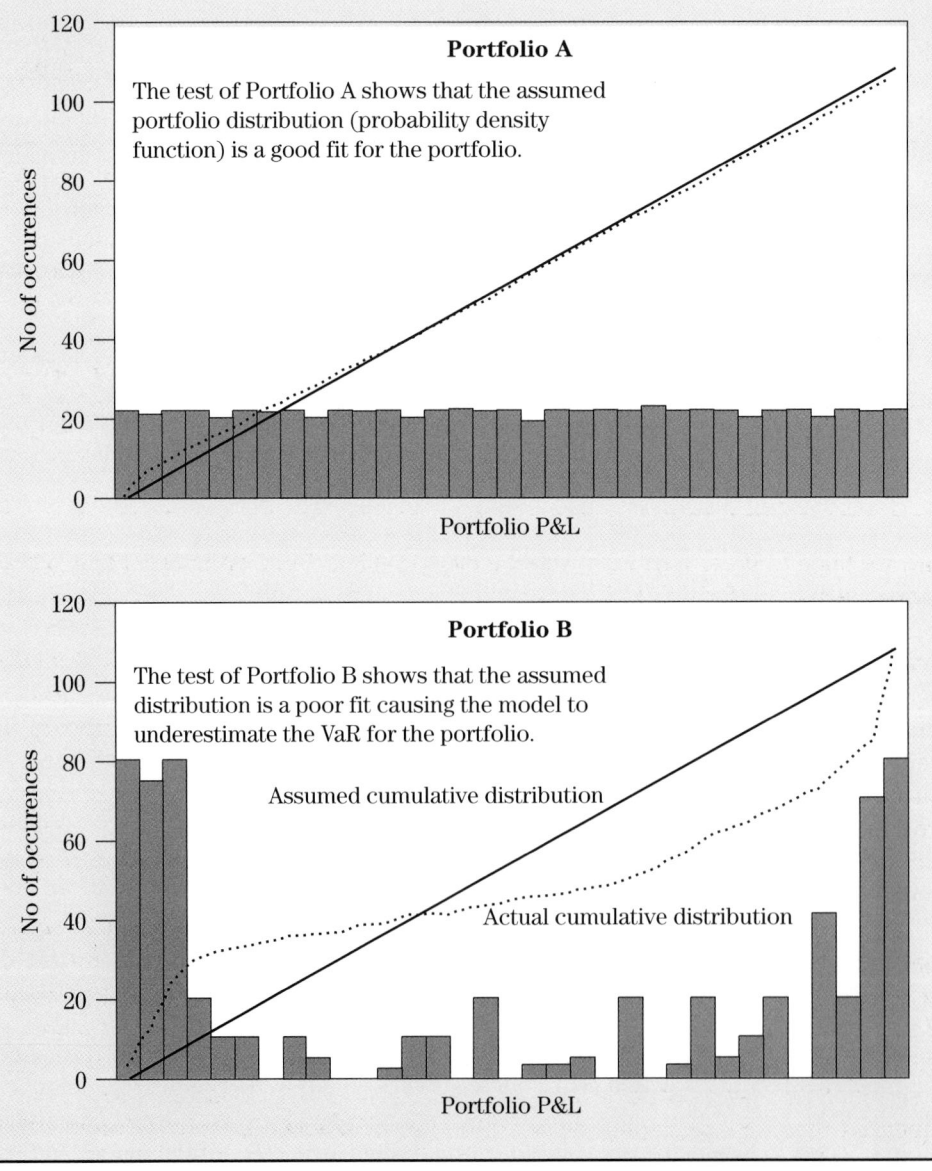

Exhibit 12.2 The regulatory framework and backtesting

Under the Basle Committee Rules (September 1997), firms that use internal VaR models to calculate their capital requirement for market risk must undertake the following procedures:

(1) Calculate a measure of the daily risk exposure (daily VaR), defined to be a loss that is not expected to be exceeded in 99 out of 100 trading days (ie a 99 per cent confidence level).

(2) Multiply the daily risk exposure estimate by the square root of 10 to arrive at an estimate of the 99 per cent risk exposure over the subsequent two-week period, or the 10-day VaR. The square root of 10 is used as the scaling factor since a VaR number is essentially a multiple of the standard deviation of the P&L distribution, but it is the variance, or standard deviation squared, of the distribution that is assumed to grow linearly with time.

(3) Compute the mean of the prior 60 daily VaR estimates.

(4) Choose the larger of (2) or (3).

(5) Determine the capital requirement by multiplying (4) by some multiplier, k, which is based on the accuracy of the bank's estimates. A value of $k = 3$ has been set as the minimum standard by the Basle Committee.

(6) Finally, review the accuracy of the estimates (and hence k) by "backtesting" these results at least quarterly. Specifically, over the prior 250 trading days, actual trading results are compared to the bank's daily VaR and the number of times that an actual loss exceeded daily VaR is noted. If the number of exceptions is four or fewer (the "green" zone), the bank's internal estimates are deemed accurate and the minimal level ($k = 3$) of reserves is required. Between five and nine noted exceptions (the "yellow" zone), some review of the bank's models is indicated and capital reserves may be raised ($k = 3.25$, for example), depending on the number and degree of the exceptions. Ten or more exceptions in 250 days (the "red" zone) is prima facie evidence (in a regulatory, not statistical, sense) of inadequate internal risk model estimates and warrants an automatic and non-discretionary increase in the multiplication factor to at least $k = 4$.

way, we hope to determine how well the model will perform with new data in a real environment. (See Exhibit 12.1.)

However, in the context of VaR methodology, and more specifically in the context of the capital adequacy rules of the Basle Committee on Banking Supervision (see Exhibit 12.2), backtesting refers to the process of comparing actual P&L with internally generated risk measures in order to test the efficacy of the internal models and thus the reliability of the resulting capital requirements. In this application, backtesting is not a one-time evaluation of a model but an ongoing process in which at regular intervals the number of exceptions (days when losses exceeded VaR) over a particular period is noted and used to judge the adequacy of capital requirements.

As a result of this set of requirements, all firms using VaR models for capital adequacy calculations will have to perform backtesting of the results to comply with the requirements of the Basle Committee. Despite the requirements set out in Exhibit 12.2, it is important that backtesting is seen as more than a regulatory burden. If used properly, backtesting of aggregate VaR models can provide valuable insights into the integrity of the risk analysis and measurement process. At the same time it is also important that we understand the statistical issues associated with performing this type of backtesting.

Type I vs. type II errors

In undertaking backtesting, as in any form of statistical analysis, we can never be certain that the correct conclusion has been drawn from the information that is available. What we are trying to establish is whether the firm's VaR model is an accurate representation of the real world (in statistical parlance, the "null" hypothesis). If our VaR model is indeed accurate and our test does not indicate otherwise, then we will make a correct decision. Likewise, if the VaR model is wrong and our test indicates as much, then we will also draw the correct conclusion.

However, it is also possible that our model is correct but our test suggests that it is understating our risk (this is referred to in statistics as a type I error). Alternatively our model may in fact be understating our risk, but the test fails to detect this (a type II error). In both these cases we would have drawn an incorrect conclusion, but the consequences of our error would be very different depending on whether we have made a type I or type II error.

In the case of a type I error, our backtest would have concluded that our risk measure is understating the probability of a given loss when, in fact, that is not the case. The consequence is that, based on the test, our risk model estimate and our capital requirement would be increased to reflect the new (though incorrect) probability of loss and VaR will thus be overstated. In the case of a type II error, on the other hand, the VaR model would be understating the true level of risk, with the result that our capital requirement will be too low, and we are likely to be "surprised" in the future by more days when we experience losses exceeding the expected VaR.

It is important to realise that in a statistical testing environment we can never know if we have made an error or a correct decision. For example, if we experience more VaR losses than we expect it could be because the established level of VaR was too low (a type II error occurred) or because we were just unlucky. All we can do is try to make our testing procedure such that we minimise the probability of making errors and then live with the consequences. Aspects of the test that affect these error probabilities include the sample size, the actual (but unknown) distribution of portfolio gains and losses, and the desired level of confidence in the VaR.

Sample size

As discussed in Chapter 7, one of the most important considerations in establishing a framework for statistical testing is to ensure the availability of a large enough set of reliable observations on which to test. Intuitively, it is obvious that to estimate very unlikely events (such as a VaR that is exceeded only 1 per cent of the time), one needs a substantial amount of data. However, when it comes to testing a VaR estimate (particularly one like the Basle Committee measure, which is based on the assumption of a 10-day holding period), this can be problematic for the following two reasons:

- First, if we were to use observations of discrete 10-day holding periods, we would require approximately 10 years worth of data in order to get 250 individual observations. Even if an institution had such data, much of it might be irrelevant because of changes in markets, financial instruments and modelling techniques over such a long timeframe.
- Secondly, and perhaps even more importantly, the portfolio needs to be relatively static over the observation period in order for backtesting to assess accurately an institution's risk estimates. Given the dynamic nature of the financial industry, trading will be continuing throughout the observation period, and the pattern of

trading is itself influenced by the ongoing gains and losses occurring in different positions in the portfolio. This means that observations taken over longer periods are likely to be significantly more "contaminated" by these dynamic effects than observations over shorter time periods.

For both these reasons, backtesting of VaR is conducted by comparing one-day estimates of risk with one-day trading outcomes.

Distributional assumptions

A second important consideration in backtesting is the shape of the distribution of the firm's trading results. If the distribution was normal (see Exhibit 12.3) was normal with a constant mean and variance, then the estimation of a reliable VaR for a given level of confidence would be a fairly straightforward statistical exercise. Moreover, because we can sum normal distributions over time, longer horizon estimates of VaR could be easily obtained from daily results by multiplying the daily result by a suitable (time) scaling factor. (This is the rationale behind multiplying daily VaR by the square root of 10 to arrive at 2-week VaR.)

In practice, however, the overall distribution of portfolio returns is not normal because the distributions of the factors or instruments that combine to yield the aggregate result are themselves non-normal. Generally, the true distribution will be more peaked around the centre with fatter tails (called "lepto kurtotic") than a normal distribution. Furthermore, the parameters of this distribution may not be stable, making aggregation over time a questionable exercise. This means that there is no reliable way to extrapolate a one-day VaR estimate to a longer horizon in such a case because if the distribution is "jumping around" in terms of location or scale, or both, then the variance won't be a linear function of time.

This said, it is still important as part of the backtesting procedure to study the form of the observed distribution of trading results so that VaR estimates can be properly tuned.

Confidence level

The degree of confidence desired in the VaR estimate is also a crucial ingredient in the backtesting procedure. As previously noted, the Basle Committee has established a 99

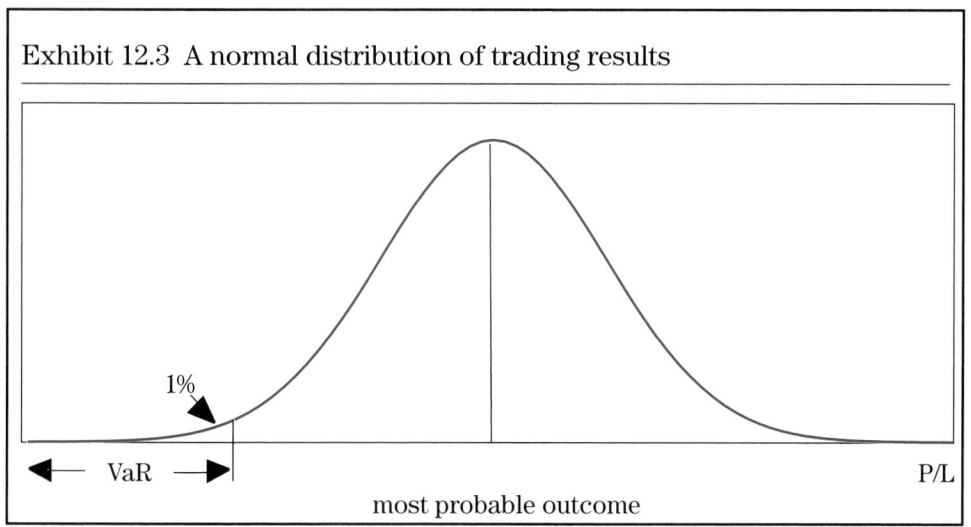

Exhibit 12.3 A normal distribution of trading results

1%

VaR

most probable outcome

P/L

per cent confidence level as the standard convention. This is tantamount to knowing the lower 1 per cent of the daily P&L distribution (as in Exhibit 12.3). But, by their definition, there are very few actual datapoints depicting trading outcomes that occur less than 1 per cent of the time. Thus, determining the amount that establishes this range is inherently more difficult than estimating a percentile closer to the centre of the distribution, beyond which we will see more outcomes.

This problem is exacerbated by the instability of the distribution (discussed earlier). A well-defined 99 per cent confidence level VaR for a given distribution could prove to be quite insufficient given a shift in the distribution to the left, which would push a greater percentage of trading outcomes beyond the VaR.

Importantly, in a backtest we should not just pay attention to the proportion of outcomes beyond the VaR in the lower tail of the distribution, but also to their magnitudes. A small number of observations that exceed the VaR by a large amount, even if they are proportionally about the number of violations expected, might indicate the presence of a significantly long lower tail and suggest that the VaR model should be adjusted accordingly.

Establishing the testing zones

The backtesting regimen established by the Basle Committee is basically an exercise in calculating binomial probabilities (see the annex to this chapter for a detailed description of the process). It should be noted, though, that this is not the only way to test whether VaR accurately assesses the lower 1 per cent of the P&L distribution. For example, a test based on the method of time-until-first-failure (TUFF), in which a sequence of days is observed until the first occurrence of loss exceeding VaR, has been described by Paul Kupiec in the Winter 1995 Journal of Derivatives, the logic of such a test clearly being that the longer one waits until a failure is observed, the lower the inferred probability of a failure occurring.

Both the binomial test and the TUFF test are aimed at determining whether a firm's VaR estimate is large enough to account for all but the worst 1 per cent of trading outcomes. They do not seek to identify other percentile points of the P&L distribution – information that is no doubt valuable to risk managers. Furthermore, the tests should not just be conducted blindly, with no qualitative assessment. A statistical test should open a discussion, not close one.

For example, a number of trading outcomes near VaR, but not exceeding it (and thus leading to a green zone test result), should still raise a cautionary flag. Likewise, a couple of very significant losses, well beyond VaR though not frequent enough to trigger a move into the yellow or red zones, might be a warning that the risk management system is not capturing some market exposure, leaving the firm at risk for a very substantial loss (for example, changes in correlations in fast moving markets may not have been properly measured).

Theoretical vs. actual P&L

Here we address the second aspect of backtesting: the analysis of the daily P&L calculations in order to establish the coherence and consistency of the risk models.

The daily P&L calculation can be thought of as the aggregation of all the cash flows that occurred during the day in question plus the change in the expected value of those that will, or might, take place in the future. It is the latter, and the assessment of its market value, that allow us to backtest the models used to value inventory positions.

Position value

Before we go on to discuss the theoretical as opposed to market value of financial instruments, we should note that there are many such instruments whose market values we take as given. They are typically very liquid, have extremely tight margins and, in general, there is no disagreement as to how they should be modelled. For example, in foreign exchange, we would never disagree with the market price of a three-month at the money US$/DM option, and in the fixed income area, we would not want to disagree with the market prices of vanilla swaps, Eurodollar futures, etc. Consequently, we should never let our valuation and risk control models disagree with these prices. Indeed, in many cases these prices would be taken as inputs to our models. In Chapter 13, we discuss pricing and price verification in greater detail. The issue that needs to be addressed here is whether our own model or the market price is the more appropriate measure of the true economic value of a position.[2]

The first factor to consider when approaching this problem is the kind of business the firm is undertaking. In the case of a firm that acts primarily as a broker, buying and selling options and underlying cash instruments in response to the (liquid) market demands, and staying well hedged, there is unlikely to be much difference between actual and theoretical P&Ls, because offsetting positions will tend to cancel out any deviations between the two. As a result, we would not expect to learn much from comparing the theoretical with the actual P&L.

The situation is likely to be very different, however, when we look at a firm that is taking positions in the market. In this case, the changes over time in the value of the portfolio should provide crucial information regarding the firm's models and the relative importance of the different sources of its revenue.

Let us now imagine a situation where the theoretical P&L disagrees with the actual (market) P&L. Furthermore, let's assume that we have identified certain kinds of options as the source of this disagreement (ie long dated options, barriers, out of the money options, etc). How would we use this information? Is it possible to determine whether the market is mispricing such options or whether or not our models are missing relevant risk factors?

If the conclusion is that the market is overpricing an option, we would buy it and hedge it. We could then run statistics over time for such options and look at our P&L. If we found that, on the average, we lost more money than the theoretical profit margin (edge) suggested by the model, we might conclude that our model is missing some key risk factor – a factor that the market itself seems to be including in the option premium.[3]

On the other hand, if we found from our statistical analysis that, on average, we were capturing a good portion of the initial theoretical edge,[4] we could conclude that our models incorporate into their dynamics some risk factors that the market is unaware of. Another possibility is that other market participants might be aware of these risk factors themselves but not of how they correlate to the other risks that are present. This would not imply that our model is "correct" in an absolute sense, but rather that its dynamics include all the relevant risk factors in a consistent manner.

Decomposing the P&L

So far we have only talked about comparing the total actual and theoretical P&Ls as two single numbers. Another crucial part of theoretical P&L calculations is to decompose the P&L into many components. This is helpful in a variety of ways. In the case where we believe that our models are essentially different from the market, we can use the P&L decomposition to better understand where the differences are coming from and to isolate which risk factor (or correlation between different risks) is being mishandled by either the market or our models. Even in the case where market and theoretical P&Ls are very similar, breaking the theoretical calculations into individual components helps clarify the different sources of revenue and their relative importance. This can enable traders and risk managers to have a clearer understanding of their positions, providing them with information on what trades to put on to be better hedged or to adjust their stance in the market.

To illustrate this process we can look at the P&L analysis in foreign exchange. Let's assume the value of the portfolio as entered into the database at the close of yesterday's trading was TV_{db}. This value should be equal to the theoretical value of the portfolio calculated with the parameters stored in the database at the closing of yesterday's trading TV_{t-1}. We can break down the P&L into the following components:

Theoretical value of the portfolio calculated with the parameters stored in the database at the closing of yesterday's trading: TV_{t-1}

+ The effect of decay, that is to say, how much our portfolio value changes when we move forward one day while all rates, volatilities and any other parameters that described the market place remain the same. One subtlety here is that, since it is the value of the forwards that stay fixed, the spot exchange rates will change by one day of carry at the appropriate interest rate; (new TV is now TV_1)

+ The effect of movements in the spot exchange rates from yesterday to today; (new TV is now TV_2)

+ The effect of movements of the rate curves from yesterday to today (new TV is now TV_3)

+ The effect of moving the volatility curves reflecting a particular view of how the volatility term structure behaves; (new TV is now TV_4)

+ The effect of moving the volatility curves from the ones used to calculate TV_4 to today's; (new TV is now TV_5)

+ Other modifications to particular deals (deals that had been entered incorrectly, misunderstandings between counterparties, etc.)

= Theoretical value of yesterday's portfolio with today's parameters $TV_t^{old\ portfolio}$

+ The contribution from the intra-day trading, ie, the new trades that were added to the book during the day. The obvious reason to separate these trades from the rest of the portfolio is that yesterday's theoretically expected P&L does not include new trades

= Today's theoretical value of the portfolio TV_t

The other dimension along which the P&L calculations are broken up is the different portions of the portfolio. Having as much flexibility as possible in this area is very important, so one can choose different ways of slicing the portfolio in order to identify the areas where discrepancies between actual and theoretical P&L arise. The choices set out in Exhibit 12.4 provide an example (based on the definitions listed above).

Notice the "Leaks" column in Exhibit 12.4. Although it has nothing to do with testing models, it nevertheless highlights a very important role that the P&L analysis performs. As already mentioned, TV_{db} is the portfolio's value as entered into the database yesterday at close of trading. When we run the P&L today, we calculate the value of the portfolio with all parameters as of $t-1$: TV_{t-1}. Yesterday's portfolio value TV_{db} should in theory be equal to the value we reported on the previous day, TV_{t-1}. If it isn't, we need to find out where the discrepancies are coming from.

Exhibit 12.4 An example of P&L analysis by portfolio constituents

Portfolio	TVdb	Leaks	Decay	Spot	Rates	DVols	ResVols	New trades	Total P&L
FX non-exotics	TV_{db}	TV_{t-1}-TV_{db}	TV_1-TV_{t-1}	TV_2-TV_1	TV_3-TV_2	TV_4-TV_3	TV_5-TV_4	new	TV_t-TV_{t-1}
Swaps & swaptions								trades	
Exotics									
Other									
Total									

There are a variety of things that could cause this. It might be somebody entering a trade with the wrong value of underlying, or booking a trade and later removing it without notifying the appropriate people, or using a different database for the yield or volatility curves, etc. Another situation where a leak will show up (not unexpectedly), is when we run the P&L across the release of a new model. This may change the values of instruments that are priced by the new model. This "leak" is expected, and the differences between the models should fully explain the values in this column. (See Chapters 11 and 15 for more discussion on how to handle these types of adjustments in the risk management process.) We have also decomposed the volatility column into two components: *Dvols* and *ResVols*. We shall come back to this later.

The example used here was for the FX business, and needs to be adapted appropriately to reflect the nature of different business areas. Thus, for example, we might need to include additional columns to reflect fixings of instruments such as average rate options – ie how the value of these options would change when an observation has been taken. Because these are OTC options, we might agree with the counterparty to mark the observation to a value slightly different from spot. In the case of equities, there should also be a column for the payment of dividends to describe how futures and options change on ex-dividend day. In the fixed-income area, there would be a column reflecting the fixing of any of the floating rates that are part of the firm's portfolio.

As stated before, one of the reasons for decomposing the P&L is to obtain a good grasp of where revenues are coming from. For instance, did we lose a lot of money because the rates went up? Or did we lose money because volatility dried up? Breaking down the P&L into individual columns is of great help when trying to answer these questions. But the second use of the different columns comes about when theoretical P&L is statistically different from actual P&L. If that is the case, we'd like to know what the root cause of the differences is. Identifying the reason for the discrepancy will help us decide whether our model is superior to the market and should be used to our advantage, or realise that it has considerable flaws and needs to be fixed.

When we find such discrepancies it is necessary to break down our data for all the days we've been calculating P&L into sub-sets that will highlight different columns of the theoretical P&L. For example, we could look for days where the rates change very little – say much less than 10 basis points. If we run statistics on this sub-set and find that the volatility terms explain most of the difference between the actual and the theoretical P&L, we might decide to revisit the assumptions the models make about volatility. This would help determine whether we should model volatility as a stochastic variable, or whether there are dynamic correlations between volatility and other parameters that our model does not incorporate.

We could also look at the spot column in addition to the volatility to check if the combination of the two was correlating closely with the P&L differences, perhaps suggesting that there are non-lognormal effects that need to be brought into consideration. Similarly we could look for trading days in our data sample where yields are the biggest component of market moves. If the rate column explains the difference between theoretical and actual P&L well on these days, we might be able to draw analogous conclusions about our models and their handling of interest rate risks. In other words, the columns in the P&L may be used to point out weaknesses (or strengths) in our models.

The examples discussed are by no means an exhaustive list of the uses that can be made of backtesting using the P&L data. Going back to the two volatilities columns of the foreign exchange example above, we might take the view that the changes in the three-month volatility drive the changes in the volatilities to all the other expirations according to a mean reverting model. To test this hypothesis we could break the volatility changes into two components – a column that calculates the changes under this mean reverting paradigm (*dVols*) and another one for the "residual" change (*resVols*) (the sum of the two columns should be equal to the change when the volatility curves move from their values at time $t-1$ to their values at time t). The better our mean reverting model describes the market, the smaller the numbers in the residual volatility column should be.

Another aspect P&L analysis can test for is the estimation of correlations and volatilities. If we take a portion of the portfolio that depends very heavily on particular correlations, such as quanto options, and analyse their P&L columns, we could learn whether our estimation of the relevant correlations is off the mark or not, revising our methodology of estimating them if necessary.

The advantage of performing these types of analyses directly on the P&L is that it brings home in hard numbers what the effect of good or bad assumptions are on the performance of the firm's portfolio.

Conclusion

It is crucial for every financial institution to understand the accuracy, consistency, and completeness of its risk measurement tools. This is important not only internally, but also is a central consideration when complying with VaR based market risk regulatory capital requirements. What is therefore essential is systematic backtesting to compare the expected changes in portfolio values as calculated by internal risk management models with the actual revenues that are generated in portfolios.

In this chapter we examined the process of comparing actual P&L with internally generated risk measures in order to backtest the reliability or efficacy of internal models. In the context of using models to generate capital requirements, the application of backtesting must be an ongoing process. We discussed comparing the theoretical and actual P&Ls to diagnose any missing risk factors. We discussed the use of the P&L decomposition that facilitates the diagnosis of the source of discrepancies between theoretical and actual P&L and highlights shortcomings in the firm's risk control models.

We observed that there is a limit to how complex a system of models can get before it becomes too cumbersome and time-consuming to be of practical use. A fully dynamic, consistent model that incorporates all the risks that are present in the marketplace is a worthy goal, but generally, practitioners stop short of that goal. Analysing the different columns of the P&L and comparing them with the actual flow of revenues is a good way to perform the cost/benefit analysis to determine whether or not a firm should invest the time and effort in moving to a higher level of sophistication. In Chapter 13 we move to the related issue of inventory price verification.

---

[1] It is important to mention here that these tests do not determine whether or not the models used by the firm are right in an absolute sense, but only whether all the risk factors are represented in a consistent manner.

[2] One of the main difficulties in comparing actual with theoretical P&L concerns over-the-counter (OTC) instruments, for which different firms might have very different models and quoted prices will generally have a wide spread (these instruments are usually illiquid). For the purposes of appraising the performance of models, we should probably mark these options to their mid-market values to avoid any biases in our comparisons. A safe procedure would be to put the instruments in a sub-class of their own and to keep in mind that, should the statistics of our P&L differ substantially from the "actual" (mark-to-market) P&L, we wouldn't be testing against a market standard something that all participants agree upon. Rather, we would be comparing our state of the art models with those of the firms we have polled. For internal management, we might just mark these options to their theoretical value and display the difference between this and their "market" value in a separate column. We should then keep a close eye on these options and analyse whether the way we think these instruments' TVs should change is in line with the columns of our P&L.

[3] The difference between expected and market P&L should be "statistically" significant, ie, larger than a specified number of standard deviations.

[4] Different types of transaction costs and market inefficiencies prevent us from capturing the whole value of our theoretical edge.

Appendix: Backtesting – establishing the testing zones

Suppose we conduct a series of repetitions (trials) of an experiment such that each trial ends in one of two mutually exclusive outcomes (heads or tails, for example), generically referred to as "success" or "failure". Assume that each trial is independent of the others and that the probability of observing a failure (denoted by p) is the same for all trials. Clearly, this implies that the probability of a success (1–p) is also constant. Define X to be the number of failures observed in n trials of the experiment (note that X can be any integer from 0 to n). In probability theory, X is said to have a binomial distribution, and a well-known formula can give us the probability of each possible outcome of X for given values of p and n. For example, if n = 4 and p = 0.30, then X can equal 0, 1, 2, 3, or 4 with the following probabilities:

X	Probability (X)	Cumulative sum
0	0.2401	0.2401
1	0.4116	0.6517
2	0.2646	0.9163
3	0.0756	0.9919
4	0.0081	1.0000
	1.0000	

Imagine a box with 30 blue marbles and 70 yellow ones of equal size and weight. If four marbles are selected, one at a time and with replacement, then X above would represent the number of blue marbles selected out of the four. Note that it is immaterial which outcome we call "success" and which we call "failure" because zero blue marbles is equivalent to four yellows, one blue to three yellows, etc, implying that the distribution above gives the probabilities of the possible number of yellow marbles too, in reverse order. The last column gives the cumulative probability of X being less than or equal to each value. Subtracting these cumulative probabilities from one thus gives the probability that X exceeds a given value. For example, the probability that X is greater than 2 = 1 – 0.9163 = 0.0837.

Now suppose we have the box of 100 marbles, only we do not know the number of blues (or yellows, of course); consider only that we have been told that the proportion of blues is $p0$. If we are not allowed to look inside the box, but can take one marble out at a time (and then replace it), we could test the (null) hypothesis that the proportion of blues equals $p0$ by conducting a sequence of n trials, observe the number of blues drawn and, based on the binomial probability of getting this number of blues in n trials with $p = p0$, decide whether we think the null hypothesis is reasonable (should not be rejected) or should be rejected because the sample evidence suggests that p is not equal to $p0$.

For example, suppose the null hypothesis is that $p = 0.01$ (ie there is one blue marble in the box) and that we conduct 250 trials. If the null hypothesis is true (ie p really is 0.01), then the probability of observing various numbers of blues is as follows:

No. of blues	Probability	Cumulative probability
0	0.0811	0.0811
1	0.2047	0.2858
2	0.2574	0.5432
3	0.2149	0.7581
4	0.1341	0.8922
5	0.0666	0.9588
6	0.0275	0.9863
7	0.0097	0.9960
8	0.0030	0.9990
9	0.0008	0.9998
10+	0.0002	1.0000

If we were to observe two or fewer blue marbles in our sample, then the high probability of this occurring (0.5432), if the null hypothesis is true, intuitively leads us to conclude that we have little basis to believe it is not true. In like manner, if we observed 10 or more blue marbles in our sample, the unlikeliness (0.0002) of this result if $p = 0.01$ suggests that the null hypothesis is not true and that p is, in fact, greater than 0.01.

Of course, we could get less than three blue marbles (out of 250) from a box that actually contains two blue marbles, three blue marbles, or even 10. We would thus make a type II error by not rejecting the null hypothesis in such cases, though the probability of making such an error obviously changes depending upon which alternative is true; it is much more likely to sample less than three blues from a box with two blues than it is from a box with 10. Intuitively, this just says that it is easier to make a type II error when the null hypothesis is wrong only by a small amount than when it is wrong by a wide margin.

This exactly mimics the procedure set up by the Basle Committee to backtest VaR, with an "exception" being equivalent to drawing a blue marble in our hypothetical experiment. The null hypothesis is that the probability of this happening is 1 per cent. The decision rules (breakpoints between the zones) were set up to control the probabilities of type I and type II errors at certain levels. The following table gives us an idea of what they are:

Probability of an exception:		0.01	0.02	0.03	0.04	0.05
No. of exceptions (out of 250 days)	Zone	Prob.	Prob.	Prob.	Prob.	Prob.
0–4	Green	0.8922	0.4387	0.1282	0.0270	0.0046
5–9	Yellow	0.1076	0.5309	0.6508	0.4284	0.1900
10+	Red	0.0002	0.0304	0.2210	0.5446	0.8054
		1.0000	1.0000	1.0000	1.0000	1.0000

The column under 0.01 gives the probabilities of being in each zone if, in fact, the probability of an exception is 0.01 (ie if VaR is correct). We see that there is a very high probability (0.8922) that the test will yield an outcome in the green zone in such a case and a comfortably small (0.0002) chance of an erroneous outcome in the red zone.

Conversely, the column under 0.03, for example, gives the probabilities of being in each zone if the probability of an exception is really 0.03 (ie VaR is too low). We see that there is a reasonably small (0.1282) probability of missing this fact by getting a green zone outcome. If VaR is so low that the probability of an exception is 0.05 (the last column), the chance is very low (0.0046) that a green zone outcome will occur and quite high (0.8054) that the test will identify that VaR is too low with a red zone result.

Calculating the probabilities

Consider n independent trials of an experiment, each of which can result in either a success (S) with probability p, or a failure (F) with probability ($1-p$). Let X be a variable that counts the number of successes in the n trials. X is called a binomial random variable. Clearly, X can take on any of the integer values from 0 to n. The probability that $X = k$ for any k between 0 and n is given by the binomial formula:

$P\{X = k\} = [C(n, k)] [pk] [(1 - p) n - k]$
where $C(n,k)$ denotes the number of ways to order k objects and $(n - k)$ objects and the formula for which is:
$C(n,k) = n!/[(n - k)!k!]$
where $n! = n(n - 1)(n - 2) \ldots (3)(2)(1)$ is n-factorial.

Note that $C(n, n) = C(n, 0) = 1$ because $0! = 1$ by definition (which just says that there is only one way to order the sequence SSSSS, for example).

The logic of the binomial formula can be seen as follows. Because multiplication is commutative (multiplication in any order yields the same result), $[pk] [(1-p)n-k]$ gives the probability of any sequence of k successes and $(n-k)$ failures over the n trials. That is, the probability of SSFFF is the same as the probability of FSFSF. $C(n, k)$ determines the number of such sequences for any n and k. Using the example of $n = 4$ and $p = 0.30$ given in the text, we can compute the probability that $X = 2$ as follows:

First, $C(4, 2) = 4!/[(4-2)!2!] = [(4)(3)(2)(1)] / [(2)(1)(2)(1)] = 24/4 = 6.$

That is, there are 6 ways to order 2 successes and 2 failures. They are SSFF, FFSS, SFSF, FSFS, FSSF, and SFFS. Obviously, for larger n and k we wouldn't want to have to list them all, but we don't have to! So:

$P\{X = 2\} = (6)(0.3)^2(0.7)^2 = (6)(0.09)(0.49) = 0.2646$

as was given in the text.

13

Inventory pricing and price verification

Introduction

As discussed in earlier chapters, clearly financial firms engage in many different activities. One important activity for many firms is buying and selling securities and contracts (eg, swaps, forwards, options and futures) and, if a firm closed out all of its positions at the end of every trading day, monitoring its financial situation would be easy. This is not typically the case, however, because firms have a certain inventory of positions that are carried over from one day to the next. Market-making activities may require a certain inventory and proprietary trading may involve holding onto certain positions. And of course firms that are in the business of managing assets may hold positions for a long time.

This chapter explores the issues relating to inventory pricing and price verification. In the first section we will address various fundamental issues regarding inventory pricing – ie how the items in a firm's inventory are valued. By "inventory" we mean long and short positions, as well as both on and off-balance sheet positions. Given the critical importance of having accurate prices, we also elaborate on how these prices are verified. Finally, we briefly discuss how to deal with aged and illiquid items – an inventory component that poses special difficulties. In an annex to this chapter we show the price verification process of a particular hypothetical option.

Inventory pricing

Marking-to-market and bid/offer pricing

For a firm's balance sheet to be accurate, inventory prices should reflect the current market value of the underlying inventory items. Financial firms typically use a daily mark-to-market policy. In practice, products should be valued on the basis of the most recent publicly available information. In the interest of conservatism, it is appropriate to value long positions at bid prices (where they can be sold) and short positions at offer prices (where they can be bought) if bid/offer spread information is available. This is referred to as bid/offer pricing. It is important to emphasise that the mark-to-market principle applies not only to actual prices but also to inputs to models that are used to value particular products (eg, volatilities).

For actively traded and exchange-traded securities, pricing is readily available from a number of sources. However, bid/offer pricing for OTC derivative products presents some complexities. For example, the pricing of every transaction in a portfolio at bid/offer would be overly prudent because it would not consider the implication of offsetting risks. Additionally, from a practical standpoint, there would be a need for not just a single discount curve, but a separate curve for cash flows to be paid and one for cash flows to be received. Moreover, the cash flows themselves might depend on both curves in a complicated manner – eg, through the forward rates. A workable alternative for OTC derivatives is to use the following two-step approach: mark at the mid-point of the bid and ask prices of the underlying instruments in combination with the establishment of a valuation adjustment.

As far as the magnitude of the valuation adjustment is concerned, it should have some relation to the magnitude of the bid/offer spreads of the underlying instruments. For example, in the swaps business the bid/offer spread for plain vanilla swaps is expressed as the difference in basis points between paying and receiving the fixed leg of the swap. Similarly, in the swaption business the spread is expressed as a number of volatility points between taking the two different sides of the trade. Generally, if a portfolio of OTC derivatives depends mostly on the movements of the Libor and Treasury yield curves and on volatilities, it would make sense to calculate the size of the valuation adjustment as some function of the interest rate exposure ("delta and gamma") and the volatility exposure ("vega"). These calculations would be applied to net exposures within predetermined maturity classes.

Regional pricing issues/policies
A complicating factor for firms with international operations is the existence of different time zones. For example, for firms with offices and trading activities in New York, London and Tokyo, the end of the trading day in one centre does not coincide with the end of the trading day in the other two centres. Does this firm mark all of its inventories at one particular point in time (eg, at the New York close) or does the firm mark its positions at the local close in each of the centres?

If a firm chooses to mark its positions on a local basis (New York is marked at the New York close, London is marked at the London close, etc), accounting issues arise. For example, there might be intra-company trades between the firm's London traders and the firm's New York traders. If those trades are not marked at the same point in time, they generally won't net out to zero, meaning that the consolidated balance sheet of the company will show a net long or short position for what is obviously a zero net position.

On the other hand, there are practical difficulties associated with global pricing at one point in time. For instance, what is the value of a particular Japanese bond at the time of the New York close? Additionally, while some products in portfolio may have active markets in multiple time zones (eg, foreign exchange), the related hedges in the portfolio may only have reliable pricing in their primary markets.

Additional valuation adjustments
Prices obtained from publicly available sources may not always reflect the true realisable value of a firm's positions, even after adjusting for bid/offer pricing. "Valuation adjustments" are created to acknowledge this fact. There is a distinction between implicit and explicit valuation adjustments. An implicit adjustment exists if a position is marked conservatively relative to its "true" value. An explicit adjustment exists if a certain amount of money is explicitly earmarked as a contingency against a particular factor.

An important type of valuation adjustment is a "liquidity adjustment". This is an adjustment that is relevant for large positions in markets where the notion of price impact is important. For example, suppose a trader holds a large position in an illiquid bond that is currently trading at a bid price of 100 (par). This typically means that a relatively small amount of this bond can be sold for 100 per bond. However, selling a large block will probably require a price concession on the part of the seller: the bond will most likely be sold for less than 100. Liquidity adjustments are nothing more than a recognition of this effect. If the trader believes that he could only liquidate his position within a reasonable period of time (eg, 30 days) at 95, he could do one of two things: either mark the bonds at 100 and establish an adjustment of 5 per bond or mark the bonds at 95. The former action would amount to an explicit liquidity adjustment and the latter action would amount to an implicit liquidity adjustment. Needless to say, greater transparency in terms of price verification and management's control over valuation adjustments would be achieved by having explicit as opposed to implicit adjustments.

A "model adjustment" is another important type of adjustment, particularly in the area of OTC derivatives where models play such an important role. At a general level, a model adjustment is simply an admission that the underlying mathematical pricing model is a simplification of the real world and that there is therefore a possibility that valuations obtained using the model are inaccurate. At a more specific level, various modelling factors are sometimes singled out as requiring adjustments. One example would be adjustments for prepayment levels, which are uncertain and often difficult to predict accurately. Another example would be spline adjustments – ie, adjustments associated with the smooth curve of discount factors associated with Treasury cash flows. The difficulties associated with the spline arise from the many degrees of freedom available for the construction of this curve, which incorporates the prices of on-the-run as well as many off-the-run government securities. Securities depending on forward rates or forward spreads are particularly sensitive to the algorithm used to construct the spline.

A type of adjustment that is relevant in the OTC derivatives business is the credit adjustment. A "credit adjustment" may be established to cover the expected losses associated with the risk that specific counterparties may fail to perform on their obligations. Such adjustments should reflect any netting agreements as well as any collateral that might be in place.

Defining marking responsibility

It is obviously important to clearly establish responsibilities for marking the firm's positions. There are basically three possibilities – either the front office, the middle office or the back office is responsible for marking-to-market. The most common arrangement is that the trading desk (front office) is responsible. Given their experience and day-to-day involvement with the markets this makes sense. However, there are also examples of arrangements where it is the middle office's or the controller's function (back office) that is actually responsible for marking. The complexity of the organisation and the products traded will generally make one structure more sensible *vis-à-vis* other methods. Clearly, if a trading desk is not itself responsible for marking its positions the need for price verification (as discussed in the next section) is not as acute as it would be otherwise. However, regardless of the actual structure, it is critical to have appropriately qualified staff performing the valuation process.

The best way to organise the marking process is to have outside market data services feed inputs to front or back-office valuation models in combination with appropriate exception reporting when outside sources are not available or appear to be inaccurate compared with typical price moves.

Frequency of marking

The usual standard is that financial firms value their positions on a daily basis. For many items this is easily done. For example, exchange-traded securities can easily be marked using the official closing price on a particular day. For other securities daily marking may be more difficult. For instance, substantial uncertainty exists about the value of certain mortgage derivatives; other examples are corporate bonds which are typically only marked weekly. It is still preferable to mark positions daily with new information being incorporated into the marks as it becomes available to ensure a consistent process.

Price verification

Under the paradigm of the front office marking its own positions, there is a particular need for verification of these prices because the compensation of a trading unit is generally positively correlated with its profits so that there might be incentives to overstate them. These conflict of interest concerns aside, the verification process is still an important component of a well-controlled environment as the marking process can be complex, requiring many sources of data and thereby increasing the likelihood of unintended error. This section surveys various approaches to price verification and discusses some of the issues related to this important topic.

Before we discuss the various methods that exist for verifying inventory prices, it is important to emphasise the difference between transaction prices and quotes. Some of the sources discussed below provide prices at which actual transactions occur. Other sources provide price quotes. These can be firm quotes at which transactions can be executed. However, it is also possible that they are no more than indications at which transactions cannot necessarily be executed, making them potentially less valuable than actual transaction prices. Having said that, we are not suggesting that there can't be flaws (eg, manipulation) associated with actual transaction prices. Indeed, judgement and experience are required to decide how much weight to attach to the various sources, depending on the particulars of a pricing question and the characteristics of the source and the market. This is not an area where a simple formula or algorithm can be applied thoughtlessly.

Price verification sources
Various sources can be used for verifying inventory prices; these sources cover both prices and inputs. The verification of inputs is an indirect way to verify a price, because there is a pricing model between price and inputs (see also the discussions later on "Model validation and change control" and "Valuation recalculations"). However, if market participants agree on a pricing model it really doesn't matter whether we quote price or input. For example, for many options the market convention is to quote volatility rather than price – it is understood that volatility is a (non-linear) function of price.

Brokers are often used as a source for various types of pricing information, such as FX rates, interest rate curves and volatilities. To avoid bias and manipulation, the information should be obtained directly from the broker and not through the trading desk. Exhibit 13.1 gives an example of a broker sheet covering indicated mid-market volatilities for a wide range of European swaptions.

For a given option maturity, each column in this matrix corresponds to volatilities applicable to different underlying swap maturities. For example, the number 13.00 in the intersection of the row labelled "10 yr" and the column labelled "6 mth"means that the indicated volatility for a 6-month swaption into a 10-year swap is 13 per cent.

Pricing services are companies that provide price information on a variety of products for a fee (eg, Bloomberg and Telerate), while exchanges (stock and futures exchanges) are another obvious source for prices.

Exhibit 13.1 Example broker sheet

SWAPTION MID-MARKET VOLATILITY INDICATIONS

		1 mth	3 mth	6 mth	1 year	2 year	3 year	4 year	5 year	7 year	10 year	
S	1yr	10.00	11.00	12.50	14.50	16.50	16.25	16.00	16.00	15.25	14.25	1yr
W	2yr	13.00	13.00	13.75	15.00	16.25	16.00	15.75	15.75	15.00	13.75	2yr
A	3yr	12.75	12.75	13.75	15.00	16.00	15.75	15.50	15.50	14.50	13.50	3yr
P	4yr	12.50	12.75	13.75	14.75	15.75	15.50	15.25	15.25	14.25	13.25	4yr
	5yr	12.50	12.75	13.75	14.75	15.50	15.25	15.25	15.00	14.00	13.00	5yr
P	7yr	12.25	12.50	13.50	14.25	15.00	15.00	14.75	14.50	13.50	12.25	7yr
E	10yr	12.25	12.50	13.00	13.75	14.25	14.00	13.75	13.75	12.50	11.25	10yr
R	12yr		12.00	12.50	13.25	13.75	13.50	13.25	12.75	12.00	10.75	12yr
I	15yr		11.50	12.00	12.75	13.25	13.00	12.50	12.00	11.50	10.25	15yr
O	20yr		11.00	11.50	12.00	12.75	12.50	12.25	11.50	11.00	9.75	20yr
D	25yr		10.75	11.25	11.75	12.50	12.25	12.00	11.25	10.75	9.50	25yr
	30yr		10.50	11.00	11.50	12.25	12.00	11.75	11.00	10.50	9.25	30yr

For a given option maturity, each column in this matrix corresponds to volatilities applicable to different underlying swap maturities. For example, the number 13.00 in the intersection of the row labelled "10yr" and the column labelled "6 mth" means that the indicated volatility for a 6-month swaption into a 10-year swap is 13%.

Industry surveys are an increasingly popular way to collect price information. These surveys are typically organised in such a way that an intermediary (eg an accounting firm) collects price quotes on particular products (eg bank loans) from several different dealers. These quotes are then averaged (possibly after dropping the highest and lowest quotes) and reported back in a confidential manner. Another source for obtaining price information is to analyse recently executed transactions. Industry publications (eg, *Derivatives Week*) provide yet another source of information on volatilities, interest rates and inputs needed for valuing basis swaps.

Finally, *cross-ruffing* (cross-checking) should be mentioned as a mechanism to obtain independent price verification. This involves the marking of a particular position by an individual who is not responsible for that position. Of course, the assumptions here are that we can reasonably assume that this individual is knowledgeable about this particular product; that they can be considered independent of the "owner" of the position and that they have an incentive to do the marking to the best of their abilities.

These mechanisms are clearly not foolproof. However, if properly applied, a combination of these methods will contribute significantly to achieving comfort with the marks established by a trading unit.

Model validation and change control
In the next chapter we discuss "model validation" as part of the overall control environment. Model validation and change control can obviously be seen as another component of price verification. Indeed, checking inputs to models is only meaningful if the model is known to be functioning properly.

Termination testing
Another price verification method is "termination testing". For example, over-the-counter swap transactions are sometimes terminated with a cash settlement prior to the originally contracted maturity date. This can happen as the result of the exercise

of some option provision in the swap contract or it can be a termination that is mutually agreed to by both parties. Whatever the reason for termination, it provides an opportunity to see whether recent marks are consistent with the amount of the cash settlement. Assuming that there was no major market dislocation between the time of the previous mark and the time of termination, a substantial discrepancy between the most recent mark and the cash settlement would be reason for investigation.

Professional counterparty collateral comparison

Another source of independent price information is provided by "collateral comparisons" of professional counterparties. In the over-the-counter market, financial firms that engage in frequent trading with other financial firms (professional counterparties) often have agreements with each other regarding collateral.

Specifically, if parties A and B have a collateral agreement with each other, this means that collateral will be posted by party A or by party B, depending on who owes whom (and also depending on how much is owed). Obviously, this arrangement is only effective if there is agreement between the two parties as to what the current NPV of the deal (or group of deals) is. Therefore, this routine provides a mechanism for comparing the NPVs of particular transactions, which can be a very useful source for identifying marking issues.

Valuation recalculations

Another important component of price verification is "valuation recalculations". This is the process whereby a party independent of the desk uses front office inputs (which are verified separately) to recalculate market values using "approved" models (see Chapter 14). This process assures that the input verification and model validation processes can be linked in an effort to validate the actual market value being reported on the firm's balance sheet.

As a side benefit to checking the real items of interest for balance sheet purposes (NPVs), valuation recalculations allow the analyst to become more intimately involved with the products in their domain. It is our experience that this has a very positive impact on both the analyst's level of job satisfaction and on their general effectiveness.

Back office expertise

Needless to say, a firm that is serious about doing price verification work should commit adequate resources to hire qualified people for this task. Once these people are in place, the firm should continue to invest in them through training programmes, mentorships, etc. As the degree of sophistication of the verification work grows, it may even make sense to establish a specialised group of people to deal with difficult verification projects. For example, Goldman Sachs has established a Derivative Price Verification Group that provides specialised pricing support to controllers on inventory items that are difficult to value (mostly derivatives). See the annex to this chapter for a case study of the type of analysis that might be undertaken.

Documentation of results

There are various reasons why it is important to document the results of the price verification process. Obviously, it allows management to monitor the results more easily. It is also a management control tool in the sense that it produces an audit trail regarding the firm's compliance with firmwide standards. Perhaps even more importantly, a careful documentation of results creates a general awareness that this type of review is institutionalised and it serves as a formal notification that this process is ongoing.

Policies on non-verifiable products

If a firm decides to trade products that cannot be priced away from the trading desk, it will need to establish procedures for dealing with this situation. Examples of such products might be certain types of CMOs. A typical approach might be the formation of a committee that periodically reviews the pricing of such non-verifiable products. To do this thoroughly is obviously a time-consuming process, providing an incentive to minimise the scope of products relegated to this unverifiable category.

Managing aged and illiquid items

Securities firms require liquid balance sheets because they need to be able to buy and sell securities easily. A liquid balance sheet means having liquid securities. Conversely, having aged items in inventory is an indicator of a potential problem, particularly if it is difficult to verify the prices of those items. Therefore, management should receive regular reports on aged items to determine whether it is comfortable with the liquidity of the balance sheet.

It is of course difficult to define what "aged" means, but as a general principle having an item in inventory for 90 days would be reason for concern in the context of a customer (flow) business. The period will clearly vary depending on the business a firm is in. Management should have some expectations as to how old a particular book should be. Ideally, it would establish limits and monitor the actual positions against those limits. In this way it can actively manage the liquidity of its balance sheet and react quickly if required by changes in the markets.

The concept of aged items is most easily applied to securities positions (as opposed to derivatives). For example, if a trader buys a 10-year bond today, it would be considered quite unusual if this same bond is still on the books a year later. On the other hand, if a trader enters into a 10-year swap, it would not at all be considered unusual if this swap remains active for a long period of time. A possible exception to this general principle might be if an aged security is part of a long-term strategy in a proprietary account, or investment account, as they often have different horizons compared with trading accounts.

Conclusion

As we have discussed, one important activity for many financial firms is the buying and selling of securities and contracts (eg, swaps, forwards, options, and futures) with other financial firms and with customers. But financial firms do not close out their positions at the end of each trading day, thus making the monitoring of a firm's financial situation difficult. Firms carry over a certain inventory of securities from one day to the next. Market-making activities may require certain inventories. Proprietary trading typically involves taking certain positions for extended periods of time.

In this chapter we have established the critical importance of putting in place robust inventory pricing policies, and their role in supporting the risk management process. As we have discussed, accurate P&L is the front line of risk management, and without reliable and high quality prices, the P&L numbers will be misleading, and could be downright erroneous.

We have outlined various sources and methods for verifying prices, and also described the concept of managing aged or illiquid inventory. In the next chapter, we discuss the notion of model risk in more detail.

Appendix: Price verification of an exotic option

Some products are not amenable to price verification using the standard approaches described in this chapter. Such cases are not uncommon in large financial firms and are most likely to be found in derivatives areas. Difficulties may stem from a complicated pay-off, a complicated model, non-observable inputs or a combination of these factors. In the absence of reliable and comparable outside price references, a critical analysis of the pricing process itself is necessary in order to assess whether marks provided by a trading unit are both reasonable and prudent. This type of analysis would have to be performed by specialists independent from the trading unit.

To illustrate this process, we briefly describe in this annex what might be done in the case of a hypothetical outperformance option. This case study illustrates the potential benefits, both from a risk management and from a control perspective, that a financial firm derives from dedicating resources to this aspect of price verification.

One final introductory comment should be that a mark coming out of a computer model is a deceptively precise number. It is important to keep in mind that for complex derivatives this mark is the result of many simplifying assumptions and subsequent mathematical derivations. These assumptions and derivations need to be made transparent by laying them out, checking them from first principles, and discussing their limitations as well as possible alternatives. The end result will then not only be another mark but also, and perhaps more importantly, a better understanding of its limitations and the associated "dollar" uncertainty.

An outperformance option

We consider an 18-month European option that has the following unit pay-off in British pounds (£) on the expiration date:

$$P = \max [0, R_1 - R_2 - 10]$$

where R_1 is the price return (in per cent) on a particular UK gilt over the life of the option and R_2 is a weighted average of the price returns (in per cent) on a set of equity indexes (see below). This is an example of an outperformance option: the option finishes in the money if the gilt outperforms the equities by at least 10 per cent. For example, if on the expiration date the realised values for R_1 and R_2 are 8 per cent and –4 per cent, respectively, then the pay-off per option is £2.

The calculation of the equity return, R_2, involves a linear combination of four separate equity index returns: the S&P 500, the TOPIX, and baskets reflecting European (excluding UK) and Pacific (excluding Japan) equities. To make matters even more complicated, all four equity components appear both in local and in currency-adjusted form (with the British pound as the currency cross). It turns out that a total of 47 variables play a role in computing P.

Price verification strategy

A common approach to check the value of a complex derivative is to proceed in two phases. In the first phase, the model and non-observable inputs used by the desk are combined in an independent implementation of the model. This verifies the implementation of the chosen model and the usage of observable inputs. If differences in price are discovered as a result of this step, the problem is often simple in nature and is easily fixed. In the second phase, the verifier starts from scratch and calculates a price using a different model, a different calibration method, and different inputs, as dictated by judgement and the characteristics of the individual transaction. If the desk "fails" the tests in the first phase, the additional effort required by the second step may not be necessary.

Model implementation and observable input verification

The first phase is relatively straightforward. We saw earlier that the pay-off function depends directly on two variables, R_1 and R_2. As such, the desk chose a bivariate lognormal framework, which is a simplifying but not unreasonable assumption. With this model, a number of inputs are necessary. These include spot values of both R_1 and R_2 plus stochastic parameters associated with the assumption of bivariate lognormality. These include the expected drifts of R_1 and R_2, their volatilities and their correlation. The desk employed a binomial approach to implement the model.

The desk values provided for the volatility of the bond and the volatility of the basket, and the correlation between the bond and the basket are 9 per cent, 15 per cent and 12.5 per cent, respectively. The corresponding option value was reported as £1.39.

Our independent work in this phase focuses on the implementation of the model and on the calculation and use of the observable inputs, which consist of the spot values and expected drifts of R_1 and R_2. We use the stochastic assumptions of the desk for both variables. We validated the calculation of the inputs, which in this case involved 47 variables (23 exchange rates, 23 equity indices, and 1 bond) and we used Monte-Carlo simulation to calculate the price. We computed a price for the option of £1.38, which is remarkably close to the desk's value.

The conclusion to be drawn from the first phase is that the transaction is properly priced, conditional on the inputs supplied by the trading desk and the bivariate valuation framework.

Full model verification

Given the idiosyncratic nature of the exact definition of this option's pay-off function, it is not possible to confirm the values of the volatility of the bond, the volatility of the basket, and the correlation between the bond and the basket by observation of the market. We therefore proceed by abandoning the bivariate valuation framework (two correlated sources of uncertainty) and value the option from first principles.

As noted earlier, the equity basket is defined in terms of the S&P 500, the TOPIX, and baskets reflecting European and Pacific equities. The European equity basket involves the national indexes of the following 13 countries: Austria, Belgium, Denmark, Finland, France, Germany, Ireland, Italy, Netherlands, Norway, Spain, Sweden and Switzerland. The Pacific equity basket involves the national indexes of 8 countries: Australia, Hong Kong, Indonesia, Malaysia, New Zealand, Philippines, Singapore and Thailand. Thus we have 23 sources of equity uncertainty. Because all of the equity components appear both in local and in currency-adjusted (£) form, we need 23 exchange rates as well. Combined with a single variable for the bond yield, this produces a model with 47 state variables. To make things tractable, we assume that this vector consisting of the equity indexes, spot foreign exchange rates and the yield to maturity, follows a multi-dimensional geometric Brownian motion.

Technical comments
Quanto adjustments to local currency indexes
The pay-off function involves non-UK indexes paid in local currencies. Under the general state variable specification described earlier, we can identify in a standard

manner the parameters of the process under the "risk-free" local currency probability measure. However, we need to adopt the perspective of a UK investor and, therefore, specify and identify the index process under the Sterling risk-free probability measure. We apply standard techniques to carry out these so-called quanto adjustments.

Modelling differences

We described earlier that the desk's modelling assumption was that the equity basket has a lognormal distribution. The value of the basket can be written as a linear combination of the value of the basket components. Assuming lognormality for the individual basket components is not consistent with the basket being lognormal, because lognormality is not closed under linear combinations. In this sense modelling the individual components is not just a refinement, it is a different modelling assumption.

There is also an issue related to the modelling of the bond price. Modelling the bond price to be lognormal is different from modelling the bond yield to be lognormal.

These types of modelling issues come up all the time, and there is often no unique solution that meets all requirements completely. Different choices can often be justified depending on the circumstances. The ultimate choice of which alternative to choose depends on judgement and how well each is supported by independent sources and empirical evidence.

Parameter calibration and valuation

A full specification of the parameters involves values for the drifts, volatilities and correlations. We can use market data to get implied estimates for the drifts and the volatilities. Because obtaining implied correlations from market data did not prove feasible, we use historical data to estimate those correlations. We then proceed and value the option using Monte-Carlo simulation.

Valuation results and sensitivity analysis

We obtain an option value of £0.81, significantly smaller than the (1.39 value obtained by the desk. Because the desk is short 500,000 units of the option, this means that it is valuing the option conservatively by an amount equal to £(500,000) × (1.39 – 0.81) = £290,000.

Differences in valuations can be translated to differences in three assumptions: the volatility of the bond; the volatility of the basket; and the correlation between the bond and the basket. We noted previously that the reference (desk) values for these quantities were 9 per cent, 15 per cent and 12.5 per cent, respectively. Our alternative valuation method yielded values equal to 7 per cent, 11 per cent and 30 per cent, respectively.

Changing the value of these three inputs one at a time (from the reference value) and leaving the others unchanged gives us additional insight as to what drives the observed valuation difference. Changing the bond volatility from 9 per cent to 7 per cent decreases the option value from £1.39 to £1.27; changing the basket volatility from 15 per cent to 11 per cent decreases the option value from £1.39 to £1.01; and increasing the correlation from 12.5 per cent to 30 per cent decreases the option value from £1.39 to £1.17. This shows that equity basket volatility is the largest contributor to the observed price difference and bond volatility is the smallest contributor. The correlation is clearly an important factor as well.

To establish the robustness of our results, we might perform additional sensitivity analyses. For example, we might calibrate the model using different estimation periods. As far as the correlation is concerned, it is well known that these quantities are often unstable and hard to estimate. In addition to using different estimation periods (say five and 10 years of observations), we could also use different data frequencies (say weekly, biweekly, and monthly sampling frequencies) to come up with a range of "plausible" values. This analysis allows us to quantify the amount of uncertainty in the underlying parameters and the corresponding uncertainty in the value of our derivative.

Disposition

Based on our results, the desk subsequently modified its input assumptions and began assuming values that were very close to the values that came out of our independent analysis.

14

Derivatives models and validation

Introduction

Imagine the following situation. A trader is structuring a complicated deal for which there is no market price available (eg, a long-dated amortising swaption in Japan). Suppose this trader has experience with such products in the US market, but is unfamiliar with the peculiarities of the current low-rate environment in the Japanese market and so simply applies the same lognormal model that "works" for a US deal.

Because this particular model does not work well in the low-rate environment of the Japanese market, this deal will not be marked properly, nor will it be hedged properly either. If viewed in isolation, this will become clear as time goes by and the trade approaches its expiration date. However, if the trader puts on similar trades and grows the book, as older deals mature it becomes obvious that this type of mispricing can escalate in a Ponzi-style fashion, remaining undetected for a long period of time. At the very least the firm could report a large hit and the debacle will be discussed in the newspapers.

How does a firm protect itself from scenarios like this? "Model validation" may be one control that minimises the risk of mismarking derivatives positions that are valued using models. The goal of model validation is to avoid situations where models are inadequate or are applied improperly. There is obviously no right model for every given situation and there will always be some uncertainty, but model validation can help identify the degree of uncertainty and the degree of sensitivity of marks with respect to modelling assumptions. As discussed in Chapters 12 and 13, backtesting and price verification are also major control methods for avoiding mismarking. Model validation backtesting and price verification are most effective when used in conjunction with each other. For example, checking inputs to a certain model is obviously only meaningful if the underlying model is known to behave properly.

The scenario sketched above is perhaps unrealistic because it is well known that a lognormal model is inappropriate in the current Japanese interest rate environment. However, this does not mean that similar cases cannot arise. In fact, the risk management function should always be on the alert to identify situations like this one. It is also worth pointing out that in today's regulatory climate, regulatory agencies and auditing firms fully expect formal model validation programs in derivatives areas that rely heavily on quantitative models for pricing and hedging. Thus, there is ample internal and external pressure to devote adequate resources to this somewhat specialised aspect of risk management.

The remainder of this brief chapter discusses model validation and model risk in more detail. The discussion on model validation is presented from the risk management point of view (the model user), whereas the somewhat more general topic of model risk is presented from the point of view of the model developer.

Model validation and related controls

As firms use mathematical models both for pricing inventories and for assessing risk exposures arising from these inventories, there is a clear need to have good controls surrounding these models and their implementation. The main model controls should typically include the following elements:
1. Documentation of a model and its implementation, including limitations;
2. Designation of responsibility for developing and testing the model;
3. Procedures for recording alterations to the model after its introduction; and
4. Policies and procedures for maintaining the systems supporting the models.

1. Documentation
Model validation is a relatively specialised task that involves the documentation of its various important aspects and implementation. Fundamentally, it includes an analysis of the financial theory and empirical work upon which the model is based. This specifically includes a summary of the assumptions upon which the model is based as well as comments on any known limitations on the domain of applicability of the model and its implementation. As an example of possible limitations of a model, some simple option formulas work relatively well for short-maturity options (eg, three months or less), but not for longer maturities. In addition to the analysis described above, a model validation report includes checks of the analytical derivation of the model used and checks any numerical solution procedures and the related computer code.

2. Responsibility for development and testing
To maintain independence between model validation and model development, the person (or team) responsible for model validation should not be the same person as the developer of the model. There are at least three ways of actually organising this in practice:
1. A member of the same group as the model developer is responsible for model validation. The advantage of this arrangement is that this person is probably quite knowledgeable about the subject, although the notion of independence might be compromised to some extent.
2. To hire an outside consultant for this task – for instance an academic or a former employee. Independence would not be an issue in this case, but the quality of work might be variable and hard to predict. There also might be an issue regarding the proprietary nature of the models, because the outsider would acquire intimate knowledge of a firm's models in a particular area.
3. To have an independent quantitative group in the back office do the model validation. Again, independence is assured, but it relies on being able to assemble, and retain, in a non-business unit a group of individuals with training in financial economics, mathematics and computer programming.

3. Alteration procedures
The financial world is a highly dynamic environment. This is also true in the state of models and their implementation. It is common for models to require subsequent

changes and enhancements. If there are no careful procedures surrounding those changes, risk may be incurred. For example, there should be clear designations as to who is authorised to make changes to the underlying source code and who is responsible for monitoring changes and possibly requiring models to be revalidated. Goldman Sachs, for example, has monthly reports that show (among other things) how many changes have been made to pricing routines that are used for production purposes, both in the current month and year-to-date. There are also specific procedures dealing with follow-up on such changes.

4. Maintaining support systems

Given resource constraints, it is often necessary to prioritise model validation activities. How do we measure which models are the most important to be validated? One approach would be to rank the various models by their frequency of use; another is to rank them by current NPV; and a third approach, possibly the most sensible, is to rank models according to some risk measure. For example, we could compute quantities such as delta and vega (both gross and net) for the various models and start with the models with the highest values for those risk measures.

Model validation can be seen as a formal process that is a sub-set of the more general process of mitigating the various types of model risk, as discussed in the next section.

Model risk

As the use of mathematical models for pricing and hedging becomes more widespread, and as these models become increasingly complicated, there is ample opportunity for something to go wrong along the way. Loosely speaking, model risk refers to the risk of losing perspective of the limitations of models in general and to the pitfalls associated with their application.

Derman[1] distinguishes a variety of different types of model risk. While acknowledging that the notion of a correct model is a slippery one, a major type of model risk is having an incorrect model for a particular situation. An example would be an attempt to value an option that depends on the slope of the yield curve with a one-factor model of interest rates. Another example would be to ignore the correlation between stock prices and credit spreads in a model to value convertible bonds. Opportunities abound for making mistakes of this nature.

Even having the "correct" model for a particular situation does not mean that there are no pitfalls. We could have the correct model, but inaccurate inputs, an incorrect solution or an inappropriate use of the model. Examples would be the specification of inaccurate volatilities and correlations, a technical mistake in the derivation of the analytic solution to the model, or choosing the wrong number of replications in a Monte-Carlo simulation, respectively. There are many opportunities for making mistakes along those lines.

Numerical solution methods might be another source of model risk. For example, under some circumstances finite difference methods may not produce accurate results. More generally, software and hardware bugs are an important source of model risk. Opportunities exist for introducing programming mistakes in the core pieces of code as well as in the interface with databases, user interfaces, trade entry screens and price feeds.

Based on his experience in the quantitative strategies group at Goldman Sachs, Derman has several suggestions to avoid these various sources of model risk. First, he stresses the importance of treating the entire process as an inter-disciplinary endeavour in which modellers, programmers and users work closely together. Obvious checks should be carried out, such as testing complex models in simple cases with known solutions, and testing the behaviour of the model on the various boundaries of the parameter region. Derman recommends a certain "life cycle" for models as far as access is concerned. The hope is that having this multi-layered screening process minimises the probability that the model behaves badly with potentially disastrous results.

As soon as the developer has tested the model, fellow developers should take a look. The next step is a release to the traders, followed by a release to salespeople. If the model has been working well for some period of time, a release to appropriate clients can then be considered. Derman concludes with the following comment: "Finally, one of the best defences against modelling error is to ensure that both models and systems are built by people who like doing it and who take pride in their work."

Conclusion

In this chapter we discussed the fragile nature of the modelling process, and the care that must be taken when both selecting the appropriate model for a particular deal and monitoring the model development process. Model validation is one control that reduces the risk of mismarking derivatives positions that are valued using models. The goal of model validation is to avoid situations where models are inadequate or are applied improperly. There is obviously no single model that is right for every given situation and there will always be some uncertainty. But model validation can help identify the degree of uncertainty and the degree of sensitivity of marks with respect to your modelling assumptions. Model validation, price verification and backtesting (discussed in the previous two chapters) are most effective when used in a complementary fashion.

We have shown that there is a clear need to have good controls surrounding these models and their implementation. These controls should typically include the following elements: documentation of models and their implementation, including limitations; designation and separation of responsibility for developing and testing models; procedures for documenting subsequent alterations to models; and procedures for maintaining the systems that support your models.

We have indicated that model risk should be managed, by which we refer to the risk of losing perspective of the limitations of models in general and to the pitfalls associated with their application. Putting proper procedures in place, and maintaining an appropriate level of awareness have become key components of an effective risk management process. In the next chapter we consider the flow of risk information.

---

[1] Goldman Sachs & Co, *Model Risk*, Risk Management Series, E. Derman, July 1996.

15

The flow of risk information

Introduction

As stated elsewhere in this book, effective risk management depends on putting the right information before the right people at the right time. Therefore it should not be surprising that implementing an effective risk management system requires a significant focus on data sources, flows and timing.

We have emphasised the essential need for accuracy of information and the ability to tie risk analysis to the firm's books and records – requirements that establish key principles for the design of risk systems. Further complicating the task is the sheer volume of information to be processed, as well as the number of different systems with which a risk system must frequently connect. These challenges emphasise the need to focus carefully on the design of information flows.

At this point, we should issue a cautionary note that this design should not be a purely technological event. Technologists ought to work very closely with risk business people in identifying and making the decisions that will be needed here. This collaboration is essential in order to achieve the desired business goals (yes, this means nobody is allowed to skip this chapter!). In the pages that follow, we discuss what data is required for risk analysis, where that data might come from, and considerations as to its storage and processing. In the course of the discussion, we develop a map of typical information flows from sources, through risk systems and ultimately into the hands of risk analysts and managers.

While we devote a portion of our discussion to flows through the risk system, our emphasis is on the flow of data into it. While a firm may choose to build or to buy its risk models and analysis systems, in any case it is necessary to integrate these modules with data that must necessarily come from in-house applications. This integration effort is not trivial; it is estimated to be as high as 65 per cent of the total cost of implementing enterprise-wide risk systems.[1] Given a recognition of the integration task, the build-or-buy decision can then be made based on cost, value, staff availability and timing considerations.

Risk data requirements

We stated earlier that the first step in risk analysis is to identify the positions. This means knowing *how much* of *what* is held *where*. In more specific terms, the *how much* translates to "position data", *what* means "product data", and *where* means "account data". Collectively, we refer to these sets of information as "portfolio data" because they describe a managed set of financial holdings. In addition, if we're going

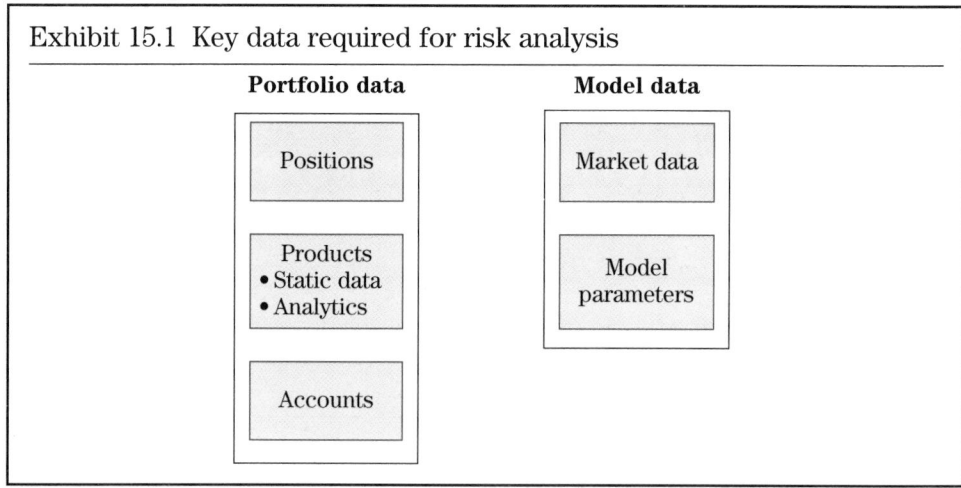

Exhibit 15.1 Key data required for risk analysis

to apply models to quantify and decompose portfolio risks, a collection of "model data" will also be required. These important categories of required data are depicted in Exhibit 15.1, which will serve as the foundation of the architectural picture of a prototype risk system that we'll develop during the course of this chapter.

Portfolio data

Positions

Oddly enough, position data itself is remarkably simple (though as we'll see shortly, it can be hard to source). We can define a position as the snapshot of a balance at a given point in time in an individual product (generally a security or other financial instrument such as an option contract) held in a given account. Therefore, position data that must be captured and maintained tends to include little more than a product identifier, an account identifier, some time-stamps (indicating the point or period in time the position represents) and a position quantity (as depicted in Exhibit 15.2).

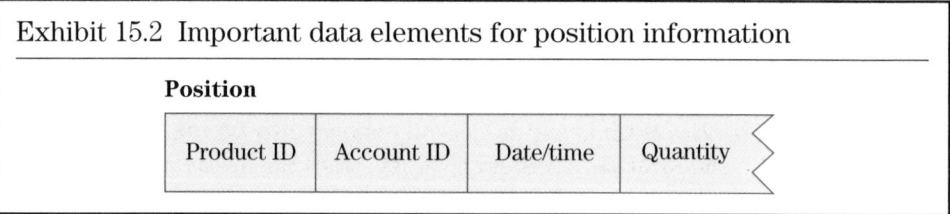

Exhibit 15.2 Important data elements for position information

We have consistently used the term "positions", rather than "transactions", for a specific reason. It has been our experience that it is far more effective to capture and store position data (ie snapshots of balances), rather than to receive individual trades or transactions. The business of assembling positions by accumulating individual transactions can be overwhelming in itself, and is best left to portfolio accounting or position-keeping systems that perform this function because they have to. If you're still on the fence on this one, imagine what happens when a single transaction is dropped. The position balance will be wrong forever, or at least until the next time a full reconciliation is performed.

The design of position time-stamps turns out to be fairly complex and surprisingly important, so an appropriately thoughtful approach should be taken. If the firm is (or will be) global in nature, the risk system design must support the fact that activity occurs during different, overlapping periods throughout the 24-hour day. Different regions have a different idea of when the "end of day" is. The first set of questions to answer concern the points in time when a risk analysis will be required. Is there interest in reporting as of the close of business in New York, including European positions as of their close (about six hours ago) and Asian positions as of their close (about half a day ago)? Is there interest in reporting risk at any particular time (eg, noon in New York) – which may include dormant end-of-day positions from some regions, but an intra-day snapshot from another region? Other obvious questions concern data availability to support these reporting needs, which we will discuss in the next main section, entitled "Sources of risk data".

It may seem obvious to respond broadly to all of these questions by saying something like, "We'd like to be able to report risk as of any time in the day, regardless of which markets are open and which are closed at that time." However, it's important to understand the implications of such a demand. First, it may simply be impossible for the firm's systems to provide such position snapshots in a timely manner. Secondly, even if the infrastructure is in place to provide the data, one should question how useful it actually is. In our experience, "real-time" risk analysis tends to be highly overrated. The vision of a war room, with instantaneous risk numbers flashing on large screens before risk managers and analysts speaking hurriedly into telephones, may in fact not be so desirable. How many risk analysts would it take to digest and make use of all that information? What corrective action, if any, would be taken based on such intra-day analysis? What if there is inaccurate, unreconciled data fed into the system and erroneously reacted to by someone on the trading floor? This can quickly render the results from the system inaccurate, and destroy hard-earned credibility. These and other practical considerations have led us towards favouring the provision of periodic (end-of-day, or intra-day where available) position level data.

Products
In comparison with position data, an enormously rich set of product information is required for risk analysis applications. This is not surprising because all the real work in estimating market risk involves knowing the special characteristics of each different sort of financial instrument (see Chapter 4).

We like to think of product data in two broad categories. The first is "static" product data, which includes all those attributes of financial instruments that are generally set once at product creation and change only occasionally subsequently. For example, typical static attributes for a bond include coupon, maturity date and currency. It is also important to consider product information that would appear on displays and reports. Such items may include descriptions, classification categories (eg, "government bond") or alternative identifiers (eg, CUSIP, SEDOL numbers). Lastly, it is important to recognise that different attributes are required for different product types, and that all instruments will not fit into a single rigid data definition.

The second broad category of product information is "analytics", which are observed or calculated attributes whose values change with market movements. The simplest example is a product's mark-to-market price, but this category also includes the other more complex analytic ratios used in risk calculations, such as a bond's duration, or an option's delta, vega and gamma.

For the most part analytics represent an approximation of the sensitivity of an instrument's price to changes in some market fundamental and therefore play a key role in risk estimation. Product analytics, in concept, change continuously, even while markets are closed. As with position information, firms must decide how frequently they wish to sample product analytics, assessing the trade-offs of benefits vs. cost and, very importantly, complexity. Once again we find that, for the most part, daily end-of-day marking of analytics suffices.

It should be understood that many analytic values do not have a single well-agreed definition. The exact values that are required must be defined very carefully to ensure that appropriate assumptions, calculations and scaling are being performed. To do this, enterprise-level risk system designers ought to work closely with business unit analytics staff in designing the interaction between product-level analytics (to be provided *to* the risk system) and risk model computations (to be performed *by* the risk system). Even the simplest of analytic values – the market price – is subject to varying interpretation, requiring that a consistent standard be defined. For this particular case, we like to use the firm's P&L standard for position marking, if such a standard exists and is enforced.

Of critical importance in defining product data is the selection of the product identifier to be used. This is the number or code by which a product can be identified across all the systems that feed information, and is often defined by the firm's product master. The product identifier is how positions are tied to product information, including analytics. It is preferable for the product identifier to be universal across all instruments. Note that often a firm will not have a consolidated product master, and must therefore rely on some of the industry standards, which would have to be architected into the system (see Exhibit 15.3).

Examples of industry standard identifiers, which are nonetheless not examples of universal product identifiers because they do not cover all instruments, are CUSIP, SEDOL, or ticker symbols. An all too common bad habit is the reuse of identifiers from "old" products as if identifiers are a scarce resource. This practice virtually guarantees misrepresenting a position as being in the wrong product at some time or another – possibly with annoying frequency. If your firm does not assign unique, universal, and non-varying product identifiers, a great deal of attention will need to be paid to the mechanisms by which the risk system will manage around this.

Accounts

While the concepts of position and product information are quite generic, it is a little more difficult to discuss account information in a way that's meaningful to different

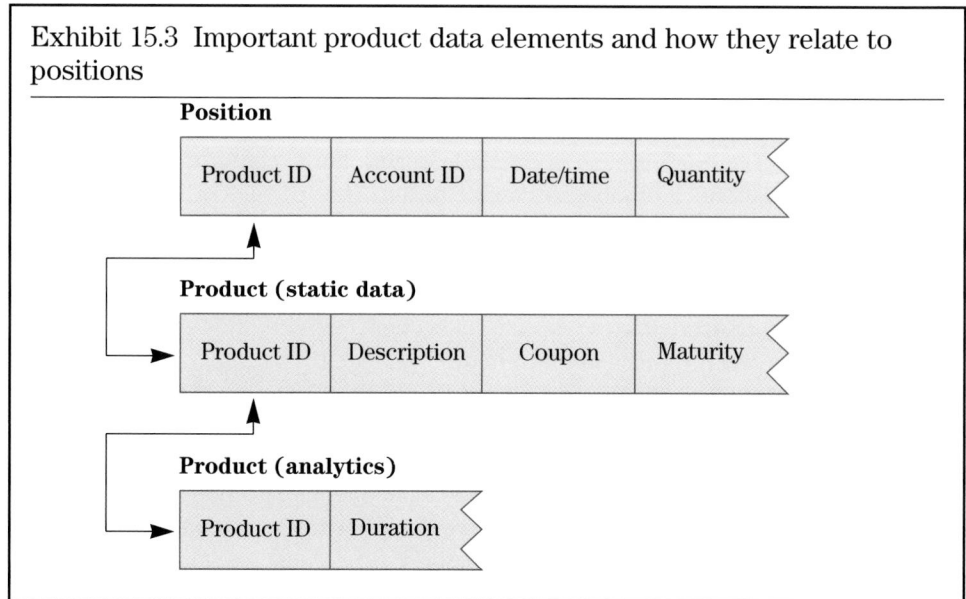

Exhibit 15.3 Important product data elements and how they relate to positions

Position

| Product ID | Account ID | Date/time | Quantity |

Product (static data)

| Product ID | Description | Coupon | Maturity |

Product (analytics)

| Product ID | Duration |

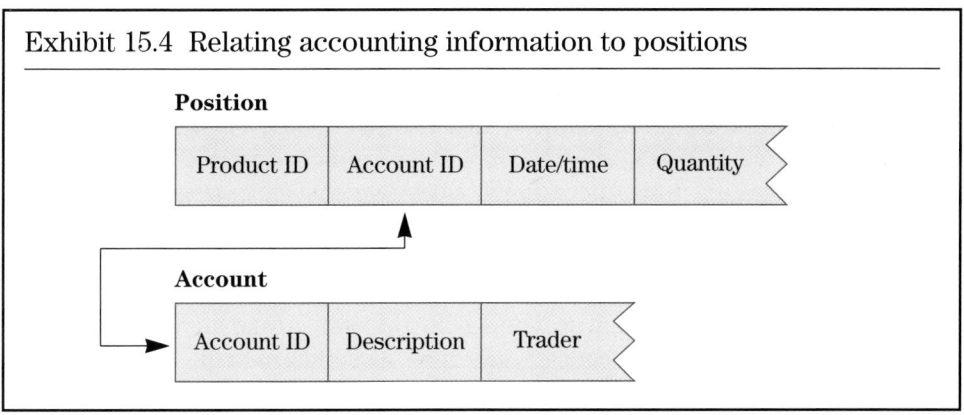

Exhibit 15.4 Relating accounting information to positions

Position

Product ID	Account ID	Date/time	Quantity

Account

Account ID	Description	Trader

types of firms. Exhibit 15.4 depicts simple account information and how it's related to positions.

The most important aspect of account information, as we're defining it here, is its use in isolating and grouping "portfolios" for which risk will be measured and reported (see Exhibit 15.5). By portfolio we mean a collection of positions that is managed as a whole. This may equate to a trader or portfolio manager's holdings or to an investment fund. In some cases, a firm may manage its risks at a more detailed

Exhibit 15.5 Aggregating positions by account into portfolios for risk measurement

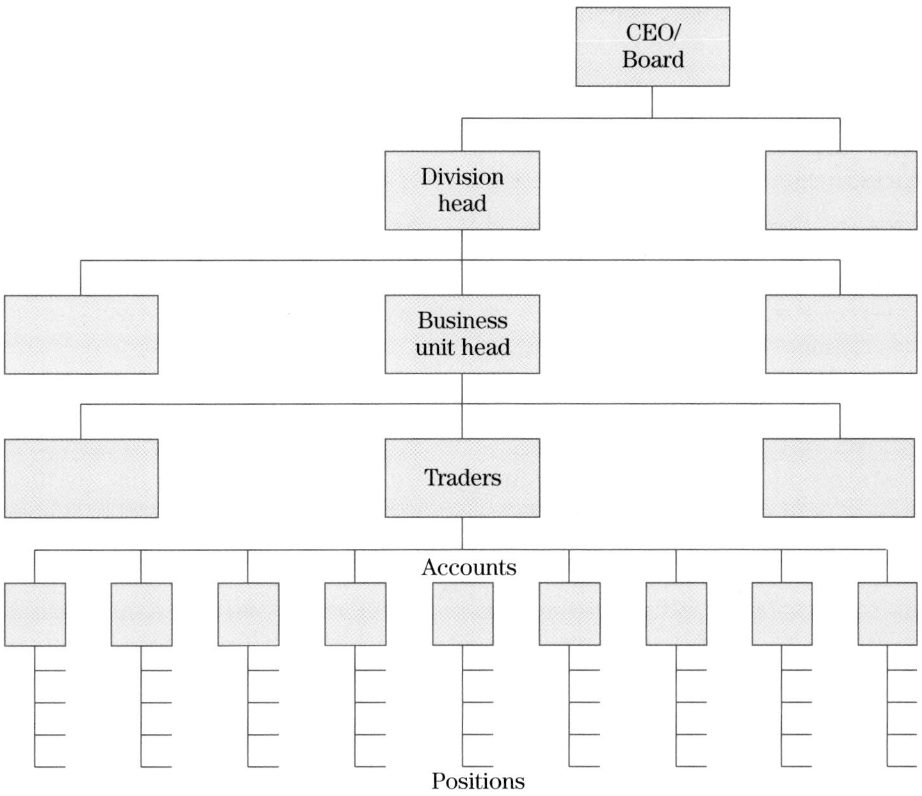

```
                            CEO/
                            Board

                Division                    [       ]
                head

    [      ]    Business           [      ]
               unit head

    [      ]    Traders            [      ]

    ──────────── Accounts ────────────

    [  ] [  ] [  ]    [  ] [  ]    [  ] [  ] [  ] [  ]

                    Positions
```

191

level, perhaps looking at portions of a trader's holdings in isolation. What is critical is that the firm decides at what levels risk will be measured and managed, and that account information be collected to enable those levels of detail to be identified.

The thought process for mapping accounts to portfolios must include the realisation that the business is likely to be reorganised over time, and that it's preferable to collect a little more detail now than have to rework systems to accommodate a change later. Even when the account data design appears to be straightforward, it is sometimes surprising just how difficult it is to locate the proper account identifiers and mappings to portfolios. The degree of difficulty is often tied to how well the account structure is defined in the firm's fundamental accounting systems (such as the general ledger) and how well this mirrors the way senior management and risk management wish to view and measure the firm. The closer the G/L view is to the risk management view, the more likely that required account data and mappings are readily available.

Model data

In Section II, we discussed various methodologies of risk measurement. Each of these techniques requires data – sometimes a significant amount – as a driver for the analysis. Model data includes both historical "market data", such as product prices or asset class returns, and "model parameters", such as yield shift scenarios or historical weighting curves that must be collected and stored.

A fundamental tenant of risk measurement is the use of an understanding of the past to build models for the future. This understanding begins by building a historical record of the market.

This historical record may include time series of prices, levels, volatilities, exchange rates, and other economic data. As we described in Chapter 13, the sources of this data typically include brokers, traders, data vendors, and exchanges. As with portfolio data, capturing model data often occurs through multiple current and historical data feeds in a broad array of formats and conventions. Because of the huge volume and volatile nature of model data, it is necessary that feed processing incorporate automated consistency checks and filters in order to ensure data quality. A review process should also be put in place to resolve exceptions, such as outliers or bad data points, which may require a judgement call.

Model parameters, such as per cent decay or overlap, which are used to generate a covariance matrix, direct how risk models are tuned for a firm's specific needs. (These parameters are referenced in Chapter 7.)

Sources of risk data

Given a good idea of what data we need, we can begin hunting around the firm's systems to find it. This search can be quite frustrating, and it is only a minor consolation that it can be quite enlightening as well. To assist with this activity, there are important considerations in evaluating sources of risk information based on *accuracy, timeliness* and *architectural concerns*. As we approach the task of sourcing data, it's worthwhile to keep in mind the old adage, "garbage in, garbage out".

Accuracy

It is attractive to divide a firm's application systems into two broad categories – "books and records" (also known as transaction processing or accounting systems) and "information" systems (typically used for decision support only). An unfortunate corollary drawn from this categorisation is that books and records systems require the highest degree of accuracy and rigorous scrutiny, and that management information systems do not. Perhaps somewhere, someone once said, "Close enough for MIS", which is interesting, because if the data isn't accurate, how can these systems be relied upon for the management decision-making process?

There are a number of reasons why risk system builders ought to avoid this misconception and realise that their applications require a near-books-and-records level of accuracy. First of all, a risk system contains complex models and creates complex end-products that, in and of themselves, are very difficult to tie directly to any known quantities. Risk measurement lives in the world of probabilities, estimation, assumptions and non-intuitive interactions between risk exposures. It is certainly difficult enough to get people to understand and buy into the analysis without the added distraction of bad raw data thrown into the mix. As we pointed out in earlier chapters, there is no easier way to lose credibility than to spend an hour explaining the non-intuitive result of a risk analysis only to find that it was really caused by a missing position on a data feed.

The greater the degree to which risk measurement is integrated into such corporate financial management processes as capital allocation (discussed in detail in Chapter 19), the greater the need for accuracy throughout risk systems. Traders or portfolio managers who are subject to market risk limits or risk-adjusted return measures will validate this requirement in no uncertain terms. In addition, as market risk measurement becomes more a part of disclosure and regulatory reporting (as discussed in Chapters 17 and 18), so the need for accuracy and reconciliation to the firm's books and records is increased. Regulators will insist on it; in fact, they are beginning to do so already. A distracting factor is that a lot of attention is usually given to the details of the risk models themselves. This is natural as there is tremendous complexity and a host of methodological decisions to be made there – not to mention that the modelling tends to be the more intriguing activity. In our experience, however, bad risk numbers are just as likely to be the product of bad or missing portfolio data as modelling errors.

We recommend receiving portfolio data from audited books and records systems (such as P&L applications or operations systems) wherever possible. Furthermore, wherever it isn't possible, it is at least critical to establish a mechanism for verifying the accuracy of the data used against the audited books on an ongoing basis. Product analytics data (with the exception of market prices) will rarely be available from books and records systems, and an independent validation will be required. But it is key to use audited positions as the basis for risk analysis, and to map in analytics using product identifiers as described earlier.

An important aspect of accuracy is completeness. If your firm is like most, there will be many situations where all positions of a given portfolio are not available from a single system. For example, positions in non-traditional products such as swaps or futures may be maintained on a separate system. Fixed income and equities products are also typically on different systems due to their unique business requirements. This is where the design process requires a lot of rigour, legwork and manual verification. A touch of the skills of Sherlock Holmes wouldn't hurt either.

In Exhibit 15.6, we have added the data feed processing steps to our architectural picture. In this diagram, we break down the feed-loading process into "feed-specific filters" and "generic loaders". This type of arrangement makes sense in typical environments where the risk system will ultimately be fed by numerous "upstream" systems, each of which may deliver data in different formats. The feed-specific filters

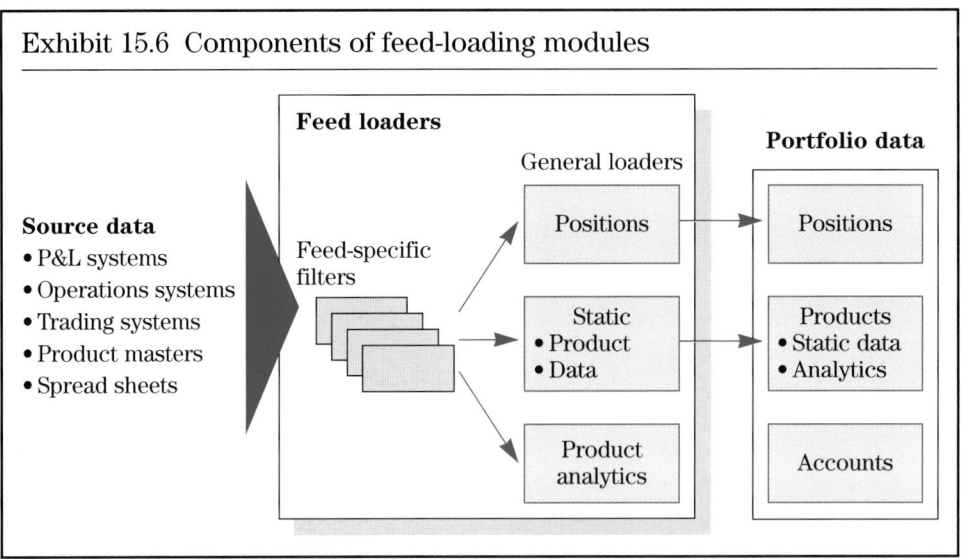

Exhibit 15.6 Components of feed-loading modules

are programmes that translate the incoming data into a single standardised format that the generic loaders recognise.

Timeliness

Because risk measurement is performed on a snapshot of a portfolio that changes over time, and against dynamic market conditions, the longer it takes to prepare and present risk results, the lower its value to end-users. Perfect risk analysis is perfectly useless if it arrives too late. In order to avoid being accused of rearranging deck chairs on the Titanic, an enterprise level risk system must tackle the challenges of data availability and synchronisation with flexibility. A further complication is that risk analysis itself tends to require conspicuous processing time, depending on the models used.

To accommodate these seemingly contradictory requirements, it may be helpful to recognise that different pieces of data are likely to be available at different times. While it's normally much simpler to manage applications that wait for all required data to arrive before beginning their processing, there may be overriding benefits in processing what you can when you can. Doing this requires maintaining information about process and data dependencies, and building flexible process scheduling (see Exhibit 15.7). We will discuss this further later on in the section on "Processing input data".

In discussing accuracy above, we strongly advocated choosing books and records sources for positions. Now comes the challenge: books and records systems typically have complex dependencies in their processing streams, and often require hours after the market close to provide data for "downstream" analysis systems such as risk. This may be exacerbated in global firms where foreign region processing depends on central office systems (eg, London or Tokyo accounts waiting for New York close to process).

Sources further upstream from the back office, such as trading systems, may appear far more attractive because they can usually provide positions information shortly after market close. Further, if they are distributed applications, they can also provide data on a timely basis for the region. Trading systems, however, also have some less-than-desirable attributes. For example, in the rush to close out at the end of a day only the bare minimum information may be entered to get the trade through the system, while product details and analytics needed for risk measurement are

Exhibit 15.7 A feed process scheduler understands dependencies among data feeds and risk processes, and directs loader activity

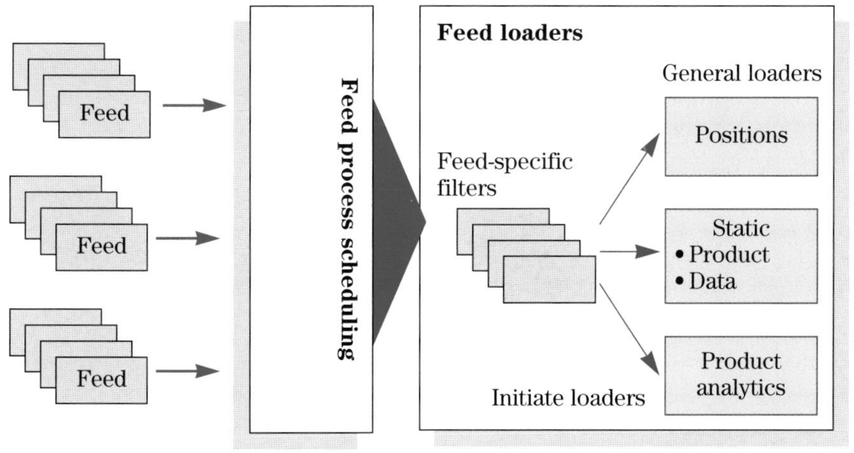

neglected. In some cases, trades may even be booked too late to be captured by the system. Risk system users and designers often must navigate this trade-off of timely versus audited source data. One possible compromise is to use both – producing a "preliminary" risk analysis based on trading system data and following up with a "final" run against books and records data. In such a design, an ongoing automated verification process should be included to ensure the preliminary run is accurate and to resolve any systemic differences.

Architectural concerns
As we mentioned, product analytics will typically come directly from trading desk systems that may lack the rigour of books and records systems. These, like spreadsheet applications, require special attention. Ask and answer the questions mentioned above. In addition, look into the ability for the source system to cut a feed as of a specified time, as typically a trading system runs on a continuous basis rather than on an end-of-day basis as "books and records" systems do. Ensure that there is a clear way to separate out the "real" analytics from the results of traders' "what-if?" analysis, because these two contexts are often intermingled in front office systems.

From the architectural perspective, having the minimum number of different data sources is certainly an advantage. This allows the application support staff to track a smaller number of dependencies, and to have fewer contacts for resolving problems that arise. Certainly, if your firm already has a good comprehensive positions and products data repository or warehouse, you are well ahead of the game (and you can consider yourself among the gifted few). For the rest of us mere mortals, it's a question of either having many data sources or very many. Actually, one disadvantage of keeping the number small, as we alluded to during the timeliness discussion, is that having more sources providing smaller feeds might allow processing to proceed more efficiently if the risk system has a flexible scheduler. Also, the risk system then becomes a bit more immune to problems occurring with individual feed sources. Of course, the likelihood of problems arising increase as the number of sources becomes greater. Additionally, in a large global firm, keeping a list of contacts for a multitude of source systems up to date may be a daunting task. And keeping the risk team knowledgeable about all of their sources may be equally challenging. Overall, it is clearly preferable to keep the number of different sources as limited as practical, but to be flexible enough to handle whatever comes your way.

Risk data storage and processing

Having defined and sourced our data, we now turn the discussion to the flow of information within the risk system. If a single principle could be applied to this topic, it would be "to automate the details and report status and exceptions". It should be clear by now that risk measurement requires the collection of enormous quantities of data from many sources. It will be impossible to maintain control over this sort of environment unless extensive automation is brought to bear.

When such complex machinery is put into place, it is necessary to report on the general health of the "factory" such that confidence in its results can be maintained, and that corrective action can be taken swiftly when necessary. Status information must be provided intelligently on an exception basis; it will be impossible to wade through detailed status on every feed and every process. We could have established "keep it simple" as the guiding principle, and we certainly expect that every risk system builder will attempt to do that to the extent possible. But we recognise that despite best efforts to do so, the system will be complex anyway. The requirements of risk measurement are not simple by any means, and the application solutions, unfortunately, can't be simple either. Keep it simple wherever possible, but don't fear complexity – manage it. One way to do this is by automating the details and reporting on status and exceptions.

Processing input data

Because any risk system is likely to be receiving data from a great number of feeding sources, and at various times of the day and night, it is essential to keep track – systematically – of what feeds are expected, when they are expected, and what time

---

Exhibit 15.8 Some additional data sourcing concerns

When it comes to IT system architecture, doing things the "right way" may initially take longer, but the returns are almost always there. Whenever possible, we highly recommend choosing strategic sources for information. These are the systems that are identified by the firm as key long-term components, are well supported and are generally close to the point where the information is captured. Because of their identification as "critical applications" to the firm, strategic systems are the ones used by the most downstream applications, and are typically more dependable.

The constraint with strategic systems is that they are sometimes in development. In these cases, you will be forced to choose "interim" sources (sometimes involving "legacy" systems or even "spreadsheets"). That's acceptable where necessary, but expect reliability to be low, limitations to be placed on modifications, and a replacement of the source at some point in the future – probably on their schedule, not your own. While the use of "spreadsheets" tends to strike fear in the hearts of IT professionals (and rightly so) there are some steps that can be taken to make life with spreadsheet feeds a little more bearable. The key is to think in the same terms as you do for any other "real" source system. Who is responsible for the system? When, and by what mechanism is the feed produced? Who is the contact person to be called when the feed doesn't arrive, or is incorrect?

they actually arrived. There is great utility in designing into the system a repository for status information along with the tools to allow various modules to easily post status to this repository. By storing feed status information, it will be easy to set alarms and report on missing feeds, as well as obtain an overall picture of which upstream systems tend to be the most problematic (see Exhibit 15.9). The "today's status" information will be critical to risk analysts in their daily production activity, while the longer-term analysis will enable developers to fine-tune the risk system for greater overall reliability.

Armed with the appropriate information about the current "health" of the system, risk analysts can make the necessary decisions to ensure the effective execution of their daily production responsibility. Given a backdrop of established goals for making risk reports available by a certain time in the morning, what choices exist for a risk analyst when some basic position information has not arrived? One choice is simply to hold up the reporting process and wait for the data. A second option might be to substitute in the previous day's positions and continue running. This decision should be made based on an understanding of the day-to-day change in the affected positions as well as their overall impact on risk.

An intermediate approach is to hold off on reporting for the affected areas, continue reporting on the portfolios for which data is ready and to substitute in yesterday's positions to be included in aggregates that include the areas of missing data. In these higher-level aggregates, the effect on risk of any given position may be small enough to warrant use of "best available" data on occasion. For the risk system, the key is to provide feed status information and the tools to implement all alternative solutions that will be employed.

Handling information storage
The name of this particular game is "flexibility". Not surprisingly, this is another of those words that can cause trepidation to system developers, and not without justification. It may be unreasonable to set a broad requirement that the system simply be flexible. It is completely appropriate, however, to define what aspects of the application require the ability to adapt to changing needs – particularly if some further colour can be provided about the nature of likely changes. For example, we know

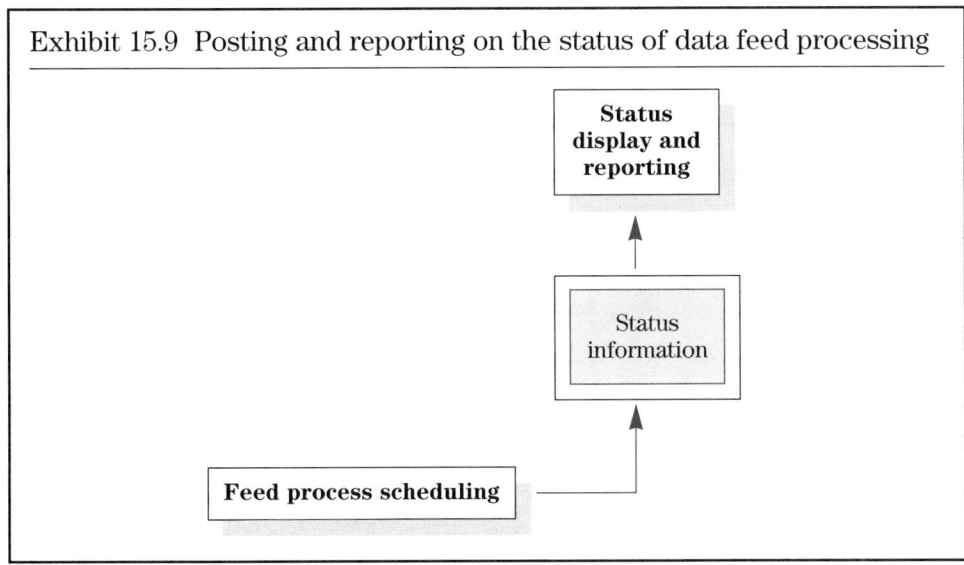

Exhibit 15.9 Posting and reporting on the status of data feed processing

Status display and reporting

Status information

Feed process scheduling

there should be an ability to easily incorporate product attributes not originally anticipated (due to new products or refinement of risk techniques). In addition, it is likely that users will want to aggregate and measure risks in ways that differ from the standard portfolio definitions.

In discussing account data requirements earlier, we commented that firms are likely to reorganise the way they think about the business over time. This indicates that the system must incorporate the ability to easily restructure portfolio definitions and how they are grouped. A particularly useful feature might allow users to routinely prepare risk analysis for standard as well as alternative groupings of portfolios. Exhibit 15.10 introduces a portfolio definition module that could be used to represent this user capability.

Careful attention should also be paid to whether risk monitoring staff should edit data within the risk application. It is clearly preferable to correct data at the entry point rather than adjusting it in a "downstream" analysis system. However, there is often a trade-off between taking control of whatever is necessary to perform the function, versus truly solving the problem of bad data. In the elusive ideal world, all data would be correct (and timely) when it reaches the risk application. In a not-so-ideal, but tolerable world, the risk application would be able to hook into corrections made upstream and have its data fixed automatically. In the real, merely adequate world, data exists in both states, but only to a certain extent. We can only emphasise that unless you are prepared to be in the data correction business, all data problems should be rigorously reported back to the sources for correction, so that the problem will not reappear on subsequent days, which also benefits the firm as a whole. This should be done even if you need to make an adjustment directly into the risk system in parallel for timeliness purposes.

Producing and distributing risk analysis

In Chapters 10 and 11 we highlighted the importance of verifying risk analysis for reasonableness before releasing the results to general distribution. Supporting this, the risk system must include a flexible, interactive reporting module that allows the risk monitoring group to view results and rerun the analysis if necessary. Another

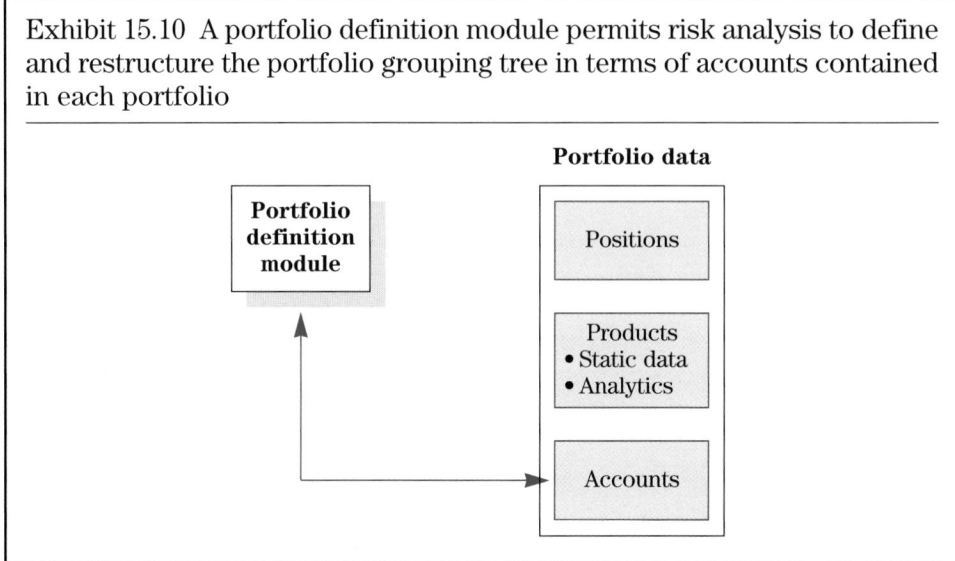

Exhibit 15.10 A portfolio definition module permits risk analysis to define and restructure the portfolio grouping tree in terms of accounts contained in each portfolio

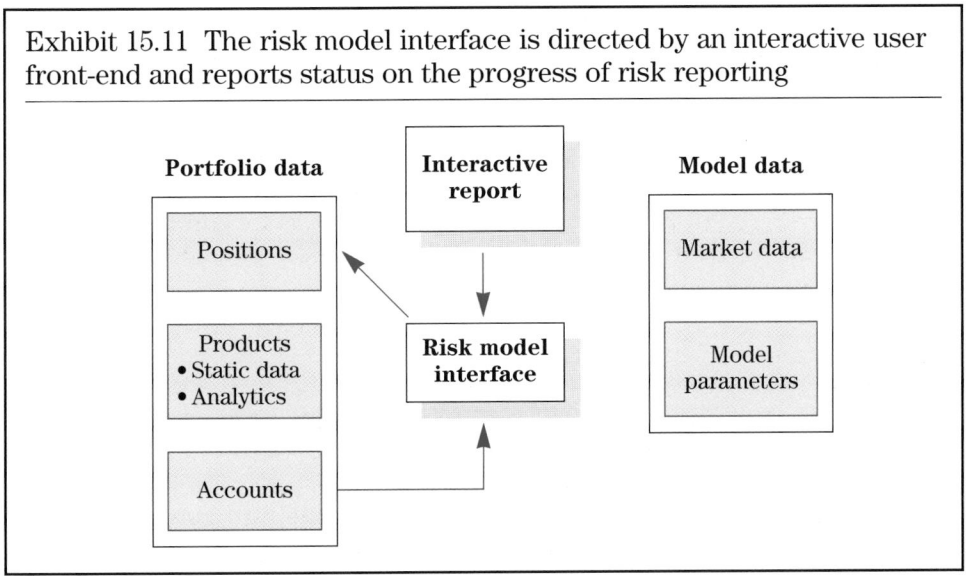

Exhibit 15.11 The risk model interface is directed by an interactive user front-end and reports status on the progress of risk reporting

important dimension of flexibility is that the system should isolate data collection from risk modelling and provide a "universal" interface to risk models. This will support the use of multiple risk models, and the easy inclusion into the overall risk tool-kit of additional models as they are developed. Exhibit 15.11 adds the risk model interface to our picture, along with an interactive user front-end that includes the ability to monitor the progress of the risk reporting process.

The model interface is really a crucial part of a risk system. Inputs into the models and how this data is used within the models must be understood very clearly – a fact that is equally important for internally developed as well as vendor-provided models. For this purpose, it is essential that the models not be considered "black boxes" – a thoughtful approach must be taken in designing the model interface. Finally, the collection of and reporting on the status of which analyses have been run and distributed provide significant value in monitoring the production process. In particular, as the size and number of portfolios to be analysed increases, the time required for running them through the models will increase, and dynamic feedback to risk analysts on progress becomes more critical.

As outlined in Chapters 10 and 11, the risk monitoring group functions as the publishers of risk analysis and related information. As such, there are two phases of report distribution – preview (where the reports are available only to the risk monitoring group) and release (where the reports are made available to all their ultimate end-users). The preview phase gives risk analysts the opportunity to verify results before releasing reports "to the world". Any distribution system should include configurable security permissions so the risk monitoring group can ensure that only the appropriate people have access to particular analyses once they are released.

There are also likely to be a large number of people around the firm who should see some risk reports, and they may have different types of workstations on their desktops. It is therefore preferable for a risk system to be able to present analysis on different computer platforms. The currently popular web-based technology is an ideal platform for report delivery in such an environment. This technology has also introduced the concept of posting information in many different formats, including reports, graphic images, spreadsheets and word processing documents. The risk analysis distribution front-end can also become an excellent repository for other risk-related reports (eg, P&L, balance sheets, trader or market commentary). Building a capability to import, store and display reports generated elsewhere in the firm into the risk delivery vehicle can be very powerful.

Conclusion

In this chapter, we reiterated that effective risk management depends on putting the right information before the right people at the right time. We focused on the specific types of data needed to perform risk measurement, and provided some ideas on where to look for that information. We then turned to describing the feed processing necessary to collect and maintain the data, and discussed the flow and use of the data throughout our prototype risk architecture. Finally, we discussed the distribution of the risk measures and analyses that are produced by risk models.

Exhibit 15.12 brings our full discussion together in a single overall architecture. By now, our picture has grown quite elaborate, but hopefully also, you've learned not to fear this necessary complexity and to look actively for tools or solutions which can contribute to managing those prices which are in the risk group's control. In addition, we hope we've kept the business people with us and have convinced you of the importance of playing a key role in defining the requirements, and in understanding the information flows, that are vital to successful enterprise-level risk system implementation. In the next chapter we digress from our focus on banks and trading firms and consider the application of risk management to other types of organisations.

---

[1] Meridien Research, Inc. 1997.

Exhibit 15.12 From source data to risk report distribution – the complete flow of information through the risk system

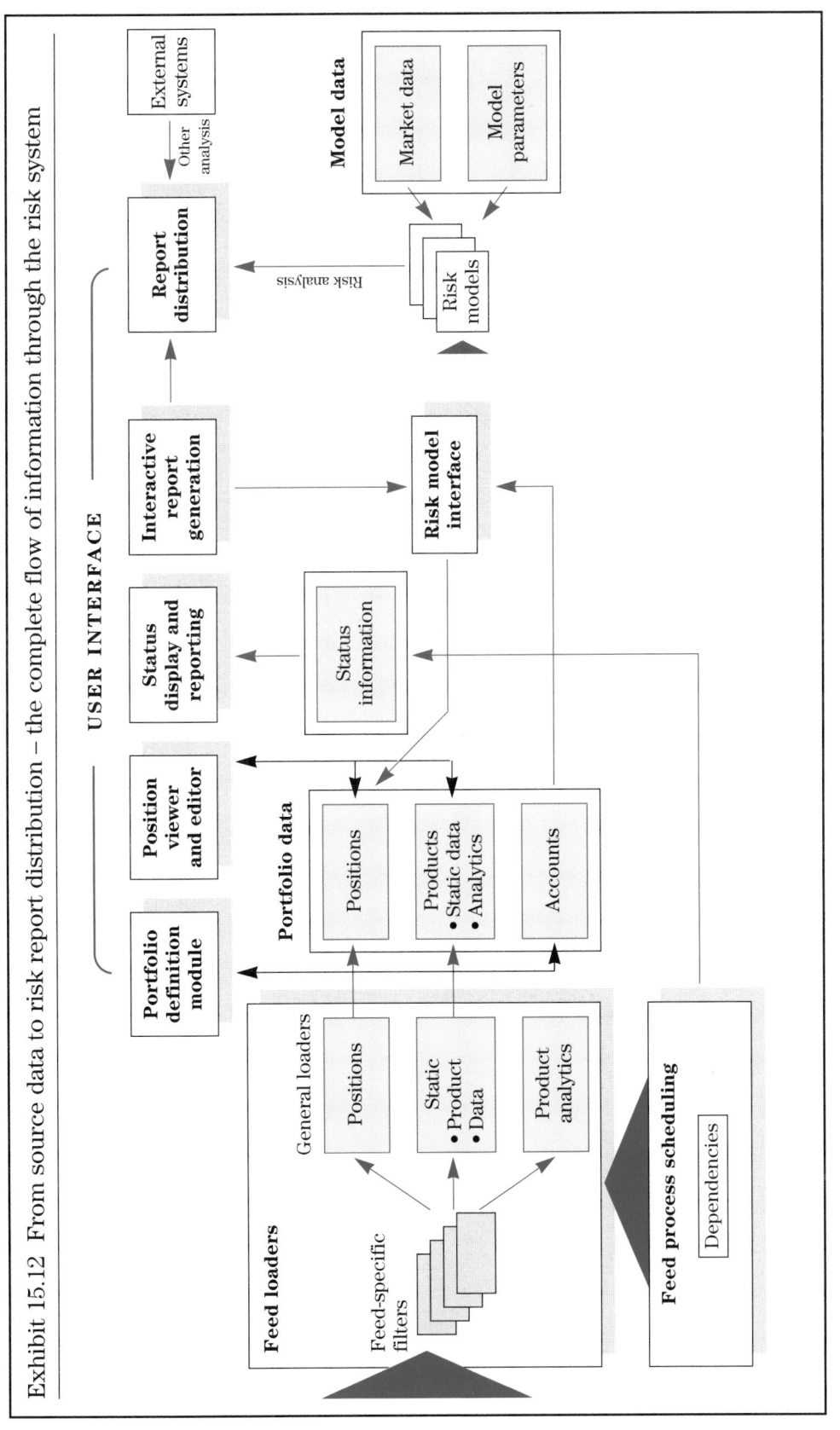

16

Risk management for other users

Introduction

While the focus of this book is mainly on risk management in the securities industry, this chapter takes a brief digression to consider some variations on this theme. In the first case study we step outside of the financial industry altogether to discuss how some of the fundamental issues and methodology of risk management are applied in a large, integrated oil company. In the example, the oil company finds its earnings to be highly vulnerable to a drop in crude oil prices and refining margins. We will describe the steps that the corporation goes through in order to develop a more active risk management strategy. In the second case, we stay within the financial industry but take a look at risk management from the perspective of an institutional investor – in this case a pension fund. Thirdly, we consider another important segment of the financial infrastructure – the central banks. Here the emphasis is on reserves management and some of the bench-marking alternatives and risk/return objectives unique to currency reserve management.

Risk management building blocks

Risk management, whether practised in the securities industry or elsewhere, typically begins with certain key building blocks. These are the starting point analyses and determinations on which an appropriate risk management structure can be built. This foundation differs among industries, sectors of industries and companies. Likewise, risk management analytics and processes differ depending on these inputs and assumptions. We begin this chapter, therefore, with a brief list of questions that any of these institutions might start with.

Identifying the key financial flows
- What are the future cash flows that need to be managed?
- What are the risk factors that are likely to impact these cash flows?
- How do sources and uses of funds inter-relate?

Determining the appropriate time horizon
- Are the risk management objectives primarily tactical (short-term) or strategic (long-term)?
- How do short-term considerations relate to longer term objectives?
- How often are risk management objectives reviewed and revised?

Setting a benchmark
- Is the risk management benchmark a financial measure, or expressed in other terms (eg, achieving non-financial corporate targets)?
- Is performance to be measured in absolute or relative terms?
- Is the benchmark in single currency or multi-currency terms?
- What is the appropriate riskless benchmark against which the effectiveness of risk management is measured?

Defining the investment objectives and attitudes towards risk
- Is the risk management objective active (ie, to enhance the risk/return tradeoff) or defensive (ie, to avoid unacceptable events)?
- What is the appetite and capacity for risk taking?
- What is regarded as acceptable for the level of risk assumed?
- How will risk taking be monitored and controlled?

In the following three examples we will show how these concepts are applied with different emphasis for each of the three entities discussed. We start with an integrated oil company.

Risk management in an integrated oil company

Introduction
The following discussion will demonstrate how some of the fundamental issues and methodology of risk management can be applied to a non-financial company – in this case a large, integrated oil company with operations and, hence, risk exposures in both the producing and refining parts of the business. As background, most oil companies use some type of "risk management", though the definition of this can differ markedly among industry participants. One useful distinction is between defensive risk management and active risk management. The balance and preference between these two strategic orientations, of course, varies by company. Some of the differences are summarised below:

Defensive risk management
The majority of oil companies have in place certain strategies that can be described as defensive risk management. These defensive measures may include operational strategies such as reducing discretionary expenditure when revenues are low, or market-based strategies such as locking in attractive levels when prices are high. A company typically has discretionary investment and expenditure plans such as refinery upgrades or exploration. The expected return on these investments can be considered the company's marginal return on capital, ie, the return that an additional dollar invested in the company would be expected to yield. When revenues are low, the company is often forced to cut down on discretionary investments. This expense reduction is a form of defensive risk management – the company is dampening the shock of lower revenues by incurring lower expenses. The cost of this risk management strategy is the opportunity of not undertaking the planned venture, in other words, its marginal return on capital. An advantage of defensive risk management is that a company pays for it only in times when revenues are low. A strong disadvantage is that at these times there may not be discretionary expenses to reduce, or the opportunity cost of reducing investments may be prohibitively high.

Active risk management

An active risk management strategy, on the other hand, focuses on enabling a company to reduce its risk to a level that it deems acceptable. These hedging strategies typically involve forward contracts, swaps, or options in order to limit the downside risk faced by the company. The level of hedging that is appropriate is derived from a benchmark, which can be developed by taking into account the strategic objectives of the company. The cost of an active risk management strategy can be thought of as a company's marginal cost of capital. If a company wishes to purchase a put option to hedge its downside risk, the premium for the option can be financed by issuing debt or other appropriate forms of financing. Active risk management strategies are generally cheaper than defensive risk management. This is because a company's marginal cost of capital is typically lower than a company's marginal return on capital.

A growing number of oil companies are turning to at least some degree of active risk management as a prudent and cost-effective method for achieving their strategic objectives. In addition to being generally cheaper than defensive risk management, an active risk strategy typically safeguards a company's capital investment plans even when revenues are low. In the rest of this section, we will see how the different components of a risk management strategy correspond to the issues facing an integrated oil company wishing to take a more active approach to its risk management activities.

Key products and financial flows

The integrated oil company that we will be discussing can be described in simple terms as follows:

- The company produces crude oil which also serves as input into its refining processes.
- In addition, the company also purchases crude oil to supplement its own production.
- The company refines crude oil to produce heating oil and gasoline.
- As a result, the company has a net exposure to gasoline-crude and heating oil-crude refining margins and to gasoline and heating oil prices.
- The company has some outstanding debt of which one portion is fixed and the other portion is floating. The company's annual debt expense is a key financial outflow.
- Aggregate corporate expenses are another financial outflow.

A flowchart is often the first step in risk analysis. It should highlight the key product flows and financial exposures as well as their relative magnitudes. The product and financial flows (simplified) are represented in Exhibit 16.1.

As shown in the exhibit, it is clear that the company's earnings are exposed to both product prices and refining margins. Companies, however, face different challenges in their efforts to maximise shareholder value. These differences are especially true in risk management where the "starting points" for various companies can be quite different. For the company we are analysing, we consider the company's profit margin in its crude oil production and refining operations and also its earnings per share (EPS) sensitivity to changes in crude prices and refining margins. A company with a high profit margin and a low EPS sensitivity will be concerned about market volatility in a different way than a company with a small margin and high EPS sensitivity. This can then be translated into a hedging approach that best corresponds with the company's particular financial situation.

Exhibit 16.1 Key product and financial flows for an integrated oil company

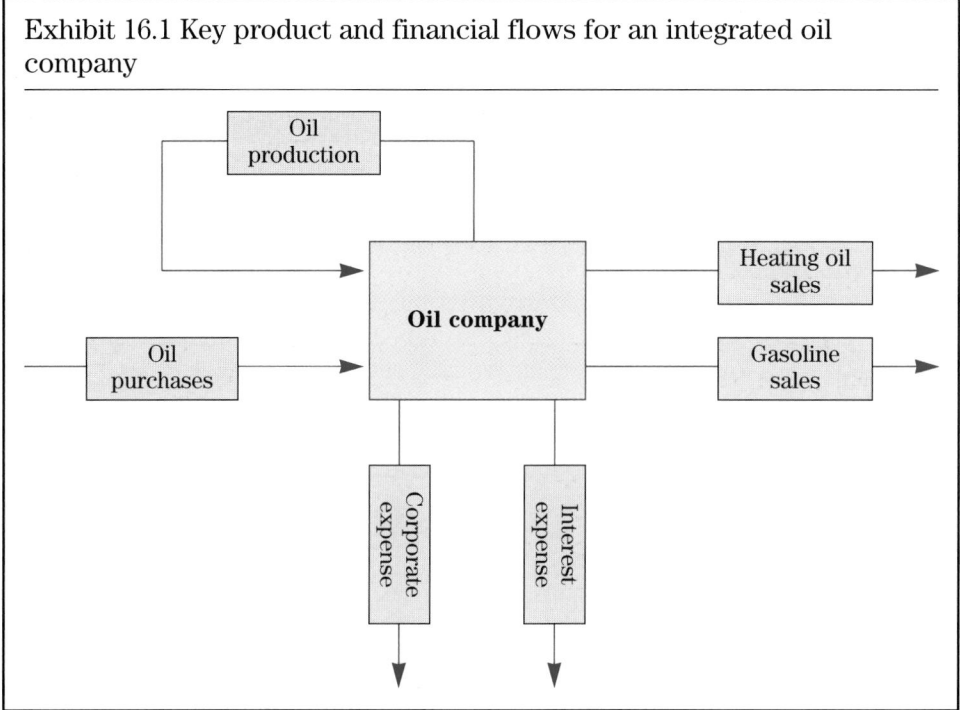

Determining the appropriate time horizon

For non-financial corporations, six months or a year is a typical time frame over which to review earnings and, hence, risk management strategies as well. This in itself makes for a very different risk management practice than in financial institutions which often mark to market on a daily basis. On the negative side, a longer time horizon may mean a weakening of the risk monitoring aspect of risk management because risks may be identified too late to take remedial action. On the positive side, however, a longer time horizon going forward often creates a tighter link between risk management and a company's operational and financial strategy. For example, a company may decide to hedge its risk exposure but only until a future date or event. Or, a strategy to buy options on a quarterly basis may need to be synchronised with expected revenue and cost projections from operations.

Setting a benchmark and related financial objectives

One of key financial guideposts in the oil industry is a company's Return on Capital Employed (ROCE).[1] ROCE is a distinguishing criteria among shareholders and investors and an important variable examined by equity analysts. Each company, in order to meet its target ROCE, would develop its risk management strategy taking into consideration its particular profit margins and income sensitivity. The optimal risk management strategy would maximise the company's chances of achieving its ROCE objective.

The ROCE objective can be translated into a corresponding Earnings Before Taxes (EBT) benchmark. Suppose, for example, that our company's primary objective is to minimise the risk of low earnings. In addition, suppose that the company would like to maintain an ROCE of at least 5.25 per cent. The following shows how an EBT benchmark of US$300 million can be calculated under certain assumptions.

Suppose that the company has a US$2500 million debt portfolio on which it expects to pay US$185 million in interest expense and US$3040 million in Stockholders Equity. Assuming 150 million shares outstanding and a 40 per cent corporate tax rate, the 5.25 per cent ROCE translates into an earnings per share benchmark of 1.20 and, hence, an EBT benchmark of US$300 million.

Of course there may be additional financial considerations and constraints that can also play a role. For example, a company will often tolerate some risk of falling short of its ROCE or EBT benchmark in order to safeguard a portion of revenues which it has earmarked for capital investment. Also, while a company may want to take a conservative stand and minimise the risk of lower earnings, it may still want to retain the upside of a potentially favourable market environment. The benchmark and related financial considerations all have an effect on the risk management strategy that is pursued and, in particular, on the hedging alternatives that may be attractive to the company.

Defining objectives and views toward risk

As discussed above, if the company's primary objective is to minimise the risk of lower earnings, it is possible to construct an efficient frontier that shows EBT and standard deviation for different hedging strategies. A representative frontier is shown in Exhibit 16.2.

The company's objectives and desired cost/risk trade-offs determine both the size of the hedging strategy and the selected point along the efficient frontier. In our hypothetical optimisation analysis, we determined that hedging heating oil with a 3-month forward swap offers an attractive trade-off between risk and return. While 100,000 b/d of this strategy slightly reduces the company's expected EBT, it also significantly reduces the standard deviation, or in other words the company's risk.

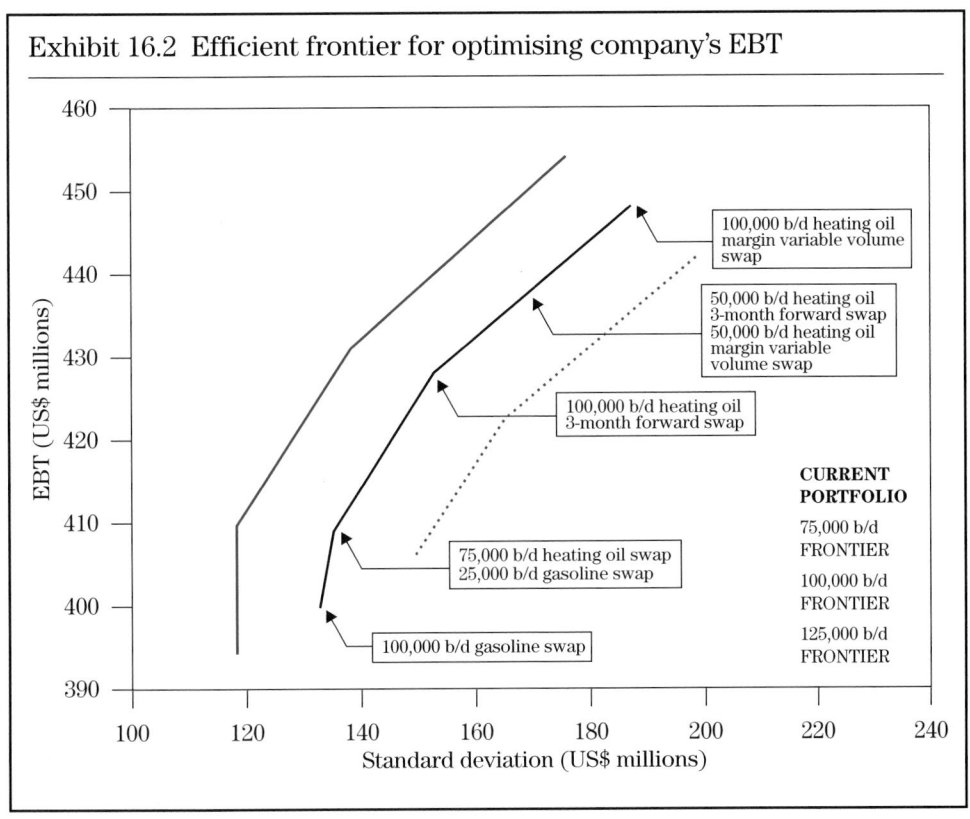

Exhibit 16.2 Efficient frontier for optimising company's EBT

In summary, oil companies are active users of risk management techniques. Risk management strategies have increasingly involved the use of various hedging alternatives. While some may argue that investors are generally aware of an oil company's risks, the counter argument has been that investors also desire predictability in their returns. This section has given a snapshot of some of the issues and analyses that this type of active risk management strategy involves.

Risk management in a pension fund

Introduction

Of approximately US$35 trillion in global securities, nearly US$8 trillion are currently in pension assets. The large size of this asset pool along with increasing pressures and expectations by pension fund sponsors has focused attention on the provision of risk management services by the custodian community to these funds. Pension funds face a highly competitive market fuelled, on the one hand, by clients' return expectations and, on the other hand, by a complex set of regulatory requirements that shape the types of investment and risk management strategies being followed.

This section discusses several aspects of risk management, as outlined in the previous section above, and how they apply to the particular circumstances that pension funds face today. In analysing key product and financial flows, the breadth of investment alternatives, including potentially volatile instruments such as derivatives, real estate, or emerging markets has held out the attraction of lucrative returns. At the same time it has heightened the awareness and use of risk measurement techniques. Regulatory requirements further shape the role that custodians play as providers of risk management information. In determining the appropriate time horizon, transaction cycles and data availability are key. The process of "setting a benchmark" raises the issue of investment performance objectives and what these should be for pension assets. Finally, in defining the pension fund's objectives and views toward risk, heightened competition and cost pressures play an important role in a pension fund's risk management activities. These will be discussed in more detail below.

Key product and financial flows

The broad determination of where risk is coming from starts with an overview of the products and financial flows involved. For pension funds over the last few years, the trend has been toward a wider breadth of investment alternatives coupled with greater depth in the types of services and information provided by custodians for their clients. Pension assets today are increasingly diversified across all markets, not only in equities and fixed income products but in so-called "alternative investments" such as real estate, hedge funds, private placement, and emerging markets.

From a risk perspective, the degree of diversification offers pension funds an opportunity to better manage the volatility of their clients' portfolio while still achieving target returns. The key word, however, is "opportunity". Alongside the potential benefits of diversification is the day-to-day reality that many of these alternative investments are extremely volatile, highly correlated with other investments in the portfolio, and often subject to regulatory and corporate focus. Hence, pension funds have found the use of risk management tools and techniques to shift dramatically from a somewhat optional to an obligatory, centre-stage aspect of their business.

Pension fund managers have responded by providing a greater depth and sophistication in their services. Risk management is one such area. At the same time, custodians have been expanding the scope of the services they offer to pension funds from their traditional custodial responsibilities into both risk monitoring and risk analysis. Risk monitoring has involved detailed tracking of market risk across fund managers, including whether risk guidelines are being adhered to and notification of violations. For many pension funds, risk monitoring responsibilities take on a broader definition than just market risk, to include legal and reputational risk. Hence, "risk management" often also covers the areas of compliance and adherence to regulatory restrictions.

Interestingly, it is also the regulatory arena that is responsible for shaping the "frontier" of risk management services provided by pension funds. Regulatory requirements govern the line between the custodian's responsibility to provide risk information to its client and the grey area of providing advice based on that information. For example, the risk models and systems used to monitor risk can often be used to do "what-if" analyses on alternative portfolio compositions. When risk levels are too high or concentrated in certain asset classes, a good risk system can help identify hedging possibilities or alternative asset allocation strategies.

Hence, the distinction between pre-trade and post-trade risk management activities becomes somewhat blurred. Regulatory requirements address the question of what constitutes a fiduciary relationship and where this relationship starts and ends. Regulations in this area, however, are under increased scrutiny and the industry is in the process of working with regulators to better define the acceptable scope of risk advisory activities.

Determining the appropriate time horizon

Most pension funds monitor risk on a monthly basis. Pension funds with risk managers, however, are aggressively working to shorten this cycle, moving towards weekly, even daily reporting. The time horizon is influenced by both the transaction cycles typically affecting most pension portfolios and the availability of data needed for more frequent risk monitoring. For many pension funds, asset allocation decisions are often made on a monthly or even quarterly basis. Hence, risk reporting and risk committee meetings follow a corresponding timetable.

A monthly reporting cycle, however, is hardly the panacea it may appear to be for complacent risk managers. While a detailed set of risk reports is only run each month, the market shifts on a daily basis and risk exposures change correspondingly. For longer risk reporting cycles, procedures need to be put into place to generate exception reports, such as when guidelines are crossed or risk "hot spots" develop. These can be difficult to catch or even track intra-month. Many pension funds, therefore, supplement monthly value at risk analyses with stress testing and scenario analysis. Monthly value at risk analysis is rarely done in a vacuum. In fact, the competitive differentiation between good and outstanding risk management capabilities at a pension fund is to a large part influenced by what goes on within a monthly risk reporting period.

Setting a benchmark

Pension funds typically benchmark performance against one or a combination of the following:

- key equity and fixed income indices (eg, S&P500, US government bond indices);
- future liability stream;
- industry average;
- top pension fund performance.

As pension fund assets have grown more liquid in recent years, competitive benchmarks have taken on greater importance. The industry leaders set the standards against which other industry participants are judged. It has grown more difficult to rely on simply making an acceptable return over a "safe" portfolio of US securities or over a future liability stream. The bull market of the 1990s made more aggressive targets the goal and more in keeping with client expectations.

While one can hardly argue against competitiveness as an important aspect of a pension fund's success, it is also the challenge of a risk management department to preserve a risk/return perspective on what constitutes an appropriate benchmark. Pegging against an aggressive competitive return normally means taking on a certain level of risk. Using a "riskless" benchmark, on the other hand, can provide a neutral reference point against which to evaluate the portfolio manager, ie, how much risk did the portfolio manager take on to achieve a given return?

Finally, the highly regulated nature of the pension fund industry needs to be taken into account when choosing a benchmark or more broadly considering investment performance objectives. Investment guidelines, compliance issues, and a changing regulatory backdrop all play a role. Normally, risk analyses can be run incorporating various specific, objective constraints. The importance of reputation, however, has often meant additional subjective consideration of what risks are acceptable and which are not.

Objectives and views toward risk
While many of the pension fund industry's objectives and views toward risk have already been mentioned above, it is important to place them in the context of an increasingly cost conscious environment. The competitive pressures driving up return expectations are similarly forcing a reduction in cost. In an effort to keep it simple and keep it low-cost, pension funds are reducing headcount, reducing the number of outside managers, and generally attempting to bring down the level of administrative overhead that has plagued the industry in recent years.

Risk management falls into an interesting category in this respect. While initially sceptical of the expenditure involved in creating a risk management function and either buying or developing risk management analytics, pension funds have become heavily focused developing risk management expertise in recent years. The industry leaders have made this a selling point with existing and prospective clients, further establishing it as a standard service that clients have come to expect. Nevertheless, the wide range of risk management services has caused some debate within the industry as to what constitutes adequate risk capabilities. At the low-cost end, a pension fund can purchase risk management software which provides simple volatility estimates, stress tests, or VaR calculations. At the high end, a comprehensive risk system can cover a wider range of assets classes, more sophisticated analytics, and client customisation. While there is fairly widespread consensus that pension funds need to provide risk management services, the industry is currently splintered by different opinions as to the level of depth required and the necessary cost.

In summary, pension fund managers are a natural user and provider of risk management services for their institutional clients. A wider range of investment alternatives, regulatory changes clarifying risk advisory participation, and a competitive environment forcing pension funds into higher value-added services have all focused attention on risk monitoring and analysis activities. Over the next decade, we expect that many of the advances in risk management capabilities will be driven by experience in this industry.

Risk management at a central bank

Introduction

All central banks, such as the Federal Reserve System in the United States or the Bundesbank in Germany, are actively involved in some type of risk management activity. As the central monetary authority in a country, a central bank is ultimately responsible for maintaining stability and control over the nation's monetary system. In particular, in times of economic and/or political turbulence, the central bank acts as a monetary ballast, a stabilising body for nation's network of member banks. In reality, however, a wide spectrum of sophistication exists among central banks and their ability to deal with risk in an appropriate manner. This includes choosing the best mix of financial assets to meet risk and return objectives. It also includes the central banks' own ability to monitor risk in an accurate and timely manner.

This discussion examines a central bank's risk management of its reserves, which are primarily composed of currency and gold. We will focus on currency, though the basic risk management methodology can also be applied to gold (or other commodities for that matter).

Exhibit 16.3 depicts several aspects of reserves management and examples of the analyses involved. As a starting point, the level of reserves is affected by a country's monetary policy. Monetary policy includes open market operations (ie, the purchase and sale of government securities), changes in the discount rate and any increases or decreases in the reserves requirements that mandate the level of reserves held by member banks within the banking system. Reserves, however, may be held in various forms – different currencies, different durations, fixed vs. floating rate obligations, and so on. Choices made regarding the appropriate mix of reserves have important risk and return implications for the central bank. Hence, a thorough risk analysis is key to this step in the reserves management process. Finally, the best strategies for determining the optimal amount and mix of reserves can still fall short if appropriate reserves monitoring is not in place. Besides reserves levels, monitoring needs to be done on expected returns and their corresponding risk levels, including currency exposure and interest rate exposure.

The rest of this section is designed to provide a flavour of the types of issues and concerns that can affect both the choice of reserves mix and risk monitoring methodology. What follows is one doorway into this complex field, using the same "risk management building blocks" that we used to structure our discussion of risk in an oil company in the first part of this chapter. These include:

- identifying the key financial flows;
- determining the appropriate time horizon;
- setting a benchmark; and
- defining the organisation's return objectives and views toward risk.

We also cover some of the practical issues involved in effectively monitoring risk in a central bank.

Identifying key financial flows

Similar to our starting point in analysing risk management in an oil company earlier in this chapter, one typically needs to begin with a clear understanding of the magnitudes and types of flows affecting the organisation. Here we examine some of the financial flows that affect reserves in a central bank. Starting from the ground up, these can include:

Exhibit 16.3 Aspects of central bank reserves management

Level of reserves	Mix	Monitoring
• Purchase and sale of government securities • Changes in the discount rate • Increases and decreases in the reserve requirement	• Currencies • Durations • Fixed vs. floating rate obligations	• Reserves levels • Returns • Risk

- *Short-term cash flow requirements.* Examples of these are external interest costs, short-term external liabilities of the government and the import cover. One rule of thumb, for example, would be to have reserves sufficient to cover three months of imports. In that case, it is necessary to explicitly consider trade flows and, in particular, any short-term variability in expected import levels.
- *Intervention requirements.* Most governments look to reserves, in part, as a potential buffer against runs on their currency. In the case of domestic capital flight, international capital flight or currency pegging, governments may choose to intervene in the currency markets. While difficult to forecast the extent of possible intervention, reserves management (especially short-term tactical strategy) needs to consider the possibility of these flows and the corresponding liquidity constraints.
- *Receipts for reserve deposits abroad.* Central banks may hold a certain portion of total reserves outside of the country. In that case, there will be a corresponding financial inflow from assets held abroad. The issue of different currencies over different maturities further complicates this analysis.
- *Servicing of external debt.* Short-term and long-term external debt obligations, paid off according to specified timetables, are a key consideration for many developing countries. A detailed analysis of these flows for a country such as Mexico, for example, is needed up front to set the stage for any subsequent risk management analysis.

Overall, reserves can be thought of as a cushion to meet temporary shortages in foreign currency needed to make payments for trade, or to pay interest, or to support the value of the currency if the need arises.

Determining the appropriate time horizon

The flow analysis above leads into some specific issues concerning the time dimension and the appropriate time horizon over which to analyse risk. The timetable of short-term, medium-term and long-term commitments of the central bank, for example, needs to be considered alongside expected receipts. Furthermore, reserves may need to be sufficiently liquid to fund uncovered or unforeseen expenditures. A central bank may, in fact, not be able to invest in long-term assets in order to protect the liquidity of its cash reserves.

For risk analysis, one might ask what the appropriate time horizon is over which to monitor volatilities and risk levels. In general, the answer to this question depends on the time that elapses between revaluations and adjustments to the portfolio. In most large securities firms, for example, revaluations and adjustments occur daily. For non-financial institutions such as the oil company discussed earlier, the time horizon will typically be longer than one day as these firms do not normally mark-to-market on a daily basis and may, in fact, be as long as a year. For a central bank, the answer of course depends on the degree to which it is dynamically buying or selling assets in its reserves portfolios as well as any major changes on the liabilities side.

Setting a benchmark

The choice of a benchmark portfolio depends on a number of factors. Hence, there is no one right answer. Often it is best to keep it simple. If the US dollar is the sole reserve currency, for example, one could benchmark to a return from holding US dollars. If reserves are held in a basket of currencies, one could benchmark to returns from holding these currencies. What follows are some basic examples of asset-based and liabilities-based benchmarks that may be appropriate for a central bank.

Asset-based benchmark alternatives
- Cash reserve weights mandated by the central bank. The central bank could keep the currency composition that it receives and invest it in short-term instruments to achieve its benchmark without risk.
- Value of reserves in a single base currency. Against this benchmark, the central bank assures itself of a risk-free position by converting all of its reserves into the base currency and investing in short-term instruments.
- Basket of currencies. The central bank may decide that there is an optimal basket of reserves it wishes to hold, possibly related to international payment needs and/or intervention currency reserves. By holding these currencies at their respective risk-free rates, the central bank meets this benchmark without risk.

Liability-based benchmark alternatives
- Liability portfolio in percentage terms. The assumption underlying this benchmark is that the reserve holdings of the central bank should reflect as closely as possible the make-up of the liability portfolio. If the liabilities of the central bank, for example, are primarily in US dollars, Deutschmarks and Japanese yen, then assets would be benchmarked against a portfolio with the same percentages.
- Liability portfolio in absolute terms, chosen by level of currency importance or riskiness. In choosing to mirror the liability portfolio in establishing a benchmark for the Central bank, the actual amounts of currency borrowed may be more important than the relative quantities. For example, if one currency is considered to be the most important to hold, the central bank may choose a benchmark that matches that currency liability in absolute terms, with less in the other currencies.
- Liability portfolio with mandate considerations. The central bank could choose the currency amounts for its benchmark portfolio by first establishing a hierarchy based on a combination of liability considerations and policy mandates. For example, the currency benchmark could be built in a two-step procedure. First, the central bank could determine minimum quantities of currency that must be held for intervention purposes. The remaining portion of the benchmark can be constructed as in one of the previous two examples, matching the liability portfolio in either percentage or absolute terms.

Defining the central bank's return objectives and views about risk

Any organisation's risk management strategy is ultimately dependent on what it considers to be acceptable returns and its appetite for risk. Return objectives may be absolute (eg, 10 per cent return, earnings sufficient to cover foreign liabilities). More typically, however, returns are measured against the chosen benchmark, as discussed above. For example, the central bank may simply stipulate that it should not lose money relative to the benchmark or, more aggressively, that it targets to earn at least 100 basis points more than the benchmark. When return objectives exceed the "risk-free" benchmark level of return, however, the central bank must establish risk guidelines that are consistent with this return.

In establishing risk guidelines, VaR methodology requires that the following determinations be made – risk level, rebalancing horizon and the confidence level. For example, the central bank may be comfortable with a VaR where one would lose no more than 100 basis points over a one-week interval with a 99 per cent confidence level. The rebalancing horizon is the shortest interval over which the bank would change its positions. Naturally, the shorter this period, the more frequently risk levels need to be calculated and monitored. In most large brokerage firms, risk is calculated and monitored daily.

For central banks, risk and return objectives are typically formulated against a backdrop of acceptable or authorised investment instruments, markets, or currencies. The mandate of the bank, for example, may stipulate a certain degree of liquidity. Minimum levels of cash reserves are often held as a safety net for intervention purposes.

Conclusion

While the focus of this book has been primarily on risk management in the securities industry, here we have taken a brief digression to consider risk management applications in other fields. We have shown, for example, that a central bank tends to focus on reserves management and return objectives consistent with its goal to manage currency reserves. An oil company is more focused on the predictability of its returns which are affected by oil prices, refining costs, and foreign exchange costs.

At the same time the key components of the risk management process can be generally classified into four tasks: identifying key product and financial flows; determining the appropriate time horizon; setting a reasonable benchmark; and perhaps most importantly, defining the organisation's objectives and views toward risk. In fact, as we have seen throughout this book, the goals of risk management tend to be quite consistent. Different institutions necessarily have different approaches or focuses in monitoring and controlling risk because their profitability is impacted differently by the risks they face. No single practice is universally effective. At the same time, a clear conclusion is that effective risk management, in today's global environment, has increasingly become recognised as a core competency of the successful international enterprise.

In the next section we consider how developments in risk management theory and practice and are influencing the broader environment in which firms now operate.

---

[1] Return on Capital Employed = (After-tax Income + After-tax Interest Expense)/(Debt + Stockholders' Equity).

Section IV

The changing world of risk management

This final section of the book considers how developments in risk management theory and practice are influencing the wider environment within which firms operate. It looks in particular at adaptations in the regulatory structure which is placing greater emphasis on the quality of risk management practices. It also considers changes in accounting and disclosure rules to provide investors with more meaningful risk profile information, and the integration risk measures into the performance measurement and capital allocation processes. Finally, in a more speculative vein, it considers what life might be like in the successful firm in the year 2008.

17

The regulation of financial firms

Introduction

The previous sections of this book have primarily addressed the challenges that are associated with implementing risk management techniques in financial firms, but our analysis of risk management would be incomplete without some consideration of the profound impact this is having on the approach to financial regulation both domestically and internationally.

As we saw in Chapter 2, the collapse of Barings in 1995 initiated intensified concern regarding the safety and soundness of financial markets. This has been a focus for discussions by the G7 heads of government at their annual summit meetings every year since 1995, with particular emphasis on improving the supervision of globally active financial firms. It has also led to increased calls for banking, securities and insurance regulators, working through their respective international organisations – the Basle Committee and the International Organisation of Securities Commissions (IOSCO) and the International and Insurance Supervisor (IAIS) – to develop a common approach to the supervision of international firms.

However, while there is broad consensus that changes must occur in the approach to regulation and the convergence between banking and securities regulators from these different disciplines, it is proving difficult to achieve in practice. This chapter outlines some of the background to the current situation in international regulation and considers what might be expected in the future.

Why regulate?

To begin our discussion it is important to consider why official regulation is so pervasive in financial markets, and why regulatory decisions play such an important part in the way in which firms are organised. There are generally acknowledged to be three primary justifications for official regulation of financial markets:

- *Systemic safety* – ensuring that the financial system itself operates in a safe and sound manner, and is protected from the risk of contagious collapses running from one firm or market to another.
- *Consumer protection* – ensuring that ordinary private users of financial markets are fairly treated by banks or advisers and are afforded some measure of protection against the risk of loss if their bank or adviser becomes insolvent.

- *Market integrity* – ensuring that financial markets operate as efficiently as possible by preventing market manipulation and promoting liquid markets where investors can deal with confidence.

In addition, when regulation moves from the domestic to the international level a powerful pressure arises for regulators to maintain competitive equality between firms from different jurisdictions, and to ensure that firms from one country or regulatory background do not enjoy an unfair competitive advantage over firms that are subject to different regulatory requirements. This consideration, which is often referred to as a "level playing field", has had a significant role in the development of international supervisory standards, most notably in the development of the regulatory system within the European Union.

Nevertheless, despite the existence of these common goals, the difference in the business activities of banks and securities firms has until recently meant that banking and securities regulation have developed along very different paths. Indeed many of the problems that have arisen historically between banking and securities regulators are a direct consequence of these different objectives and priorities.

Banking regulation

The history of banking regulation lies in the experience that many countries have had of the economic costs of bank failures. The need for effective bank regulation on these grounds is evidenced by an IMF survey published in 1996 that estimated that over 50 per cent of all countries worldwide have experienced serious banking sector problems at some point since 1980. In many cases these losses have run into billions of dollars and have had a severe impact on the real economy. Banking regulators have therefore always had a dual concern – to protect the depositors in the bank and to protect against the risk of a systemic collapse. This also explains why central banks have historically taken a close interest in issues related to banking supervision because of their interest in systemic safety and in the integrity of the payments systems in which banks play a crucial part.

The linkage between banking and systemic risk is well described by Goodhart et al[1]: "The key point is that banks are subject to contagious deposit runs which can cause solvent banks to become insolvent both because a large proportion of their assets are not easily marketable (and, probably to a lesser extent, because the panic drives down the value of marketable assets). The value of a bank's loans is based on inside information possessed by the bank which cannot credibly be transferred in a secondary market. Put another way the value of a bank's assets is usually greater on a going concern basis than on a break up of the bank. In particular the failure (losses) in one bank will (rightly or wrongly) cause outsiders to revise their view of the value of other banks' assets".

In response to these considerations, the approach of banking supervisors has been built around the need to protect against the risks in the core credit business of a bank, and to put in place depositor protection arrangements (usually in the form of publicly underwritten deposit insurance funds). The main components of the banking supervisors' approach are:

- Strict entry level requirements, so that the supervisor can ensure that the management of a bank is honest and competent.
- Capital adequacy rules that have been set at a level to ensure that the bank is able to survive a deterioration in the quality of its loan book.

- Limitations on concentrations in lending.
- Close attention to the possible impact of connected business activities, both through limits on lending to connected parties and through the practice of consolidated supervision of banking groups.[2]

The issues that concern banking commissions have also influenced the style and approach with which they have undertaken their task. The priority of the banking regulator is to preserve the worth of the bank by ensuring as far as possible that it remains a going concern. Consequently, the authorities are closely involved in the management of orderly workouts of problem cases, which have to be managed on as confidential a basis as possible in order to avoid the risk of the situation being exacerbated by a run on the institution. This approach to regulation is characterised by the choice of the term "supervision" to describe the activity of the banking authority as opposed to "regulator" which is the term more commonly used to describe securities authorities.

These considerations, combined with the fact that from an early stage banks frequently operated across borders through branches rather than through locally incorporated subsidiaries, led banking supervisors to be the first to recognise the need for international co-operation and harmonisation of standards. The Basle Committee on Banking Supervision was originally set up by the Governors of the Group of Ten countries in 1975 to consider common issues in the supervision of cross-border banking business.

From an early stage, the work of the Committee was motivated by the need to ensure that banks active in the international market should be subject to common regulatory standards in order to avoid a competitive market in regulation. This led to the publication in 1988 of *International Convergence of Capital Measurement and Capital Standards,*[3] which set out for the first time the 8 per cent standard for regulatory capital for internationally active banks; this has subsequently become the benchmark for bank capitalisation worldwide.

Securities regulation

In contrast with banking supervision, the origins of securities regulatory regimes have typically been associated with problems of fraud and misappropriation. The Securities and Exchange Commission (SEC) in the United States for example was set up to deal with the problem of fraudulent prospectuses in the bull market of the 1920s, and has always held the protection of US investors as its pre-eminent objective. The Securities and Investments Board in the United Kingdom, while established much more recently in 1986, was created in response to concerns about the misappropriation of investors funds by a number of small investment advisers in the early 1980s. Similarly, the Securities and Futures Commission in Hong Kong was set up to prevent a repeat of the excesses which accompanied the collapse of the Hong Kong markets in 1987.

The different priorities and concerns of securities regulators have also meant that they have developed different techniques from those of banking supervisors. The greater focus on customer protection and fair dealing has meant that securities regulators place more emphasis on enforcing conduct of business rules through publicity, using the public announcement of fines and disciplinary action in order to encourage compliance. The use of the term regulation as applied to the securities regulator by contrast with the term supervision as applied to the banking supervisor reflects this difference of approach.

Exhibit 17.1 Capital requirements to capture credit risk (simplified)

The Basle accord requires the capital to be equal to at least 8% of the total sum of risk weighted assets:

$$\text{Required Capital} \geq 8\% \text{ of } \Sigma \text{ risk weighted assets}$$

The risk weighted assets are calculated as follows:

On-balance-sheet items (simplified[a])

Risk weighted value	=	0%	Cash held Claims on OECD central governments	x	claim's value

```
Risk              0%    Cash held
weighted                Claims on OECD central governments
value       =     20%   Cash in process of collection
                        Claims on multilateral development banks
                        Claims on OECD banks
                        Claims on non-OECD banks, maturity ≤ 1 year
                        Claims on non-domestic OECD public-sector entities
                  50%   Loans fully secured by mortgages on residential property     x   claim's value
                  100%  Claims on private sector
                        Claims on non-OECD banks, maturity > 1 year
                        Claims on non-OECD central governments
                        Plants, equipment and other fixed assets
                        Real estate
                        Corporate bonds
                        all other assets
```

[a] for more details see International Convergence of Capital Measurement Standards, BIS-Basle Committee, 1988.

Off-balance-sheet items (simplified[b])

```
Risk              0%    Claims on OECD central governments
weighted          20%   Cash in process of collection
value       =           Claims on multilateral development banks
                        Claims on OECD banks                                    mark-to-
                        Claims on non-OECD banks, maturity ≤ 1 year       x     market
                        Claims on non-domestic OECD public-sector entities      replacement
                  50%   Claims on non-OECD banks, maturity > 1 year             value[c]
                        Claims on non-OECD central governments                  + Add-on[d]
                        Claims on all other counterparties
```

[b] for more details see International Convergence of Capital Measurement Standards, BIS-Basle Committee, 1988 + amendment Treatment of Potential Exposure for Off-Balance-Sheet Items, Basle Committee, 1994.
[c] bilateral netting agreements are allowed to be taken into consideration provided certain criteria are fulfilled; for interest rates and foreign exchange related contracts a simpler calculation method can be used alternatively (original exposure method), where the credit equivalent amount is derived by multiplying the notional principal amounts by an conversion factor, which depends on maturity and type of product (see Treatment of Potential Exposure for Off-Balance-Sheet Items, Basle Committee, 1994 for more details).
[d] the Add-on is an additional amount to cover potential future credit exposure, it is derived by multiplying the total notional principal amount by an add-factor which depends on maturity and type of product. In case of netting the add-on factor is reduced (see Treatment of Potential Exposure for Off-Balance-Sheet Items, Basle Committee, 1994 for more details).

The differences are also reflected in the varied approaches to capital adequacy requirements and the protection of customers' property. Thus, while in the case of banking supervision there has always been a close link between the objective of protecting customers' funds and the need to maintain a bank on a going concern basis, the same has not been true for securities firms. The approach of securities regulators has instead been to ensure as far as possible that customers funds are not affected by the insolvency of a securities firm. Consequently, the securities regulators' approach to protecting customers' assets has been built around two complementary techniques:

- Rules that require the segregation of clients' money assets and positions from those of the firm, so that the customer is not financially at risk in the event of the insolvency of a broker-dealer.
- Capital adequacy rules designed to ensure that the firm can be wound down at any time without loss to the firm's creditors (other than those who have provided it with its capital funds).

The approach to constructing capital adequacy rules for securities firms was initially established by the SEC in its net capital rule for broker-dealers. Under this system, a firm was required to maintain a cushion of capital equivalent to the "haircut" or mark-down which the SEC judged would be required if the firm had to liquidate its positions in a distressed market. Consequently, highly liquid, low volatility securities such as government bonds were accorded a relatively small haircut, whereas more volatile or concentrated positions were accorded higher haircuts. Moreover, in keeping with the objective of the rule, which was to maintain high levels of liquidity in broker-dealers, fixed assets such as property were deducted from the available capital. However, in contrast with the rules for banks, the SEC did allow firms to include forms of committed short dated subordinated debt in their capital base on the basis that this was available to help to maintain the liquidity of the firm.

Exhibit 17.2: Simplified net capital requirement formula

+ Ownership equity
+ Subordinated debt
= Total capitalisation
- Deductions for illiquid assets, credit exposure and operational inefficiencies
= Tentative net capital
- Haircuts for market exposure
= Net Capital
- Minimum requirement
= Excess net capital

The SEC net capital rule worked reasonably well while US broker-dealers held relatively small proprietary positions. However, by the mid-1980s, as the newly established UK securities regulators began considering the appropriate capital rules for firms authorised under the Financial Services Act, it was already coming under criticism from the larger firms. They felt that it failed to recognise the diversification benefits in large portfolios, particularly those including options.

This led to the second phase in the development of capital rules for market risk in securities firms, which was the introduction in 1988 of the position risk requirement for firms authorised in the UK by The Securities Authority (TSA).[3] The TSA rules were still based on the principle of ensuring that the firm could be wound down without loss to its customers, but they recognised for the first time the development of portfolio theory in risk management. The rules permitted firms to recognise certain offsets and hedges across their portfolio, both in their equity and fixed income businesses. The rules also introduced for the first time the possibility for firms to calculate their exposure to market risk in their options portfolio by reference to the results of their in-house option pricing models.

The TSA rules were widely welcomed when they were introduced but, unlike the position with respect to international banks, there was no immediate pressure for an international harmonisation of capital rules for securities firms as a result of different rules in different countries. This reflected the fact that, unlike the position in the banking market, there was relatively little cross-border competition between securities firms at that time. As a result, there was no great pressure on the securities regulators to establish an equivalent standard to the Basle Capital Accord for banks. Consequently, although the securities regulators, like the banking supervisors, also established an international organisation – the International Organisation of Securities Commissions (IOSCO) – its primary focus was on issues related to cross-border co-operation in the enforcement of conduct of business and insider dealing rules rather than on the arrangements for supervising securities firms, which was regarded as primarily a local matter for individual regulators.

The European Union and the Capital Adequacy Directive

The idea that it was possible to set different capital adequacy standards for banking and for capital markets was, however, coming under increasing pressure within Europe. The project to establish a European single market by the beginning of 1993 included a proposal to open up the market in financial services to allow banks to offer services in different EU countries without being subject to local capital adequacy or registration requirements. This proposal created the prospect of the European universal banks, which had always been active in their domestic securities markets, gaining access to a cross border securities markets on the basis of a banking licence (and bank-based capital adequacy standards), unlike the situation in the UK or the US, where securities business required a separate licence. In response to this prospect, the UK lobbied for the parallel Investment Services Directive to be adopted which would permit securities firms authorised within the European Union to compete with the universal banks by offering investment services on a cross-border basis as well. The directive also set out to establish the basis on which securities regulators in the different EU countries would be able to continue to enforce their conduct of business rules.

The prospect of the two single market directives, one for banks and the other for investment firms, set the stage for the first international attempt to adopt a single common capital standard for banks and securities firms. This arose because the competition provisions of EU law required that if securities firms were to be offered free access to provide their services on a cross-border basis, there should be common minimum standards of capital adequacy within the EU for securities firms However, at an early stage of discussion, it became clear that the EU countries that operated with the universal banking model would not agree to a separate capital standard for securities firms, as they believed that this could give an unfair competitive advantage. The securities firms, for their part, pointed out that under the existing capital adequacy standards, banks were not required to hold any capital to protect against the market risks in their securities business. It therefore became inevitable that the EU would have to adopt a directive on capital adequacy for both banks and securities firms in order to ensure that there was agreement on the two single market directives.

The Basle/IOSCO project

The prospect of an EU directive setting common capital standards for market risk for both banks and securities firms set in train the first (and to date only) attempt to establish common ground between the Basle Committee and IOSCO on capital adequacy standards for banks and securities firms. The attempt was based on the recognition by the Basle Committee that the increasing involvement of banks in the securities business would require an update to the 1988 Accord to incorporate market risk.

The proposal that formed the basis for the agreement attempt (which has become known as the "building block" approach) was initially put forward by Jerry Corrigan, at the time the chairman of the Basle Committee, and Sir David Walker, then chairman of the Securities and Investments Board in the UK. The proposal, which was relatively simple in design, was to divide a bank or investment firm's business into two components – its "banking book" and its "trading book". It was then proposed that the existing Basle Committee standards should apply to the banking book, while a capital requirement based on modern portfolio theory (similar to the SFA capital adequacy rules) should apply to the trading book.

Within the trading book, separate charges would be made for the general market risk component and for the issuer-specific risk component of the portfolio. However, while this compromise was broadly acceptable to the Basle Committee and to the European securities regulators, it posed significant problems for the SEC who had at that time still not accepted the validity of many of the haircuts implied in the SFA capital rules. The SEC chairman, Richard Breedon, was therefore faced with a proposal for an international standard for capital adequacy which, if applied to the SEC net capital rule, could have resulted in a reduction in the capital requirement for a number of large US broker-dealers.

Breedon's final decision that the SEC would not agree to the new common standard was taken in the course of IOSCO's annual conference in London in 1992. This led to a highly publicised speech by Sir Leon Britton, the EU Commissioner responsible for the Single Market Project, in which he took issue with Breedon over his claim that the new standard was unsafe and confirmed the EU's intention to proceed with the Capital Adequacy Directive. Nevertheless, the failure of the Basle/IOSCO project in 1992 can in retrospect be seen as something of a turning point in regulatory thinking about market risk, as it represented the high-water mark of uniform prescriptive capital standards for market risk.

The Basle Committee and internal models

Although the building block approach was adopted by the EU in 1993 as the basis for the Capital Adequacy Directive, it was never adopted in that form by the Basle Committee. Indeed, it was the industry's response to the consultation paper that the Basle Committee published in 1993 proposing to adopt the same approach, which initiated a completely new direction in thinking about capital for market risk. The overwhelming message from the industry to the Committee was that the prescriptive standards implied by the building block approach were less accurate in measuring a firm's exposure to market risk than their own internal value at risk models. Instead, the industry argued strongly that the supervisors should consider basing their capital standards on the results of such models.

The Basle Committee's response was to set up a task force to examine the way that different firms' value at risk models performed and to consider how a regulatory capital standard might be formulated based on those models. The results of this exercise led to the announcement in December 1995 of a two-track approach to the calculation of capital requirements for market risk (to come into effect from 1 January 1998). One approach for firms without models is based on the building block or "standardised" approach and is similar to that in the CAD, but an alternative, models based approach is available for firms that meet certain qualitative standards for their risk control system. For these firms, the capital requirement will be the higher of:

- the previous day's VaR; and
- a moving average of the previous 60 days' VaR multiplied by three.[4]

The Basle Committee also placed considerable emphasis on the results of backtesting (see Chapter 12), and reserves the right for supervisors to impose a higher multiplier (known as the "plus factor") in the event that a firm's model does not predict actual trading results sufficiently accurately.

In addition, for firms with models that measure exposure to specific issuer risk as well as to general market risk, the Committee agreed after some further consideration that they would also be allowed to use the results of these models to calculate their capital requirement for specific risk as well, subject to a multiplier of four. (For further discussion of the issues associated with modelling specific risk see Chapter 9).

But perhaps more significant than the quantitative standards is the fact that the Basle Committee recognised formally for the first time the importance of the internal control environment in determining the capital standard for banks. As a result, banks that wish to use their internal models for calculating capital adequacy are required to meet the following predefined qualitative standards:

- The bank must have an independent risk control unit that reports directly to senior management and undertakes a daily evaluation of model outputs and the relationship between risk exposures and trading limits.
- The risk control unit must undertake regular backtesting of model results against actual and hypothetical portfolios.
- Senior management and the board of directors must be actively involved in the risk control process.
- The internal model must be an integral part of the bank's process for planning, monitoring and controlling market risk.
- Trading limits should be set in a manner that is consistent with the bank's model and is well understood by traders and senior management.
- Model results must be supplemented by a rigorous programme of stress testing.
- The bank must have a well-documented risk management manual and ensure compliance with internal procedures.
- Internal audit should review the adequacy of the bank's risk measurement system and its overall risk management process at least once a year.

More recently still, and partly as a result of the general recognition of the superiority of an internal models based approach to calculating capital, banks have begun to argue that the Basle Committee should also consider adopting a models based approach to calculating the capital requirement for credit risk in place of the standardised 8 per cent requirement established in the 1988 Capital Accord. This debate is still at an early stage as this book goes to press, but we anticipate increased interest in such an approach as banks improve their ability to model credit risk in line with their capabilities in market risk.

The Derivatives Policy Group and the SEC

At the same time that the Basle Committee was developing its model-based approach to market risk for banks, there was an increasing concern about the SEC's net capital rule. In the US the SEC was responsible for setting the capital adequacy standard for securities firms with large derivatives portfolios. The problem was clearly evidenced by the decision of all the major firms to establish affiliated companies that were not subject to SEC regulation so they could undertake this activity. These firms were referred to as "swaps affiliates" because they took advantage of a 1992 decision by the CFTC, generally referred to as the "swaps exemption", which exempted over-the-counter derivative transactions in interest rate and foreign currency products from official regulation by either the SEC or the CFTC.

This enabled the firms to build up sizeable derivative portfolios without facing the high capital charges that would have been necessary if the business had been conducted by a registered broker-dealer. As a result, by the end of 1994 the swaps affiliates of the six largest US securities firms had grown to the point where their portfolios were significantly larger than the portfolios held within the regulated firm. This development drew attention both from the banking industry, which argued that the lack of official regulation and capital adequacy requirements afforded the securities firms a competitive advantage (banks were not yet required to hold capital for the market risk in their derivatives portfolios, but had a capital requirement for their credit risk), and from the General Accounting Office (GAO). Its 1994 report pointed out the potential regulatory gap arising from the sizeable trading volume of unregulated affiliates.[5]

Following the GAO report, and with the active encouragement of the chairmen of the SEC and the CFTC, the six largest US securities firms set up the Derivatives Policy Group (DPG) in August 1994 to establish a voluntary framework for the official oversight of their unregulated affiliates. The DPG focused on the following four areas where it identified scope for improvements in the information available to the SEC and the CFTC about the firms' derivatives activities:

- management controls;
- enhanced reporting;
- evaluation of risk in relation to capital; and
- counterparty relationships.

The recommendations of the DPG with respect to capital measurement for market risk were remarkably similar to those included in the Basle Committee, with the proposal that firms should employ VaR models to measure their market risk, using a 2-week holding period and a 99 per cent confidence level, although the report stopped short of recommending a multiplication factor to convert the VaR model outputs into a capital standard.

With respect to credit risk, however, the DPG rejected the Basle Committee approach for calculating the credit risk in their derivatives portfolio. Instead, they proposed using net exposures multiplied by observed default ratios for current credit exposures, and a "models" approach for potential future exposure and a two-week maximum loss calculation for each counterparty multiplied by the counterparty's default probability. But like the Basle Committee, the DPG report also placed its primary emphasis on the regulator's ability to form an overall view of the quality of firms' management control environments rather than on calculation of capital requirements.

Following publication of the DPG report, the SEC has received regular reports from the six firms setting out the VaR measures for their unregulated subsidiaries, and as a result has considerable information about the reliability of the different firms' models. Partly as a result of this experience, in late 1997 the SEC issued two important new papers on capital. The first proposed introducing a models-based capital regime for OTC derivatives dealers that chose to register with the SEC. The second invited comments on capital requirements for broker dealers. In both cases the SEC proposed using broadly similar standards for model recognition to those adopted by the Basle Committee.

Precommitment: An alternative approach to setting capital standards

In parallel with the initiative of the Basle Committee to set standards for firms' internal models for market risk capital, a different and potentially competing approach was being advocated by two economists from the Federal Reserve Board in Washington. In an article published in *Risk Magazine* in 1995, Paul Kupiec and Jim O'Brien argued that the supervisors should not get involved in setting standards for internal models, but should instead simply rely on firms to "precommit" sufficient capital to cover their own assessment of the risk that they faced. Under this proposal, the amount of precommitted capital should be publicly available, and the supervisors would be able to penalise a firm that precommitted insufficient capital to cover its actual risk. The authors argued that this would allow the firms to use whatever methodology they regarded as most appropriate and would preclude supervisors from having to make judgements about the relative merits of different measurement systems.

The article gave rise to an extended debate about the relative merits of precommitment and the Basle Committee approach. Kupiec and O'Brien quickly conceded that precommitment could not operate in a vacuum, with any firm that chose to being able to volunteer a precommitment number whether or not it was substantiated by a robust measurement methodology. As a result, however, one of the purported merits of the approach, namely that supervisors would be relieved of the need to judge firms' internal systems, was brought into question because supervisors would still have to make a judgement as to whether a firm had a sufficiently reliable internal system to qualify to use the precommitment approach in the first place.

Notwithstanding these issues, however, the precommitment proposal attracted considerable attention from both academics and the industry as a potentially more flexible approach than that proposed by the Basle Committee, and one which relies more clearly on market disciplines and disclosure to reinforce the regulatory process. As a result, a number of firms have engaged in tests of the approach with the US regulators in order to compare the results with trading results and with the Basle model requirements.

Risk management and the supervision of global firms

The change in thinking, characterised by the Basle Committee's move from its original proposal on market risk in 1993 to its models-based approach in 1995 and by the DPG report/SEC proposals, is representative of a broader shift in regulatory thinking in recent years. The change is particularly evidenced by their view on supervision of large international financial institutions. As the collapse of Barings in early 1995 demonstrated (see Chapter 2), capital adequacy measures are of limited value when a firm's internal controls are inadequate. Barings also clearly indicated that potential systemic disruptions could arise in securities markets as well as in traditional banking activities.

The concern in this area has been summarised by Howard Davies, the chairman of the Financial Services Authority in the United Kingdom in the following terms:

> Systemic risk is still primarily transmitted through the banking system. But the world's banks are increasingly the dominant factor in the world's securities markets. And, in addition, the world's major non-bank securities houses have themselves become core participants in the world's wholesale financial markets. If one of them were to become insolvent the effects would be widespread and that process would be magnified if several such houses were to be affected simultaneously.

It is this concern about potential systemic disturbances that led the G7 heads of government to take a closer interest in financial supervision since 1995, and also led the Joint Forum of banking securities and insurance regulators, which was formally established in 1995, to consider how the techniques for overseeing the activities of large international firms might be improved. In its response to the 1997 Denver Summit, the Joint Forum recognised the importance of achieving an overall assessment of the quality of risk management within a group and emphasised the importance of improving the arrangements for co-operation and communication between the regulators of different entities within the group. The approach proposed by the Joint Forum was also supported by the industry in a paper from the Institute for International Finance, published in February 1997, which advocated a common risk-based approach to the supervision of globally active financial firms.

But despite a general recognition of the need to move towards a common risk-based approach to supervision, progress to date has been constrained by the fact that individual regulators are limited in their resources and in their ability to extend their activities beyond their own jurisdiction and their own legal scope. These problems were touched on by the Fed chairman, Alan Greenspan, in a speech in April 1997 that addressed the problems of implementing a framework for global supervision:

> Another question is whether supervisory authorities have the expertise and resources to provide meaningful oversight and develop accurate assessments of the risk-taking activities of large diversified globally active financial institutions. If the answer is no, as might well be the case, should we nevertheless convey to market participants the sense that we are in fact adequately supervising such activities?

Nevertheless, speaking only one week later, Greenspan recognised the need for further change as follows:

> If market forces are driving financial firms towards centralised decision making regarding risk, pricing and other operational issues, it will be difficult at best to implement a decentralised approach to prudential regulation, however attractive its apparent simplicity. Similarly, in the face of continual market driven innovations in banks' risk management systems,

regulatory approaches based on rigid, one size fits all rules are likely to become quickly outdated, ineffectual, and worse, potentially counterproductive.

It was partly in recognition of the difficulties that national regulatory authorities faced in this area that a Group of Thirty study group on systemic risk chaired by John Heimann of Merrill Lynch (and containing both regulators and industry practitioners) recommended that the industry itself should take the initiative in addressing this issue. The report, which was published in July 1997, proposed that each globally active firm should have a single lead regulator worldwide. It also recommended the establishment of agreed standards of best practice in risk management, as well as common worldwide audit standards for internal control and standards for public disclosure and reporting to regulatory authorities.

Conclusion

We have focused throughout this book on developing risk management techniques, here we turned our discussion to the profound impact that these relatively recent practices are having on the approach to financial regulation both domestically and internationally.

The approach proposed by the Group of Thirty has given rise to considerable debate about the relative role of the industry and of official regulators in establishing standards of best practice in risk management.

As we go to press, the nature of the follow up to the report is still to be determined. However the Group of Thirty hopes to commence work on establishing these standards in the middle of 1998, and if it is successful in this initiative it could prove to be the first step towards a genuinely worldwide regulatory framework to meet the needs of the global market place. Next we consider risk management's equally profound impact on the international standards for reporting and disclosure.

---

[1] C. Goodhart, P. Hartmann, D. Llewellyn, L. Rojas-Suárez and S. Weisbrod, "*Financial Regulation: Why, how and where now?*", Routledge: London, forthcoming 1998.

[2] The banking supervisory approach is well summarised in *Core Principles for Effective Banking Supervision* – the Basle Committee, 1997.

[3] More often referred to as the "Cooke Standard" after Peter Cooke, the then chairman of the Basle Committee.

[4] In 1990 TSA merged with another self-regulatory body, The Association of Futures Brokers and Dealers, to form The Securities and Futures Authority (SFA).

[5] The standard also requires a 10-day holding period, a 99 per cent confidence interval and a minimum observation period of one year.

[6] Technically, the unregulated subsidiaries of US broker-dealers were subject to a modicum of official oversight under the Market Reform Act following the collapse of Drexel Burnham Lambert. The SEC had the right to request information but did not supervise or set capital standards.

18

Reporting and disclosure

Introduction

Shareholders' primary interests these days seem to be in understanding the profitability of business areas and sectors within banks and they are demanding full disclosure of management account profitability, return on risk-adjusted capital and better discussion and analysis of future business prospects. Questions often surround businesses that do not meet their cost of equity and whether cash cows will continue to be cash cows in the future. While risk and how successful management has been at controlling that risk are matters of concern, no real consensus exists on how that does or should translate into share price. Some market participants hold that disclosure of this information is irrelevant (especially in today's bull markets where share prices of financial institutions are highly correlated with the market as a whole); others find that the effect is negative as it exposes risks in a market that still hasn't achieved harmonisation of disclosures; still others argue that it is a distinct competitive advantage that sets the well-managed firms apart from the others. Analysts, in practice, appear to put most of their emphasis on three factors – strategy, quality of management and volatility of earnings.

How does disclosure impact evaluation of these three factors? First, conveyed properly, analysis of risk exposures and risk management tells a lot about a firm's strategy in the use of derivatives and how well management has controlled the risk of the organisation. Increased disclosure also indicates how comfortable management is with its own risk management practices and how convincingly it can translate them into increased analyst and shareholder perception of the quality of management. In the future good risk management metrics may be required by shareholders or at very least, will be conspicuous by their absence. These are not the critical issues, however, as there are just as many other factors that signal soundness of business strategy and quality of management in financial institutions. It is the third point that is most significant – the ability of good risk management to reduce the volatility of earnings inherent in derivatives.

Here, the evidence is young. Since the advent of market risk techniques there have been only a limited number of market events which have allowed the practical testing of VaR's ability to measure risk. Further, VaR itself only gives an estimate of loss within an established confidence level and what investors really want to know is how major market changes will affect earnings (ie, "tail risk"). Experience with VaR and other advanced forms of risk management such as stress testing, do not yet give us well-supported answers to these questions. Market analysts thus feel that a healthy dose of scepticism is warranted. In fact, most believe it will take several more years of experience, greater disclosure levels and a greater awareness of risk management among investors, before the market is willing to place value directly on risk management itself.

In the meantime, those banks and companies that are confident in their risk management practices continue to disclose greater amounts of more meaningful information and exploit short-term perception gains. The market itself will determine whether these gains are turned into substantive long-term value for shareholders.

Derivatives – reporting and disclosure

Arthur Levitt, chairman of the US Securities and Exchange Commission, recently quoted British writer W. Somerset Maugham's witticism that "There are three rules for writing a novel. Unfortunately, no one knows what they are". This is equally true of reporting and disclosure of derivatives and the risks associated with them. And while this book is focused on the many financial products that constitute risk for financial institutions, we deal here with a few of the issues in accounting for some particularly tricky instruments.

Regulators, accounting bodies, tax authorities, exchanges, analysts and investors have all struggled to keep up with the pace at which derivatives have proliferated. The global nature of the growth and management of these financial instruments have meant that stakeholders have had to work together as never before in coming to grips with an effective means of regulating their use by financial institutions.

An ensuing global debate has emerged over how far reporting and disclosure standards must be harmonised. Embodied in this discussion are matters of national sovereignty, shareholder rights, the definition of proprietary information, competitiveness of national markets and, ultimately, the need to maintain liquid, competitive and sound global markets. What is clear is that all of the stakeholders are demanding greater and more transparent levels of information commensurate with the industry's growing ability to quantify and manage the risks involved. Some national standard-setters appear willing, if necessary, to go their own way while others are striving aggressively for harmonisation in what seems primarily an effort to maintain the global competitiveness of their national markets. Whatever the incentives, it would seem evident that the world's markets will be more transparent, and thus safer and more liquid, if a consensus on key accounting and disclosure matters can be reached.

In a March 1997 interview, Sir Bryan Carlsberg, Secretary General of the International Accounting Standards Committee (IASC), asserted that it would be surprising if, very soon after the turn of the century, we don't get to an agreement on one system of accounting standards for publicly held companies. Industry opinion, at least with respect to derivatives, appears to support this. A survey conducted for the IASC by Axel Vietze of the University of St. Gallen in Switzerland revealed that of 136 responding companies, 75 per cent believed that harmonisation of accounting standards for derivatives was important to their businesses. However, few agree on what this means in practical terms!

How well have the various regulators and accounting bodies lived up to the challenge? Some could argue that significant progress has been made in a very short period by looking at the evolution of reporting and disclosure practices over the past several years, while even critics have to concede that it is a wonder that any progress at all has been made given the hurdles involved in seeking an internationally acceptable solution. This chapter attempts to trace recent progress and make sense of today's current morass, taking note of each of the principal stakeholders' positions and how these positions may impact future developments.

International accounting principles: Convergence?

Much of today's international accounting practice is built on historical cost conventions developed for manufacturers. These principles in many cases ignore derivatives altogether (eg, the initial cost of a forward contract is zero!). Also reflecting historical developments, accounting principles differ among securities companies and banks in some countries (such as the US); this has become increasingly troubling given the blurring of lines between these two types of financial institutions. Current debate in accounting circles attempting to resolve these issues centres on not if, but how and where to recognise these instruments in the financial statements.

Principles of accounting valuation

With the myriad accounting standards for financial instruments in place around the world today, and in some instances the complete lack thereof, even professional accountants cannot keep track of how to account for X financial instrument in Y country. (To make things a little clearer for the non-accountant, there are essentially three means of accounting for these products, as set out in Exhibit 18.1.)

To a certain extent at present, the old accounting norms hold true. That is to say, European and, to a large degree, Asian countries currently favour accrual principles based upon historical statutory and tax reporting conventions, while Anglo-Saxon principles, when not explicitly stated otherwise, favour fair value in an effort aimed at protecting shareholder interests. However, treatment within countries as well as internationally can be confusing.

As a simple example, an interest rate swap entered into by US bank in New York may be accounted for under mark-to-market (when considered a trading position) or

---

Exhibit 18.1 Accounting for financial instruments

Method	Description
Fair value (mark-to-market)	Derivatives are carried on the balance sheet at replacement value with changes recognised in earnings or in stockholder's equity
Accrual	Each net payment/receipt which is due or owed under the derivative contract is recognised in earnings during the period which the payment/receipt relates (eg, payment of a fixed leg on a swap contract will be accrued over the period for which it is payable)
Deferral (hedge)	Gains and losses are deferred from the P&L on the balance sheet and recognised in earnings in conjunction with the underlying item (eg, for a manufacturer, the gain/loss on an FX forward hedge would be recognised when a PC is recorded as a sale by a manufacturer)

deferral (when used for asset/liability management purposes) depending upon the nature and purpose of the transaction. The problem is that short of authoritative comprehensive guidance covering all derivatives, each bank has to read between the lines and come up with its own policy for how to account for the instrument, some banks taking a more restrictive interpretation of existing literature than others.

Now take, for example, a French bank doing business in Tokyo that centralises options exposures for risk management purposes in New York and reports for group purposes under IAS. The bank enters into an interest rate option contract in Tokyo to hedge its rates exposure in Japan. Four sets of financial accounting rules may apply to this single transaction – Japanese, French, US and IAS. The problem is that the same transaction may be valued three different ways depending upon the rules that surround it.

Each of these standard-setting policies has its own interpretations for when to value an option under each method. Relevant questions may be:

Exhibit 18.2 Accounting treatment under different systems

Accounting treatment	IAS	US	France	Japan
Interest and currency swaps	• No current authoritative standard - disclosure only	• MTM unless meets certain deferral criteria (rules are not robust)	• Accrual unless substantiated otherwise by meeting a series of tests	• Accrual
Interest rate futures and options	• No current authoritative standard - disclosure only	• MTM unless certain criteria met qualifying for deferral (rules are not robust)	• *Exchange traded:* MTM • *OTC:* Accrual	• Accrual
Foreign currency spots and forwards	• MTM unless meets certain hedge criteria	• MTM unless meets certain deferral criteria	• MTM/accrual/ deferral depending on instrument	• Accrual
Securities portfolios	• *Current assets:* MTM or lower of cost or market • *Long-term:* costs, in the case of equities, revalued of lower of cost or market on a portfolio basis	• *Trading:* MTM • *Held for sale:* MTM with gains/losses to equity • *Long-term:* Amortised cost	• *Trading:* MTM • *Held for sale:* Amortised cost less provisions • *Long-term:* Amortised cost	• *Bond:* Cost or lower of cost or market • *Equity:* Lower of cost or market

- Does it qualify as an accounting hedge under each standard's rules?
- If so, how is the underlying exposure accounted for in each case?
- Is it traded on an exchange?
- Is it a liquid or illiquid instrument?
- Is it an off-market transaction?
- Is it covered by a netting agreement?
- On which product desk is it traded?

While not a comprehensive comparison, Exhibit 18.2 shows some of the inconsistencies in place for financial institutions.

To be sure, harmonisation will not eliminate all of the issues associated with accounting for financial instruments, but it would prevent coming up with different accounting treatments based on the same answers! Note that for a multinational bank, this is not only an accountant's nightmare, it also augments the risk of loss due to operational risk.

Valuation principle proposals

Given the sampling of the above valuation issues, it is no surprise that the raging debate among international standard-setters encompasses accounting for these instruments. Much of the current international co-operation is thanks to IOSCO, which has challenged IASC to come up with mutually acceptable International Accounting Standards (IAS) for use in multinational securities offerings and other international security offerings by the spring of 1998.

The European Commission has also jumped on the bandwagon by announcing that rather than amend existing EU directives independently, the EC would associate with the joint work being undertaken by IOSCO and IAS. It seems that the EC believed that divergence from the IASC/IOSCO approach would only serve to undermine the IASC efforts, make European markets less attractive, and potentially, by default, propel US GAAP and therefore US securities markets into the driver's seat.

Given that much of the impetus for harmonisation resulted from the US goal to make its securities markets more accessible to foreign registrants, this was probably a wise decision. The US, for its part, also realised that maintaining its hard line on requiring non-US companies registered in the US to report under US GAAP could potentially jeopardise its leading role. Thus, it seems, harmonisation is to everyone's benefit by creating a level playing field through which companies have access to capital markets around the world based purely upon competitiveness and liquidity. The SEC, supported by President Clinton and the Financial Accounting Standards Board (FASB), has identified the following three elements as necessary for the IAS standards to gain acceptance in the US:

- the core standards must constitute a comprehensive, generally accepted basis of accounting;
- the standards must be of high quality; and
- the standards must be rigorously interpreted and applied.

While not insisting on the hegemony of US standards, American standard-setters have made it clear that they expect the standards must be of a sufficiently high quality to meet acceptance in the US and that they are not about to be jettisoned in favour of IAS. Following that, the FASB's push in adopting its own comprehensive standard covering financial instruments by the autumn of 1997 seems in part designed to influence the eventual IAS statement. In addition, as evidenced by the third requirement above, auditors and regulators will be called on to ensure enforcement in interpretation and application of the standards issued by the IASC – a matter that was also raised indirectly by the Core Principles for Effective Banking Supervision which the Basle Committee issued in April, 1997.

How far apart are the US and IAS proposals?
Four basic issues surround the debate on accounting for financial instruments:

1. From an accounting perspective, is fair value accounting the most representative of economic substance?
2. If so, where should gains and losses be reported (income statement or shareholders' equity)?
3. What qualifies as a hedge and should the accounting treatment be consistent with the underlying item being hedged?
4. If fair value may not be appropriate in certain circumstances, to what extent should disclosure of fair value be required?

Broadly speaking, all of the national standard-setters now agree that for trading instruments the correct treatment is fair value (even though their standards may not yet reflect that agreement (eg, Japan). The issue around fair value accounting really surfaces when discussing hedge accounting. The US FASB and IASC have been able to move closely together on this and each have proposals outstanding (see Exhibit 18.3).

While there remain less important accounting and disclosure issues to be resolved, Exhibit 18.3 shows a great degree of commonality. However, both sides have

Exhibit 18.3 IAS and US areas of agreement

Financial instrument uses (areas of agreement)	Summary of IAS and US proposals	
	Valuation	*Where recognised?*
Hedges of anticipated transactions	Fair value	Outside statement and profit and loss in a separate statement of comprehensive income. When the anticipated transaction is recognised or no longer anticipated the hedge is recognised in the profit and loss statement.
Hedges of an asset/liability or firm commitment	Fair value	In profit & loss and offset by gain/loss on the hedged item
Hedges of investments in foreign entities	Fair value	Outside statement and profit and loss in a separate statement of comprehensive to match the required treatment of exchange differences on translation
Other financial instruments	Fair value	Profit and loss statement

their opponents and neither proposal is assured of issuance. In August 1997, US Federal Reserve chairman, Alan Greenspan, called on the FASB to ditch the above proposal on the basis that it would not improve accounting for derivatives and would constrain prudent risk management. Industry participants have also applied pressure on FASB as they believe that markets will not respond kindly to the increased volatility of earnings. Others, including the SEC, support the proposal and question why the changes should have such a dramatic effect on US companies when disclosure of fair value is already required.

Internationally, other opponents of the current harmonisation efforts under way suggest that accounting standards need not be harmonised to provide adequate investor information and support cross-border listings but that they should be made more comparable through comprehensive disclosure of accounting valuation principles and fair value amounts in the footnotes. In this way, IOSCO could refrain from interfering with the roles of national standard-setters and regulators. Proponents of this argument also have support from national accounting standards committees that need to push through standards quickly to ensure that at least minimum market-based information is available to investors to enable them to reach their own conclusions about the use of derivatives within companies. Insisting on uniformity is believed to delay and jeopardise the aim of greater transparency.

While progress has been achieved through voluntary disclosure and the efforts of national standard-setters, the *1996 Survey of Disclosures About Trading and Derivatives Activities of Banks and Securities Firms* report issued jointly by the Basle Committee on Banking Supervision and IOSCO showed that, of the 79 internationally active institutions surveyed, only 13 (16 per cent) disclosed the amount of deferred gains or losses on financial instruments in the financial statements and only 24 (30 per cent) disclosed the amount of unrealised gains or losses! Interestingly, the disclosure leader for reporting of deferred gains and losses was not the US as one might suspect, but Italy, and by a long way. The US did lead the category in showing the amount of unrealised profit and loss, however. Similarly low results were reported for banks and securities companies identifying the impact of derivatives on revenues.

It seems evident that current accounting and disclosure rules with respect to valuation of derivatives are inadequate to protect and inform investors and regulators and must be brought at least to a reasonable level of international comparability. Whether this is achieved through harmonising accounting practices or requiring a greater level of international disclosure remains to be seen, but is surely less important than delivering financial statements that as a whole convey the economic substance of a company's affairs.

Risk disclosures

Achieving more meaningful accounting and disclosure regarding the valuation of financial instruments used by firms in managing their risk profiles is a critical component of assessing an institution's earnings performance. Equally important is evaluating the level of risk that the institution takes to achieve those earnings. Risk disclosures are even less robust on the whole than those of accounting. Market risk has received most of the attention and significant progress has been made here. Operational risk, however, is the subject of appreciably less discussion, which is surprising in that it has resulted in the biggest derivatives bungles (eg, Barings, Sumitomo, etc). The reason is simple – there is no accepted comprehensive way to measure it. Financial institutions have spent millions developing market risk methodologies (the most common being VaR) over the past 10 years, but few have robust operational risk management systems that translate into earnings and internal capital charges. One of the easiest ways to focus someone's attention is by putting a dollar sign in front of a number, but most banks cannot yet do that. The FDICIA Act in the US, which requires external auditors to report on a bank's system of internal controls, has at least raised sensitivity towards and awareness of the issue. Outside of the US very little progress has been made. However, once accounting and market risk disclosure rules have been sorted out, operational risk will surely hit the issue list in a big way. In fact, proactive banks are already addressing the problem.

Most of the literature and current regulatory requirements, therefore, focus on market and credit risk.

Fisher Report

One of the first studies of market risk disclosure was the report on *Public Disclosure of Market and Credit Risks by Financial Intermediaries* (commonly referred to as the Fisher Report) which was issued by BIS in September 1994. The Fisher Report was issued by G10 banks with the intention of stimulating further debate rather than providing authoritative guidance, although it did offer several alternative approaches for disclosure. The concerns of the committee were effectively that there was a growing gap between how management assessed and managed its financial risks and the information available to outsiders in evaluating the financial institution resulting in a potential misallocation of capital. In summary, the report recommended that all financial intermediaries, regulated and unregulated, provide the following:

- The market risks in their relevant portfolio or portfolios, as well as firms' actual performances in managing market risks in these portfolios.
- The counterparty credit risks arising from their trading and risk management activities, including current and potential credit exposure as well as counterparties' creditworthiness, in a form that permits evaluation of firms' performances in managing credit risk.

While falling short of prescribing the actual form or level of disclosure, the report illustrated six possible templates of market risk and three possible levels of credit risk disclosure. It was believed at the time that a consensus had not yet developed on how to measure the market and credit risks associated with derivatives and it was better to encourage firms to disclose these risks using their own management systems rather than wait for an international consensus to develop. The Fisher Report was successful in fulfilling its purposes of heightening the level of discourse and disclosure on the subject (as evidenced by the trends highlighted in the joint Basle Committee/IOSCO survey discussed below) and it put a stake in the ground for benchmarking future progress.

IAS/FASB

For their part, the IASC and FASB have been slow to respond to market and credit risk disclosure challenges because they have been embroiled in the debate over accounting issues. IAS-32 requires disclosure about the exposure of an entity's financial instruments to interest rate risk while the FASB Statement 119 encourages but does not require information about the market risk of derivatives (see Exhibit 18.4). Overall, IAS-32 would appear to be stronger than US GAAP in this regard, although neither require comprehensive disclosures.

Exhibit 18.4 IAS and FASB market risk requirements

Market risk requirements	IAS	FASB
General	• Applies to all financial instruments	• Applies only to instruments with off-balance sheet risk and derivatives
Quantitative	• Exposure to interest rate risk for each class of financial instrument including contractual repricing or maturity dates • Suggested disclosure of interest rate sensitivity information	• Encouraged but not required hypothetical effects on equity or annual income of several possible changes in market prices
Qualitative	• General discussion required	• Discussion of market risk for each category of derivative financial instrument

Basle Committee/IOSCO

Survey of Disclosures about Trading and Derivatives Activities of Banks and Securities Firms

The Basle Committee and IOSCO annually publish a survey of disclosure, covering a cross-section of the 79 biggest banks and securities companies in the G10 plus Hong Kong. It is intended to summarise trends in disclosure practices and encourage further progress towards transparency and international comparability. The survey covers five broad areas of derivatives disclosure: qualitative information; gross position indicators; credit risk; market risk; and earnings information. All of these areas have shown significant increases in the level of disclosures the past few years, although much important information is still notably lacking. A short summary by area from the latest November 1997 survey is set out in the following subsection:

- *Qualitative information on risk.* Unsurprisingly, this is the category of greatest disclosure incidence as it is relatively the most generic and least controversial. Objectives of trading and non-trading of derivatives as well as general discussion of risks (including specific risks such as credit and market) showed very high rates of inclusion in disclosures (80–90 per cent). Low incidence rates were observed of operational (51 per cent) and liquidity risks (62 per cent) as well as disclosure of areas of accounting policy issues (market valuation reserves, hedge accounting, terminations and credit losses). Disclosure of accounting policies is driven very much by standard-setting bodies; US and Canadian banks have the highest disclosure incidence but securities firms still lag in certain areas.
- *Gross position indicators.* Information on notional amounts was disclosed by all firms surveyed although most recognise that this information is almost useless on its own. The biggest area for improvement noted was disclosure distinguishing between trading and non-trading positions with respect to maturities, fair values and related hedge exposures. Again US banks showed the highest incidence of disclosure while US security firms fell behind in their non-trading disclosures.

- *Credit risk.* This still has a low disclosure incidence with less than half of the institutions showing even their current credit exposures. Only 14 of the 79 disclosed actual credit losses (up from 10 in the year before), not one financial institution indicated the volatility of its current exposures and only 21 of the 79 disclosed potential credit exposure (up from 15 in the year before). US banks fared no better than their international counterparts in disclosure of credit risk. However, trends indicate a growing awareness in the industry of the significance of this risk.
- *Market risk.* Disclosure of market risk improved significantly (in the 1996 survey only 46 per cent of the surveyed firms were found to have disclosed VaR data such as daily exposures, by 1997 this number had risen to 63 per cent). The number of incidents where the daily change in portfolio value has exceeded the VaR-number, however, were reported only by 15 firms (10 in 1996). Still very low, but much better than in the year before, is the number of firms disclosing scenario analysis on trading derivatives (13 in 1997, up from six in 1996). Disclosure by securities houses is poor, none of the Japanese securities houses and only one US securities house have disclosed market risk information. Among banks, the US, Swiss and Japanese banks provided the most information. Japanese market risk disclosures are perhaps the most surprising since these banks are widely believed to be the furthest behind in this area.
- *Earnings information.* Most institutions provided some disclosure of information on trading income although few provided meaningful breakdowns of the impact on total revenues, business area breakdowns or the amount of deferred gains and losses.

Overall, the 1997 Basle Committee/IOSCO survey showed that significant progress has been made but that reporting and disclosure of derivatives and the risks associated with them is still in a startup phase.

New SEC requirements

In January 1997 the SEC issued its report on *Disclosure of Accounting Principles for Derivative Financial Instruments and Derivative Commodity Instruments and Disclosure of Quantitative and Qualitative Information About Market Risk Inherent in Derivative Financial Instruments, Other Financial Instruments and Derivative Commodity Instruments*, effective for periods ending after 15 June 1997. The accounting policy requirements embodied in the report serve to require greater disclosure over how and when derivatives are valued under the three methods described earlier – ie, fair value, accrual and deferral. It does not, however, alter current FASB rules on valuation itself; it simply aims for greater transparency over current institutional practice and extends the requirements to commodity derivatives.

The market risk requirement imposes registrants to disclose quantitative information about market risk sensitive information using one or more of three alternatives:

- Tabular presentation of fair value information and contract terms relevant to determining future cash flows, categorised by expected maturity dates.
- Sensitivity analysis expressing the potential loss in future earnings, fair values or cash flows from selected hypothetical changes in market rates and prices.
- Value at risk disclosures expressing the potential loss in future earnings, fair values or cash flows from market movements over a selected period of time and with a selected likelihood of occurrence.

Registrants are required to categorise market risk into trading and non-trading purposes, providing separate quantitative data for each market risk exposure category (ie, interest rate risk, foreign currency exchange rate risk, commodity price risk, and other relevant market risks, such as equity price risk). Registrants may use different disclosure alternatives for each of the separate disclosures.

The new SEC proposal again shows the willingness of regulators to compromise, allowing management to present what it believes to be the most relevant and meaningful in the circumstances, but at the same time requires a more forward-looking view of risk that users of the financial statements may apply to assess a firm's future performance.

Other stakeholder views: Analysts and shareholders

The old adage that if you ask someone if he wants something, he will probably answer yes, generally holds true for analysts and shareholders too. We will first look at suggested disclosures by analysts in the United States and then discuss briefly how useful practitioners actually believe the information is.

Association for Investment Management and Research

For the past few years the Association for Investment Management Research (AIMR) has called for increased disclosure of derivatives activities. It has published a set of

---

Exhibit 18.5 Suggested AIMR disclosures

For each type of instrument	• notional values • fair values (including methods) • credit and market risk • cash requirements • accounting policies including balance sheet classification • potential counterparty accounting loss
For concentrations of credit risk	• collateral policy and arrangements • amount of losses
For trading derivatives	• average fair values • net gains or losses, by class, business activity, risk
For non-trading derivatives held	• objectives of holding the derivatives • description how each instrument is reported including measurement policies
For derivatives used in hedging anticipated transactions	• description of anticipates transactions • description of classes of instruments used to hedge • amount of deferred hedging gains/losses • events triggering recognition of gains/losses
Other	• description of current positions and activity over period • projected effects of market changes on equity or income • a gap analysis of interest rate repricing or maturity dates • duration of the instruments • value-at-risk from the derivatives

guidelines intended to assist companies in determining which disclosures the analysts require (see Exhibit 18.5).

The recommendations largely follow required or suggested disclosures by FASB but go further in requesting some market risk data. Noticeably, operational and liquidity risk disclosures are absent and credit risk disclosures appear relatively modest.

Conclusion

In summary, accounting and reporting disclosure of derivatives has made significant progress over the past few years. Innovation, however, still outpaces the ability of stakeholders to keep up. Increasingly, levels of required disclosure as well as heightened expectations of voluntary information have been encouraged while regulatory and accounting bodies wade through the multitude of issues surrounding this area. Although national governing bodies (regulators, accounting bodies and tax authorities) have divergent national interests, all insist on greater transparency if not uniformity of treatment in financial accounts.

These divergent interests temporarily inhibit progress and create additional interim risks that smart firms are able to exploit by using disclosure as a competitive advantage. Ultimately, given the risks involved, we shall likely reach a consensus on key issues of accounting and disclosure for derivatives. After addressing the current accounting and market risk disclosure issues, stakeholders are likely to focus more on operational risk as well as interim reporting issues. While no amount of disclosure can prevent material losses from occurring, it is important that stakeholders understand management's philosophy and policies surrounding risk, how well risk has been historically managed and how future risks are being controlled. Current disclosures clearly do not meet these tests. In the next chapter we will discuss risk management applications in capital allocation for the maximisation of shareholder value.

19

Managing risk capital

Introduction

The focus of most of this book so far has been on the practical application of risk management techniques for the purposes of measuring, managing and containing risk. In this chapter we look at the role risk management plays in internal capital allocation decisions within financial firms and in the wider context of maximising shareholder value.[1] While efficient capital allocation does not guarantee success, failure to make the best returns possible on the resources invested by shareholders will almost certainly guarantee sub-optimal performance in an increasingly competitive market-place. Allocating capital even on a relatively rudimentary basis – such as capital adequacy regulations – goes a long way to improving the efficiency of resource utilisation.

In many ways, the challenge for the management of financial firms is no different from that which faces the management of any other company. However, there are a number of factors that are particular to financial companies because of the nature of their business and the structure of their balance sheets. Textbook techniques in corporate financial management have to be adapted. We need to understand what these differences are in order to understand why risk-based capital allocation techniques play such an important role in ensuring effective resource allocation within a firm.

Why are financial firms different?

The primary focus in corporate financial management is to maximise the risk-adjusted returns generated for the providers of capital. In applying this objective, an investment should generate a positive net present value after discounting the expected cash flows. In order, therefore, to measure how much value has been generated, and where, we need to know three things:

- the returns earned (or expected to be earned);
- the amount of capital actually invested or tied up in a particular business, portfolio, transaction, etc; and
- the appropriate risk-adjusted cost of the capital involved.

In the case of a non-financial firm, these three factors are relatively straightforward to measure. The returns are the cash flows generated by the investment, the capital is the amount of funding that the investment requires and the cost of capital can be derived from the market price of the firm's stock. However, because a financial firm is itself in the business of raising and investing money, the position is much less clear cut.

In the first place, it is not always easy to define clearly what the return on a particular investment is, because this itself depends on the risk decisions that the firm takes. So, for example, if a US-based firm acquires a Japanese yen asset (say a five-year Japanese Government Bond, JGB) the return it makes on that investment will depend on three things:

- the rate of return on the JGB in yen;
- the way in which the position has been funded (ie, whether the maturity of the funding is the same as the maturity of the asset); and
- the movements in the exchange rate between the US dollar and the Japanese yen.

It is, of course, possible for the firm to hedge any of these exposures thus influencing its overall return.

Similarly, the amount of capital tied up in a financial investment is not always easy to measure for a financial institution. For a non-financial company, the amount of capital allocated to an investment can be equated more or less to the cost of the investment. Moreover, because the cost of capital for a non-financial firm can be assumed to be indifferent to the level of leveraging, the return on capital should be unaffected by decisions about the amount of debt or equity that the firm has on its balance sheet. However, in the case of financial firms the position is very different. Banks, securities firms and insurance companies are all highly leveraged institutions, which make money out of managing the liability side as well as the asset side of their balance sheets. Consequently for financial institutions, we must clearly differentiate between the refinancing (cash) requirement of a transaction, and the capital allocated to that transaction. The driving force behind most of the development of internal risk capital models has been to determine how much capital is actually tied up in a particular transaction, portfolio, business, etc, and it is this question that will occupy most of the rest of this chapter.

Before moving on to this issue, however, we need to address very briefly the third component in our value generator – ie, the cost of the capital invested (recall the value-generating principle under which the returns earned must exceed the cost of the capital invested). In many cases, the application of the capital asset pricing model will provide a good indication, although this is usually dependent on having beta factors derived from quoted stock prices. Where these are not available (if the institution is not quoted, or when we wish to look at the component businesses, which may have different levels of risk and therefore different capital costs), we may need to use the betas of proxy or benchmark institutions.[2]

Investment vs. allocation of capital

Because financial institutions need to distinguish between the process of funding an investment and the process of allocating capital to it, a further important consideration arises – how do they maintain a clear distinction between the process by which the firm's capital is physically invested in assets of a particular character, and the way in which it is allocated to the business areas.

This issue is of particular significance for financial firms whose balance sheets display significant interest rate sensitivity. For example, if a firm decides to invest its capital directly in a business area, that business can then use the capital as "free funds" to finance its business assets. The firm now has an interest rate sensitive asset (eg, a 10-year bond or loan) and a non-interest rate sensitive liability (capital). As a result of this process, the firm has effectively taken a decision to invest its capital directly into 10-year assets.

The choice of period over which a firm invests its capital can have a very material influence on its earnings. This can be seen in the following example. Firm A does not have any guidelines as to how its capital should be invested. If capital makes up 8 per cent of the assets on the balance sheet, then each asset is effectively financed 92 per cent by borrowings and 8 per cent by non-interest-bearing capital. Exhibit 19.1 shows the interest rate sensitivities that arise if these loans are made for 5 years when the 5-year rate is at 10 per cent (we assume that the loans pay interest annually).

Note that, as interest rates fall, the value of the assets rise (Firm A is earning 10 per cent on something that, if entered into at the new level of interest rates, would only be yielding 9 per cent). The value of the liabilities also rises – a loss – as it is now borrowing at 10 per cent when it could be borrowing at 9 per cent. The opposite happens when interest rates rise. The value of the capital remains unchanged – it is not interest rate sensitive. In this case, the capital has been effectively invested at the five-year rate.

Now consider Firm B. This firm enters into exactly the same transactions, but forces its businesses to match-fund all assets and liabilities, and invests all of its capital in 30-year Treasury bonds. Let us also assume that the 30-year bond yield does not change in tandem with the five-year rate (in practice, the long end of the yield curve is

Exhibit 19.1 Firm A's interest rate sensitivities

| | Value per US$100 at different interest rates | | |
	9%	10%	11%
Value of loans	103.89	100.00	96.30
Value of borrowings	-95.58	-92.00	-88.60
Net assets	8.31	8.00	7.70
Value of capital	8.00	8.00	8.00
Revaluation of net assets	0.31	0.00	-0.30
Net worth	8.31	8.00	7.70

Exhibit 19.2 Firm B's interest rate sensitivities

| | Value per US$100 at different interest rates | | |
	9%	10%	11%
Value of loans	103.89	100.00	96.30
Value of borrowings	-103.89	-100.00	-96.30
Value of bond	8.00	8.00	8.00
Net assets	8.00	8.00	8.00
Value of capital	8.00	8.00	8.00
Net worth	8.00	8.00	8.00

indeed much less volatile than the short end), and that the bond yield remains unchanged. The resulting sensitivity to changing interest rates is shown in Exhibit 19.2.

Because the bond value remains unchanged and the interest rate sensitive items are fully matched, the bank's value does not change with shifts in the five-year rate. Of course, Firm B is still exposed to interest rate risk, but this risk is now related to the 30-year bond yield, and has nothing to do with the sensitivity of the loan activity. Note that we can still say that Firm B has underpinned the loan business with 8 per cent capital – it has simply decoupled the issue of underpinning (allocation) from the issue of asset and liability management (investment).

We can thus see that the choice of investment for a firm's capital can have a marked impact on its earnings and value. It is therefore imperative that the decisions on the investment of capital be clearly distinguished from the process of allocating capital to businesses. If the individual businesses are allowed to decide how to invest the capital, they are most likely to use it as "free" funding of their respective products, with little regard to the interest rate exposure of the firm as a whole.[3]

The allocation of capital

Having dealt with the question of establishing a framework for determining a firm's capital investment objectives, we turn to the question of how this capital should be allocated to the different business areas. The important point to note here is that this is a notional or pro forma calculation of the amount of capital required to underpin a particular business. This is distinct from the investment of capital in that no actual cash investment takes place. No funds are actually transferred to the business in the course of the capital allocation process.

The notional calculation can be driven by any one of a number of different methods, as examined later, and is often used as the basis of performance measurement. In particular, it is very important that management does not just allocate out the total capital on a pro-rata or other such basis, as this provides no incentive for businesses to maximise their return. Instead, management must define a methodology under which capital will be imputed to businesses and then allocate the appropriate amount of capital. It has to be recognised at the outset that a process of this sort may not result in the full amount of the firm's capital being allocated. Any excess capital is not attributable to the businesses, but is a "spare" corporate resource that earns only the risk-free rate of return.

One way of envisaging this process is to think of the capital invested in risk-free bonds, which are then held as collateral to underpin the various activities of the firm. The investment of the capital is in a long-term riskless asset, whereas the allocation of the capital is in risky businesses. This view is consistent with the decoupling of the interest rate risk in the investment from the interest rate risk in the business activities demonstrated in the previous section. However, it gives rise to a further area of confusion – the difference between net and gross returns on capital (ROC).

Net vs. gross ROC
The problem stems from the fact that the decision about the funding of a business has been separated from the decision about capital allocation to the business. Consequently, the question arises concerning who should benefit from the income that the firm obtains from investing its capital. If the business areas' performance is measured on a net (ie, fully funded) basis, the income of the business areas will be less than the income of the firm as a whole by the amount of income imputed to arise

from investing the capital. Alternatively, if performance is measured on a gross basis (ie, after crediting back the return on capital employed) the results will tend to favour those businesses that have a higher requirement for capital relative to those with a lower requirement. A gross measure does provide a more ready basis for comparison with other businesses that have free capital to support their business.

There is no right or wrong answer on this issue. It is a matter of management preference as to which measure suits a firm best, and indeed both can be used in parallel within the same firm. Nonetheless, it is important for the firm to be aware of the potential impact this decision can have on the results of different business areas.

If calculated properly, the following rule will always hold true:

Net ROC + Risk-free rate = Gross ROC

Measuring risk-adjusted return on capital

Having segregated the impact of the investment of capital, we can now turn our attention to the measurement of returns generated through the allocation of capital. In all cases, the approach taken will be a variation of the primary goal of financial management – ensuring that the return earned is greater than the cost of the capital tied up. In its simplest form:

Return ÷ Capital allocated ≥ Cost of capital

Issues in measuring return

There is one important correction that needs to be made at the outset here, which is normally omitted in accounting definitions of return: the difference between expected loss and unexpected loss. Expected loss is a cost of doing business, and should be deducted from the measure of return. Capital, on the other hand, exists to enable us to absorb risks – ie, it covers unexpected loss. In the case of market risk the expected loss is zero because markets can go up as well as down with equal probability. (In fact, one could argue that there is even an expected gain in market risk: just by holding a position in risky assets, we would expect to earn a yield over the risk-free rate at which the position was refinanced.) In the case of credit risk, however, we would always expect a certain level of credit losses, and we should charge these to the business as a deduction from return, even if actual credit losses are lower than the expected amount.

A further issue with the definition of return is the level at which we stop going down into more detail in the profit and loss account. The primary measurement yardstick used – whether returns exceed the cost of capital – assumes a net profit after tax, because the return to an investor is nearly always calculated on this basis. However, this might be perfectly appropriate for a whole business division, but is hardly going to be feasible at the level of the individual trading book, as issues such as allocated overhead, tax rates, etc play an important role. Generally, it is most appropriate to move up the P&L account as we move down through the organisation structure. Thus while an individual trader might be measured purely on the performance of his or her trading book compared with the capital required, a larger profit centre might be measured after deducting some measure of direct costs, and so on. Hurdle rates of return will need to be adjusted during this process, as a target of 10 per cent post-tax return on equity for a business division will imply a much higher pre-tax, pre-overhead return from an individual trader, account officer, etc.

Exhibit 19.3 Essential components of asset volatility approaches

| Current value of portfolio | × | Sensitivity of portfolio to change in underlying factors (default rates, financial market prices, etc.) | × | Potential change in underlying factors | = | Value at risk |

Different measures of capital

Turning to the denominator of the equation, capital, there are a number of different measures that can be used: regulatory capital, risk capital, funding capital, and so forth. It may be appropriate to use more than one such measure, depending on the constraint that needs to be optimised. A firm facing an acute shortage of regulatory capital might be well advised to ignore risk capital, at least temporarily, to concentrate on getting its regulatory capital usage back under control.

We can distinguish between two different approaches to risk capital – an "asset volatility" approach and an "earnings volatility" one.[4] (We use the term "assets" in a broad sense here, meaning essentially any series of expected cash flows, and not just in the accounting sense.) Under an asset volatility approach, we understand a derivation of capital required by assessing the sensitivity of the value of assets to a movement in underlying market prices. Value at risk is such an approach, but it should be noted that regulatory capital is just a cruder version of the same technique. Exhibit 19.3 shows the generic VaR formula: first, we calculate the sensitivity of a particular asset to a change in an underlying market parameter, then we multiply this by the potential change in that parameter over a given time horizon and within a given confidence interval.

The earnings volatility approach takes a different tack, however: it is based on the historical volatility of the earnings of a business. Capital is defined as an amount that would need to be invested to hedge against the downside risk in earnings, assuming that the historical pattern is a valid indicator of future volatility. In simple terms, capital can be thought of as investment in a risk-free financial instrument, such as a government bond, which guarantees a yield sufficient to cover the potential downfall in earnings within a certain confidence interval. A more sophisticated way of approaching this is to think of a series of put options on the earnings of the business, which can be exercised if the returns fall below a given level. The amount of capital required is the cost of purchasing such options.

The principal differences between the asset volatility and earnings volatility approaches are, first, that the latter is based entirely on an historical view of actual revenues rather than an assessment of potential future changes in value; and second, that the asset volatility approach is built up by aggregating individual risk positions. The earnings volatility approach has the advantage that it implicitly reflects all risks entered into, not just those that can be explicitly modelled, thus avoiding problems in aggregating different VaRs, especially across different businesses with heterogeneous risks that make themselves felt over different time horizons. The major drawback with the earnings volatility approach is that it only gives an indication of riskiness without providing any levers for managing those risks. The advantages and disadvantages of each approach are summarised in Exhibit 19.4. In practice, many

Exhibit 19.4 Advantages and disadvantages of asset volatility vs. earnings volatility approaches

Asset-volatility approach	Earnings-volatility approach
+ Allows ex-ante assessment of likely risks	- Allows only an ex-post observation of actual riskiness
+ Provides a detailed explanation of where risk is coming from	- Cannot analyse by itself the causes of volatility
- Requires explicit modelling of all risks (which may not all be identifiable/modellable)	+ Automatically covers all incurred risks, whether individually measurable or not
- Expensive to set up and run (computing power, data capture, etc.)	+ Very inexpensive and easy to calculate
- Does not allow aggregation of non-homogeneous risks (especially with non-comparable holding periods)	+ Allows a group-wide comparison of riskiness across all businesses

institutions will use both, or will at least use an earnings volatility approach to "backtest" the VaR models to ensure that the latter can explain earnings volatility to a sufficient degree (see Chapter 12).

The generic RAPM model

Having thus derived an appropriate measure of return and capital, we can now progress to establishing risk-adjusted performance measurement (RAPM). Again, there are a number of options to choose from, and the alphabet soup generated by practitioners and consultants has added to the confusion: RAROC, RORAC, RARORAC and so on. In practice, there is usually very little difference between these models, and a generic RAPM approach might look something like this:

RAPM = Return (ie, Revenues – Costs – Expected losses) ÷ Risk capital

The risk capital that can be used in the denominator could be a bottom-up VaR type of measure, which would be best suited for use within and across homogeneous businesses, or an earnings-at-risk type of measure, which would be best suited for making more strategic decisions when comparing businesses with each other.

Impact of diversification

Having now established a definition of return, a definition of capital and simple ratio for performance measurement purposes, we have one final problem to deal with – the impact of diversification. This problem arises from the fact that the risk capital of an organisational unit will nearly always be less than the sum of the risk capital of the component parts. For example, the FX trading area might have risk capital derived on a VaR approach of US$100; the interest rate trading area might have risk capital of US$200, derived on a similar basis. The combined risk capital will only be US$300 under a worst case assumption – ie that the relevant FX and interest rate positions are perfectly correlated. Under any other assumption – for example a bottom-up variance/covariance approach or a simple assumption of zero correlation – the combined risk will be less than the sum of the parts.

The same applies to the earnings volatility approach. Because this is derived by compiling a probability distribution of revenues or earnings, the correlation effect will be the same: unless all of the component businesses are perfectly correlated with each other, the standard deviation of a combined distribution will be less than the sum of the standard deviations of the components.

This causes an immediate problem – how do we allocate our capital across businesses if the sum of the capital used by the businesses is greater than the total available capital? If we allocate the available capital to the businesses based on their stand-alone risk capital requirement, we could actually allocate much less capital than we have available, because we will not have accounted for the diversification effect. We therefore need to convert the stand-alone, undiversified risk capital of a single business into a diversified measure by adjusting for the correlation between the individual business and the organisation as a whole. This then gives us a measure of diversified risk capital – the amount of the overall capital utilised by the individual business.

From a performance measurement point of view, however, the only parameter that the business unit head can control is the capital relating to their risks – they cannot control the correlation between their business and the organisation as a whole. So the correct measure of performance should be based on the undiversified risk capital. How do we then reconcile the differing goals of capital allocation (on a diversified basis)? The solution to this conundrum is to allocate available capital based on a diversified basis, and then to convert this back into an undiversified basis using the historical correlation as a guide. We can then compare actual performance on an undiversified basis with the capital allocated on that basis.

For example, consider an organisation that has three businesses, A, B and C. These businesses use 100, 200 and 50 units of risk capital, respectively. The correlation factors of these businesses with the organisation as a whole are 0.4, 0.9 and 0.4. The overall risk capital of the organisation – 240 units – is shown in Exhibit 19.5.

Now consider that the organisation needs to reduce its capital allocation to only 200 units. To do this, it will first have to look at the returns earned by its businesses on a risk-adjusted basis, and should logically reduce the capital allocation to the business that is generating the lowest return per unit of capital. If the reduction in allocation is done on the basis of the undiversified RAPM ratio, as Exhibit 19.5 illustrates, the capital reduction would be spread equally across Businesses A and B, as they both have the same ratios. Applying a capital reduction of 20 to each, we would need to reduce the capital allocation to Business A by 50 (20 divided by 0.4) and to Business B by 22.2 units (20 divided by 0.9). Assuming that the returns earned

---

Exhibit 19.5 Diversified and undiversified risk-adjusted returns

	Return	Undiversified risk capital	Undiversified RAPM	Correlation factor	Diversified risk capital	Diversified RAPM
Business A	10	100	10.0%	0.4	40	25.0%
Business B	20	200	10.0%	0.9	180	11.1%
Business C	10	50	20.0%	0.4	20	50.0%
Group	40	350			240	16.7%

Exhibit 19.6 Capital reduction based on undiversified measure

	Return	Undiversified risk capital	Undiversified RAPM	Correlation factor	Diversified risk capital	Diversified RAPM
Business A	5	50	10.0%	0.4	20	25.0%
Business B	17.8	178	10.0%	0.9	160	11.1%
Business C	10	50	20.0%	0.4	20	50.0%
Group	32.8	278			200	16.4%

Exhibit 19.7 Diversified and undiversified risk-adjusted returns

	Return	Undiversified risk capital	Undiversified RAROC	Correlation factor	Diversified risk capital	Diversified RAROC
Business A	10	100	10.0%	0.4	40	25.0%
Business B	15.6	156	10.0%	0.9	140	11.1%
Business C	10	50	20.0%	0.4	20	50.0%
Group	35.6	306			200	17.8%

remain in the same proportion to the capital allocated, the overall return of the organisation actually falls slightly, to 16.4 per cent (see Exhibit 19.6).

However, if we apply the capital reduction based on the diversified RAPM ratio, we would apply all of the reduction to Business B. Again assuming that the returns remain in the same proportion to the capital allocated, the overall return of the organisation improves to 17.8 per cent, as is shown in Exhibit 19.7.

In this example we kept the returns in each business at a constant percentage of the undiversified risk capital: typically, a business will be made up of transactions with differing profitability and the capital allocation will need to take this into account. We should also note at this point that this kind of calculation will only work with marginal changes in capital allocation: any significant change in the capital allocated will cause a change in the correlations of all of the businesses, as the business mix in the organisation as a whole will have undergone significant change. In practice, optimal capital allocation tends to be an iterative process, constantly adjusting the allocations based on recent experience.

The capital allocation process

As just noted, optimal capital allocation requires repeated adjustments of the allocations based on recent experience, rather than a "green-field" type of calculation. This is due not only to the fact that the dynamics of diversification change in non-foreseeable ways with the mix of transactions and businesses – making an optimal ex-ante allocation almost impossible – but also to the pragmatic fact that the institution already consists of a complex web of open transactions and client relationships, which cannot be altered overnight.

Capital allocation processes can be divided into two classes – a "passive" approach and an "active" approach. Under the "passive" heading are grouped all capital allocation processes that derive an amount of capital attributable to a firm as a whole or to a particular business, transaction, etc, but which do not attempt to steer this number. In its simplest form, this can be the statement of regulatory capital requirements submitted by a bank to its supervisor. This might be further supplemented by an alternative definition of capital, such as risk capital, and may be broken down by business units. A further stage in the evolution of the process might be the application of the imputed capital in a performance measurement context.

An "active" approach to capital allocation uses the process to influence business results: adjusting the capital allocated to particular businesses and encouraging managers to maximise returns on this allocated capital. This approach allows the management of the bank to adjust, for example, the risk capital available to businesses.

The switch from a passive approach to an active one is dependent on the capital allocation methodology's acceptance by managers as a formal part of the performance measurement process. Without this, the imputation of capital to a business remains an academic exercise – business heads will not feel bound by the imputed capital, and any attempt to steer the performance of the bank by changing the allocation will have no impact.

Two steps in the transition from a passive to an active approach can be envisaged. First, the calculations are broadly circulated and discussed and management's acceptance of the methodology is gained. This can be done, for example, by stating broad return expectations as part of the planning process. In a second step, the imputed ROC (or risk-adjusted measure) becomes a formal component of the performance-related compensation of business managers, and perhaps even at lower levels within the organisational hierarchy. The bank is now able to take a more active role in capital allocation decisions, and the link to performance measurement ensures that business managers have an incentive to maximise the return on the resources given to them. These steps are summarised in Exhibit 19.8.

Building a dynamic capital allocation process
Having established a system of capital-based performance measures and linked these to compensation, the bank is now in a position to build a dynamic capital allocation process. The first step in the process is to determine the capital available for allocation.

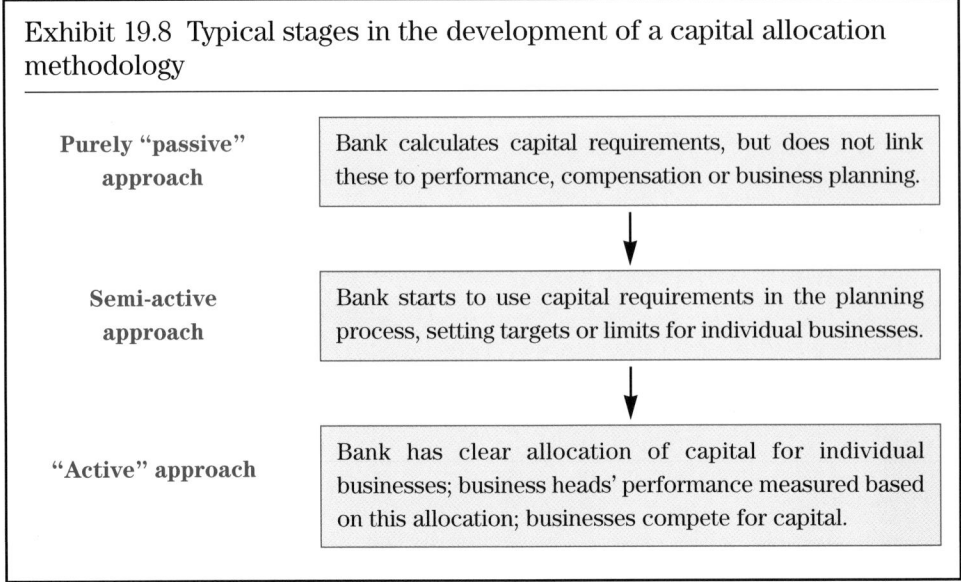

Exhibit 19.8 Typical stages in the development of a capital allocation methodology

Purely "passive" approach	Bank calculates capital requirements, but does not link these to performance, compensation or business planning.
Semi-active approach	Bank starts to use capital requirements in the planning process, setting targets or limits for individual businesses.
"Active" approach	Bank has clear allocation of capital for individual businesses; business heads' performance measured based on this allocation; businesses compete for capital.

This may simply be the available regulatory capital, but is preferably a more sophisticated calculation, taking into account the risk appetite of the organisation and determining the amount of risk capital that management wishes to make available.[5]

Having established the amount of capital available, it is important to set targets for the returns that management expects. These targets may be different for different businesses. Different levels of risk will require different hurdle rates (the riskier the earnings stream, the higher the required return) and management may also wish to invest in strategic projects (such as new businesses) which will not yet generate the required return. It may also be desirable to maintain a certain level of diversification across businesses, even if some of these are not as profitable as others.

In a third step, management will allocate capital to businesses. This is an incremental process because capital already committed to a business cannot be withdrawn overnight. Thus the capital allocation process involves "fine tuning" over time. Businesses that employ too much capital will be given slightly less, forcing the business managers to reduce the number of new engagements as old engagements mature, whereas businesses to be built up will gradually receive more capital.

The fourth step in the allocation loop is to measure the performance generated on the capital employed. This in turn provides input to the next round of allocation, as management adjusts its expectations and thus the amount of capital allocated to each business. Typically, the allocation process will be performed annually, as part of the bank's planning/budgeting cycle. Swiss Bank Corporation combines a three-year planning horizon with a one-year, more detailed, budget. Capital is allocated annually, with the rolling three-year plan enabling management to steer longer-term investment and set expectations well in advance.

The performance measurement process will typically be more frequent than the capital allocation process – it should be an integral part of the firm's internal management reporting (quarterly, monthly, or even weekly/daily for trading activities). The periodic performance measurement needs to focus on the ROC numbers generated, to ensure that the firm is constantly working towards its stated goals. In extreme cases, management may need to readjust the capital allocation during the year – for example, if the performance of the business significantly deviates from expectations. At Swiss Bank Corporation, in addition to the regular monthly management information that includes (annualised) ROC metrics, detailed quarterly analyses are also produced covering such questions as:

- How much capital do we currently have available?
- How much capital are we currently utilising?
- What is our forecast availability and usage over the coming quarters (particularly important when management are contemplating acquisitions)?
- What returns have we earned on the capital allocated?
- What changes in capital allocation do we recommend?

The analyses will cover more than one definition of capital (regulatory capital and risk capital are the two standards; these are supplemented by other definitions on an ad hoc basis to support strategic decisions).

Conclusion

At the current pace of change, it may be impossible to forecast what the financial world will look like 20 years from now, certain events seem more likely than others.

As firms are faced with new competitors from both beyond their national borders as well as from outside their traditional industry, and as the financial services industry continues to convulse with acquisitions and mergers, it is safe to bet that those firms that appear to have provided the best returns to investors of the future will be the ones that have showed their ability to utilise their capital most efficiently, and acted decisively to ensure that this happened.

In Chapter 20 we will begin a hypothetical discussion on what the future might hold for the rapidly accelerating field of risk management.

---

[1] The principles discussed in this chapter are examined in more detail in *Managing Bank Capital*, Matten, C., published by J. Wiley & Sons Ltd, 1996, ISBN 0-471-96116-7.

[2] An approximation for deriving betas from revenue volatility can be found in Matten (see note 1), pp.95–101.

[3] The important thing to note here is that the decision on the appropriate investment rate for capital does not need to prevent capital being used in practice as a source of financing for the business areas. This can be achieved by an internal transfer pricing process that ensures that the businesses are charged with the appropriate yield for the bank's desired investment horizon, and the interest rate "mismatch" or "gapping" analysis treats this as a loan by Treasury to the business at the appropriate duration.

[4] Both of these techniques are examined in full detail in Matten (see note 1).

[5] A further discussion of risk measurement and capital allocation methodologies can be found in *Building a coherent risk measurement and capital optimisation model for financial firms*, Tim Shepheard-Walwyn and Robert Litterman on FRBNY website.

20

Life in the year 2008

Introduction

Throughout this book we have discussed many aspects of managing risk in practice. We have outlined how risk management has evolved; defined market risk and various methodologies for measuring it; described the structure and processes of the risk management function; and articulated methods for applying risk management information, such as capital allocation and regulatory reporting. Our intent in writing this book however was not to strictly document the current and near-term environment, but also to think about what the future might bring.

With that in mind, we spent some time considering our thoughts on the changing world of risk management. The possibilities are vast, and certainly, as with all attempts to predict the future, we may be right about some things and wrong about others. Some things may happen sooner, some later, and some not at all. So, like the oracles of ancient Greece, we also have tried to avoid being too categorical in our predictions and have intentionally left some room for interpretation in our discussion of how the risk management landscape might change over the next five to ten years – in methodologies, and in usage as a common language and as a business management tool. We begin this chapter with a discussion of potential future trends in risk management and conclude it in the mode of Chapter 1, with a depiction of a pivotal event in the life of a firm of the future.

Future trends in risk management

While it is true that enormous strides have been made to date in risk management, it is our suspicion that this area will evolve as rapidly in the future as technology has evolved in recent years. Certain risk management development trends are already clear, and we have attempted to characterise some of them, and to extrapolate them into the future.

In technology, for example, almost every day there is some new breakthrough. The whole technology field has been driven by increases in the speed of processing and reductions in the cost of storage. The reasons for this are two-fold – (a) the large number of people thinking about technology questions, and (b) the base of tools and knowledge that have already been built up, allowing for accelerated innovations. These technology innovations are in turn driving and facilitating firmwide risk management.

So in the risk management arena a similar phenomenon is beginning to occur. The need for risk management has been accepted and the initial concepts have been developed. Now that a base of tools and knowledge has been established and the number of people focusing on risk management has multiplied, we expect to see the same kind of rapid, almost exponential progress that has occurred in the technology world.

General trends

Given the current direction, we anticipate that globalisation will have increased dramatically 10 years from now, facilitated by cross-border mergers and alliances, the gradual migration towards regulatory consistency and the increased use of the Internet. For example, given current consolidation trends, it is frequently suggested that there will be a limited number of successful global financial services firms in the future. These firms will be both vast and complex, increasing the importance of sophisticated risk management tools and consistent risk management practices as a basis for managing diverse global businesses.

To enable cross-border acquisitions to work, risk management needs to become a common language. As described in Chapter 18, a lexicon of risk management standards will need to be applied for global consistency. Imagine a large global entity that acquires a number of smaller firms in different countries with the goal of diversifying its business risk. If the risk, and the diversification benefits, of these acquisitions are not quantified in common terms, these businesses become difficult to manage along with the rest of the portfolio of businesses. They could actually introduce risks rather than reducing them, and management would have no mechanisms to recognise the problems in time to correct them.

So along with the search for a common risk lexicon, and the consolidation of diverse types of financial businesses, methods for comparing different businesses in common terms will continue to expand. Let's take a hypothetical example of an insurance company expanding into banking and brokerage; these business models, and their accompanying profitability measures and risk tolerances, are very different. The evaluation of risk on commercial loans is very different from that of the risk on life insurance liability streams, or on a new form of OTC derivative. But senior management will need the ability to quickly and consistently compare them. In this manner, common risk measurements and integrated risk and profitability reporting will become key decision-support tools for understanding all types of businesses.

Based on these assumptions, we would expect the successful firm to be a global one. It will be in diverse businesses, and in many countries, and common terms for evaluating the risks of these businesses will have been agreed upon and implemented. A mindset focused on considering the risk component in all activities will have been absorbed into the firm's culture. The global risk management staff will be fully trained and supported by sophisticated tools. The risk management function will be tightly integrated with P&L reporting, and an integrated Sharpe ratio will be used to measure businesses and overall volatility of earnings. Information will pass back and forth in common terms between the risk management function and the business units, and they will work in partnership to balance risks and returns.

In this context, perhaps risk management will become an additional tool to help firms manage the predictability of future earnings, thereby increasing control over their own destiny. For example, while accounting reports on what has happened, risk management attempts to project what could happen in the future, both in terms of the range and direction of future revenues and the contribution of various businesses to revenue stability.

Accurate firmwide risk measures will allow a variety of analyses that senior management, investors and regulators currently only dream about. For example, as introduced earlier, we anticipate a tightening of the connection between risk and profit/loss reporting. In this manner, risk moves significantly closer to becoming part of the books and records of a firm. Calculating P&L daily is already standard practice and regulatory reporting of daily P&L, when large losses occur, is on the horizon. This linkage will lead to increased usage of risk and return measures as a business management tool, also supporting the decision-making process for allocating capital.

Risk capital is one of a firm's scarce resources. The cost of capital is directly related to a firm's risk profile. As discussed in Chapter 19, firms today measure return on capital in order to identify businesses that should be increased versus businesses that should be reduced or otherwise restructured. In the future we might expect risk capital to be charged to a business unit, based not on its individual volatility, but rather on its contribution to the total risk capital of the firm. In this way businesses can be evaluated not on the dubious basis of return on capital without regard to the risk incurred, but rather based on profitability after all potential or realised costs – ie, economic value – where the costs are inclusive of risk capital charges. Risk measures will be evaluated on a par with profitability measures and operational costs to develop a view on a business unit's overall economic value.

In addition to using risk to evaluate the economic value of a business, internal and external audits of risk management systems and processes are already the norm, supporting the notion of the business-critical nature of risk information. We expect the required disclosures and audits to become even more comprehensive and pervasive. Calculation and retention of firmwide VaR for accounting and regulatory purposes is already being considered. We might even expect the balance sheet to be supplemented by a business unit VaR report. In the light of current trends, net capital requirements will certainly include a significant component based on value at risk.

Further risk measures
There is already a trend to include more and more types of risk in "market" risk systems. In general, accurate VaR measures are only available where transparent market data exists. New and diverse risks are starting to be priced, however, which will lead to increased data availability. Especially with the development of new types of derivatives, we have moved from a world in which only spot prices of equities, government bonds, commodities and currencies were accurately recorded on a regular basis, to a world in which many other risks are valued. Forwards and options provide pricing (and therefore risk measures) for many dimensions of financial risk. But there are a growing number of volatilities, credit spreads, catastrophe bonds and other new and creative instruments that seek to measure and price a whole series of additional risks. Once we have a price for a type of risk, we can begin to measure it.

This pricing need not be limited to market or credit risks, but in theory a methodology could be developed for pricing operational risks or other business risks. For example, many businesses currently spend hard currency buying insurance for fraud risks; somehow the insurance industry has developed actuarial statistics enabling it to set a price for this type of insurance, and firms have made an intuitive assumption about the price they are willing to pay for comfort in this area. With operational risk more broadly, the first step might be to define a standard set of agreed upon risk factors, such as number of errors, reconciliation exceptions, or fails outstanding, which can then be captured and tracked over a period of time. The operational risk of a particular business could then be determined, and charged back as a cost of doing business. In this manner, if a particular business is efficient and easy to process, its operational risk charge will be lower; if it is complex and difficult to support, the risk charge could be quite high. We could envision this type of decision being included in the list of risk considerations for starting a new business or beginning to trade in a new or complex product.

Macro scenario analyses (as described in Chapter 8) should also play a larger role in the future, and ultimately be facilitated by automation (although the subjective evaluation of results will continue to require human intervention). We could imagine a series of automated scenarios being developed and run periodically against a firm's businesses. These scenarios could be used to project the market and credit exposure to events such as large market moves or significant situations in particular countries or currencies. These macro scenarios should accompany the risk/return measures for senior management's review of businesses for capital allocation.

Risk reporting

As risk management measures become common on financial statements and in annual reports, we may start to see the emergence of publicly available "risk statements". In this context, there is likely to be a continued move towards standardising accepted methods of measurement, so that risk statements can be compared between firms on a global basis. From the regulatory angle, as discussed in Chapter 18, we have already seen co-operative efforts between the regulators, and perhaps a common worldwide risk regulator will emerge to ensure consistency of both risk reporting and risk processes. In the future, we anticipate that risk reporting standards will facilitate consistent usage and understanding of risk measures.

Customers will demand risk reporting along with performance reporting. We are already seeing this trend emerge among institutional investors, as well as the beginnings of interest in measuring risk at the retail level. Envision a future where a retail customer can pull up a consolidated portfolio of mutual funds, stocks and bonds on-line, and see up-to-date performance and risk measures. This is really not too far-fetched and could easily become a competitive necessity given current trends. For example, the NASD recently agreed to allow bond mutual funds to report a risk or volatility rating along with a performance measure. The main concerns about the use of this number are ensuring that it is accurate, that it is being correctly used for marketing, and, perhaps most difficult to assess, that it is being correctly interpreted by the public. The challenge is not the technology, it is customer education and support regarding the interpretation of the numbers.

Risk technology

As discussed earlier, technological advances have already paved the way for the calculation of firmwide VaR. Additional advances will allow for more accurate and complete measurement. The volume of data that can be stored, processed and presented, and the complexity of the analyses that can be performed, will grow dramatically as disk space and computing power continue to expand. For example, we would expect to see firmwide data warehouses storing not only inventory positions and prices, but also analytics; perhaps even validated models will be stored and accessible from multiple systems. We might expect to link real-time position data together with a mapping of risk exposures to market data to allow real-time projection of P&L. Some of these innovations are not that far away. As we are already seeing, the Internet is enabling the distribution of vast amounts of information, and we expect the Web to become the delivery vehicle of choice for the results of risk analyses as well.

Let us look ahead for a moment to the technology world we might live in ten years from now, as that will have a significant impact on our ability to manage risk.

Sometimes the best way to envision the possibilities the future holds is to consider how far things have changed in the ten years that have come before. Ten years ago, PCs were not even consistently used in business, and mainframes were still the norm. Compare that with where we are today, and then consider the exponential progress that is now occurring routinely. Just a few years ago, it was remarkable that storage and computing power could double every 18 months. Now, the timeframe is closer to six months. So the potential for ten years from now, given a world that continues to be conducive to technological innovation, could be off the charts. Nevertheless, let's at least try and imagine it.

The Internet is now accessible from anywhere in the world, either through a direct connection or an optical or radio signal, with irrefutable security. Hand-held devices are common, and confidential messages and information can be sent to remote locations, triggered by a particular event or scenario. So if the CEO is off travelling, an instantaneous transmission of the projected impact of a market event on 10 subsidiaries can be fired off automatically by a warning trigger in the system. The CEO can take action directly by opening a simultaneous on-line dialogue with the heads of the 10 subsidiaries. The group's consensus is that the entity is currently covered by offsetting positions, but when projecting forward the implications of the event, certain trades should be put on to reduce the forward risk. The trades are fired off automatically to global exchanges, with automated confirmations coming back, tagged with the CEO's authorised password.

This is a nice vision, but despite the advances in computing power, the real challenge in this picture will be integrating data from diverse sources and supporting compatibility between diverse technologies. As we see today in established markets such as US Treasuries, standardisation has taken hold. However, there will always be new and innovative products presenting interesting potential returns, but also presenting booking and risk measurement challenges. And as long as there are differences in financial practices around the world (such as payment and settlement methods), this kind of seamless vision will not be fully achievable. This is why we often reiterate that risk management is a constantly evolving process, because it must continue to handle new products, new markets and new ways of measuring risk.

Many open questions

Notwithstanding all the advances to date, it is still a long road to full acceptance of risk management methods and technology by all firms with exposure to risks. In the light of this, perhaps another measure of progress will be the degree of implementation and standardisation of risk management globally. We certainly anticipate that the current regulatory initiatives will have a direct and beneficial impact on acceptance of risk management principles; however, the maximum benefit will be derived if firms adopt risk management as a critical component of active business management, not strictly to comply with regulatory requirements. In other words, there are still many open questions. For example:

- How pervasive will risk management be in different businesses and markets, both financial and non-financial?
- How rapidly will the common language of risk be understood and implemented on a global basis?
- Can firms, and the people within them, adjust to this new way of thinking?
- Can they utilise risk management tools effectively to help manage their businesses?
- What methodologies will be developed for measuring other types of risk, and how will they be implemented?

We have tried to paint a picture here of what a successful global firm will look like in the future, and how that firm conducts itself during a major event it is involved with. The reader will note that our picture of the future relies heavily on enabling technology, and that we have combined the functions of P&L reporting and risk management into a single group. Please join us as we update the scene we depicted in Chapter 1, and travel ahead to an event in the life of a firm in the year 2008.

The setting: The year 2008

During the intervening years since 1998, the number of financial firms has polarised to a handful of diversified mega-firms and some small specialised boutiques. Given current consolidation trends, the large firms are typically involved in most financial services businesses to varying degrees. Although large and far-flung, the successful firm must be able to respond nimbly to the risks implied by market events and new business opportunities. As the global playing field has grown more uniform, market practices and regulation have converged on a single standard. New and innovative products continue to be introduced to measure and price risks that weren't even recognised 10 years ago. And of course technology has advanced dramatically, supporting these business changes.

Our firm of the future – we'll call it "FutureCo" – is a large diversified financial firm, with activities in banking, securities, asset management and insurance, operating on a global basis. The largest portion of FutureCo's business is in securities and asset management, with a smaller concentration in banking and insurance. The firm's concentration is also primarily in institutional businesses, with only a marginal contribution from retail. FutureCo has good capabilities in many countries around the world, but still needs to strengthen certain areas in order to be strong globally. Profitability has been steady and buoyant, without large and unpredictable spikes. The firm attributes this to its focus on managing both risk and return in its diverse businesses.

In FutureCo, risk management has long been considered an essential competency and is tightly integrated into the business. Senior management has fully absorbed and condoned risk as a common language and a key component of the firm's culture. Every business and opportunity is assessed on both a risk and a return basis. To support this view, the P&L reporting and risk management functions have been combined into a single group – for our depiction, called the "Risk/Return" group. Members of the group generate risk and return information for a variety of constituents (both internal and external) and also perform scenario analyses and assess new business ventures from all angles. This group is therefore integral to the support of strategic management decision making.

Because a key component of effective risk management is the ability to quickly assess and communicate information, the Risk/Return group's capabilities have been enhanced to include video conferencing, hand-held computing devices and other advanced tools, so information can be rapidly shared with the appropriate people. Depending on their role and location, some even work from home via video link. For smaller offices without staff on site, interaction is also through video link. The general philosophy is that while technology has obviated the direct need to be on site, physical presence continues to support the acceptance of the risk culture.

The firm's global risk and P&L data is processed in a single system, so the information for each office is combined into a global view; however, the risk and P&L team also needs to be aware of product, business unit or local market activity, and the potential impact on the firm's risk. They use a number of methods to identify these, including video, e-mail, event-driven alerts and various other system warnings. For example, over the years, diverse sets of scenarios have been developed by country, by product and by business, which are triggered by market events. These scenarios can be easily expanded to include new events or to support the analysis of a new business venture.

The event

The event in our depiction is a major acquisition of another large firm. Over the years, FutureCo has grown organically as well as through small acquisitions in other countries, but an acquisition of another global firm is now being considered. FutureCo's intent in this venture is partly for diversification and partly to grow certain businesses. For example, while there are overlaps, FutureCo's business is more heavily tilted towards institutional securities and asset management, while the target firm, code-named "Phoenix", is more oriented towards retail banking and insurance. FutureCo is very strong in the Americas and central Europe, whereas Phoenix is stronger in Asia, Africa and eastern Europe.

The acquisition must be addressed on multiple dimensions. As in 1998, many disciplines are required to support the due diligence process. At FutureCo, risk management is considered to be an essential element both in assessing the target and in quantifying the impact on, and potential diversification benefit to, existing businesses. Following this line of thinking, the acquisition decision process always includes a risk assessment, both in terms of projected business risk and the target's existing risk management capabilities. Because of this, the Risk/Return group plays a key role in the assessment process.

Over the years, the group has developed a number of tools to greatly increase the speed and the consistency of their risk assessments. During a risk assessment, each business unit is evaluated based on its current and projected contribution to risk and return, along with its risk capital allocation, just as an internal business would be. Because the merger implementation process would include a risk culture exchange and the integration of risk systems and data, the extent of this effort is also evaluated. The resulting analysis is used to identify any major issues, and to establish a final price for the largest global acquisition to date.

Scene 1: The Risk/Return group gets a call

The Risk/Return group is now spread around the world, with analysis staff in all major offices. Since the integration of the P&L and risk functions, the combined group is now responsible for projecting future P&L and risk, as well as confirming and reporting on what has actually occurred. They work closely with the business units and the risk committee to measure risk-adjusted performance and to allocate capital. They also work closely with their colleagues from other areas of the firm, such as legal, compliance, operations and internal audit, to ensure all dimensions of risk are considered.

As noted earlier, the Risk/Return group often participates in new business or acquisition assessments, and has developed a number of supporting tools. On this particular Monday, Gerry, one of the co-heads of the Risk/Return group, gets a call from John, the head of Strategic Planning.

John: "Gerry, Hi! Interesting news! The firm's assessing a major acquisition opportunity. We need your team to lead the global risk assessment, similar to the others you've done. But this one is larger than any we've considered before, so you may have to expand your standard plan."

259

Gerry: "OK. I'll get a team focused on it. What's the timeframe?"

John: "Oh, ASAP, of course. When is it ever otherwise? The good news is that we're getting you guys involved early in the process, because there may be significant exposure on this one. We also want you to vet the overall business concept, to see if we'll really get the diversification benefit we think we will."

Gerry: "Do you have any briefing material? That'll help us get a sense of the resources we'll need, as well as how to flesh out the plan."

John: "Sure, I'll send it now." (John forwards an e-mail to Gerry while they talk). "You'll find a number of exhibits in it – covering their business units, historical revenues and projections. By the way, the code-name is "Project Phoenix", just so you know if you get any mystery e-mails. Please also post Francine, as I think the P&L side of the team will need to get focused on this one as well."

Gerry immediately calls a video conference to post Francine and the risk/return managers globally. Depending on the time of day, some of them connect to the call from home. Gerry stresses both the goals of the acquisition and the scale. He also forwards the e-mail containing the briefing document, which gives them an initial sense of Phoenix's business as well as some of FutureCo's drivers for the acquisition. It is clear that this will not be a standard risk assessment, in part due to its size and global nature, and in part due to FutureCo's combined motivations of business expansion and diversification.

The standard plan will need to be expanded to consider all assessment dimensions, including implementation. The plan covers topics such as risk culture, risk processes, and the supporting risk technology and measurements; the risks typically include market, credit, operational and legal. Reputational risk is also considered, as it will impact the perception and therefore the value of FutureCo in the market-place. Business units from Phoenix can then be superimposed on to FutureCo's existing businesses to determine the potential diversification, or the potential magnification, of various risks.

A core team of Terry, Karen and David is assigned to expand the plan and come up with the resource assignments and information requirements.

Scene 2: The first steps of the plan are initiated

The three of them first consider what should be covered. It is clear that they will need to learn more about the structure, the businesses and the capabilities of Phoenix. By searching through various on-line data sources, they quickly gather information from articles, financial and risk statements, global regulatory reports, and the historical activity between FutureCo and Phoenix, as captured in the credit component of the risk system. Because Phoenix is a public company, they can begin to monitor the daily change in risk and return of the various business units. In their search, they try to get a sense of how Phoenix has managed its own risk over the years by plotting trends in the published data.

A picture of Phoenix begins to develop, including where some of its potential risks might be and what categories of information will be required for the assessment. The implementation effort is also considered – ie how long, complex and costly will the merger process be, how advanced is Phoenix's risk culture and technology, what level of integration will be required, will Phoenix retain its own risk technology or will FutureCo's system be more effective? If Phoenix retains its own system, how will summary level data be reported?

Terry: "So the steps we've defined so far include assessing the risk culture and processes at various sites globally, the risk system, and the risk/return measurements from the business units and what their typical exposures are. So far, my read on the culture and processes from the regulatory audits is quite clean, but we also need to consider how they will align with us. Anything else you can think of?"

Karen: "We need to quantify the risks and diversification benefits by business unit, to make them comparable with the way we measure things. That may turn out to be a challenge, because they're concentrated in different businesses to ours. Then we can run a scenario analysis on the combined firm. If we can get the numbers to work, we could easily do a heat map of the whole thing to identify problem areas."

Terry: "So I guess we should have separate teams to look at the various aspects. We need to be sure we can reconcile all the information, so we should define things up front as much as we can before we send people all over the world to visit the sites. The visits should really just be to verify what we have discovered from our information sources, and to get a sense of the consistency of the risk culture. Anything else that comes to mind?"

David: "I was just wondering how quickly we can get on-line access to their risk information? That would help a lot in this process. They should be able to give us secure access, so we can review the major risk factors at least, and start overlaying them."

Karen: "That would help a lot. My sense from the research is that they have decent systems, and they have combined risk and return, which is also good news. Plus the regulatory reports indicate that they conform to the global standards. I just think that since their businesses are so different from ours, I'm not sure how comparable they will be. I assume they have a greater emphasis on credit risk than we would but I guess that's also where some of the diversification benefits come in."

Terry: "I think we can do a lot of this in parallel, and feed everything back as we learn more. Let's also schedule a daily video call, at a time that works for all time zones."

They split up to head the various review teams. Terry focuses on the risk culture and processes; Karen focuses on developing the methodology to measure business units of the combined firm on comparable terms; David focuses on considering the implementation effort and risks. They also set up a global database and a common site for documents, data and notes, so all information can be accessed by the team.

Scene 3: The team works on the assessment process

The two assessment teams (we'll call them the "Qual" team and the "Quant" team) begin the assessment process. Terry and the Qual team will review the risk culture and processes; Karen and the Quant team will measure the historical risks and returns, and apply them to FutureCo's businesses. The goal is to evaluate, in qualitative and quantitative terms, the risk and performance of each business unit, and to develop an assessment of the overall economic value of each, and of the entity as a whole. David and the rest of the implementation team will work also in parallel with effort.

The Qual team splits up to visit various sites around the world. Standard assessment questions will be asked at each location, and the team will use its judgement and experience to evaluate the environment and the culture. At each site, all aspects of risk and performance are assessed – market, credit, operational and legal. They also get an initial sense of the risk culture, how pervasive it is, and how similar or different it is from FutureCo's. This could be as simple as terminology differences, or as complex as diametrically opposed. One thing they have learned from experience is not to take risk culture on face value – often the real circumstances take some time to uncover.

Terry: "So if a concentration limit in a loan portfolio is exceeded, what steps are taken?"

Phoenix staff member: "Actually, we have warnings by various market segments which alert us well before the limit is exceeded. This is mainly because in the loan business there is typically a pipeline of loans waiting for approval, so we can't immediately stop. Also we can't cover all of our risks in the secondary market, or sell off the loans quickly."

Terry: "And if there is a warning?"

Phoenix staff member: "Depending on the magnitude of the portfolio of loans, we'll alert the market segment manager and the division head. They will evaluate the potential returns, and the historical risk/return ratio. They may decide they're comfortable with that level of risk, but may also mark the portfolio in the system as being on warning. The system will also provide them with a number of alternative ways to mitigate the risk, which they can take action on if they want to."

Terry: "Who gets the initial warning?"

Phoenix staff member: "Actually, all the loan officers see it. We like them to be aware immediately if there is an issue. They also have tools to review their existing loans, along with the pipeline and the prices in the secondary market."

The Qual team continues with this line of questioning in a number of business units globally. They feed the information they gather into the central project database, and also communicate it on the daily calls. The goal is to both assess the risk culture and to independently confirm the trends identified by the Quant group.

While the Qual team is performing the site assessment, the Quant team is getting actual feeds of risk and return at the portfolio level from the Phoenix risk systems. They need to analyse this data in order to assign appropriate risk factor proxies to make them consistent with FutureCo's current businesses. This team's key goal is to produce measurements at sufficient granularity and consistency to allow assessment of each business unit's risk, and well as it's potential future contribution to the overall risk of the combined firm. Karen enlists Eric to help on the analysis.

Karen: "Fortunately, the majority of the historical risk factor data we need is already in our database, because we've accumulated the industry standard risk factors over the years. In most cases, Phoenix also used the standards, which will help with the accuracy of our approximations."

Eric: "We also set up a new tree structure for Phoenix, so we can look at their risk and returns by business unit as a stand-alone entity, and then we can overlay them on to our businesses. We can also run scenario analyses for the combined firm, to project the possibilities in terms management is accustomed to seeing."

Karen: "We actually may need to add some additional analyses, because their business concentrations and risks are so different to ours. We have to consider the diversification benefits too, to see if they are truly there once we combine the businesses. We should be able to do that easily in the system, as long as our proxy assumptions are correct."

Eric: "I agree, but I still think we'll need to do some refinement after the first pass, to make sure we're accurately capturing the risks and potential returns. For example, the weights in the various risk factors may need to change because of the differences in the businesses. But that's part of the standard process."

The Quant team continues its analysis of the data, and begins to generate preliminary results to share with Gerry and Francine.

The third major component of the plan is to assess implementation risk. Phoenix might fit well from a business diversification perspective, but the cultures and technology of the two firms might be so far apart that the largest risk is a costly and time-consuming merger integration process. While Phoenix has conformed to industry standards in most cases, the actual implementation of the standards may be very different, and may be costly to adjust. The implementation team needs to assess how far apart the risk measurement methodologies and the risk culture are, and how difficult it will be to integrate the technology, not only of risk, but of other functions as well. David enlists Joanne, who has worked on other merger implementations, to assist in this activity.

David: "We've updated the implementation plan to adjust for the larger scale of this acquisition, but we still need to refine it for Phoenix's different businesses."

Joanne: "OK. So the current categories we have include, in addition to the standard legal and logistical changes, assessing and selecting the technology for overlapping businesses, converting data to common systems, aligning the risk culture, and adjusting the risk and return reporting processes, as well as capital allocation and regulatory reporting. Any initial take on where the problems will be?"

David: "Well, the limits-setting process will be a challenge, again because of the difference in the businesses. But as long as we have senior management commitment, it should work."

Joanne: "How about on the technology end?"

David: "Nothing that is jumping out at us, but there will be significant data conversion issues. The only reason those will be reduced somewhat is again because of the diversity of the businesses. In many cases, the choice of the preferred system to use will be straightforward because each firm is active in different areas. But we haven't discovered any obvious show-stoppers so far."

The three teams continue their efforts, working to rapidly develop an initial opinion, and a framework for measuring the risks, and potential returns, of the combined firm. They begin to develop conclusions for their presentation to senior management.

Scene 4: A major market event
While the assessment team is actively involved in their three-pronged process, word comes that there has been a severe hit in the major credit markets around the world, precipitated by a significant rating downgrade of a large financial firm. The team has to rapidly determine the impact of this event on the models they have developed of the future combined firm, to see both how accurate their risk/return projections were, and to see if any diversification benefit would have been gained. There is an immediate concern that this event could derail the acquisition.

It quickly becomes clear that while the credit businesses of FutureCo were adversely affected due to a large swing in the institutional markets, the relatively stable retail credit businesses of Phoenix remained unchanged. Yet, since the cause of the rating downgrade was a large impact on the downgraded firm's insurance business due to a major earthquake, Phoenix's sizeable catastrophe bond portfolio does drop in value. During the sell-off in catastrophe bonds, however, large institutional investors start buying up more traditional bonds, which provides a benefit to FutureCo's bond business. The net result is that the combined firm remained relatively flat in this period of volatility, without significant impacts, at least at the macro level.

The assessment team re-aligns its analysis results based on the new market inputs. The team finds the market event to be very telling in its apparent confirmation of the diversification benefits of the combined firm. It was also helpful to monitor how Phoenix responded to all of the events in terms of both operational capabilities and the cultural response. While not conclusive, because many of the details were not being measured, it certainly confirms some of management's expectations.

Scene 5: The team presents its conclusions
In just a few short weeks, the risk/return assessment team was able to develop a cohesive picture of the acquisition target, and to prepare presentation materials for the acquisition committee summarising the conclusions. The speed and comprehensive nature of their assessment was clearly supported by the technology and risk assessment methodologies that FutureCo had in place, as well as the common industry standards that both FutureCo and Phoenix had complied with. In particular, the acceptance of risk and return measures within the cultures of both firms made the assessment process easier, and will undoubtedly support the implementation process.

The team's conclusions are categorised and quantified in terms of diversification benefit, major risk exposures and potential implementation risk. The team has discovered some issues that will impact the final deal negotiated with the target.

Gerry: "So in broad terms, we have been able to quickly confirm that there should be a diversification benefit from going forward with this acquisition. The major risk exposures seem to be in areas where our businesses overlap, as well as in some of the underdeveloped markets.

Now, if you look at the heat map of the combined firms, both before the market event and after, you can easily see where the concentrations are, and where some of the diversification benefit would have been picked up.

On the whole, Phoenix has sound risk management practices, and a fairly consistent risk culture, both of which conform to global standards. They have active limits in most businesses, down to a reasonable level, and they allocate capital to businesses based on their Sharpe ratio and their diversification benefit to the firm, similar to our methodology.

However, we did conclude that our risk management technology is a bit more robust, and we would recommend converting Phoenix on to our systems, which will be quite an effort due to the diversity of the businesses. In that context, we would recommend negotiating the question up front before concluding the deal. We also identified a few isolated business units that have not been included in the risk system, which will need to be worked on unless these businesses are to be divested.

There's also some implementation risk in some of the countries where we are not strong, as in some cases we're not familiar with the regulatory environment. We may want to put on some operational risk futures in those areas to mitigate the risk.

Additional implementation risk may occur during the transition period, especially in terms of operational controls, as we convert all the entity names and set up combined procedures. That's really no different from any other acquisition, except for the size."

The acquisition committee ultimately approves the acquisition, and begins to prepare the general announcements that will be made.

Scene 6: Project Phoenix is announced to the market
The acquisition is floated out to the market, starting with the regulators and the ratings agencies, to garner some initial reactions. A statement is made as to the motivation of diversifying business risks in order to benefit from the market's perception that sound risk management enhances a firm's value.

Initial feedback is positive, although there is some concern regarding the size of the merger, as this will create the largest global firm to date. Also, the global regulators still need to approve the deal. The positioning as a risk reducer is perceived as a clear benefit, although there are always those who question the ability of any two firms to pull off such a large merger.

Scene 7: Implementation begins
The Risk/Return group de-briefs and begins to get ready to execute the implementation process. They will have to work on multiple fronts, both in terms of finding a way to report the daily risk and return of the combined firm, and beginning to set and manage limits, adjust the risk and return reporting processes, and integrate the systems.

Francine: "Well, now that the merger has been approved, we can get down to the real work. We will need to move quickly to start capturing the risk and return data."

Gerry: "I think we'll need to do the combined management reporting on risk and performance through a manual effort at first. Then we can set up a parallel task of determining how to integrate the systems. The good news is that through our assessment analysis, we have an initial framework established."

Francine: "We need to move quickly to make combined capital allocation and limits decisions along with the standard staffing and business overlap decisions. That will help us manage the risk of the combined entity during the transition."

Gerry: "Well team, just to wrap up the assessment phase, the feedback from senior management was very positive. They were impressed by how fast we were able to respond on all of the different fronts, and they also feel that they have a more complete view and confirmation of the potential risk and return of the combined entity. Great job!"

Conclusion

And so we conclude our brief journey into the future. Our reality is changing so quickly that some of the things we have envisioned will probably be starting even as we go to press, while others may be completely redirected by events in the global market-place. Suffice it to say that even today the discipline of risk management has proven its potential benefits to those firms who practice it actively. Firms can no longer reasonably expect to be active in our complex markets without as many tools in the arsenal as possible to manage both risk and return. That being said, we would anticipate a broadening and deepening of the practice of risk management for many years into the future.